ASTONISHING X-MEN

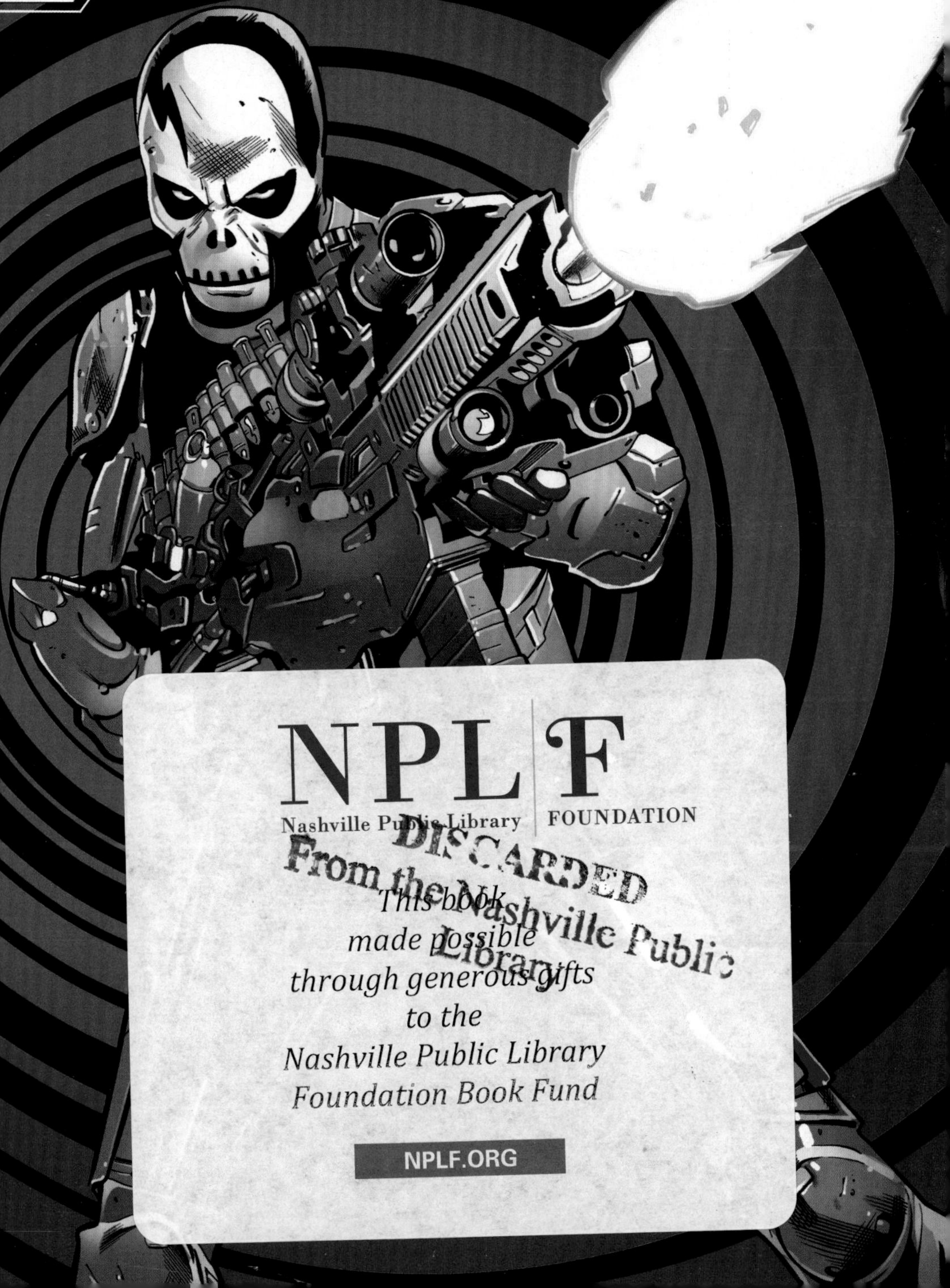

ASTONISHING X-MEN BY MATTHEW ROSENBERG: UNTIL OUR HEARTS STOP. Contains material originally published in magazine form as ASTONISHING X-MEN #13-17 and ANNUAL #1. First printing 2018. ISBN 978-1-302-91296-3. Published by MARVEL WORLDWIDE, INC., a subsidiary of MARVEL ENTERTAINMENT, LLC. OFFICE OF PUBLICATION: 135 West 50th Street, New York, NY 10020. Copyright © 2018 MARVEL No similarity between any of the names, characters, persons, and/or institutions in this magazine with those of any living or dead person or institution is intended, and any such similarity which may exist is purely coincidental. **Printed in Canada.** DAN BUCKLEY, President, Marvel Entertainment; JOHN NEE, Publisher; JOE QUESADA, Chief Creative Officer; TOM BREVOORT, SVP of Publishing; DAVID BOGART, SVP of Business Affairs & Operations, Publishing & Partnership; DAVID GABRIEL, SVP of Sales & Marketing, Publishing; JEFF YOUNGQUIST, VP of Production & Special Projects; DAN CARR, Executive Director of Publishing Technology; ALEX MORALES, Director of Publishing Operations; DAN EDINGTON, Managing Editor; SUSAN CRESPI, Production Manager; STAN LEE, Chairman Emeritus. For information regarding advertising in Marvel Comics or on Marvel.com, please contact Vit DeBellis, Custom Solutions & Integrated Advertising Manager, at vdebellis@marvel.com. For Marvel subscription inquiries, please call 888-511-5480. **Manufactured between 11/15/2018 and 12/17/2018 by SOLISCO PRINTERS, SCOTT, QC, CANADA.**

10 9 8 7 6 5 4 3 2 1

ALEX SUMMERS — THE MAN CALLED HAVOK. A FITTING NAME FOR SOMEONE WITH THE ABILITY TO EMIT POWERFUL PLASMA BLASTS...AND WHOSE LIFE HASN'T ALWAYS BEEN THE PICTURE OF ABSOLUTE CONTROL — ESPECIALLY SINCE ALEX HAD HIS MORAL COMPASS FORCIBLY INVERTED, COMPELLING HIM TO DO EVIL RATHER THAN GOOD. BUT ALL OF THAT IS OVER NOW. HAVOK IS READY TO BE AN X-MAN AGAIN!

ASTONISHING X-MEN

UNTIL OUR HEARTS STOP

MATTHEW ROSENBERG
WRITER

---------- ISSUES #13-17 ----------

GREG LAND
WITH **NEIL EDWARDS** (#15)
PENCILERS

JAY LEISTEN
INKER

FRANK D'ARMATA
COLOR ARTIST

GREG LAND
WITH **JAY LEISTEN** (#16-17)
& **FRANK D'ARMATA** (#13-17)
COVER ART

---------- ANNUAL #1 ----------

TRAVEL FOREMAN
ARTIST

JIM CHARALAMPIDIS
COLOR ARTIST

ROD REIS
COVER ART

VC's CLAYTON COWLES
LETTERER

ANNALISE BISSA
& DANNY KHAZEM
ASSISTANT EDITORS

DARREN SHAN
EDITOR

JORDAN D. WHITE
X-MEN GROUP EDITOR

X-MEN CREATED BY **STAN LEE** & **JACK KIRBY**

COLLECTION EDITOR **JENNIFER GRÜNWALD** ▪ ASSISTANT EDITOR **CAITLIN O'CONNELL**
ASSOCIATE MANAGING EDITOR **KATERI WOODY** ▪ EDITOR, SPECIAL PROJECTS **MARK D. BEAZLEY**
VP PRODUCTION & SPECIAL PROJECTS **JEFF YOUNGQUIST** ▪ SVP PRINT, SALES & MARKETING **DAVID GABRIEL**
BOOK DESIGNER **JAY BOWEN**

EDITOR IN CHIEF **C.B. CEBULSKI** ▪ CHIEF CREATIVE OFFICER **JOE QUESADA**
PRESIDENT **DAN BUCKLEY** ▪ EXECUTIVE PRODUCER **ALAN FINE**

13

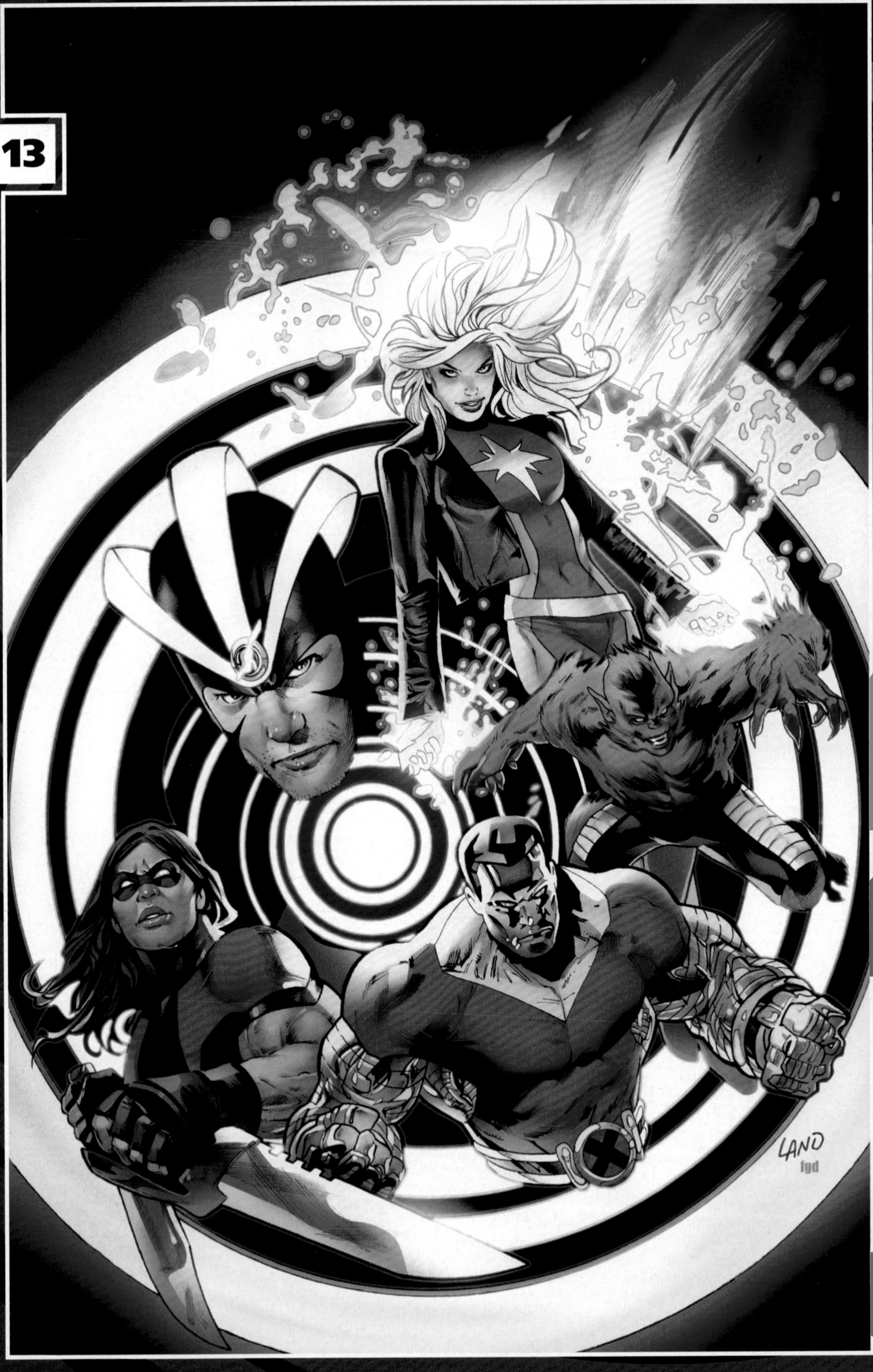
LAND
fgd

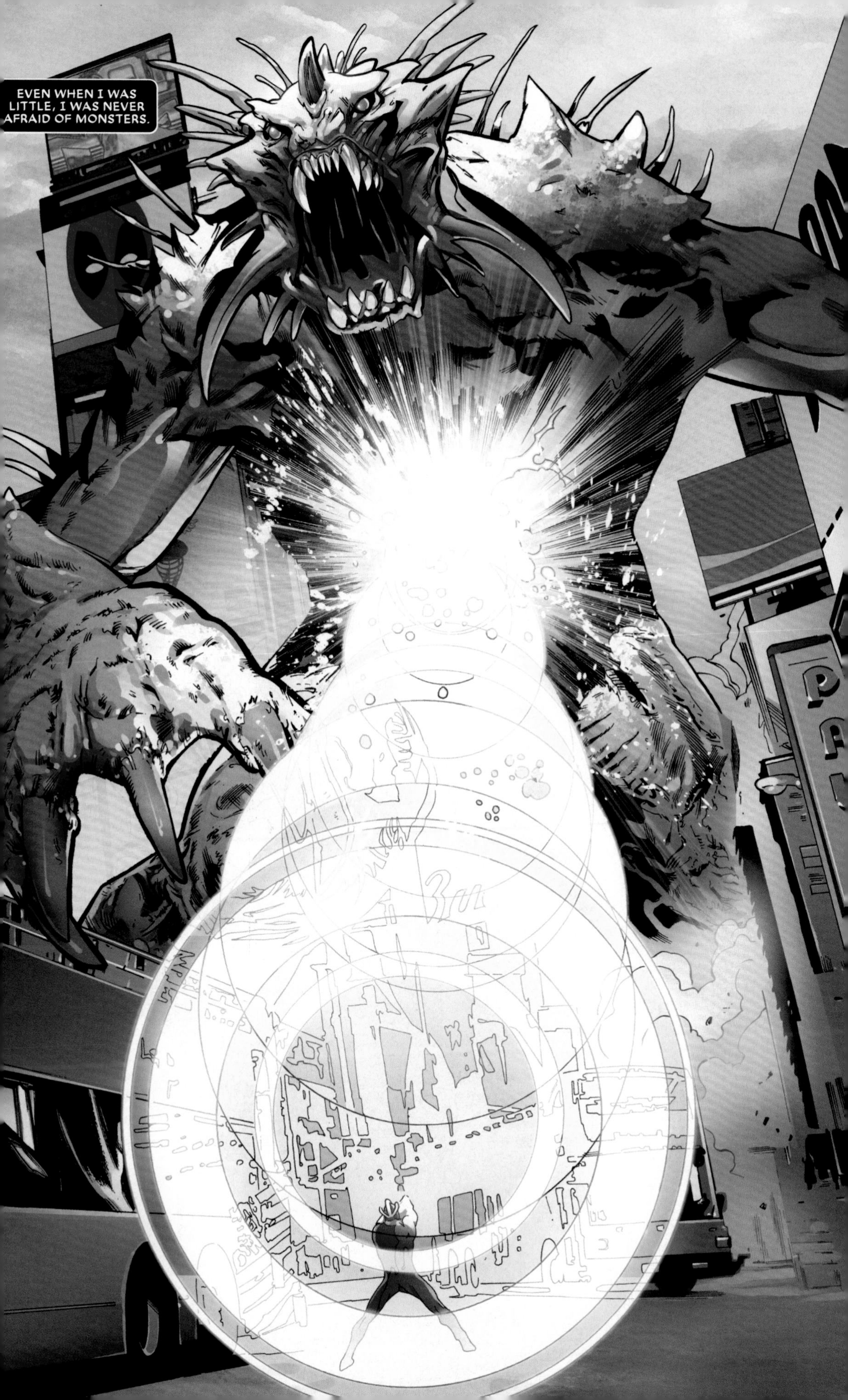
EVEN WHEN I WAS
LITTLE, I WAS NEVER
AFRAID OF MONSTERS.

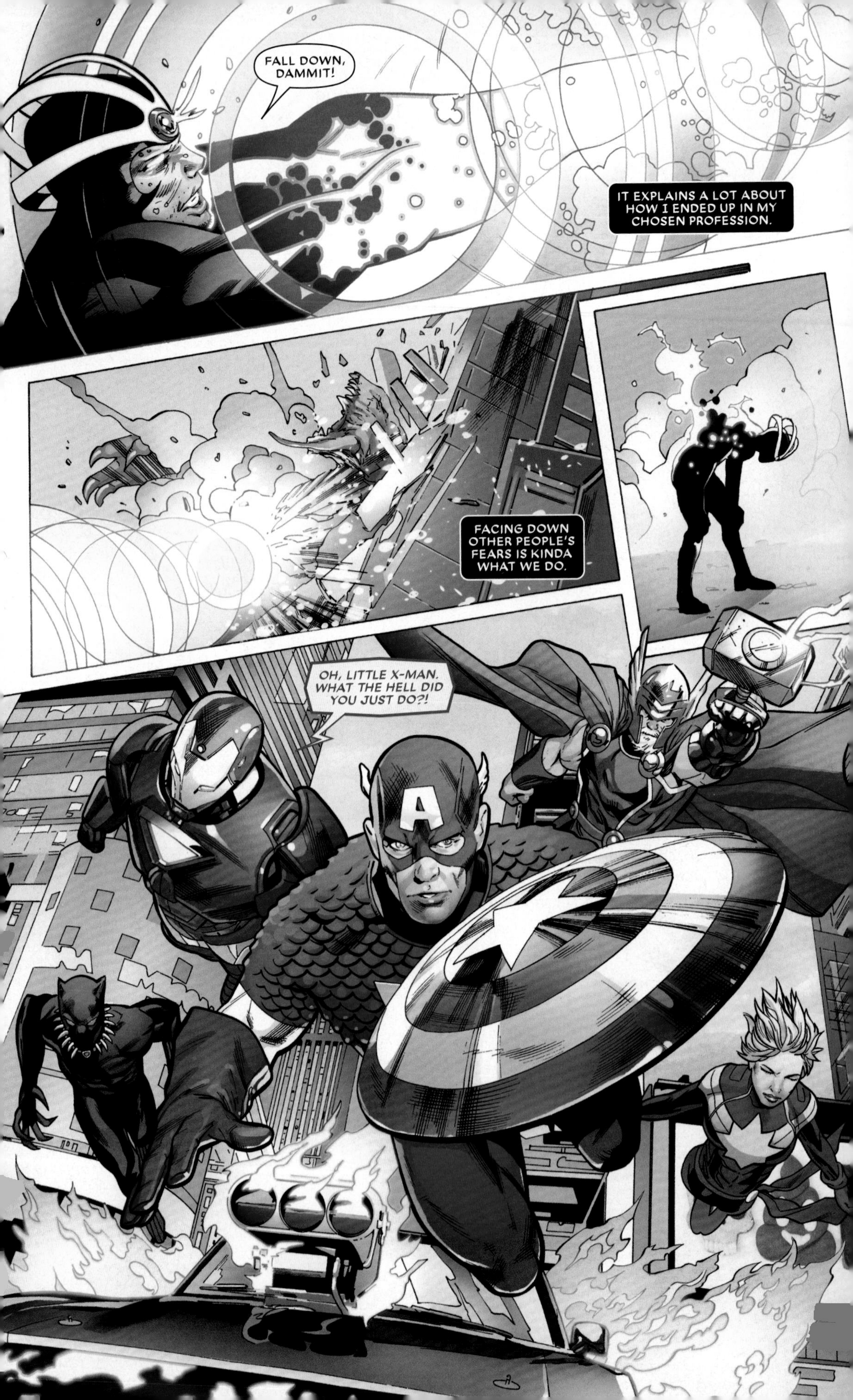
FALL DOWN, DAMMIT!
IT EXPLAINS A LOT ABOUT HOW I ENDED UP IN MY CHOSEN PROFESSION.
FACING DOWN OTHER PEOPLE'S FEARS IS KINDA WHAT WE DO.
OH, LITTLE X-MAN. WHAT THE HELL DID YOU JUST DO?!

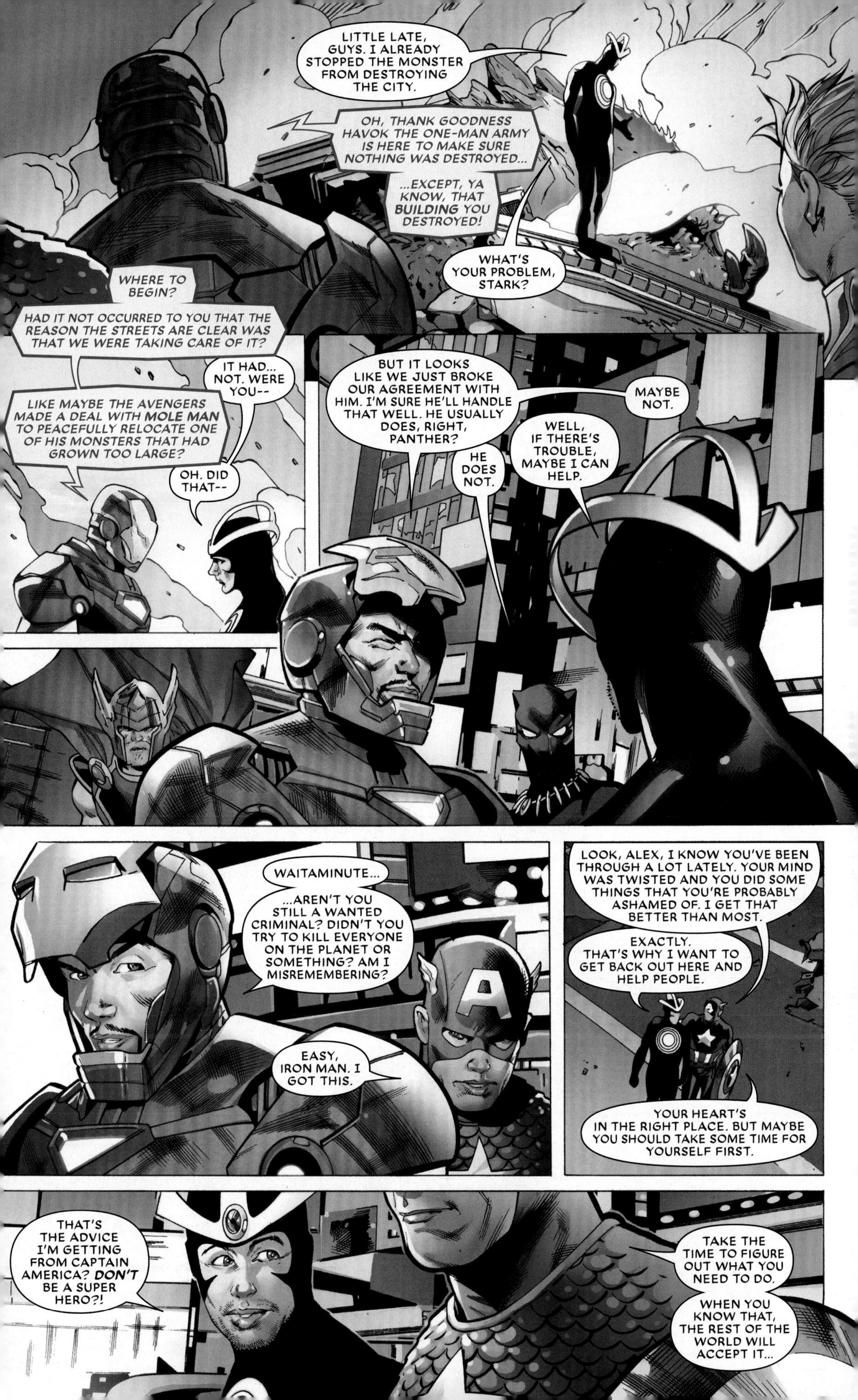
LITTLE LATE, GUYS. I ALREADY STOPPED THE MONSTER FROM DESTROYING THE CITY.
OH, THANK GOODNESS HAVOK THE ONE-MAN ARMY IS HERE TO MAKE SURE NOTHING WAS DESTROYED...
...EXCEPT, YA KNOW, THAT BUILDING YOU DESTROYED!
WHAT'S YOUR PROBLEM, STARK?
WHERE TO BEGIN?
HAD IT NOT OCCURRED TO YOU THAT THE REASON THE STREETS ARE CLEAR WAS THAT WE WERE TAKING CARE OF IT?
IT HAD... NOT. WERE YOU--
LIKE MAYBE THE AVENGERS MADE A DEAL WITH MOLE MAN TO PEACEFULLY RELOCATE ONE OF HIS MONSTERS THAT HAD GROWN TOO LARGE?
OH. DID THAT--
BUT IT LOOKS LIKE WE JUST BROKE OUR AGREEMENT WITH HIM. I'M SURE HE'LL HANDLE THAT WELL. HE USUALLY DOES, RIGHT, PANTHER?
HE DOES NOT.
MAYBE NOT.
WELL, IF THERE'S TROUBLE, MAYBE I CAN HELP.
WAITAMINUTE...
...AREN'T YOU STILL A WANTED CRIMINAL? DIDN'T YOU TRY TO KILL EVERYONE ON THE PLANET OR SOMETHING? AM I MISREMEMBERING?
EASY, IRON MAN. I GOT THIS.
LOOK, ALEX, I KNOW YOU'VE BEEN THROUGH A LOT LATELY. YOUR MIND WAS TWISTED AND YOU DID SOME THINGS THAT YOU'RE PROBABLY ASHAMED OF. I GET THAT BETTER THAN MOST.
EXACTLY. THAT'S WHY I WANT TO GET BACK OUT HERE AND HELP PEOPLE.
YOUR HEART'S IN THE RIGHT PLACE. BUT MAYBE YOU SHOULD TAKE SOME TIME FOR YOURSELF FIRST.
THAT'S THE ADVICE I'M GETTING FROM CAPTAIN AMERICA? DON'T BE A SUPER HERO?!
TAKE THE TIME TO FIGURE OUT WHAT YOU NEED TO DO.
WHEN YOU KNOW THAT, THE REST OF THE WORLD WILL ACCEPT IT...

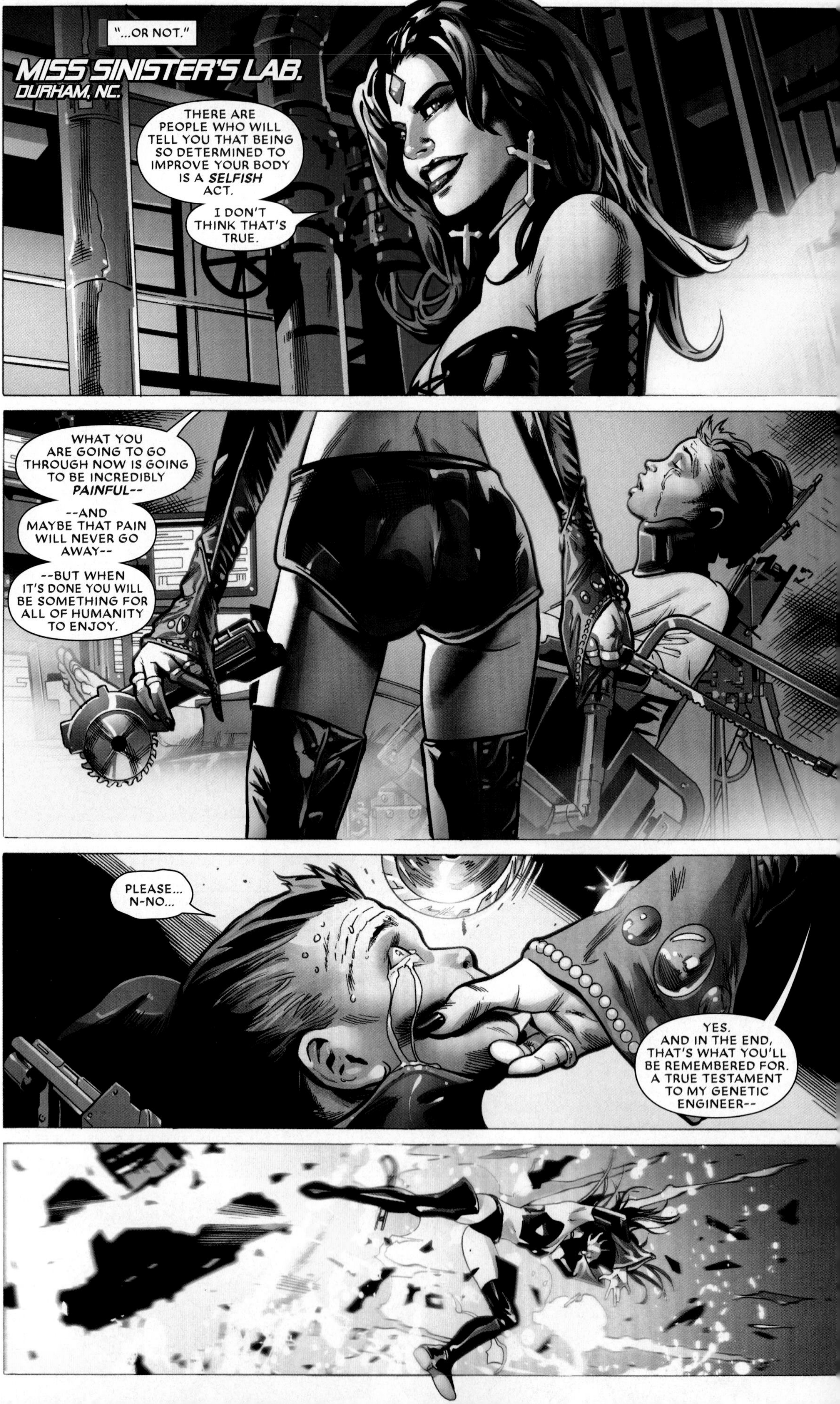
"...OR NOT."
MISS SINISTER'S LAB.
DURHAM, NC.
THERE ARE PEOPLE WHO WILL TELL YOU THAT BEING SO DETERMINED TO IMPROVE YOUR BODY IS A SELFISH ACT.
I DON'T THINK THAT'S TRUE.
WHAT YOU ARE GOING TO GO THROUGH NOW IS GOING TO BE INCREDIBLY PAINFUL--
--AND MAYBE THAT PAIN WILL NEVER GO AWAY--
--BUT WHEN IT'S DONE YOU WILL BE SOMETHING FOR ALL OF HUMANITY TO ENJOY.
PLEASE... N-NO...
YES. AND IN THE END, THAT'S WHAT YOU'LL BE REMEMBERED FOR. A TRUE TESTAMENT TO MY GENETIC ENGINEER--

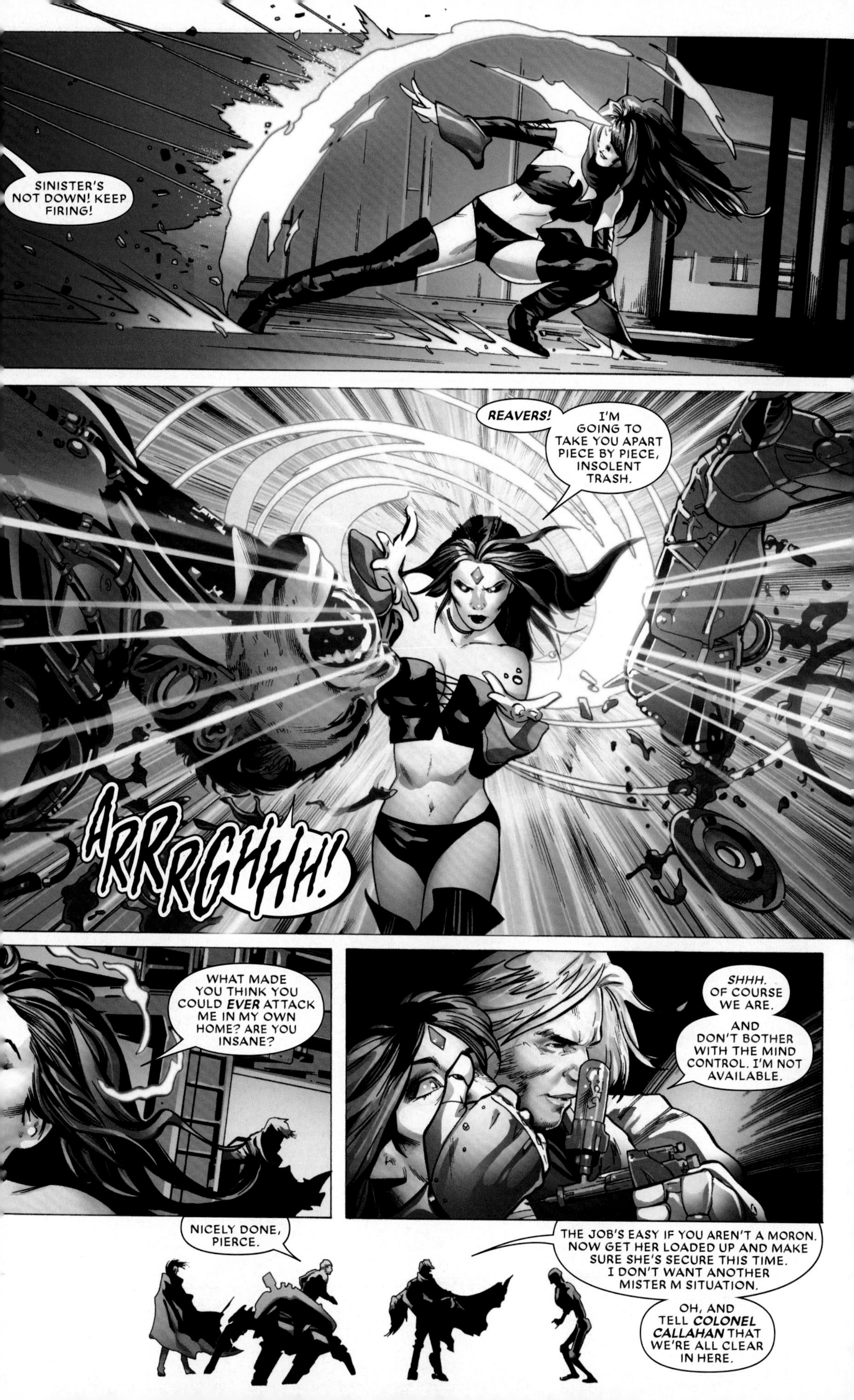
SINISTER'S NOT DOWN! KEEP FIRING!
REAVERS!
I'M GOING TO TAKE YOU APART PIECE BY PIECE, INSOLENT TRASH.
ARRRGHHH!
WHAT MADE YOU THINK YOU COULD EVER ATTACK ME IN MY OWN HOME? ARE YOU INSANE?
SHHH. OF COURSE WE ARE.
AND DON'T BOTHER WITH THE MIND CONTROL. I'M NOT AVAILABLE.
NICELY DONE, PIERCE.
THE JOB'S EASY IF YOU AREN'T A MORON. NOW GET HER LOADED UP AND MAKE SURE SHE'S SECURE THIS TIME. I DON'T WANT ANOTHER MISTER M SITUATION.
OH, AND TELL COLONEL CALLAHAN THAT WE'RE ALL CLEAR IN HERE.

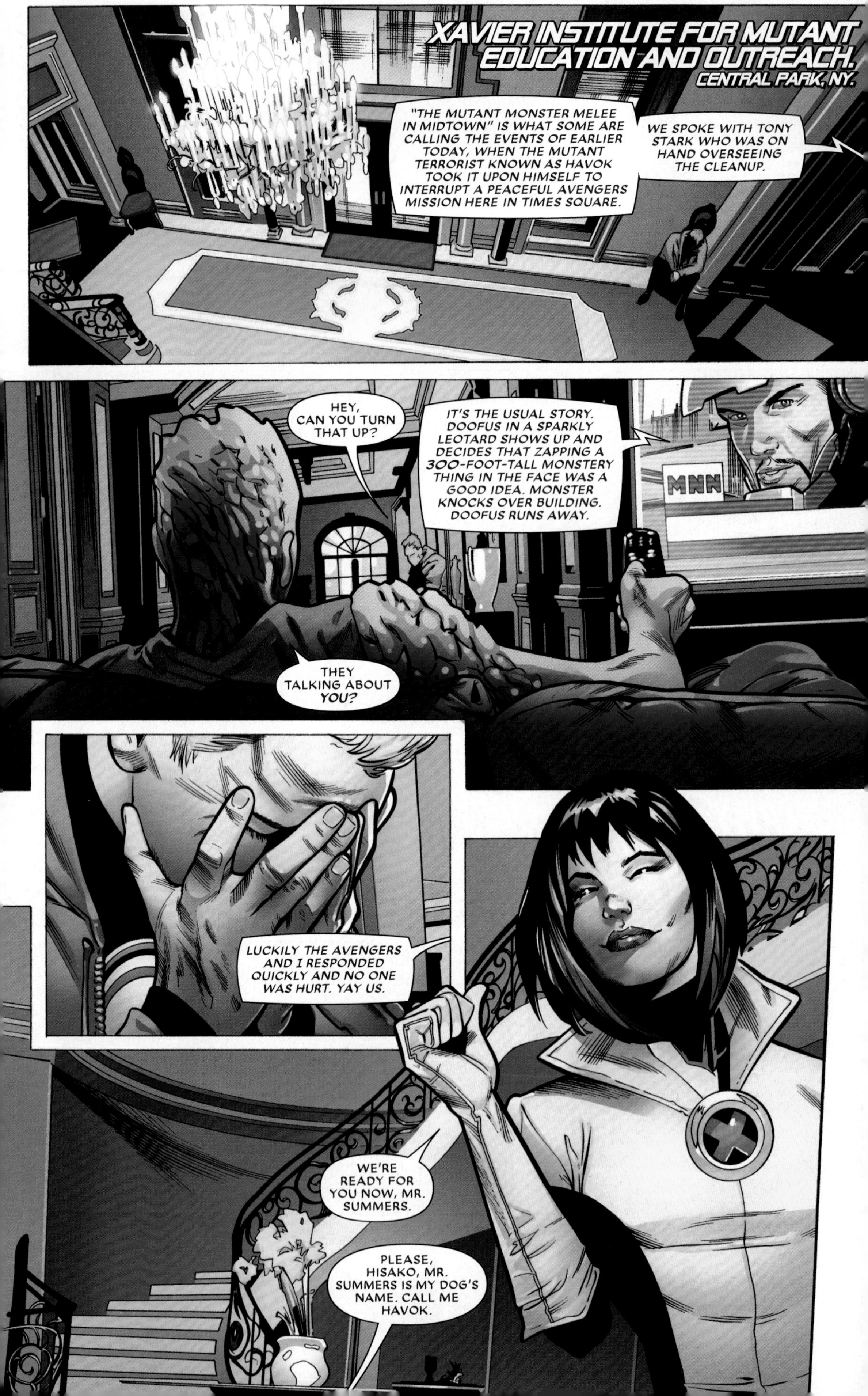
XAVIER INSTITUTE FOR MUTANT EDUCATION AND OUTREACH.
CENTRAL PARK, NY.
"THE MUTANT MONSTER MELEE IN MIDTOWN" IS WHAT SOME ARE CALLING THE EVENTS OF EARLIER TODAY, WHEN THE MUTANT TERRORIST KNOWN AS HAVOK TOOK IT UPON HIMSELF TO INTERRUPT A PEACEFUL AVENGERS MISSION HERE IN TIMES SQUARE.
WE SPOKE WITH TONY STARK WHO WAS ON HAND OVERSEEING THE CLEANUP.
HEY, CAN YOU TURN THAT UP?
IT'S THE USUAL STORY. DOOFUS IN A SPARKLY LEOTARD SHOWS UP AND DECIDES THAT ZAPPING A 300-FOOT-TALL MONSTERY THING IN THE FACE WAS A GOOD IDEA. MONSTER KNOCKS OVER BUILDING. DOOFUS RUNS AWAY.
MNN
THEY TALKING ABOUT YOU?
LUCKILY THE AVENGERS AND I RESPONDED QUICKLY AND NO ONE WAS HURT. YAY US.
WE'RE READY FOR YOU NOW, MR. SUMMERS.
PLEASE, HISAKO, MR. SUMMERS IS MY DOG'S NAME. CALL ME HAVOK.

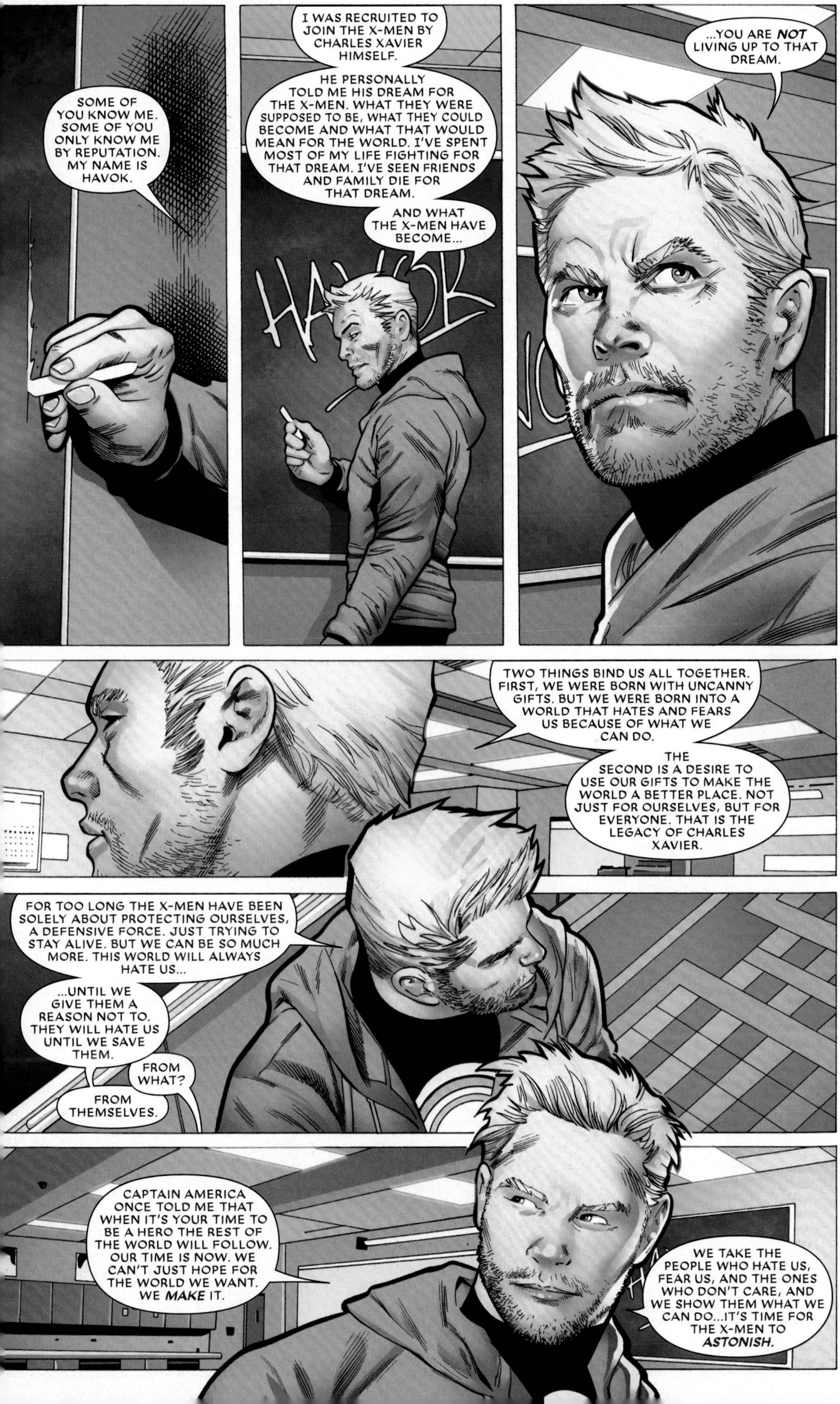
SOME OF YOU KNOW ME. SOME OF YOU ONLY KNOW ME BY REPUTATION. MY NAME IS HAVOK.
I WAS RECRUITED TO JOIN THE X-MEN BY CHARLES XAVIER HIMSELF.
HE PERSONALLY TOLD ME HIS DREAM FOR THE X-MEN. WHAT THEY WERE SUPPOSED TO BE, WHAT THEY COULD BECOME AND WHAT THAT WOULD MEAN FOR THE WORLD. I'VE SPENT MOST OF MY LIFE FIGHTING FOR THAT DREAM. I'VE SEEN FRIENDS AND FAMILY DIE FOR THAT DREAM.
AND WHAT THE X-MEN HAVE BECOME...
HAVOK
...YOU ARE ***NOT*** LIVING UP TO THAT DREAM.
TWO THINGS BIND US ALL TOGETHER. FIRST, WE WERE BORN WITH UNCANNY GIFTS. BUT WE WERE BORN INTO A WORLD THAT HATES AND FEARS US BECAUSE OF WHAT WE CAN DO.
THE SECOND IS A DESIRE TO USE OUR GIFTS TO MAKE THE WORLD A BETTER PLACE. NOT JUST FOR OURSELVES, BUT FOR EVERYONE. THAT IS THE LEGACY OF CHARLES XAVIER.
FOR TOO LONG THE X-MEN HAVE BEEN SOLELY ABOUT PROTECTING OURSELVES, A DEFENSIVE FORCE. JUST TRYING TO STAY ALIVE. BUT WE CAN BE SO MUCH MORE. THIS WORLD WILL ALWAYS HATE US...
...UNTIL WE GIVE THEM A REASON NOT TO. THEY WILL HATE US UNTIL WE SAVE THEM.
FROM WHAT?
FROM THEMSELVES.
CAPTAIN AMERICA ONCE TOLD ME THAT WHEN IT'S YOUR TIME TO BE A HERO THE REST OF THE WORLD WILL FOLLOW. OUR TIME IS NOW. WE CAN'T JUST HOPE FOR THE WORLD WE WANT. WE ***MAKE*** IT.
WE TAKE THE PEOPLE WHO HATE US, FEAR US, AND THE ONES WHO DON'T CARE, AND WE SHOW THEM WHAT WE CAN DO...IT'S TIME FOR THE X-MEN TO ***ASTONISH.***

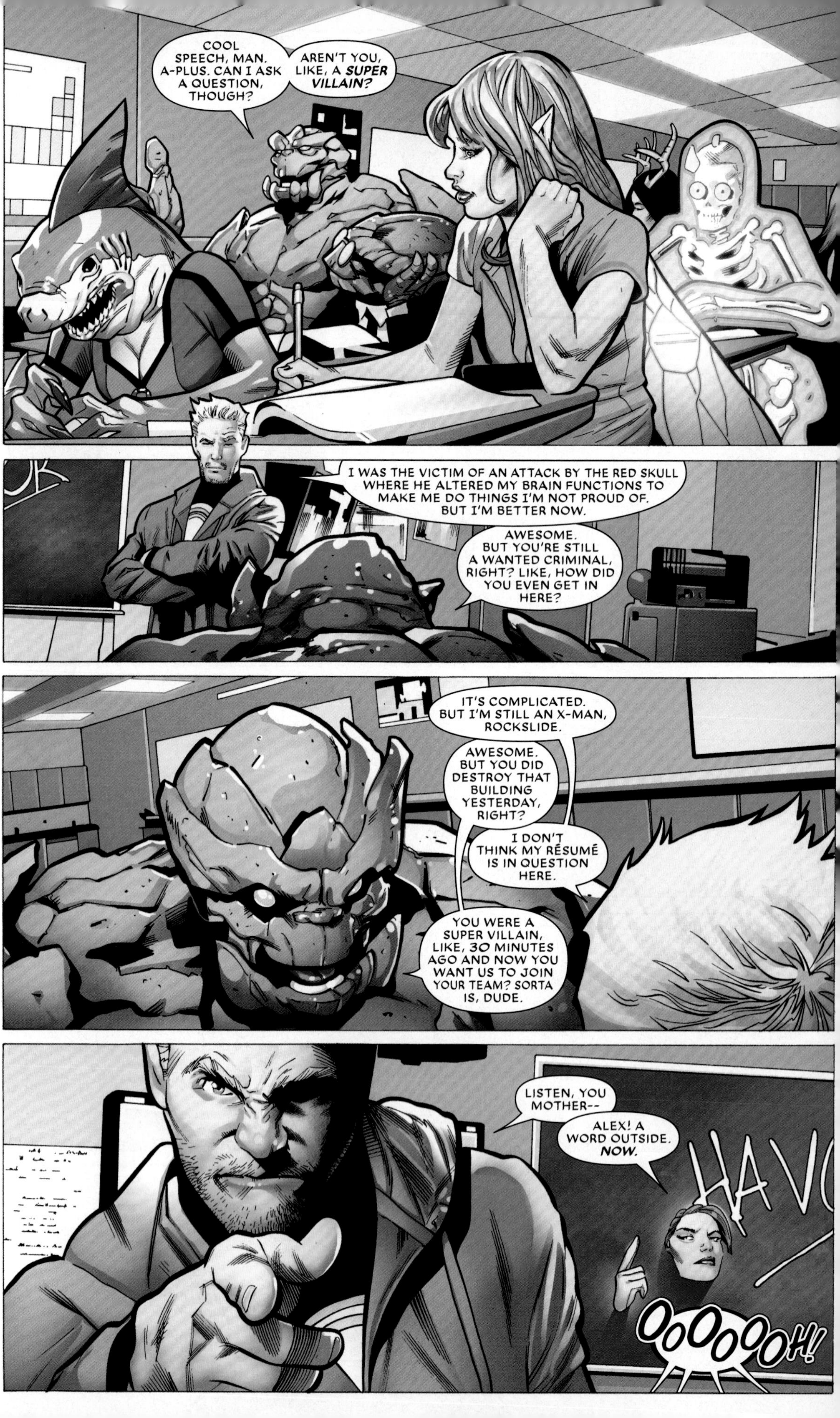
COOL SPEECH, MAN. A-PLUS. CAN I ASK A QUESTION, THOUGH?
AREN'T YOU, LIKE, A SUPER VILLAIN?
I WAS THE VICTIM OF AN ATTACK BY THE RED SKULL WHERE HE ALTERED MY BRAIN FUNCTIONS TO MAKE ME DO THINGS I'M NOT PROUD OF. BUT I'M BETTER NOW.
AWESOME. BUT YOU'RE STILL A WANTED CRIMINAL, RIGHT? LIKE, HOW DID YOU EVEN GET IN HERE?
IT'S COMPLICATED. BUT I'M STILL AN X-MAN, ROCKSLIDE.
AWESOME. BUT YOU DID DESTROY THAT BUILDING YESTERDAY, RIGHT?
I DON'T THINK MY RÉSUMÉ IS IN QUESTION HERE.
YOU WERE A SUPER VILLAIN, LIKE, 30 MINUTES AGO AND NOW YOU WANT US TO JOIN YOUR TEAM? SORTA IS, DUDE.
LISTEN, YOU MOTHER--
ALEX! A WORD OUTSIDE. NOW.
HAV
OOOOOOH!

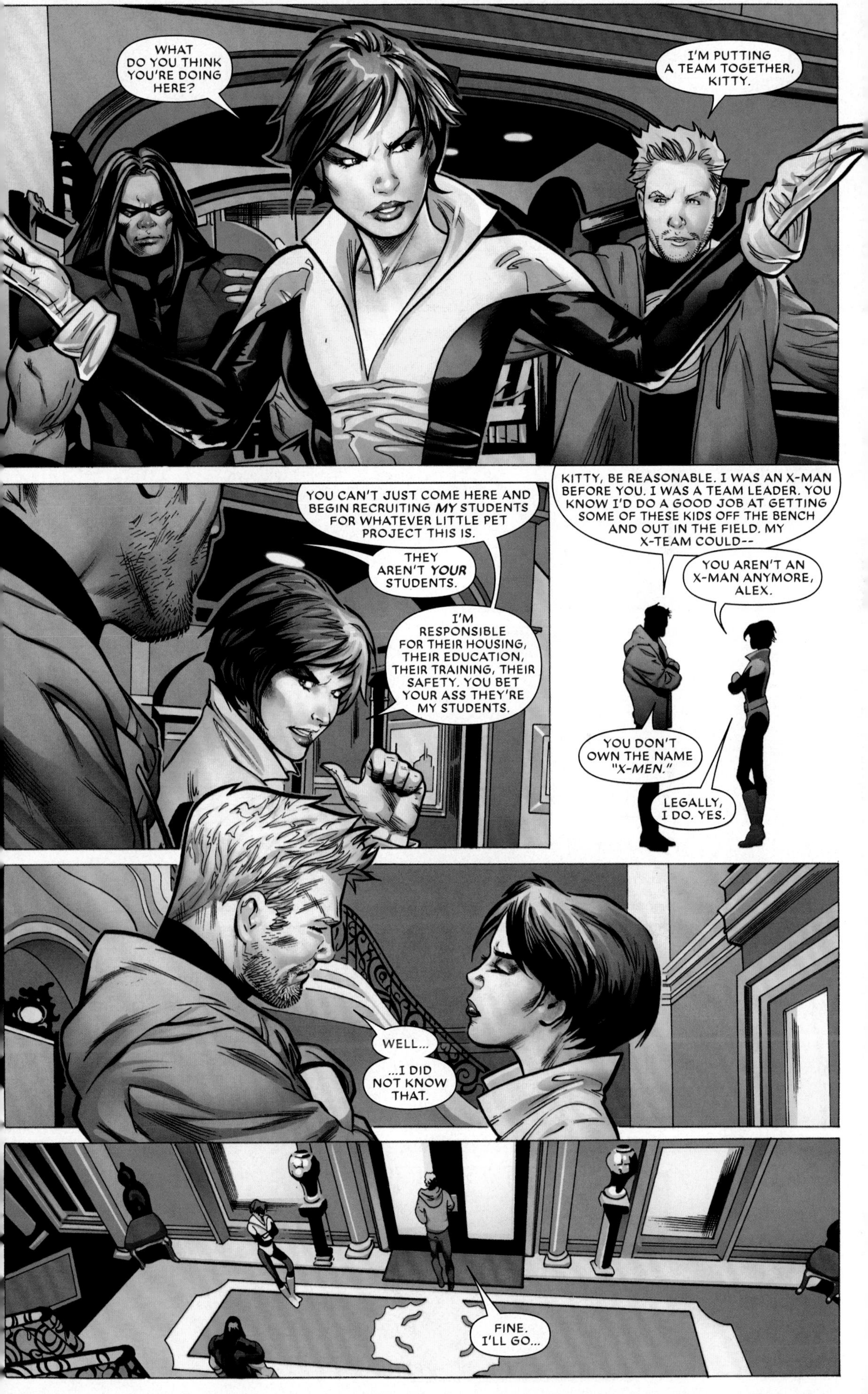
WHAT DO YOU THINK YOU'RE DOING HERE?
I'M PUTTING A TEAM TOGETHER, KITTY.
YOU CAN'T JUST COME HERE AND BEGIN RECRUITING *MY* STUDENTS FOR WHATEVER LITTLE PET PROJECT THIS IS.
THEY AREN'T *YOUR* STUDENTS.
I'M RESPONSIBLE FOR THEIR HOUSING, THEIR EDUCATION, THEIR TRAINING, THEIR SAFETY. YOU BET YOUR ASS THEY'RE MY STUDENTS.
KITTY, BE REASONABLE. I WAS AN X-MAN BEFORE YOU. I WAS A TEAM LEADER. YOU KNOW I'D DO A GOOD JOB AT GETTING SOME OF THESE KIDS OFF THE BENCH AND OUT IN THE FIELD. MY X-TEAM COULD--
YOU AREN'T AN X-MAN ANYMORE, ALEX.
YOU DON'T OWN THE NAME "*X-MEN.*"
LEGALLY, I DO. YES.
WELL...
...I DID NOT KNOW THAT.
FINE. I'LL GO...

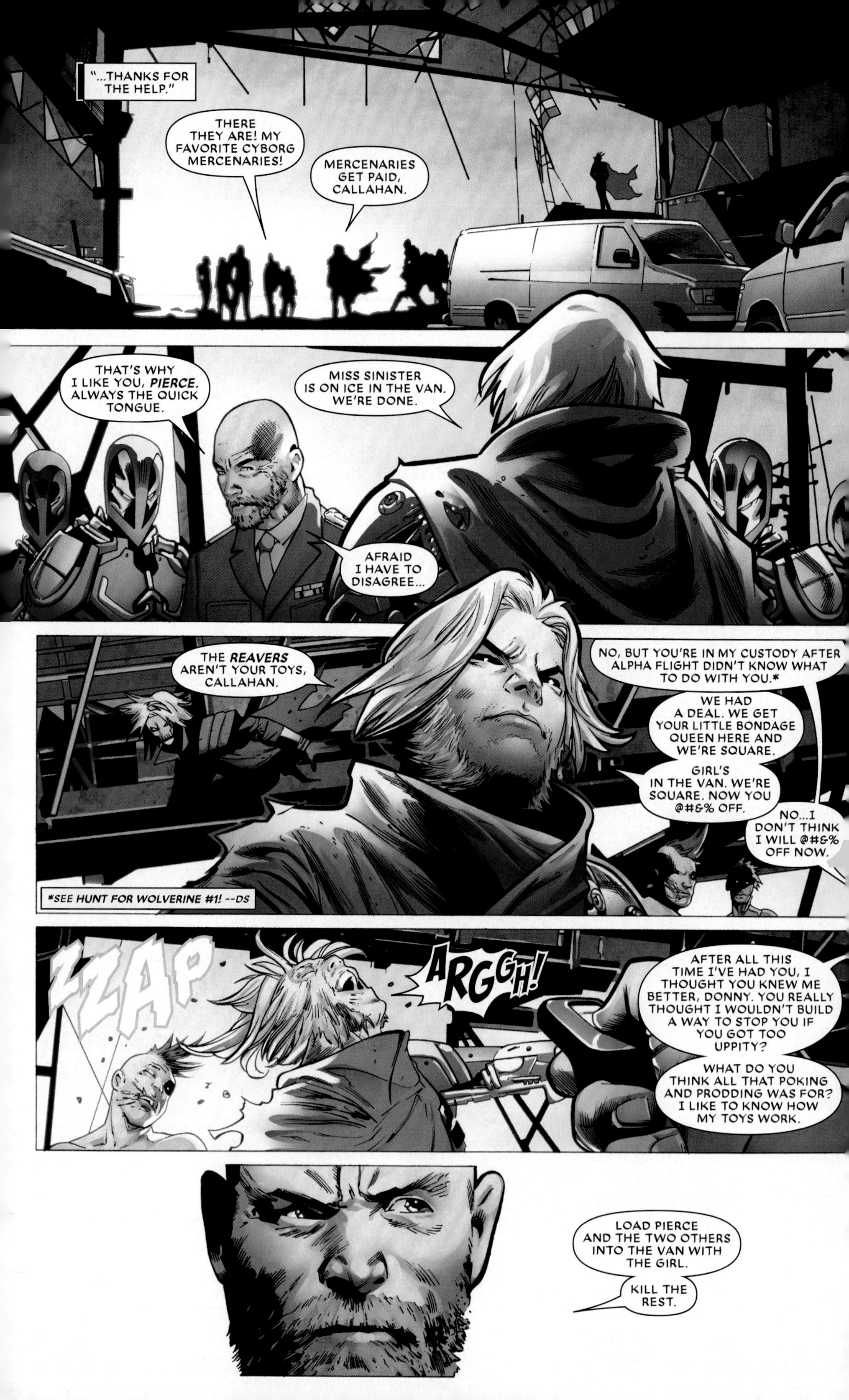
"...THANKS FOR THE HELP."
THERE THEY ARE! MY FAVORITE CYBORG MERCENARIES!
MERCENARIES GET PAID, CALLAHAN.
THAT'S WHY I LIKE YOU, PIERCE. ALWAYS THE QUICK TONGUE.
MISS SINISTER IS ON ICE IN THE VAN. WE'RE DONE.
AFRAID I HAVE TO DISAGREE...
THE REAVERS AREN'T YOUR TOYS, CALLAHAN.
NO, BUT YOU'RE IN MY CUSTODY AFTER ALPHA FLIGHT DIDN'T KNOW WHAT TO DO WITH YOU.*
WE HAD A DEAL. WE GET YOUR LITTLE BONDAGE QUEEN HERE AND WE'RE SQUARE.
GIRL'S IN THE VAN. WE'RE SQUARE. NOW YOU @#&% OFF.
NO...I DON'T THINK I WILL @#&% OFF NOW.
*SEE HUNT FOR WOLVERINE #1! --DS
ZZAP
ARGGH!
AFTER ALL THIS TIME I'VE HAD YOU, I THOUGHT YOU KNEW ME BETTER, DONNY. YOU REALLY THOUGHT I WOULDN'T BUILD A WAY TO STOP YOU IF YOU GOT TOO UPPITY?
WHAT DO YOU THINK ALL THAT POKING AND PRODDING WAS FOR? I LIKE TO KNOW HOW MY TOYS WORK.
LOAD PIERCE AND THE TWO OTHERS INTO THE VAN WITH THE GIRL.
KILL THE REST.

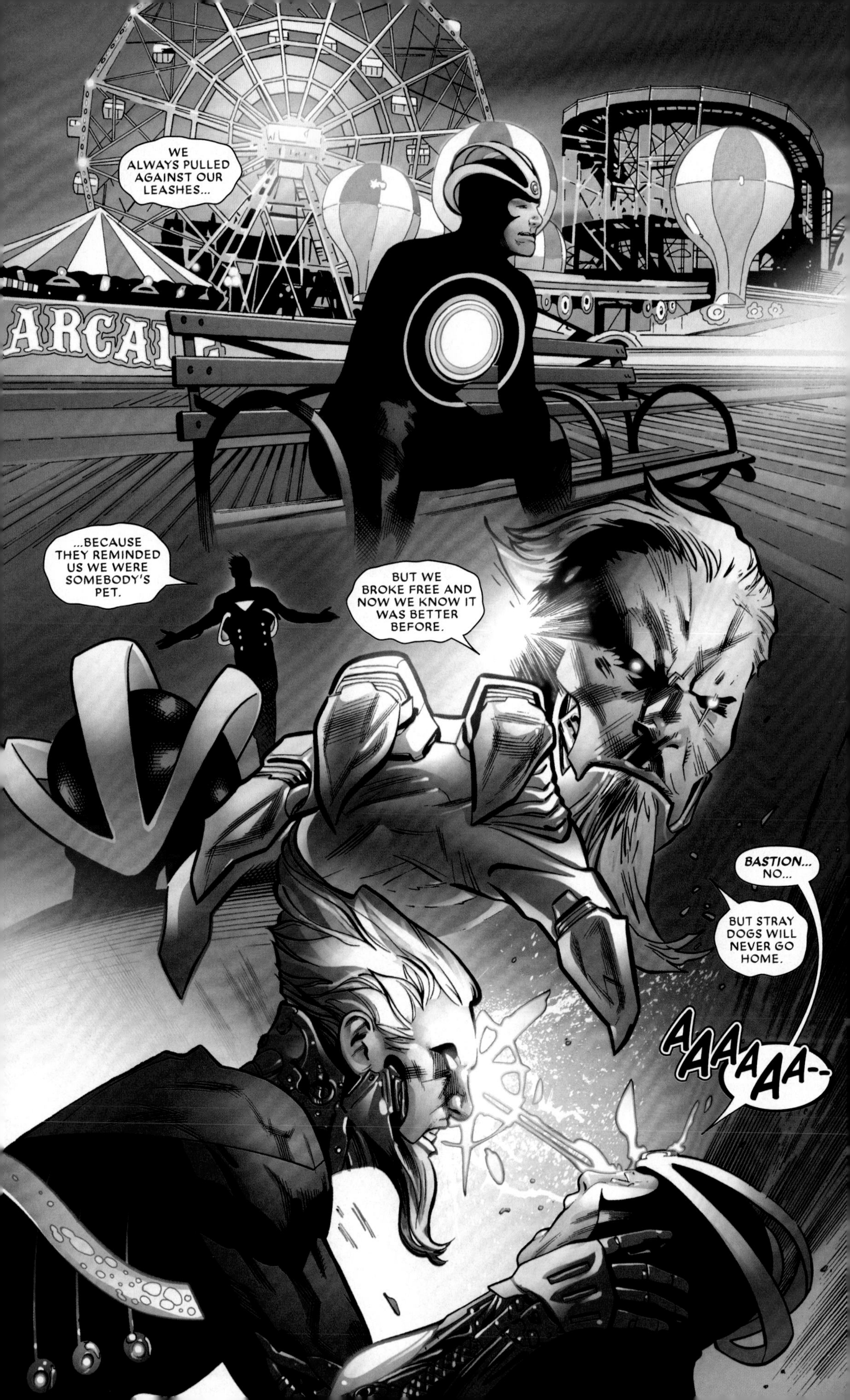

ARCADE
WE ALWAYS PULLED AGAINST OUR LEASHES...
...BECAUSE THEY REMINDED US WE WERE SOMEBODY'S PET.
BUT WE BROKE FREE AND NOW WE KNOW IT WAS BETTER BEFORE.
BASTION... NO...
BUT STRAY DOGS WILL NEVER GO HOME.
AAAAAA--

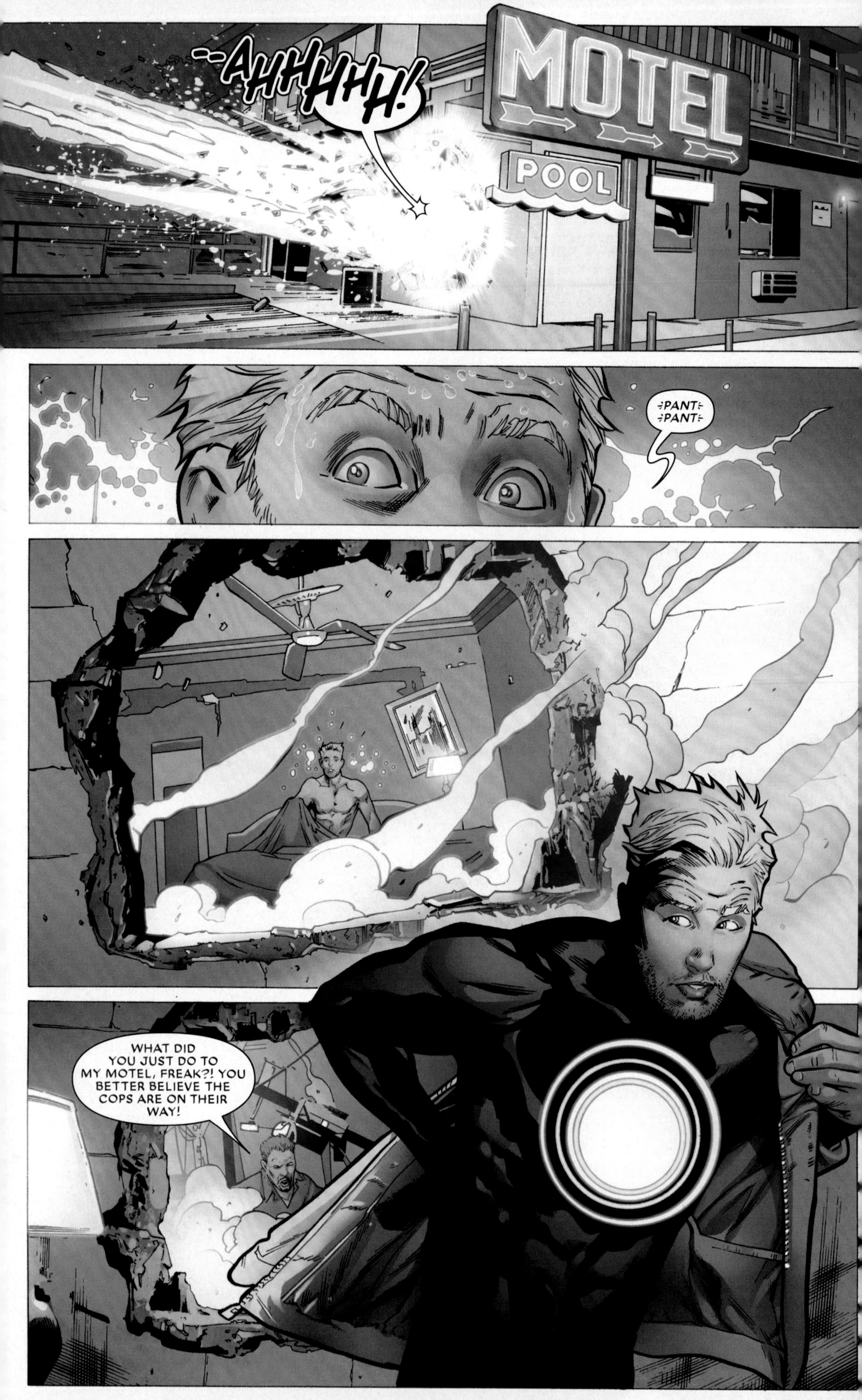
--AHHHHHH!
MOTEL
POOL
PANT PANT
WHAT DID YOU JUST DO TO MY MOTEL, FREAK?! YOU BETTER BELIEVE THE COPS ARE ON THEIR WAY!

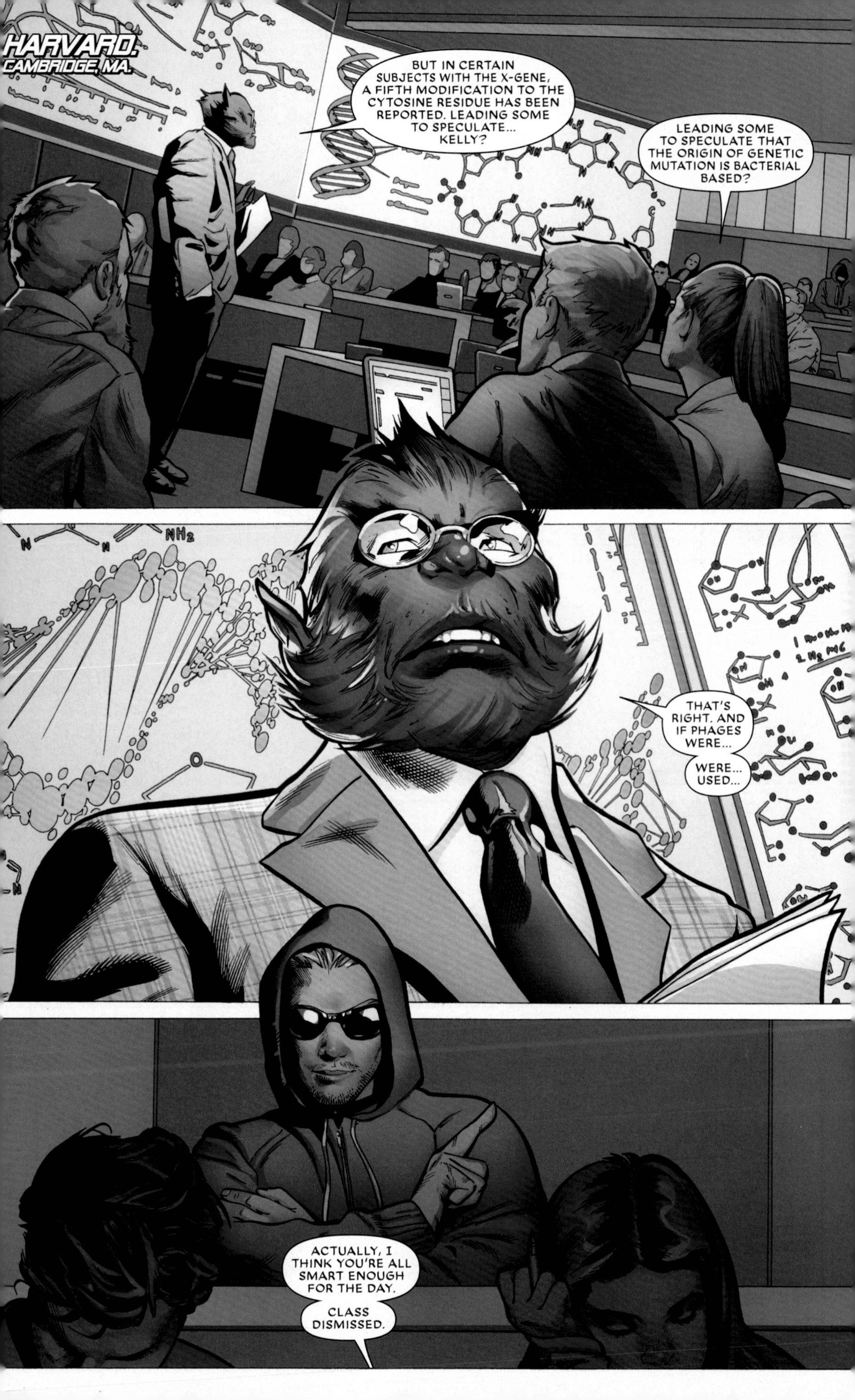
HARVARD. CAMBRIDGE, MA.
BUT IN CERTAIN SUBJECTS WITH THE X-GENE, A FIFTH MODIFICATION TO THE CYTOSINE RESIDUE HAS BEEN REPORTED. LEADING SOME TO SPECULATE... KELLY?
LEADING SOME TO SPECULATE THAT THE ORIGIN OF GENETIC MUTATION IS BACTERIAL BASED?
THAT'S RIGHT. AND IF PHAGES WERE...
WERE... USED...
ACTUALLY, I THINK YOU'RE ALL SMART ENOUGH FOR THE DAY.
CLASS DISMISSED.

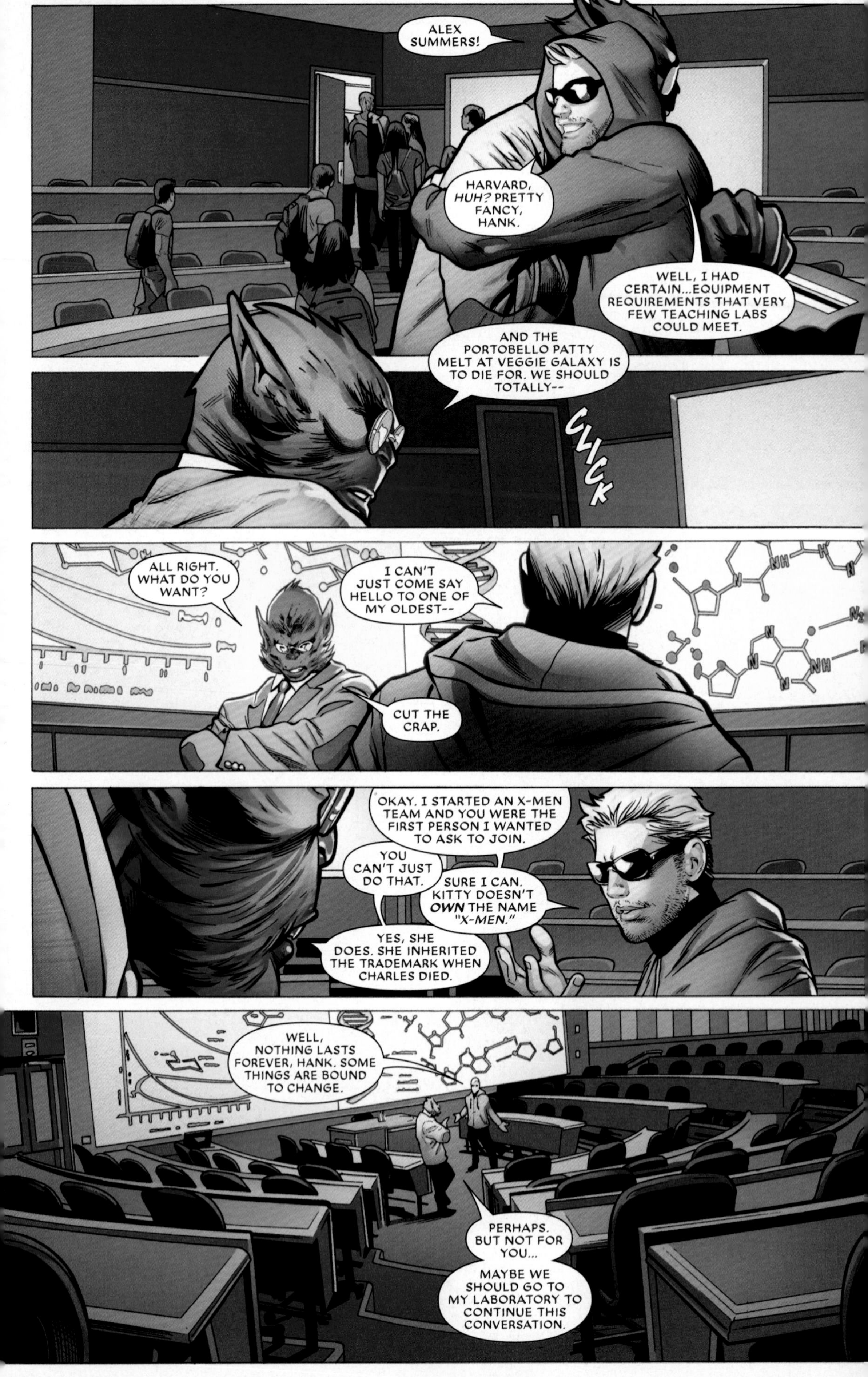
ALEX SUMMERS!
HARVARD, HUH? PRETTY FANCY, HANK.
WELL, I HAD CERTAIN...EQUIPMENT REQUIREMENTS THAT VERY FEW TEACHING LABS COULD MEET.
AND THE PORTOBELLO PATTY MELT AT VEGGIE GALAXY IS TO DIE FOR. WE SHOULD TOTALLY--
CLICK
ALL RIGHT. WHAT DO YOU WANT?
I CAN'T JUST COME SAY HELLO TO ONE OF MY OLDEST--
CUT THE CRAP.
OKAY. I STARTED AN X-MEN TEAM AND YOU WERE THE FIRST PERSON I WANTED TO ASK TO JOIN.
YOU CAN'T JUST DO THAT.
SURE I CAN. KITTY DOESN'T OWN THE NAME "X-MEN."
YES, SHE DOES. SHE INHERITED THE TRADEMARK WHEN CHARLES DIED.
WELL, NOTHING LASTS FOREVER, HANK. SOME THINGS ARE BOUND TO CHANGE.
PERHAPS. BUT NOT FOR YOU...
MAYBE WE SHOULD GO TO MY LABORATORY TO CONTINUE THIS CONVERSATION.

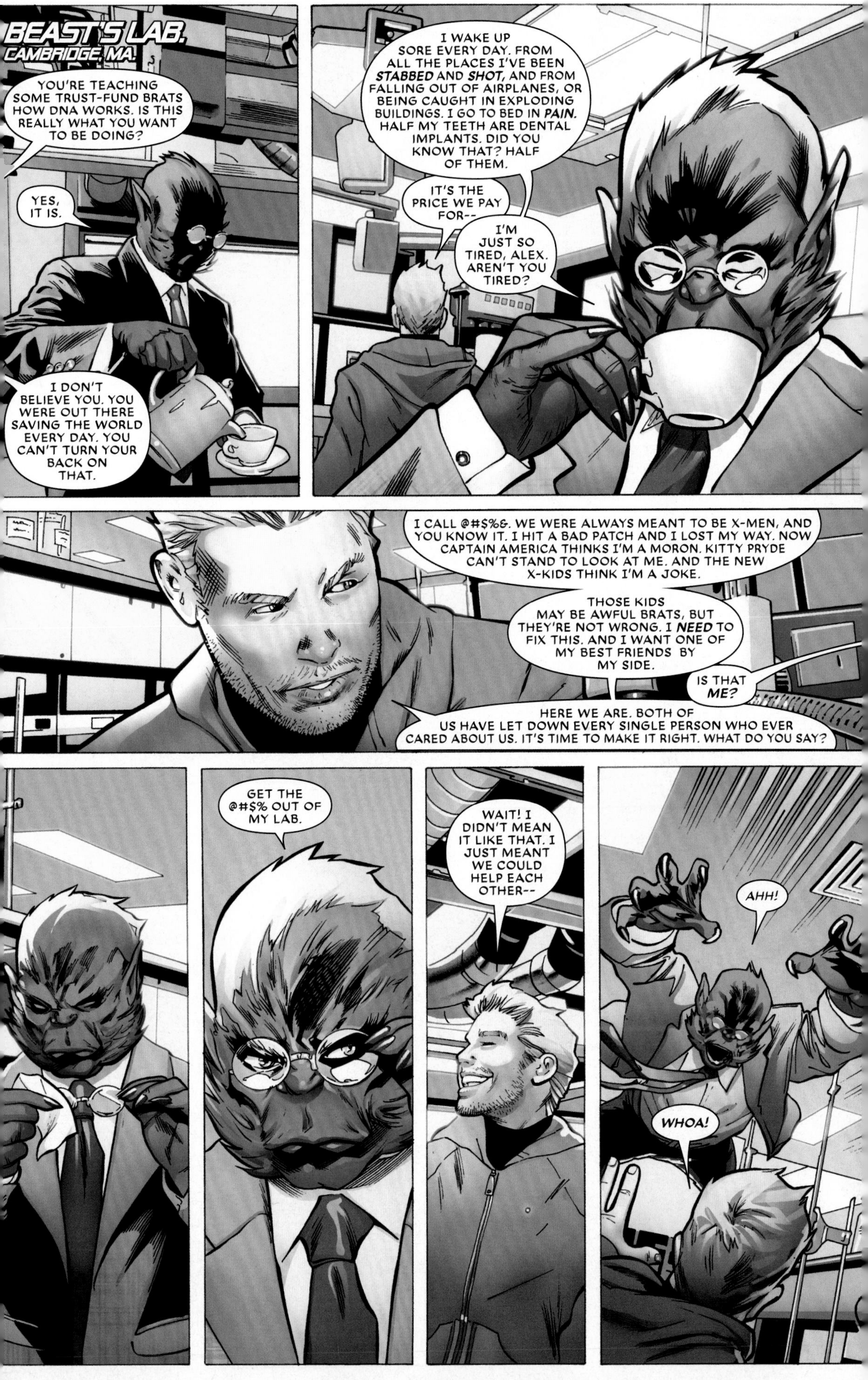
BEAST'S LAB. CAMBRIDGE, MA.
YOU'RE TEACHING SOME TRUST-FUND BRATS HOW DNA WORKS. IS THIS REALLY WHAT YOU WANT TO BE DOING?
YES, IT IS.
I DON'T BELIEVE YOU. YOU WERE OUT THERE SAVING THE WORLD EVERY DAY. YOU CAN'T TURN YOUR BACK ON THAT.
I WAKE UP SORE EVERY DAY. FROM ALL THE PLACES I'VE BEEN STABBED AND SHOT, AND FROM FALLING OUT OF AIRPLANES, OR BEING CAUGHT IN EXPLODING BUILDINGS. I GO TO BED IN PAIN. HALF MY TEETH ARE DENTAL IMPLANTS. DID YOU KNOW THAT? HALF OF THEM.
IT'S THE PRICE WE PAY FOR--
I'M JUST SO TIRED, ALEX. AREN'T YOU TIRED?
I CALL @#$%&. WE WERE ALWAYS MEANT TO BE X-MEN, AND YOU KNOW IT. I HIT A BAD PATCH AND I LOST MY WAY. NOW CAPTAIN AMERICA THINKS I'M A MORON. KITTY PRYDE CAN'T STAND TO LOOK AT ME. AND THE NEW X-KIDS THINK I'M A JOKE.
THOSE KIDS MAY BE AWFUL BRATS, BUT THEY'RE NOT WRONG. I NEED TO FIX THIS. AND I WANT ONE OF MY BEST FRIENDS BY MY SIDE.
IS THAT ME?
HERE WE ARE. BOTH OF US HAVE LET DOWN EVERY SINGLE PERSON WHO EVER CARED ABOUT US. IT'S TIME TO MAKE IT RIGHT. WHAT DO YOU SAY?
GET THE @#$% OUT OF MY LAB.
WAIT! I DIDN'T MEAN IT LIKE THAT. I JUST MEANT WE COULD HELP EACH OTHER--
AHH!
WHOA!

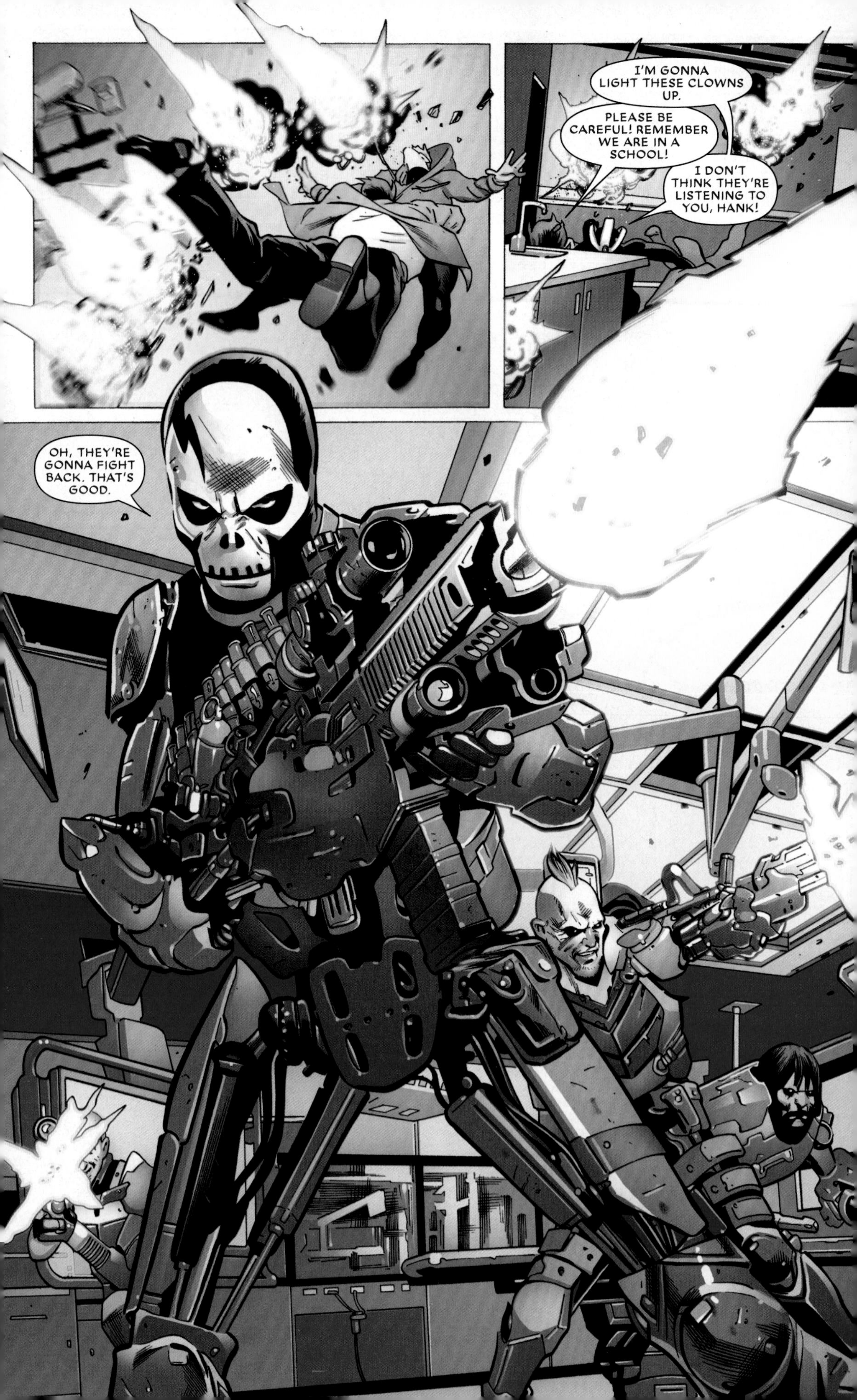
I'M GONNA LIGHT THESE CLOWNS UP.
PLEASE BE CAREFUL! REMEMBER WE ARE IN A SCHOOL!
I DON'T THINK THEY'RE LISTENING TO YOU, HANK!
OH, THEY'RE GONNA FIGHT BACK. THAT'S GOOD.

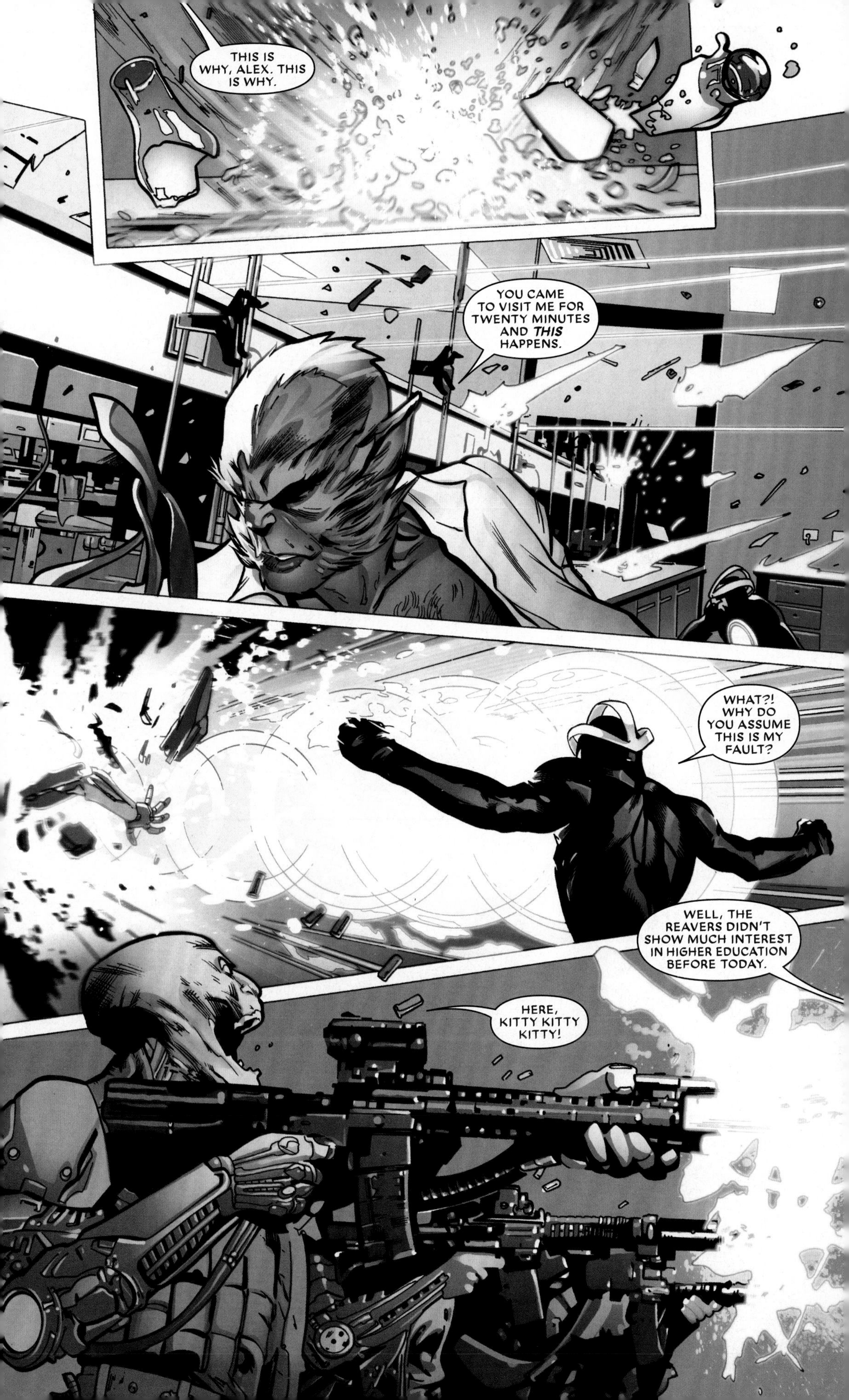
THIS IS WHY, ALEX. THIS IS WHY.
YOU CAME TO VISIT ME FOR TWENTY MINUTES AND *THIS* HAPPENS.
WHAT?! WHY DO YOU ASSUME THIS IS MY FAULT?
WELL, THE REAVERS DIDN'T SHOW MUCH INTEREST IN HIGHER EDUCATION BEFORE TODAY.
HERE, KITTY KITTY KITTY!

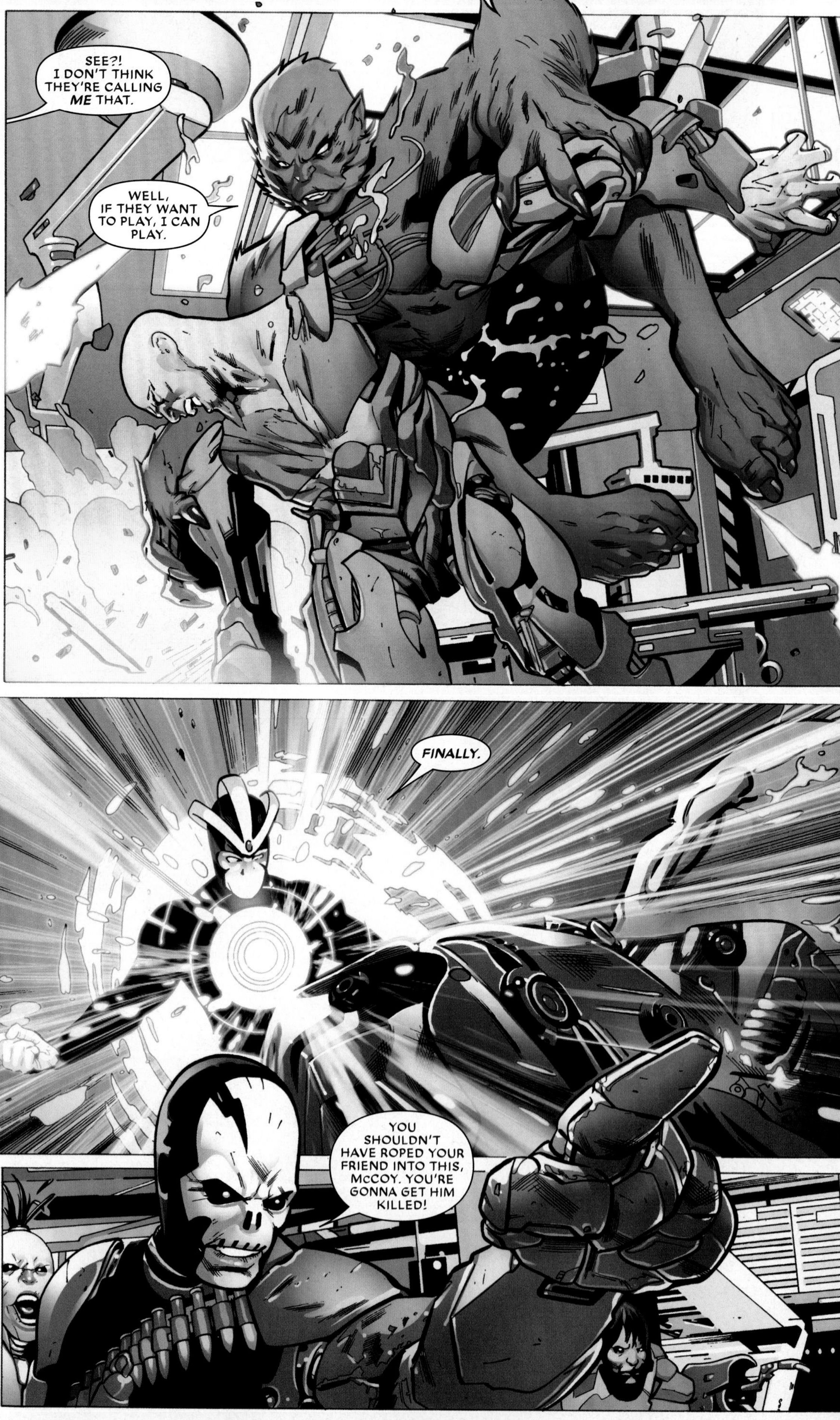
SEE?! I DON'T THINK THEY'RE CALLING *ME* THAT.
WELL, IF THEY WANT TO PLAY, I CAN PLAY.
FINALLY.
YOU SHOULDN'T HAVE ROPED YOUR FRIEND INTO THIS, McCOY. YOU'RE GONNA GET HIM KILLED!

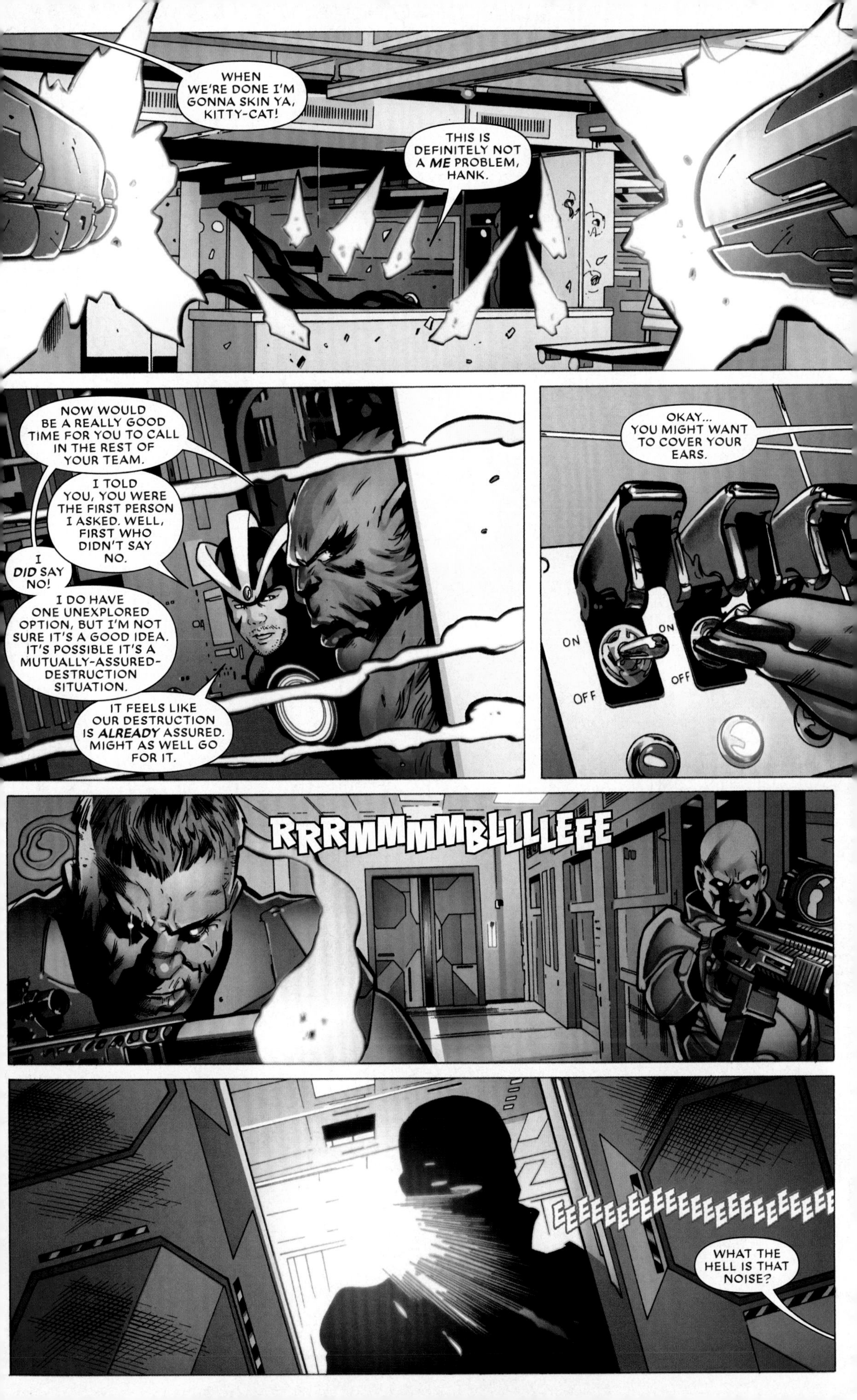
WHEN WE'RE DONE I'M GONNA SKIN YA, KITTY-CAT!
THIS IS DEFINITELY NOT A *ME* PROBLEM, HANK.
NOW WOULD BE A REALLY GOOD TIME FOR YOU TO CALL IN THE REST OF YOUR TEAM.
I TOLD YOU, YOU WERE THE FIRST PERSON I ASKED. WELL, FIRST WHO DIDN'T SAY NO.
I *DID* SAY NO!
I DO HAVE ONE UNEXPLORED OPTION, BUT I'M NOT SURE IT'S A GOOD IDEA. IT'S POSSIBLE IT'S A MUTUALLY-ASSURED-DESTRUCTION SITUATION.
IT FEELS LIKE OUR DESTRUCTION IS *ALREADY* ASSURED. MIGHT AS WELL GO FOR IT.
OKAY... YOU MIGHT WANT TO COVER YOUR EARS.
ON
OFF
ON
OFF
RRRMMMMMBLLLLEEE
EEEEEEEEEEEEEEEEEEEEEE
WHAT THE HELL IS THAT NOISE?

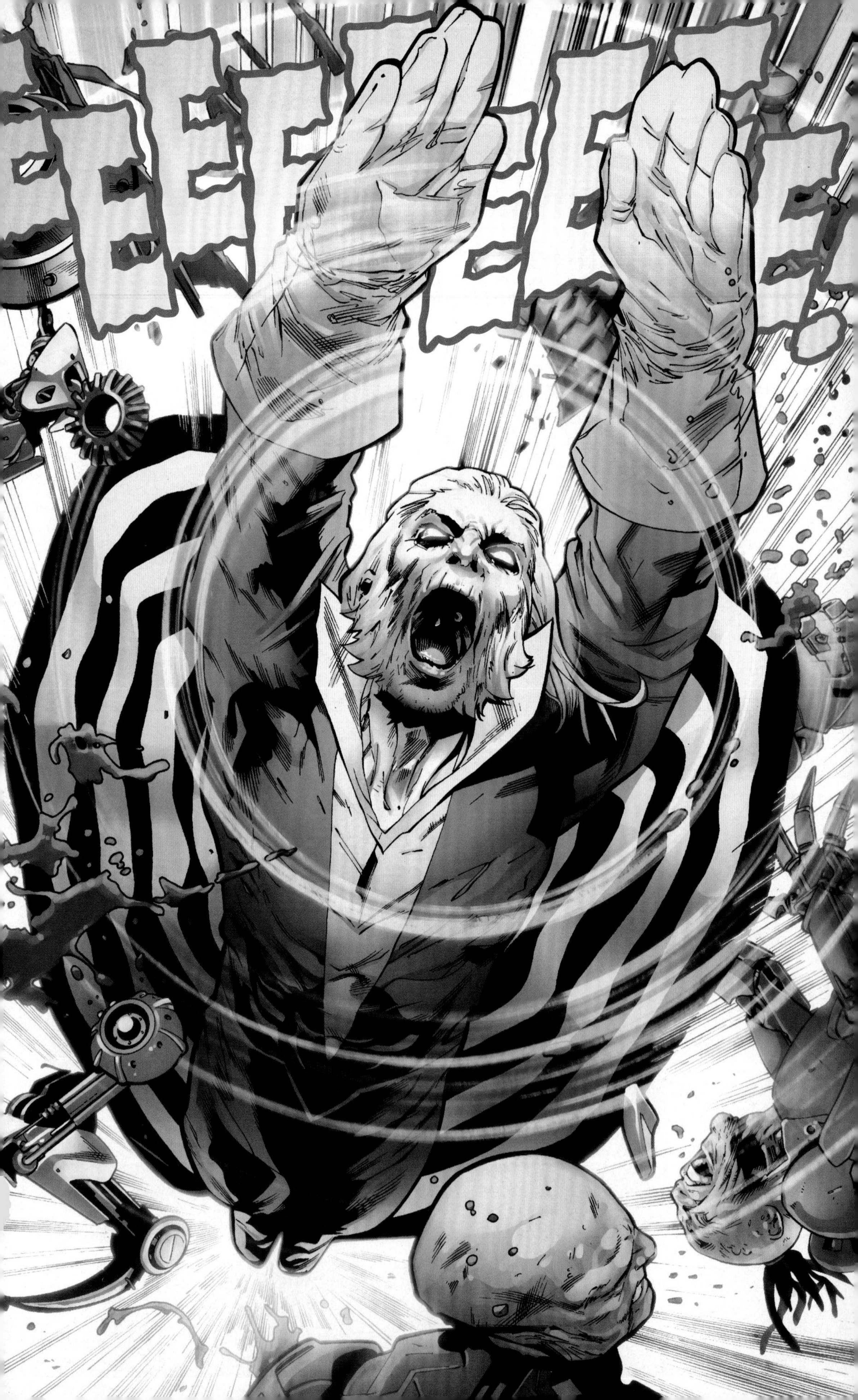

14

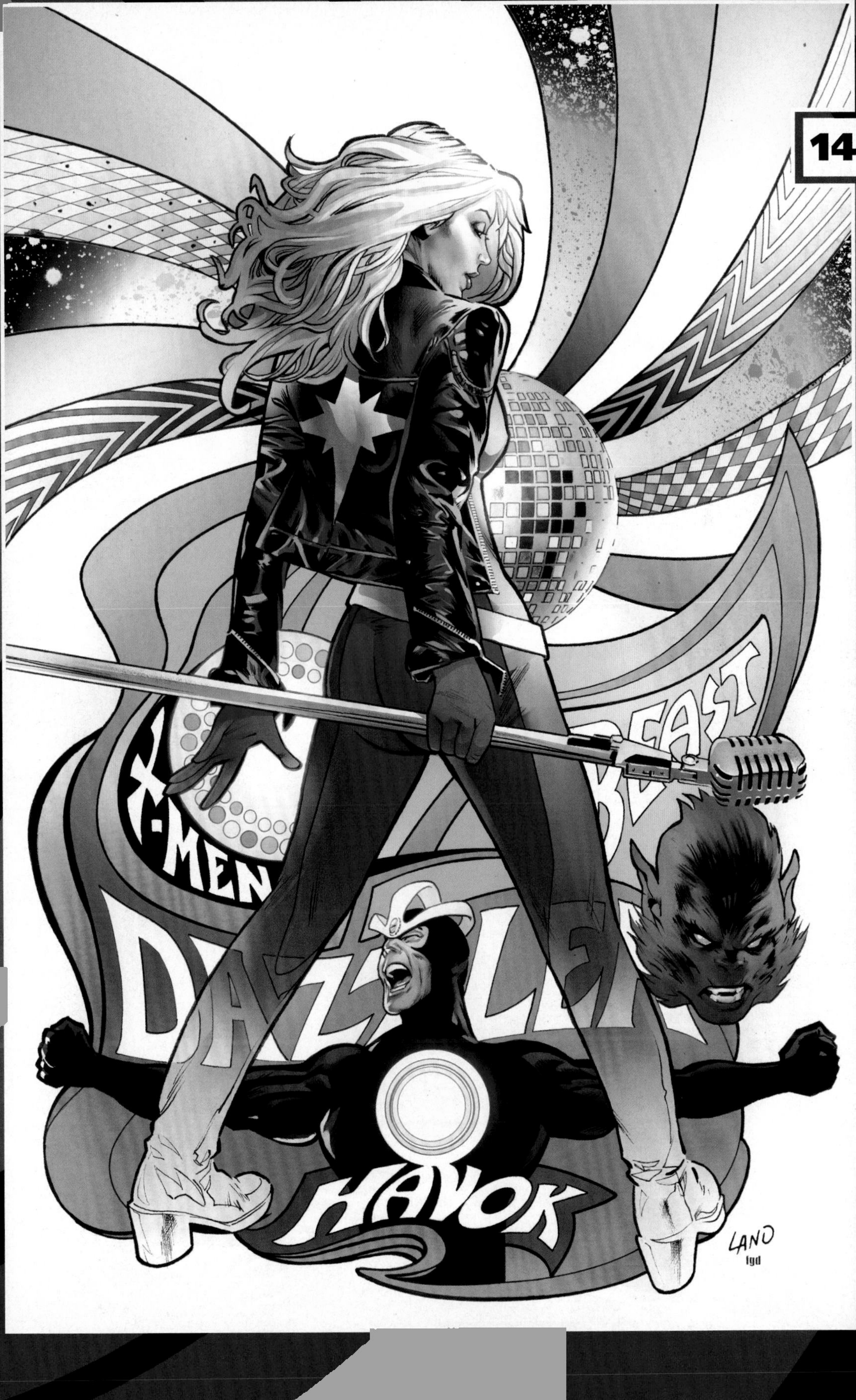
X-MEN
BEAST
HAVOK
LAND

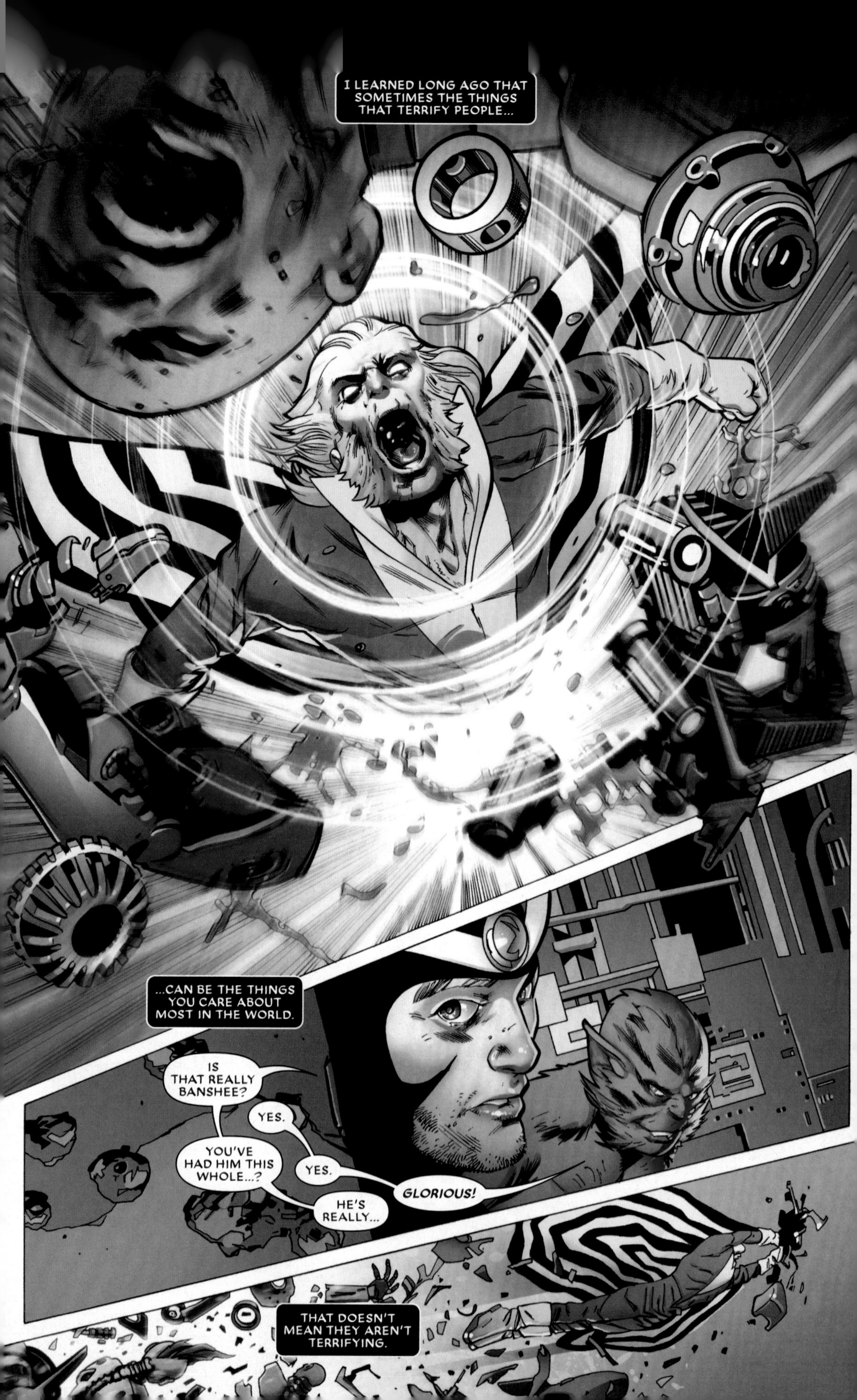
I LEARNED LONG AGO THAT SOMETIMES THE THINGS THAT TERRIFY PEOPLE...
...CAN BE THE THINGS YOU CARE ABOUT MOST IN THE WORLD.
IS THAT REALLY BANSHEE?
YES.
YOU'VE HAD HIM THIS WHOLE...?
YES.
HE'S REALLY...
GLORIOUS!
THAT DOESN'T MEAN THEY AREN'T TERRIFYING.

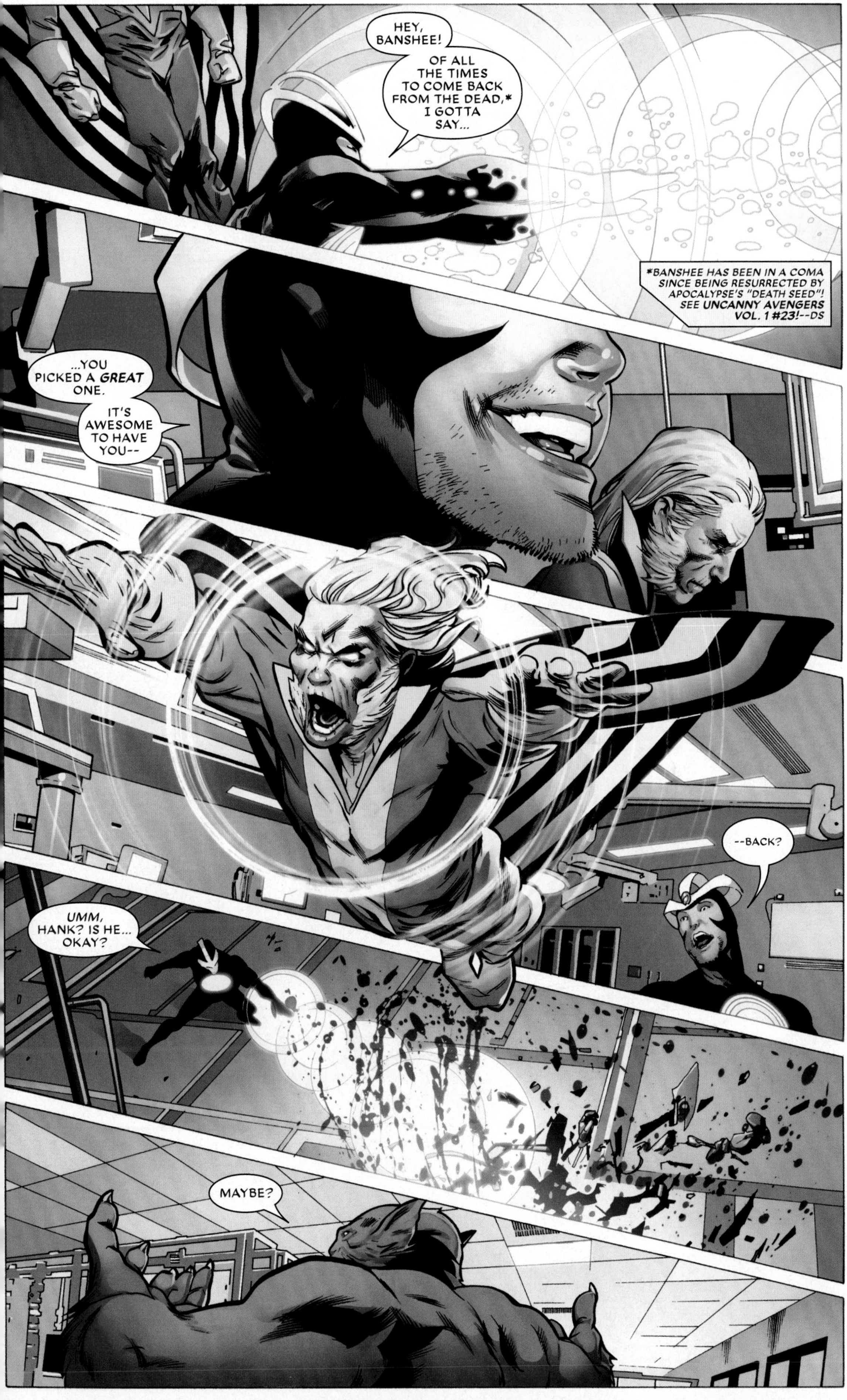
HEY, BANSHEE!
OF ALL THE TIMES TO COME BACK FROM THE DEAD,* I GOTTA SAY...
*BANSHEE HAS BEEN IN A COMA SINCE BEING RESURRECTED BY APOCALYPSE'S "DEATH SEED"! SEE UNCANNY AVENGERS VOL. 1 #23!--DS
...YOU PICKED A GREAT ONE.
IT'S AWESOME TO HAVE YOU--
--BACK?
UMM, HANK? IS HE... OKAY?
MAYBE?

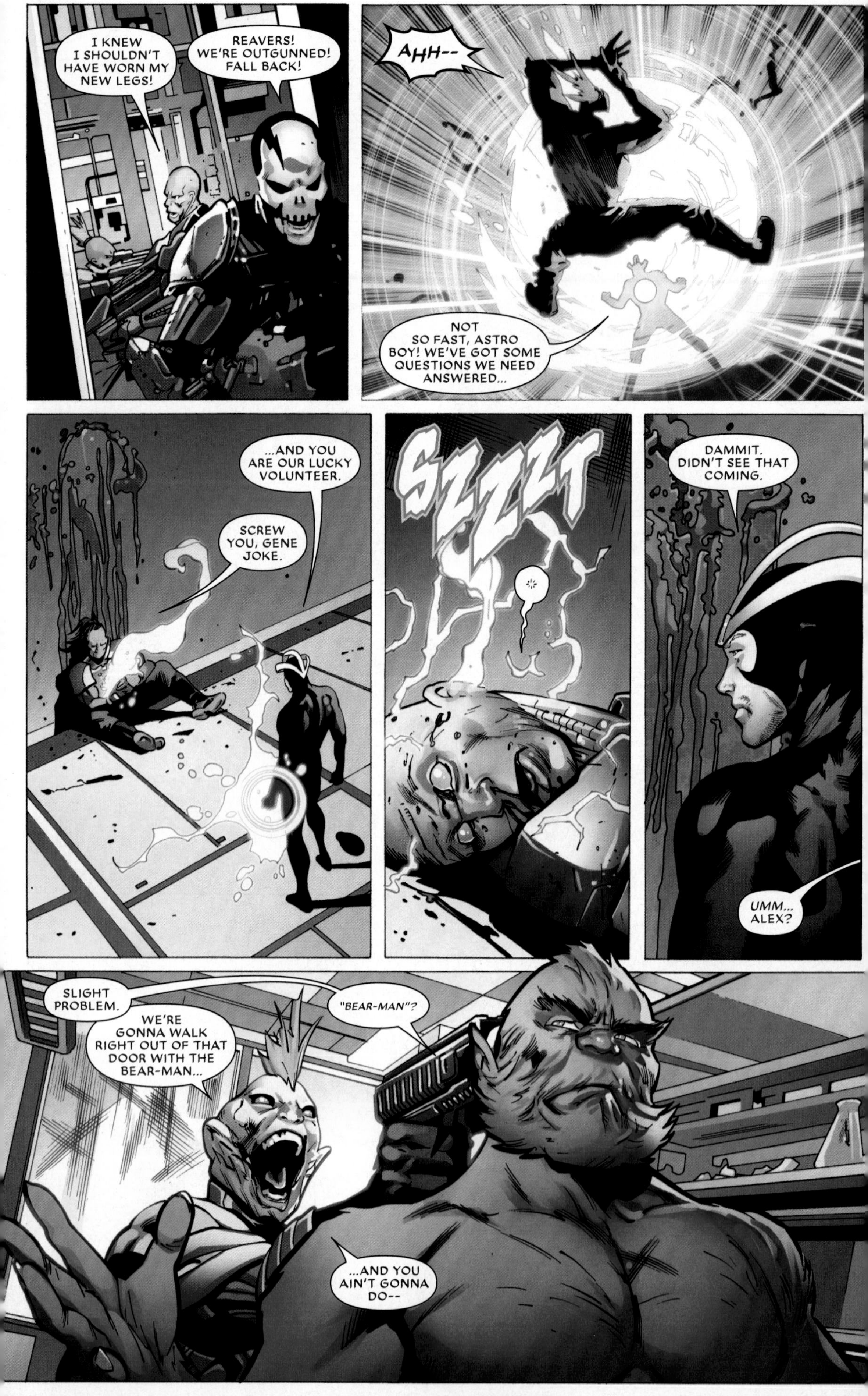

I KNEW I SHOULDN'T HAVE WORN MY NEW LEGS!
REAVERS! WE'RE OUTGUNNED! FALL BACK!
AHH--
NOT SO FAST, ASTRO BOY! WE'VE GOT SOME QUESTIONS WE NEED ANSWERED...
...AND YOU ARE OUR LUCKY VOLUNTEER.
SCREW YOU, GENE JOKE.
SZZZT
DAMMIT. DIDN'T SEE THAT COMING.
UMM... ALEX?
SLIGHT PROBLEM.
"BEAR-MAN"?
WE'RE GONNA WALK RIGHT OUT OF THAT DOOR WITH THE BEAR-MAN...
...AND YOU AIN'T GONNA DO--

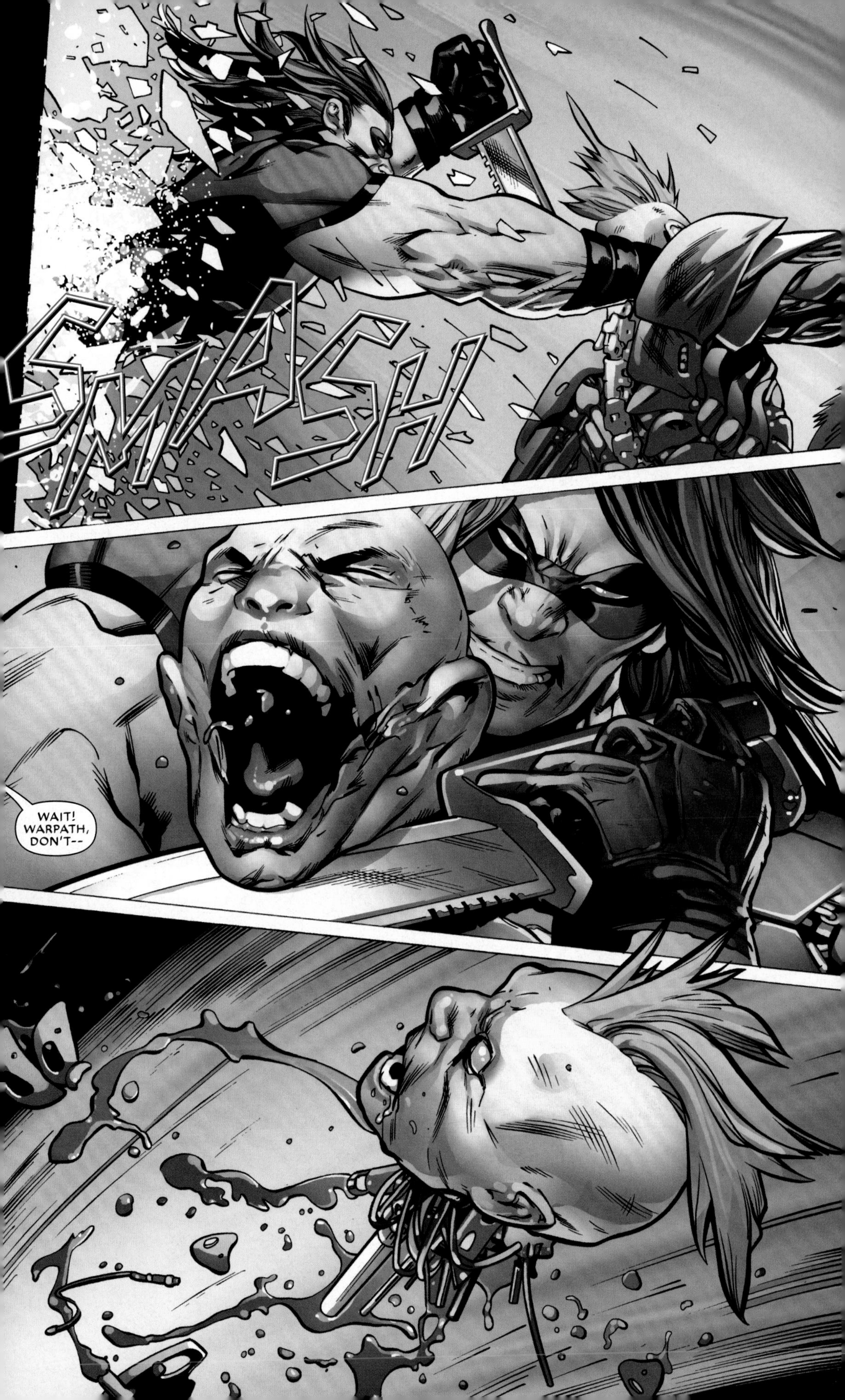
SMASH
WAIT! WARPATH, DON'T--

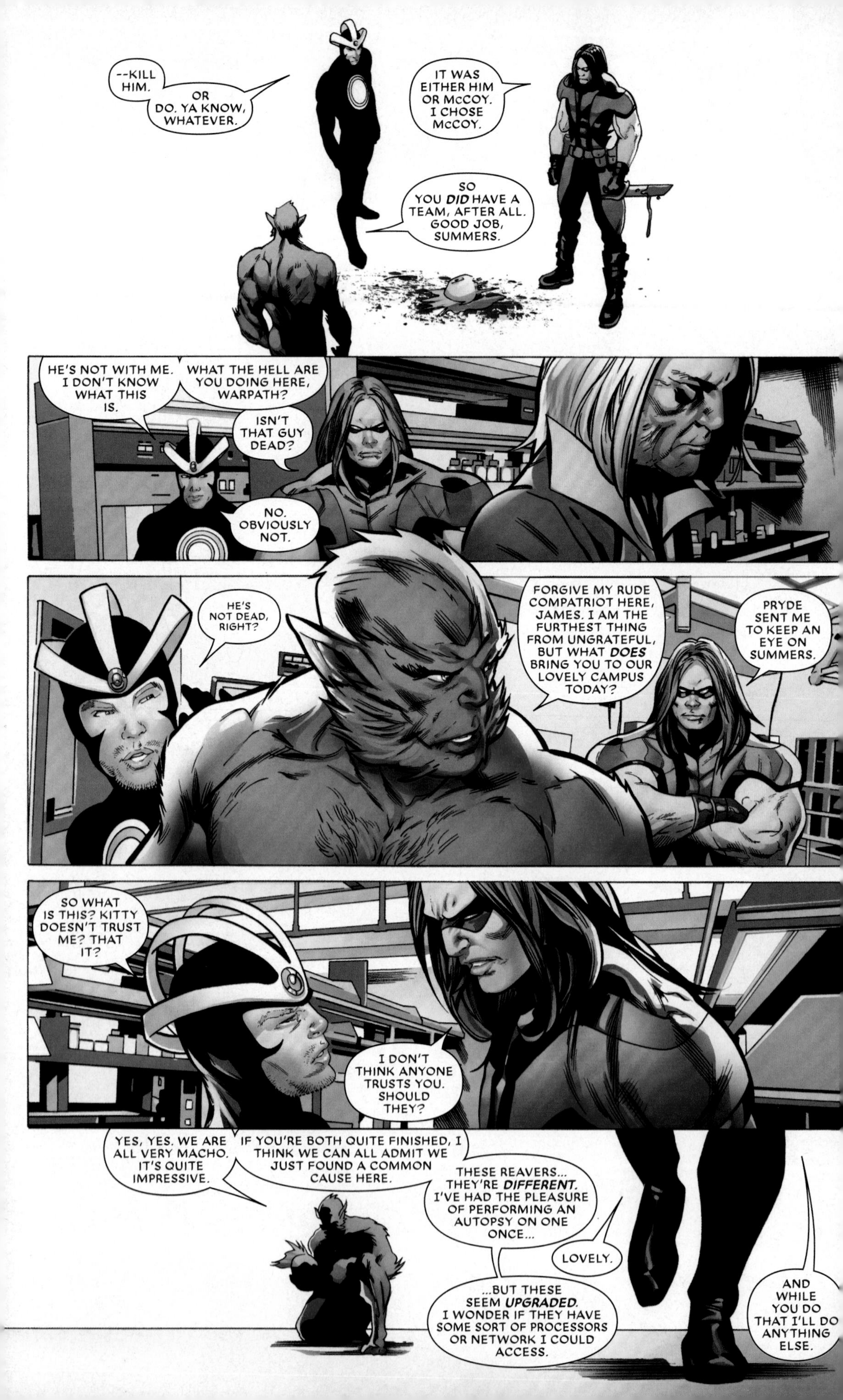
--KILL HIM.
OR DO. YA KNOW, WHATEVER.
IT WAS EITHER HIM OR McCOY. I CHOSE McCOY.
SO YOU DID HAVE A TEAM, AFTER ALL. GOOD JOB, SUMMERS.
HE'S NOT WITH ME. I DON'T KNOW WHAT THIS IS.
WHAT THE HELL ARE YOU DOING HERE, WARPATH?
ISN'T THAT GUY DEAD?
NO. OBVIOUSLY NOT.
HE'S NOT DEAD, RIGHT?
FORGIVE MY RUDE COMPATRIOT HERE, JAMES. I AM THE FURTHEST THING FROM UNGRATEFUL, BUT WHAT DOES BRING YOU TO OUR LOVELY CAMPUS TODAY?
PRYDE SENT ME TO KEEP AN EYE ON SUMMERS.
SO WHAT IS THIS? KITTY DOESN'T TRUST ME? THAT IT?
I DON'T THINK ANYONE TRUSTS YOU. SHOULD THEY?
YES, YES. WE ARE ALL VERY MACHO. IT'S QUITE IMPRESSIVE.
IF YOU'RE BOTH QUITE FINISHED, I THINK WE CAN ALL ADMIT WE JUST FOUND A COMMON CAUSE HERE.
THESE REAVERS... THEY'RE DIFFERENT. I'VE HAD THE PLEASURE OF PERFORMING AN AUTOPSY ON ONE ONCE...
LOVELY.
...BUT THESE SEEM UPGRADED. I WONDER IF THEY HAVE SOME SORT OF PROCESSORS OR NETWORK I COULD ACCESS.
AND WHILE YOU DO THAT I'LL DO ANYTHING ELSE.

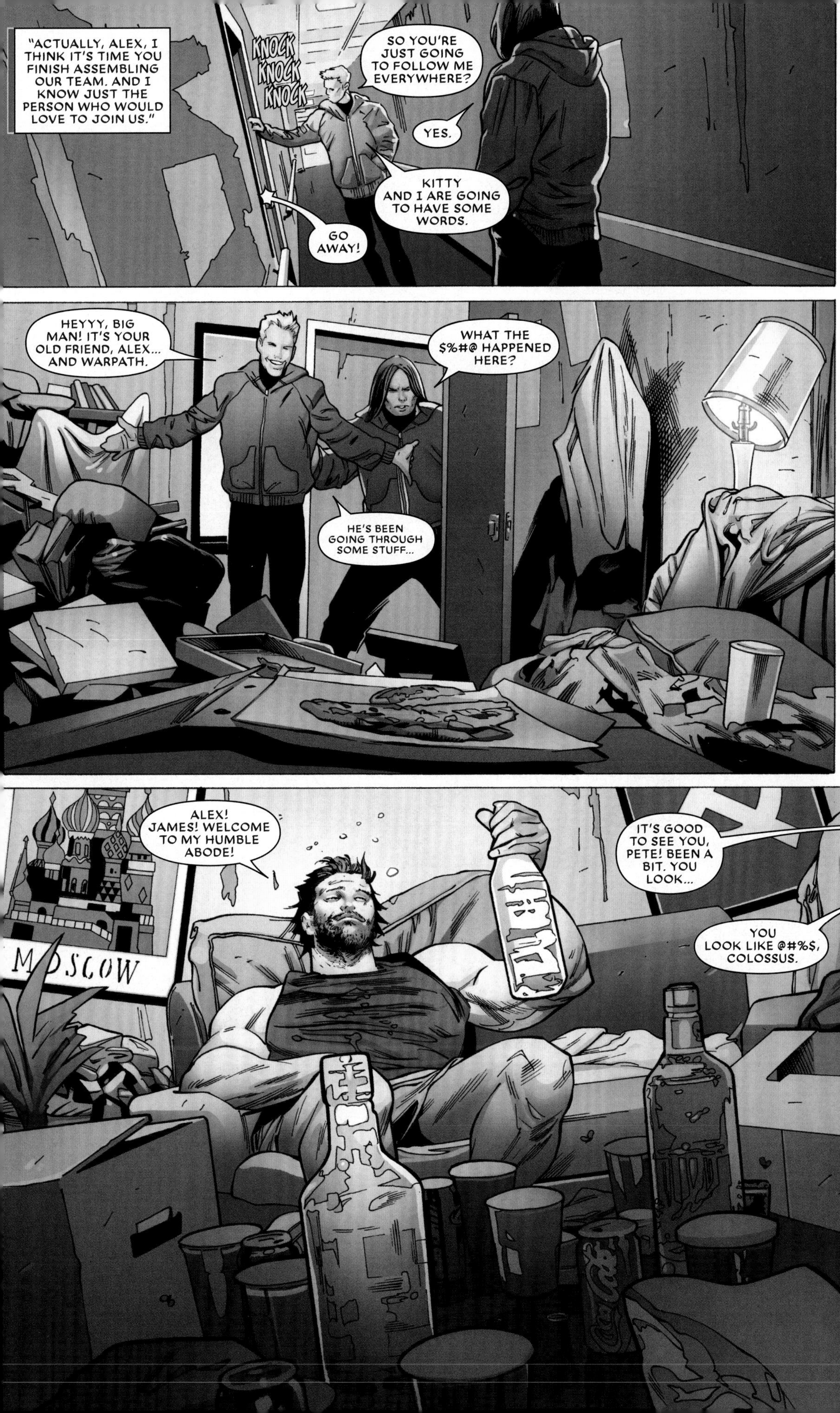
"ACTUALLY, ALEX, I THINK IT'S TIME YOU FINISH ASSEMBLING OUR TEAM. AND I KNOW JUST THE PERSON WHO WOULD LOVE TO JOIN US."
KNOCK KNOCK KNOCK
SO YOU'RE JUST GOING TO FOLLOW ME EVERYWHERE?
YES.
KITTY AND I ARE GOING TO HAVE SOME WORDS.
GO AWAY!
HEYYY, BIG MAN! IT'S YOUR OLD FRIEND, ALEX... AND WARPATH.
WHAT THE $%#@ HAPPENED HERE?
HE'S BEEN GOING THROUGH SOME STUFF...
ALEX! JAMES! WELCOME TO MY HUMBLE ABODE!
MOSCOW
IT'S GOOD TO SEE YOU, PETE! BEEN A BIT. YOU LOOK...
YOU LOOK LIKE @#%$, COLOSSUS.

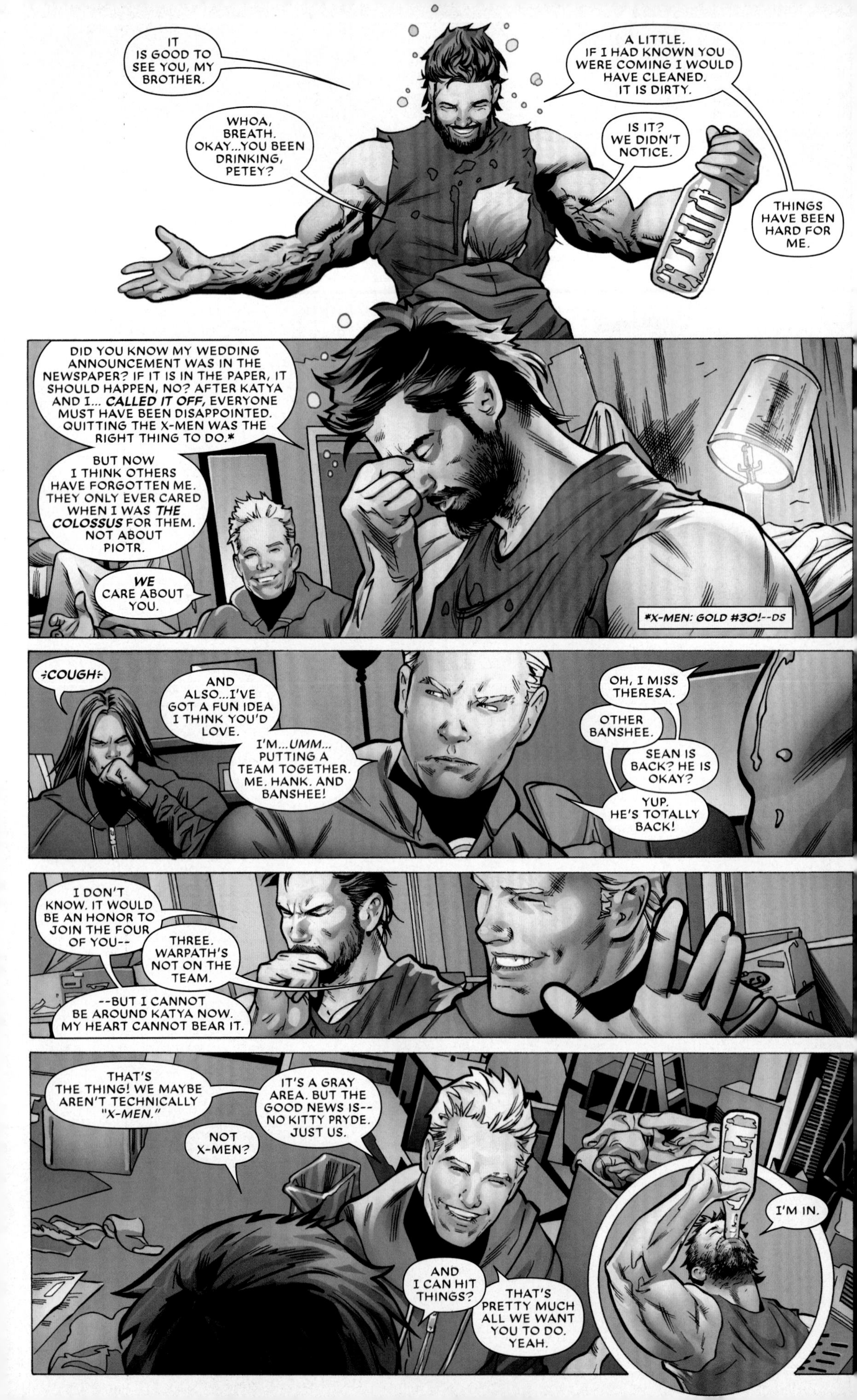

IT IS GOOD TO SEE YOU, MY BROTHER.
A LITTLE. IF I HAD KNOWN YOU WERE COMING I WOULD HAVE CLEANED. IT IS DIRTY.
WHOA, BREATH. OKAY...YOU BEEN DRINKING, PETEY?
IS IT? WE DIDN'T NOTICE.
THINGS HAVE BEEN HARD FOR ME.
DID YOU KNOW MY WEDDING ANNOUNCEMENT WAS IN THE NEWSPAPER? IF IT IS IN THE PAPER, IT SHOULD HAPPEN, NO? AFTER KATYA AND I... CALLED IT OFF, EVERYONE MUST HAVE BEEN DISAPPOINTED. QUITTING THE X-MEN WAS THE RIGHT THING TO DO.*
BUT NOW I THINK OTHERS HAVE FORGOTTEN ME. THEY ONLY EVER CARED WHEN I WAS THE COLOSSUS FOR THEM. NOT ABOUT PIOTR.
WE CARE ABOUT YOU.
*X-MEN: GOLD #30!--DS
COUGH
AND ALSO...I'VE GOT A FUN IDEA I THINK YOU'D LOVE.
I'M...UMM... PUTTING A TEAM TOGETHER. ME. HANK. AND BANSHEE!
OH, I MISS THERESA.
OTHER BANSHEE.
SEAN IS BACK? HE IS OKAY?
YUP. HE'S TOTALLY BACK!
I DON'T KNOW. IT WOULD BE AN HONOR TO JOIN THE FOUR OF YOU--
THREE. WARPATH'S NOT ON THE TEAM.
--BUT I CANNOT BE AROUND KATYA NOW. MY HEART CANNOT BEAR IT.
THAT'S THE THING! WE MAYBE AREN'T TECHNICALLY "X-MEN."
IT'S A GRAY AREA. BUT THE GOOD NEWS IS-- NO KITTY PRYDE. JUST US.
NOT X-MEN?
I'M IN.
AND I CAN HIT THINGS?
THAT'S PRETTY MUCH ALL WE WANT YOU TO DO. YEAH.

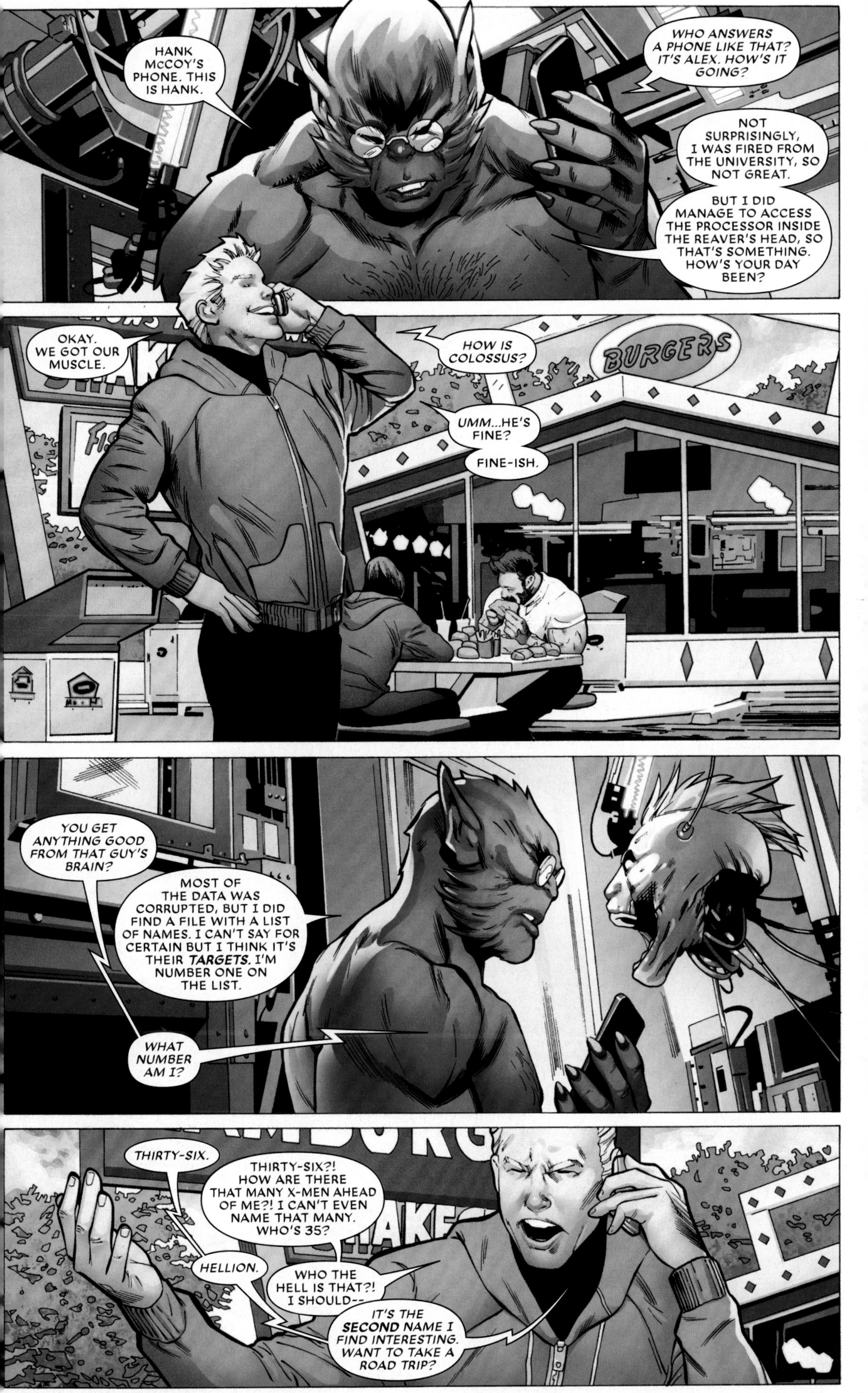
HANK McCOY'S PHONE. THIS IS HANK.
WHO ANSWERS A PHONE LIKE THAT? IT'S ALEX. HOW'S IT GOING?
NOT SURPRISINGLY, I WAS FIRED FROM THE UNIVERSITY, SO NOT GREAT.
BUT I DID MANAGE TO ACCESS THE PROCESSOR INSIDE THE REAVER'S HEAD, SO THAT'S SOMETHING. HOW'S YOUR DAY BEEN?
OKAY. WE GOT OUR MUSCLE.
HOW IS COLOSSUS?
UMM...HE'S FINE?
FINE-ISH.
BURGERS
YOU GET ANYTHING GOOD FROM THAT GUY'S BRAIN?
MOST OF THE DATA WAS CORRUPTED, BUT I DID FIND A FILE WITH A LIST OF NAMES. I CAN'T SAY FOR CERTAIN BUT I THINK IT'S THEIR TARGETS. I'M NUMBER ONE ON THE LIST.
WHAT NUMBER AM I?
THIRTY-SIX.
THIRTY-SIX?! HOW ARE THERE THAT MANY X-MEN AHEAD OF ME?! I CAN'T EVEN NAME THAT MANY. WHO'S 35?
HELLION.
WHO THE HELL IS THAT?! I SHOULD--
IT'S THE SECOND NAME I FIND INTERESTING. WANT TO TAKE A ROAD TRIP?

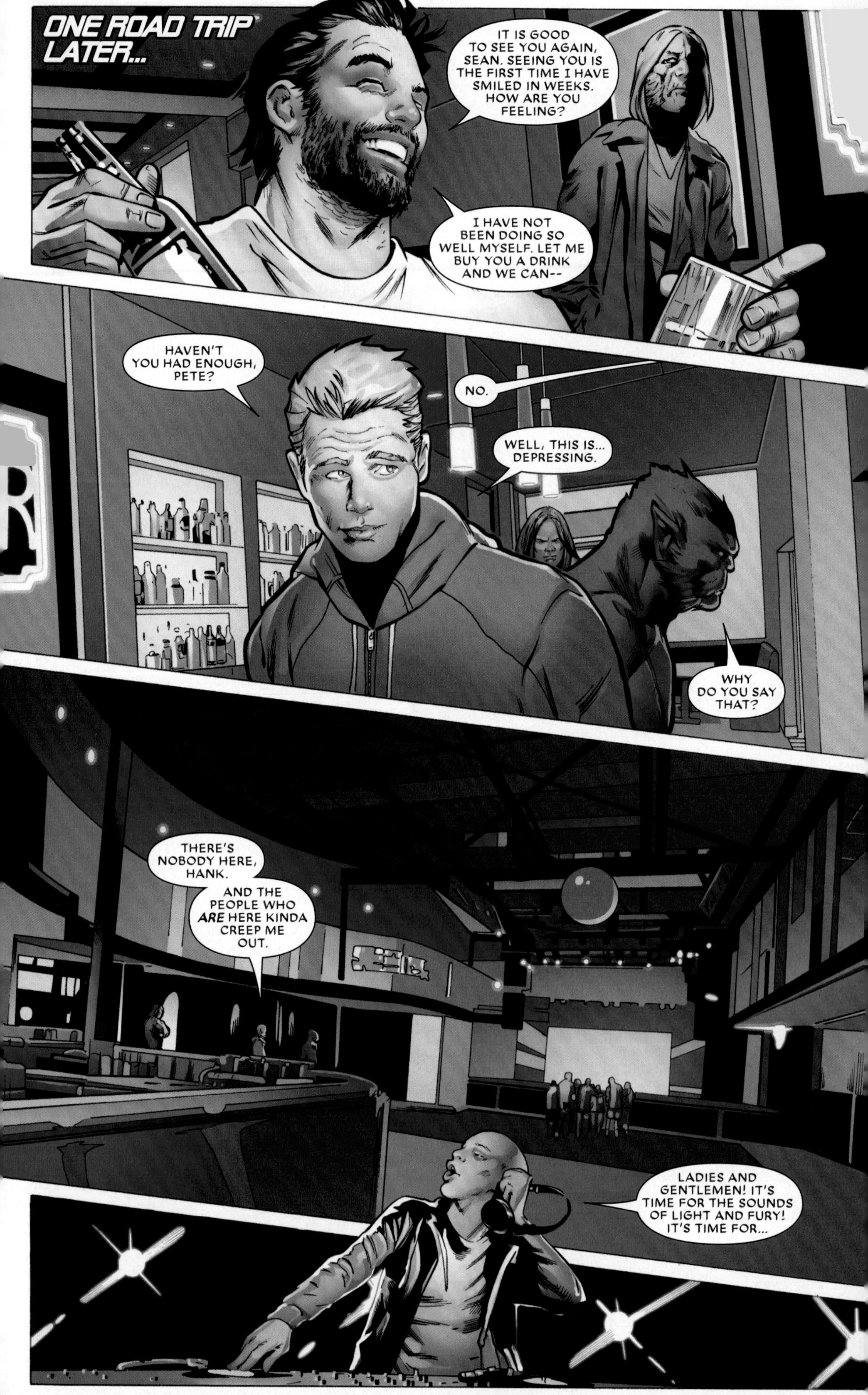
ONE ROAD TRIP LATER...
IT IS GOOD TO SEE YOU AGAIN, SEAN. SEEING YOU IS THE FIRST TIME I HAVE SMILED IN WEEKS. HOW ARE YOU FEELING?
I HAVE NOT BEEN DOING SO WELL MYSELF. LET ME BUY YOU A DRINK AND WE CAN--
HAVEN'T YOU HAD ENOUGH, PETE?
NO.
WELL, THIS IS... DEPRESSING.
WHY DO YOU SAY THAT?
THERE'S NOBODY HERE, HANK.
AND THE PEOPLE WHO *ARE* HERE KINDA CREEP ME OUT.
LADIES AND GENTLEMEN! IT'S TIME FOR THE SOUNDS OF LIGHT AND FURY! IT'S TIME FOR...

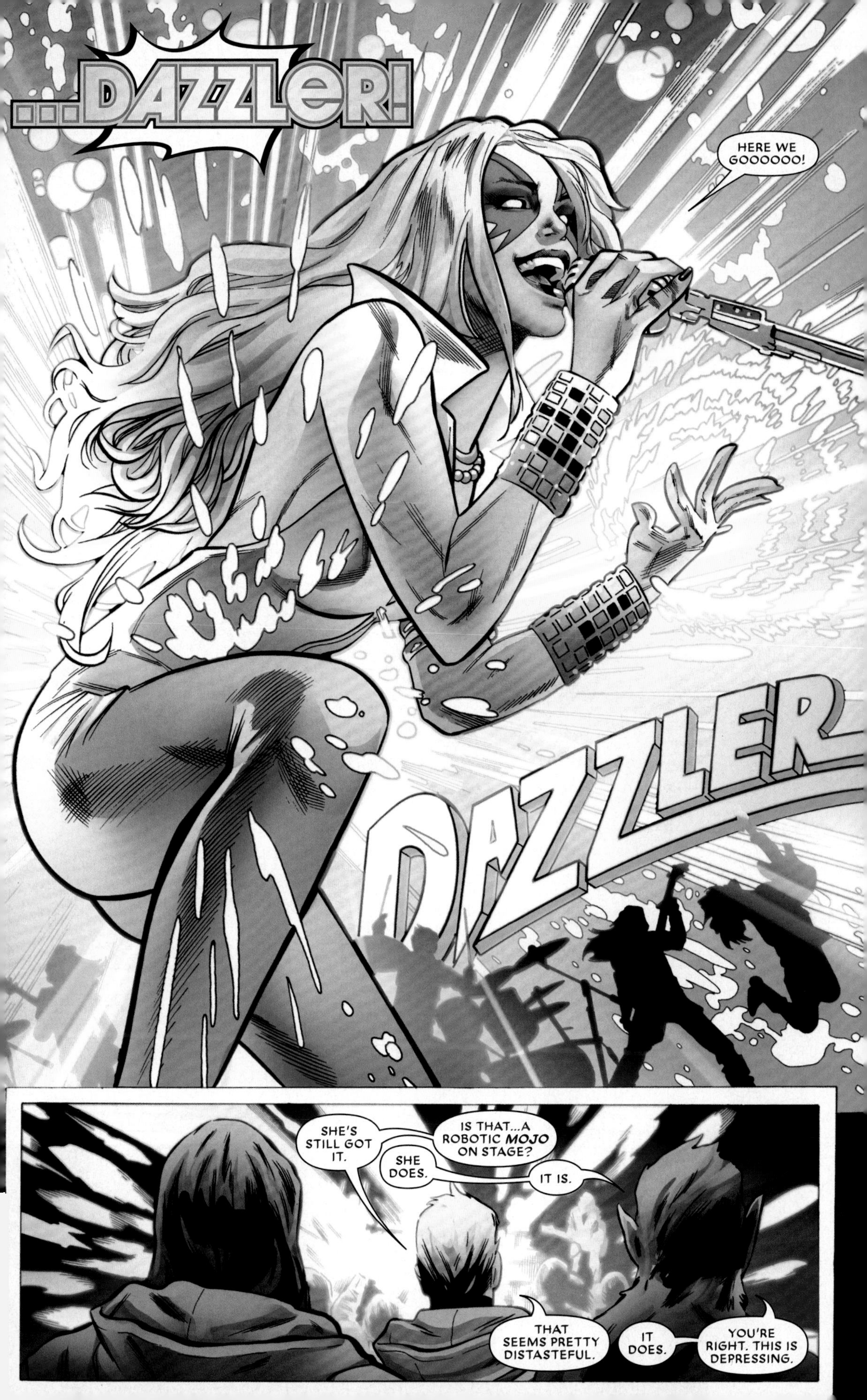
...DAZZLER!
HERE WE GOOOOOO!
DAZZLER
SHE'S STILL GOT IT.
IS THAT...A ROBOTIC MOJO ON STAGE?
SHE DOES.
IT IS.
THAT SEEMS PRETTY DISTASTEFUL.
IT DOES.
YOU'RE RIGHT. THIS IS DEPRESSING.

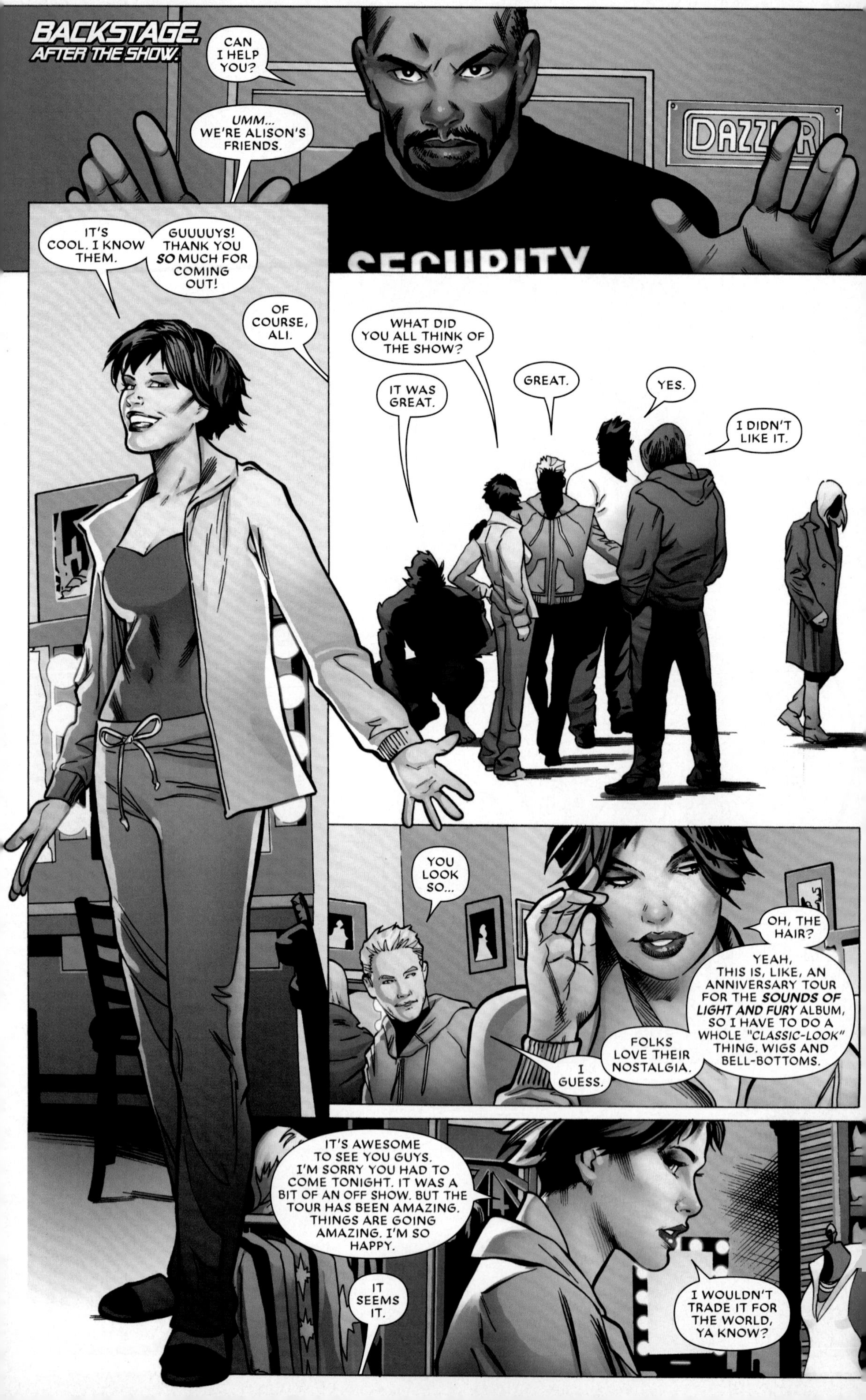

BACKSTAGE. AFTER THE SHOW.
CAN I HELP YOU?
UMM... WE'RE ALISON'S FRIENDS.
DAZZLER
SECURITY
IT'S COOL. I KNOW THEM.
GUUUUYS! THANK YOU SO MUCH FOR COMING OUT!
OF COURSE, ALI.
WHAT DID YOU ALL THINK OF THE SHOW?
IT WAS GREAT.
GREAT.
YES.
I DIDN'T LIKE IT.
YOU LOOK SO...
OH, THE HAIR?
YEAH, THIS IS, LIKE, AN ANNIVERSARY TOUR FOR THE SOUNDS OF LIGHT AND FURY ALBUM, SO I HAVE TO DO A WHOLE "CLASSIC-LOOK" THING. WIGS AND BELL-BOTTOMS.
FOLKS LOVE THEIR NOSTALGIA.
I GUESS.
IT'S AWESOME TO SEE YOU GUYS. I'M SORRY YOU HAD TO COME TONIGHT. IT WAS A BIT OF AN OFF SHOW. BUT THE TOUR HAS BEEN AMAZING. THINGS ARE GOING AMAZING. I'M SO HAPPY.
IT SEEMS IT.
I WOULDN'T TRADE IT FOR THE WORLD, YA KNOW?

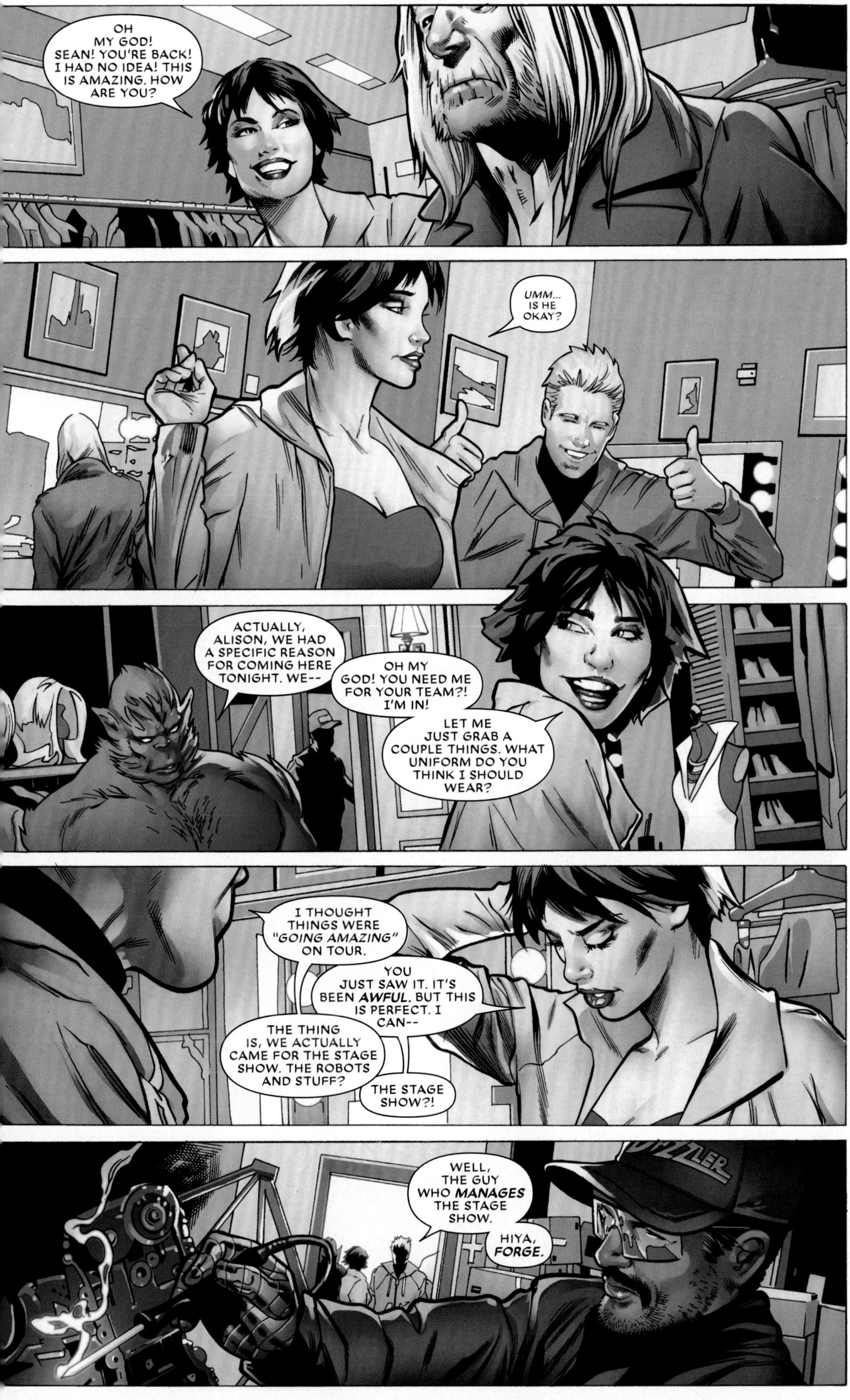
OH MY GOD! SEAN! YOU'RE BACK! I HAD NO IDEA! THIS IS AMAZING. HOW ARE YOU?
UMM... IS HE OKAY?
ACTUALLY, ALISON, WE HAD A SPECIFIC REASON FOR COMING HERE TONIGHT. WE--
OH MY GOD! YOU NEED ME FOR YOUR TEAM?! I'M IN!
LET ME JUST GRAB A COUPLE THINGS. WHAT UNIFORM DO YOU THINK I SHOULD WEAR?
I THOUGHT THINGS WERE "GOING AMAZING" ON TOUR.
YOU JUST SAW IT. IT'S BEEN AWFUL. BUT THIS IS PERFECT. I CAN--
THE THING IS, WE ACTUALLY CAME FOR THE STAGE SHOW. THE ROBOTS AND STUFF?
THE STAGE SHOW?!
WELL, THE GUY WHO MANAGES THE STAGE SHOW.
HIYA, FORGE.
DAZZLER

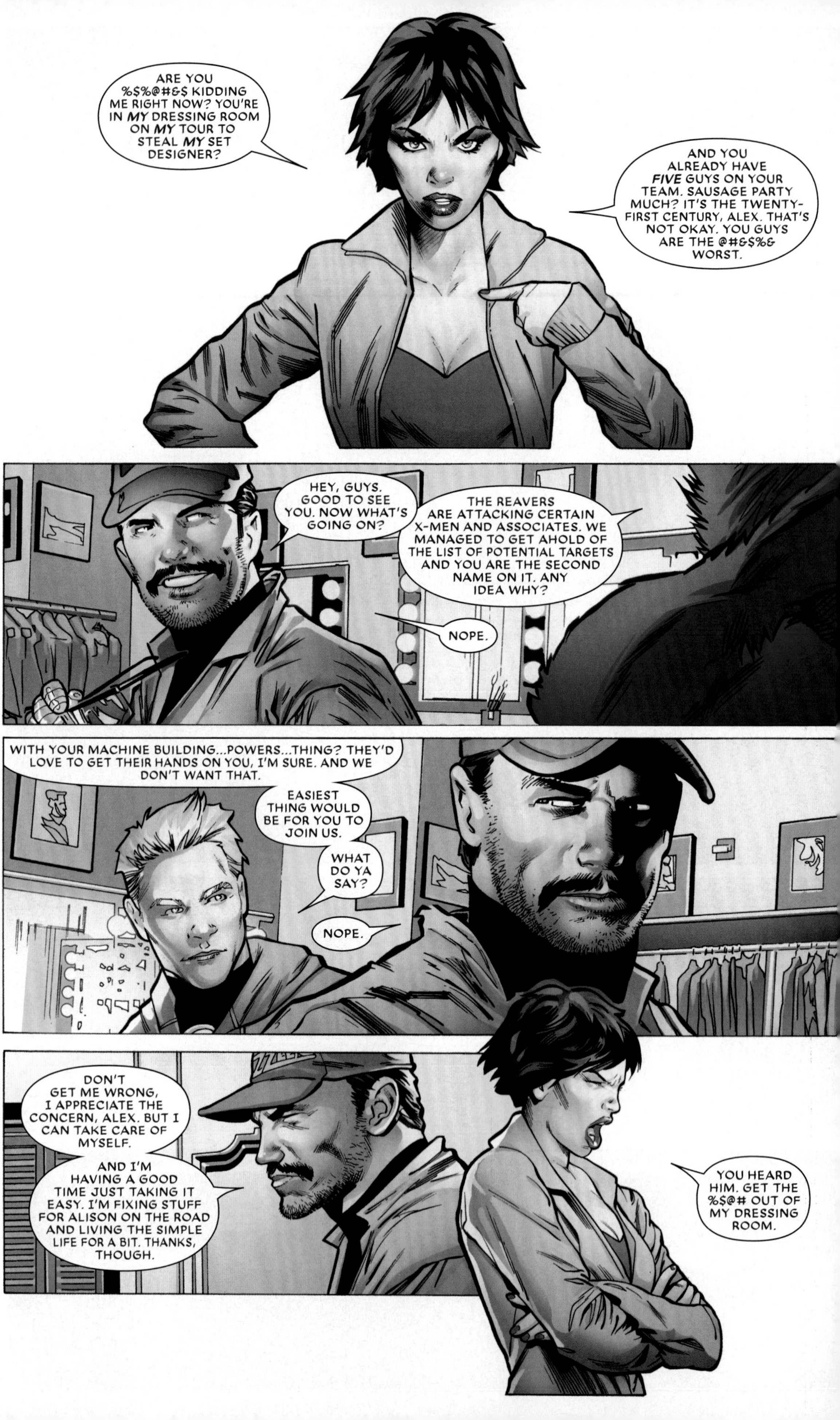
ARE YOU %$%@#&$ KIDDING ME RIGHT NOW? YOU'RE IN MY DRESSING ROOM ON MY TOUR TO STEAL MY SET DESIGNER?
AND YOU ALREADY HAVE FIVE GUYS ON YOUR TEAM. SAUSAGE PARTY MUCH? IT'S THE TWENTY-FIRST CENTURY, ALEX. THAT'S NOT OKAY. YOU GUYS ARE THE @#&$%& WORST.
HEY, GUYS. GOOD TO SEE YOU. NOW WHAT'S GOING ON?
THE REAVERS ARE ATTACKING CERTAIN X-MEN AND ASSOCIATES. WE MANAGED TO GET AHOLD OF THE LIST OF POTENTIAL TARGETS AND YOU ARE THE SECOND NAME ON IT. ANY IDEA WHY?
NOPE.
WITH YOUR MACHINE BUILDING...POWERS...THING? THEY'D LOVE TO GET THEIR HANDS ON YOU, I'M SURE. AND WE DON'T WANT THAT.
EASIEST THING WOULD BE FOR YOU TO JOIN US.
WHAT DO YA SAY?
NOPE.
DON'T GET ME WRONG, I APPRECIATE THE CONCERN, ALEX. BUT I CAN TAKE CARE OF MYSELF.
AND I'M HAVING A GOOD TIME JUST TAKING IT EASY. I'M FIXING STUFF FOR ALISON ON THE ROAD AND LIVING THE SIMPLE LIFE FOR A BIT. THANKS, THOUGH.
YOU HEARD HIM. GET THE %$@# OUT OF MY DRESSING ROOM.

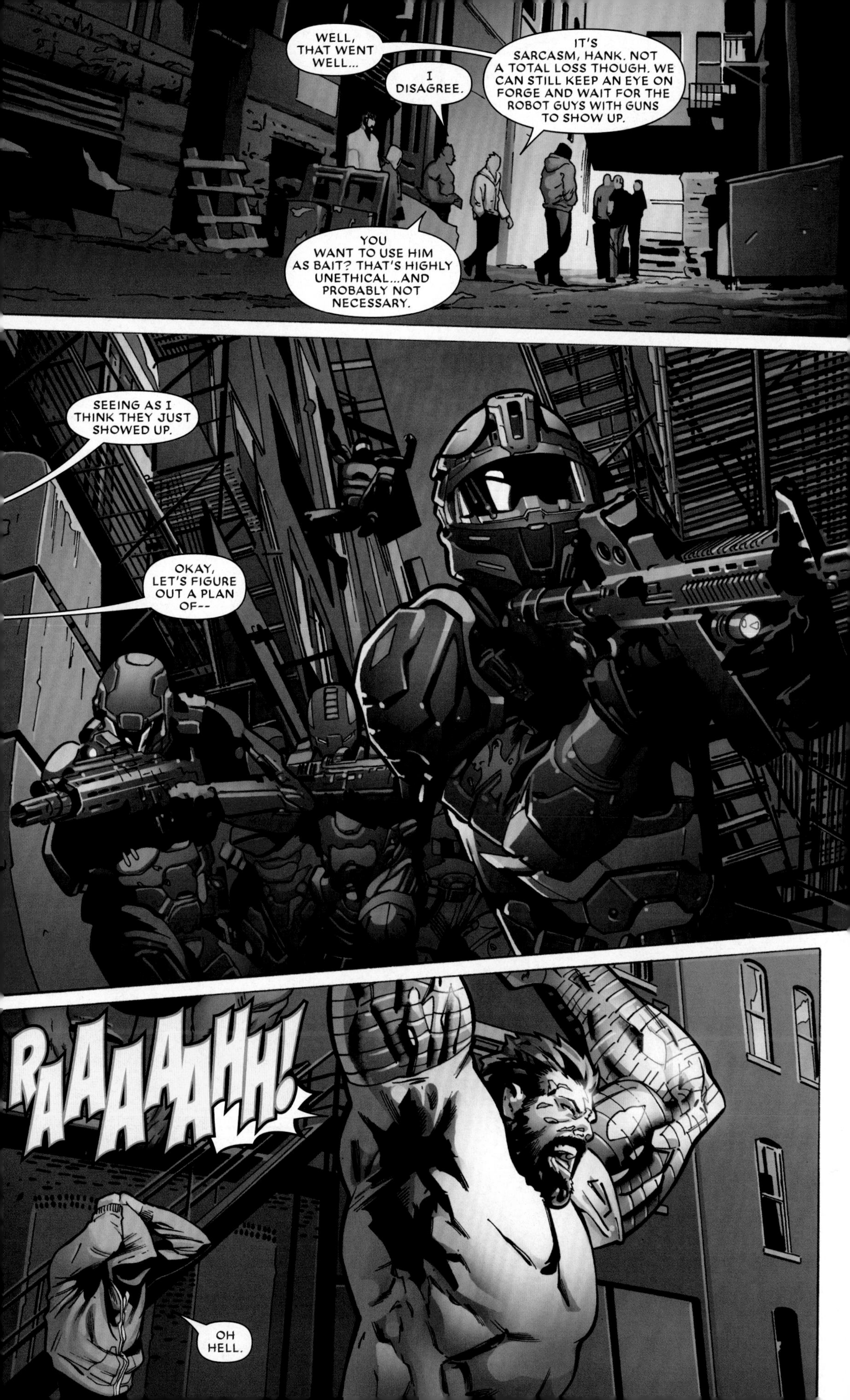
WELL, THAT WENT WELL...
IT'S SARCASM, HANK. NOT A TOTAL LOSS THOUGH. WE CAN STILL KEEP AN EYE ON FORGE AND WAIT FOR THE ROBOT GUYS WITH GUNS TO SHOW UP.
I DISAGREE.
YOU WANT TO USE HIM AS BAIT? THAT'S HIGHLY UNETHICAL...AND PROBABLY NOT NECESSARY.
SEEING AS I THINK THEY JUST SHOWED UP.
OKAY, LET'S FIGURE OUT A PLAN OF--
RAAAAAHH!
OH HELL.

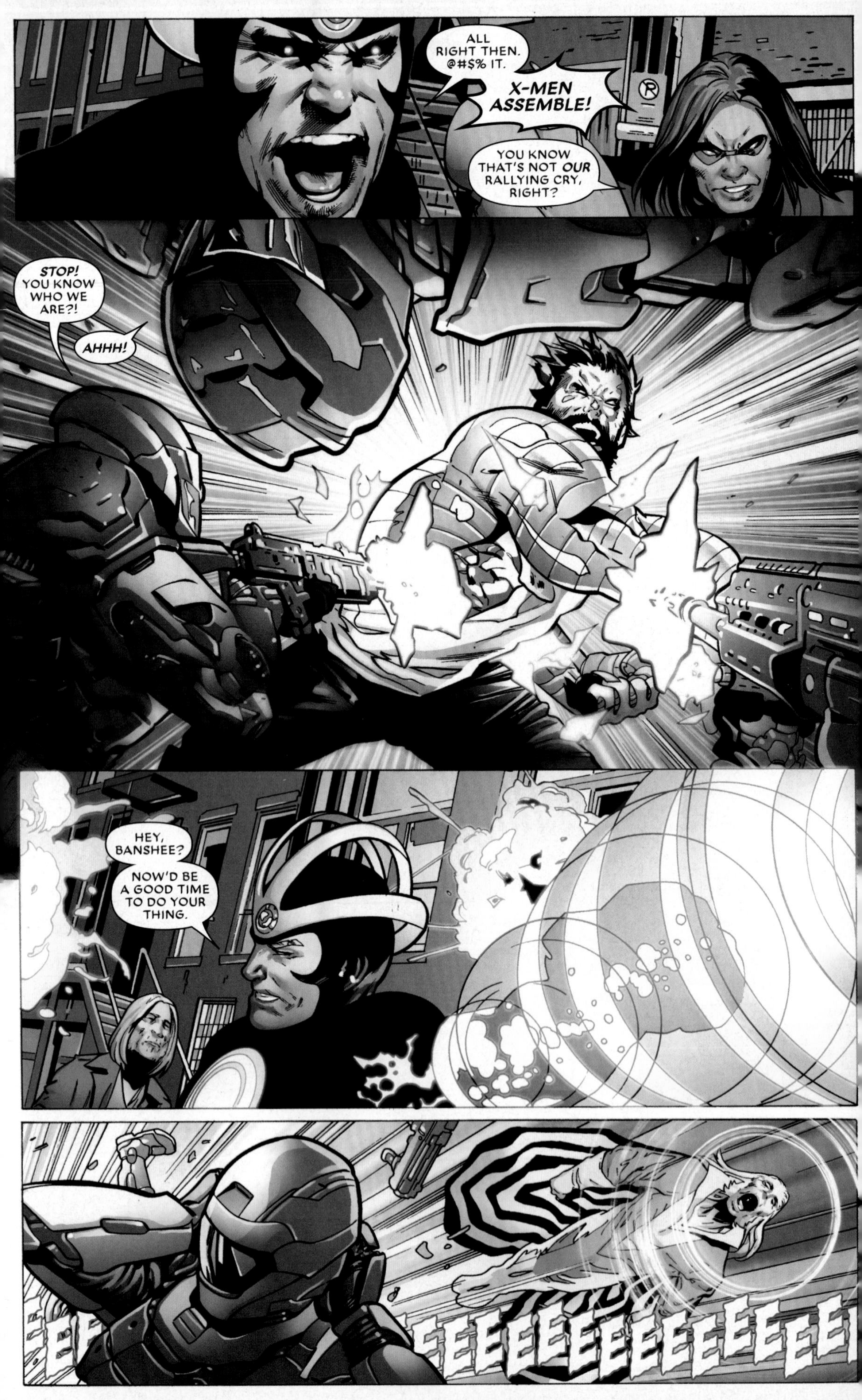
ALL RIGHT THEN. @#$% IT.
X-MEN ASSEMBLE!
YOU KNOW THAT'S NOT *OUR* RALLYING CRY, RIGHT?
STOP! YOU KNOW WHO WE ARE?!
AHHH!
HEY, BANSHEE?
NOW'D BE A GOOD TIME TO DO YOUR THING.
EEEEEEEEEEEEEEEEE

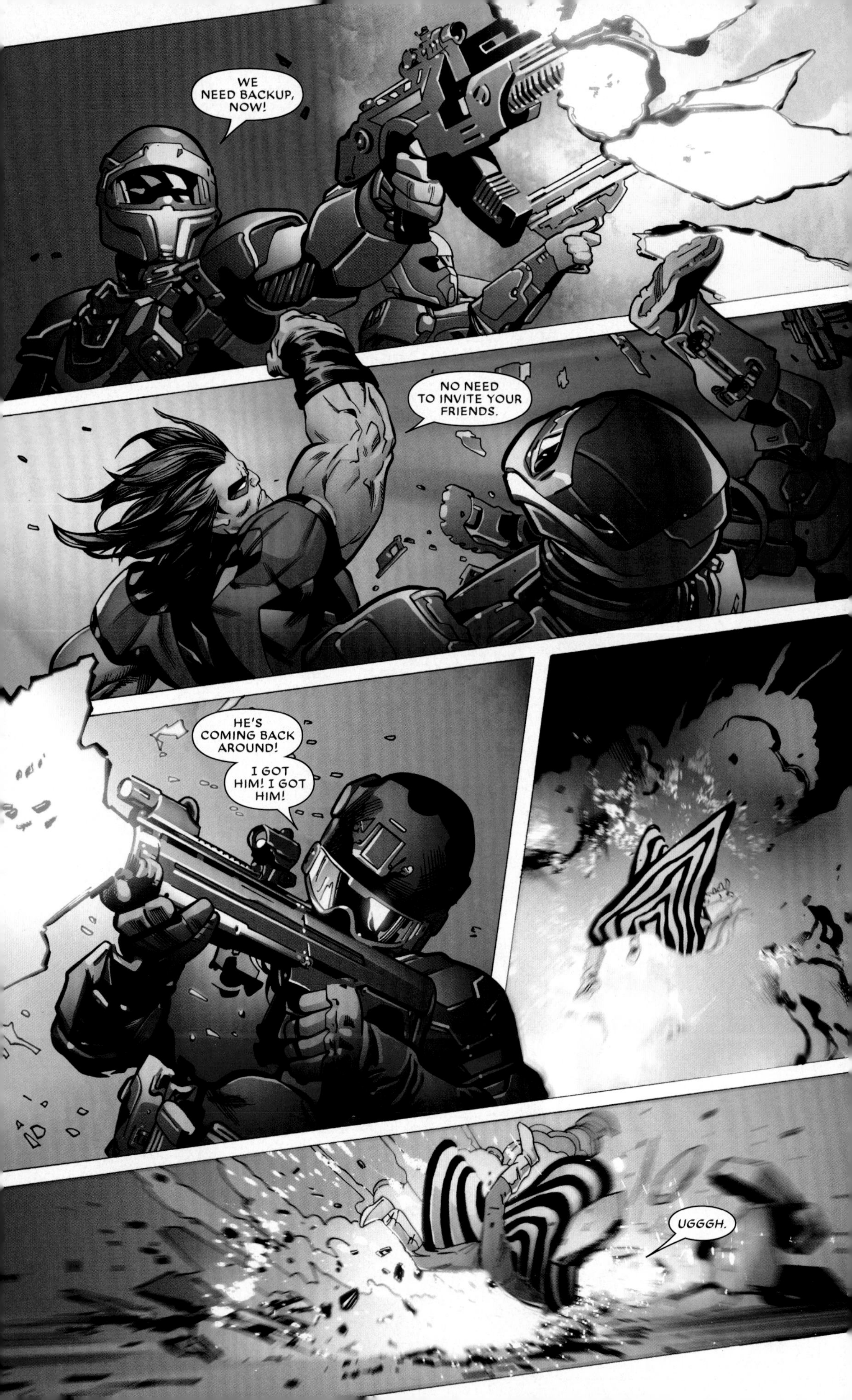
WE NEED BACKUP, NOW!
NO NEED TO INVITE YOUR FRIENDS.
HE'S COMING BACK AROUND!
I GOT HIM! I GOT HIM!
UGGGH.

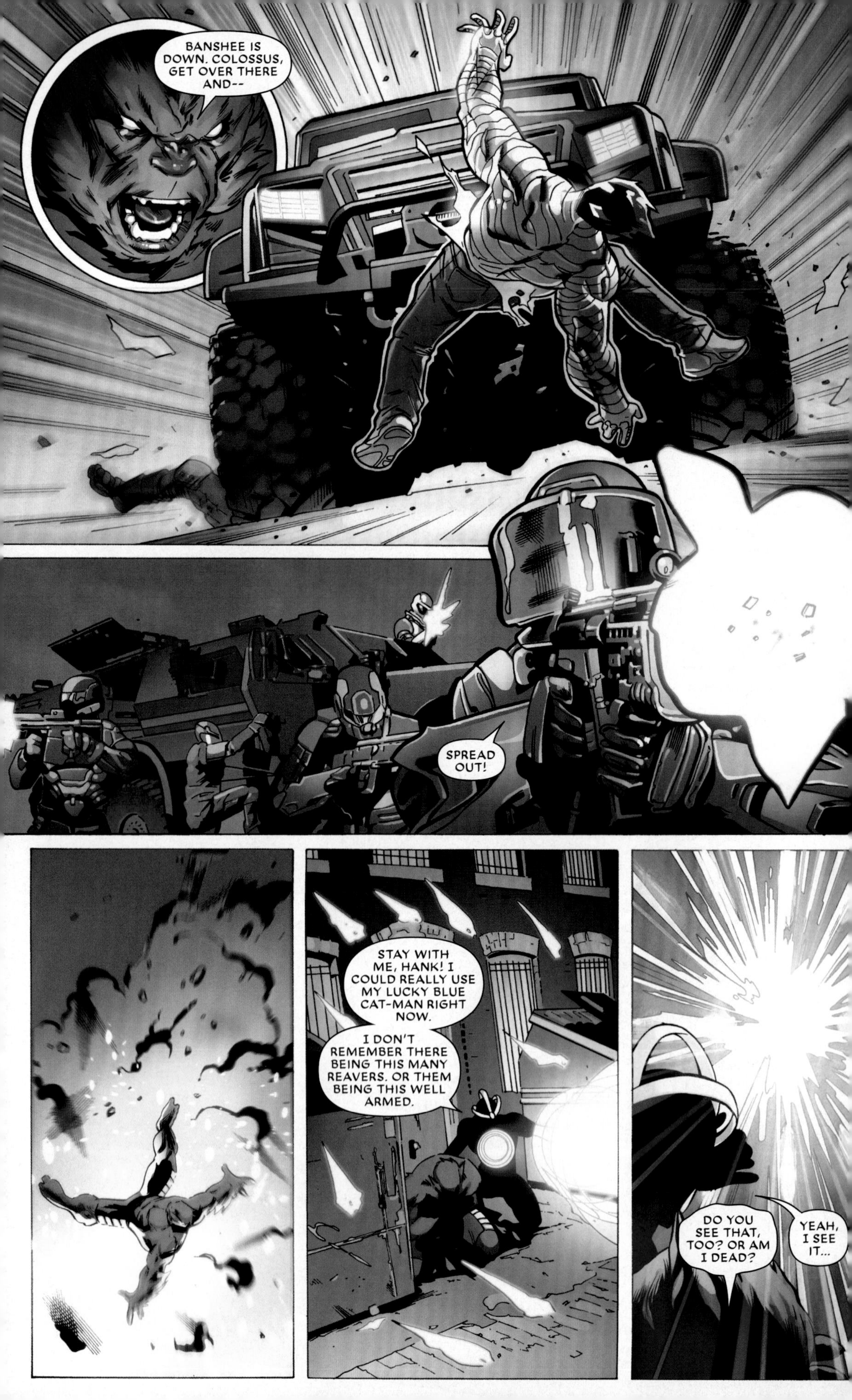
BANSHEE IS DOWN. COLOSSUS, GET OVER THERE AND--
SPREAD OUT!
STAY WITH ME, HANK! I COULD REALLY USE MY LUCKY BLUE CAT-MAN RIGHT NOW.
I DON'T REMEMBER THERE BEING THIS MANY REAVERS. OR THEM BEING THIS WELL ARMED.
DO YOU SEE THAT, TOO? OR AM I DEAD?
YEAH, I SEE IT...

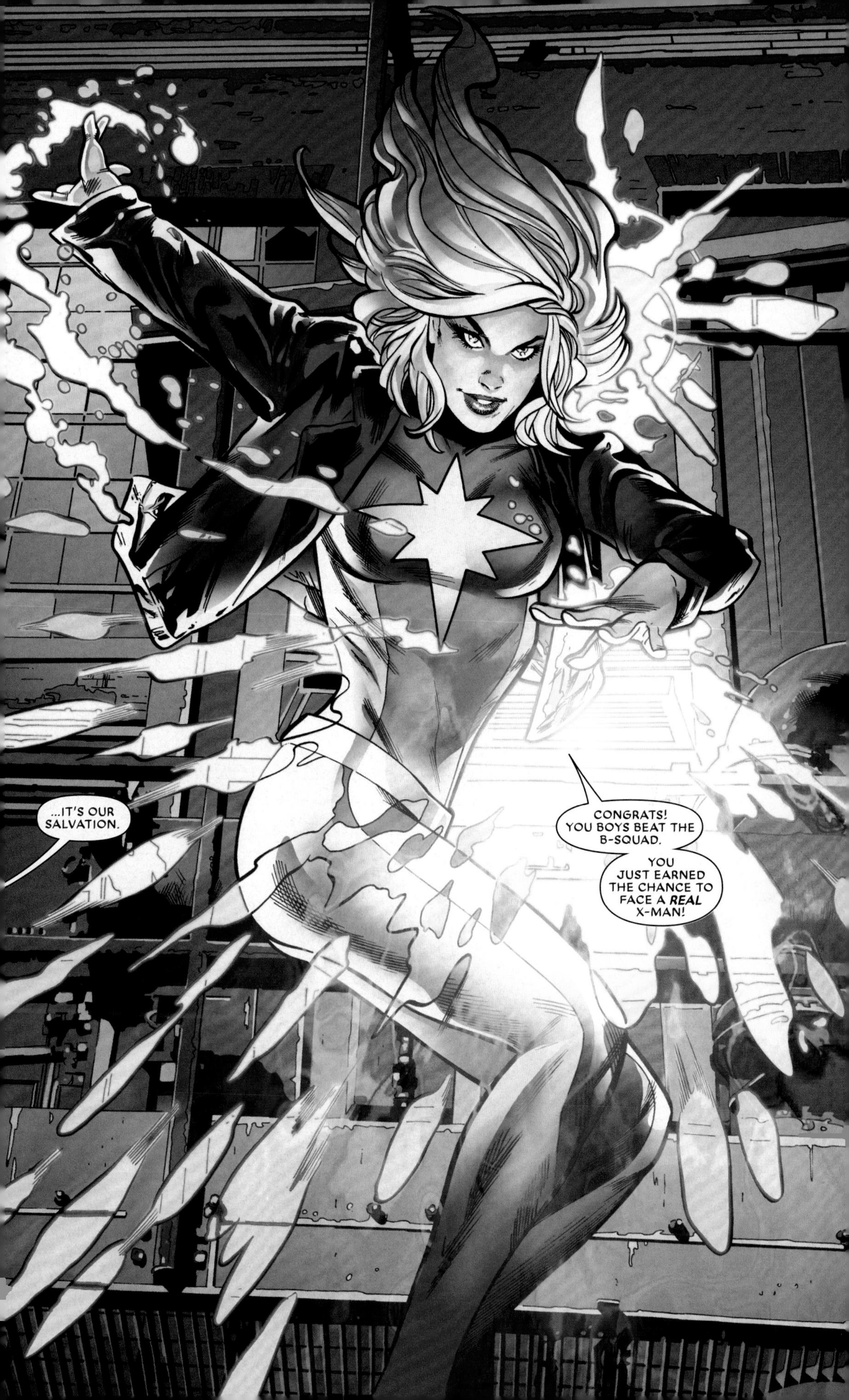
...IT'S OUR SALVATION.
CONGRATS! YOU BOYS BEAT THE B-SQUAD.
YOU JUST EARNED THE CHANCE TO FACE A *REAL* X-MAN!

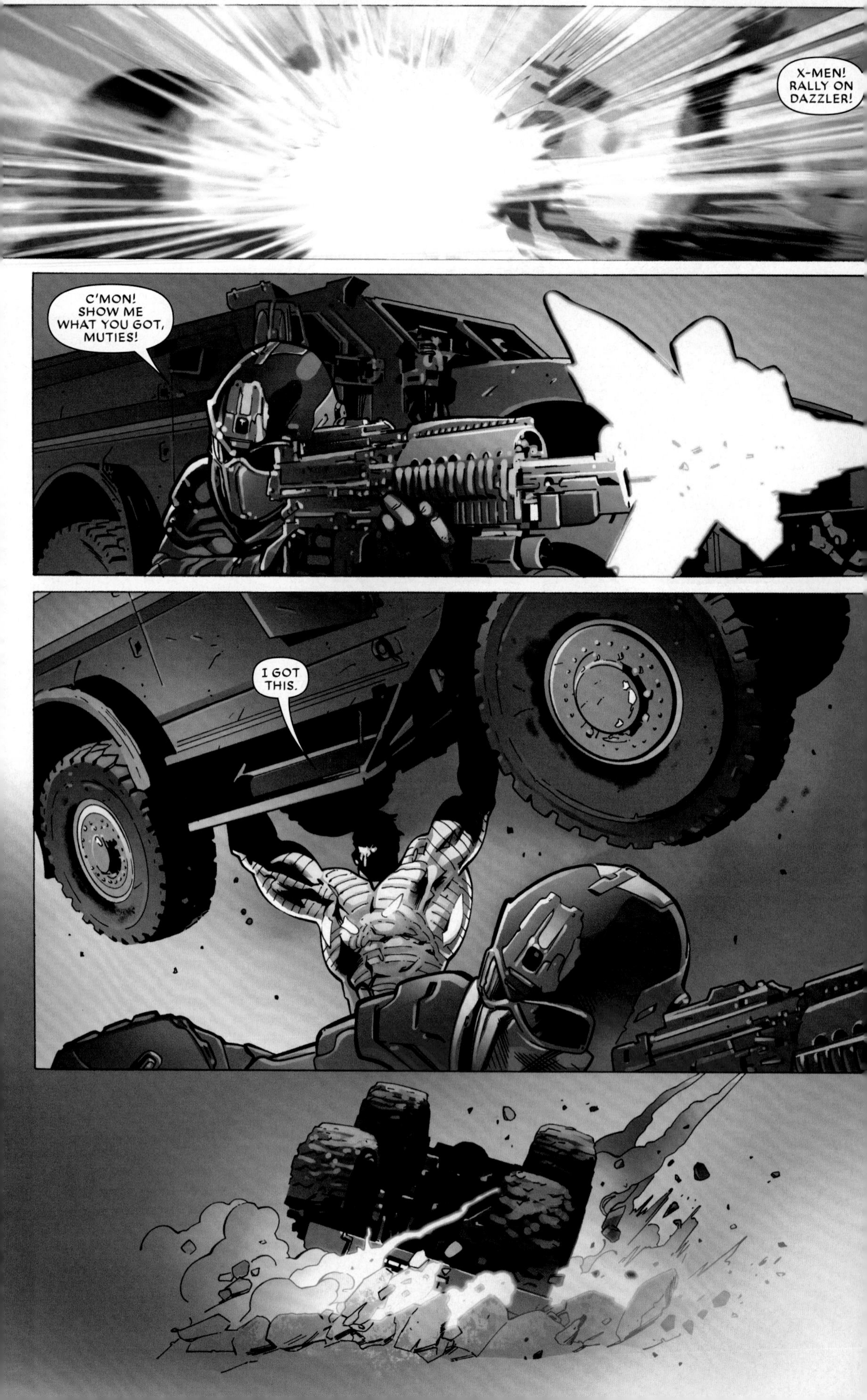
X-MEN! RALLY ON DAZZLER!
C'MON! SHOW ME WHAT YOU GOT, MUTIES!
I GOT THIS.

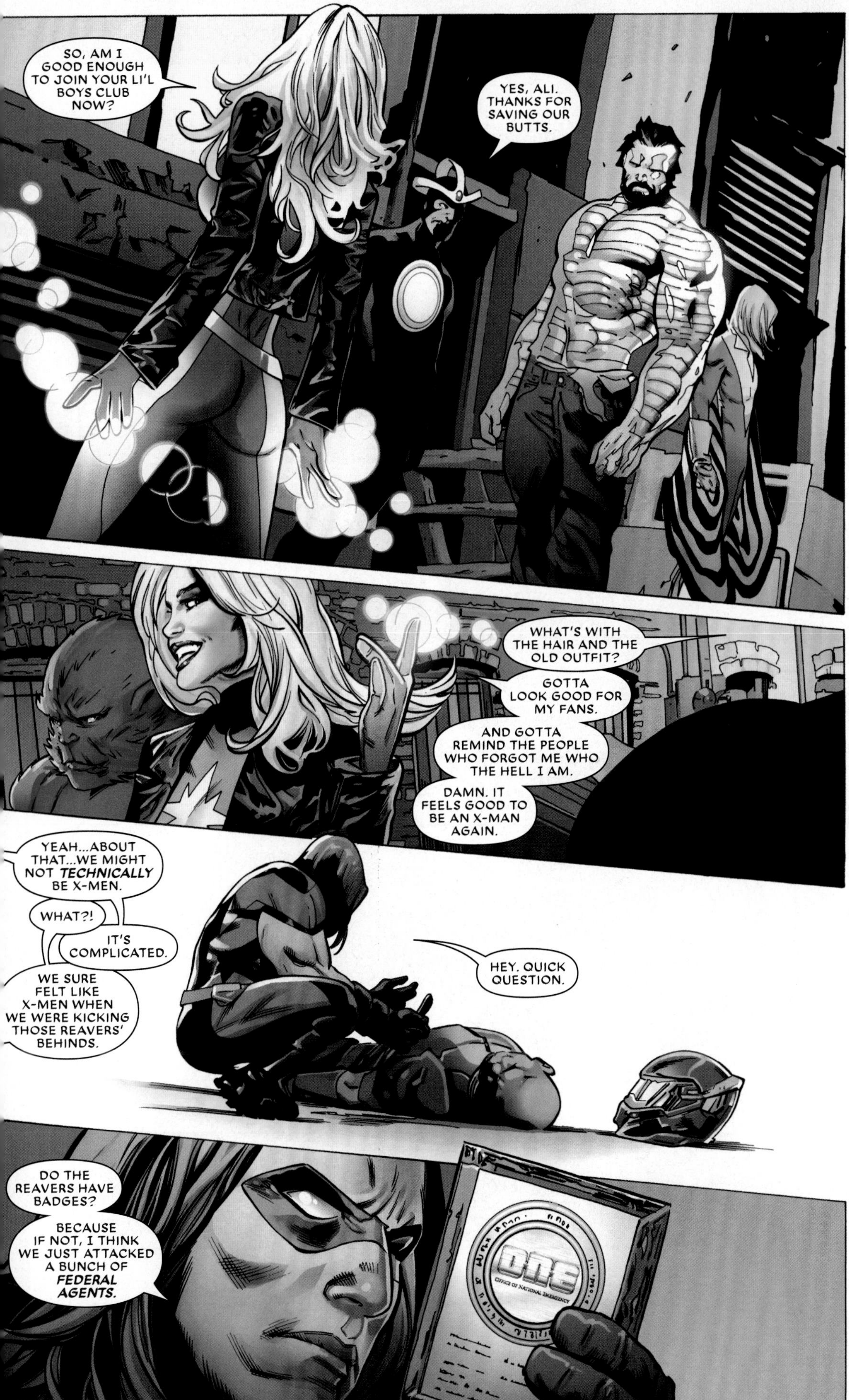
SO, AM I GOOD ENOUGH TO JOIN YOUR LI'L BOYS CLUB NOW?
YES, ALI. THANKS FOR SAVING OUR BUTTS.
WHAT'S WITH THE HAIR AND THE OLD OUTFIT?
GOTTA LOOK GOOD FOR MY FANS.
AND GOTTA REMIND THE PEOPLE WHO FORGOT ME WHO THE HELL I AM.
DAMN. IT FEELS GOOD TO BE AN X-MAN AGAIN.
YEAH...ABOUT THAT...WE MIGHT NOT *TECHNICALLY* BE X-MEN.
WHAT?!
IT'S COMPLICATED.
WE SURE FELT LIKE X-MEN WHEN WE WERE KICKING THOSE REAVERS' BEHINDS.
HEY. QUICK QUESTION.
DO THE REAVERS HAVE BADGES?
BECAUSE IF NOT, I THINK WE JUST ATTACKED A BUNCH OF *FEDERAL AGENTS.*
ONE
OFFICE OF NATIONAL EMERGENCY

15

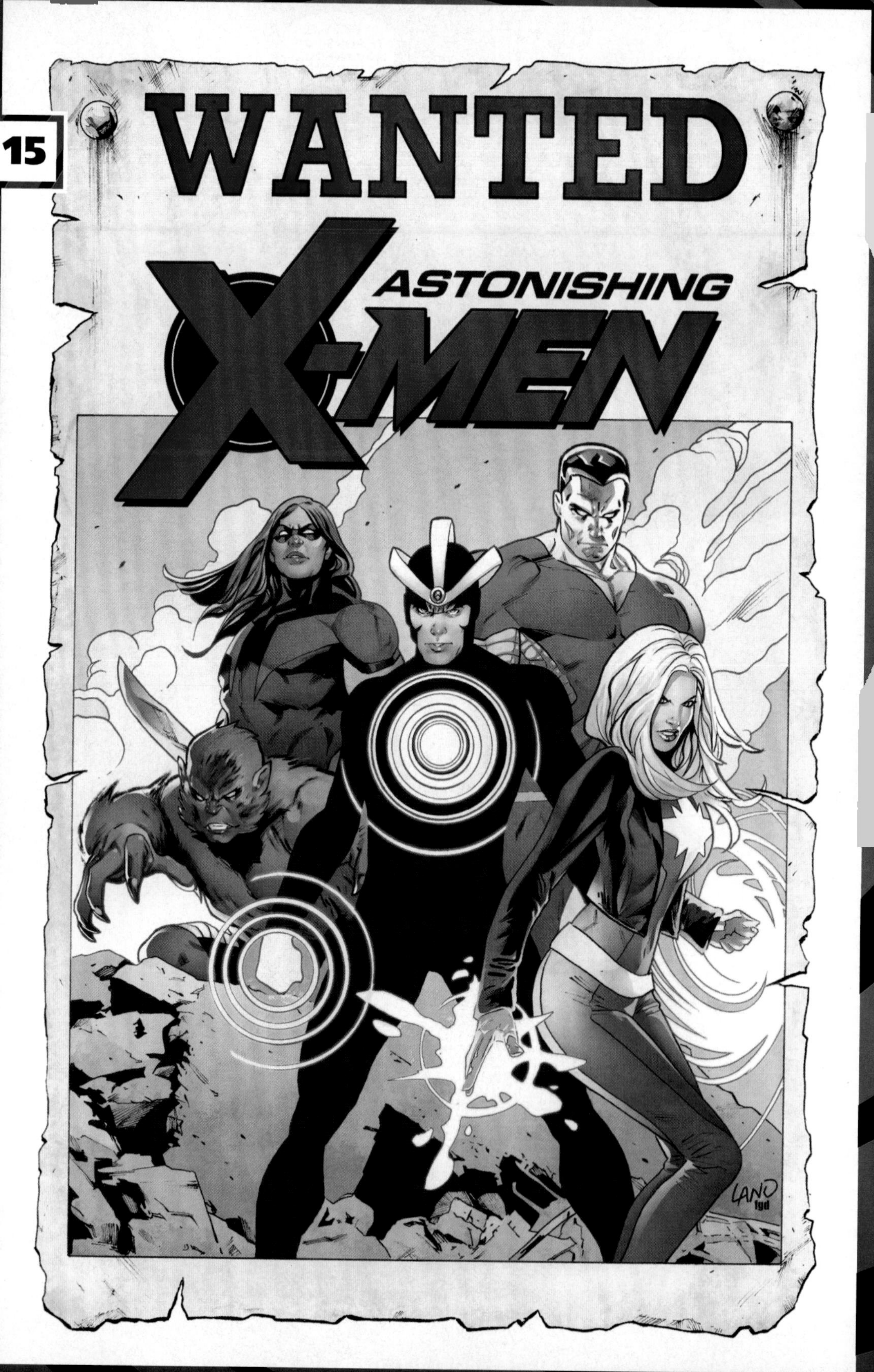
WANTED
ASTONISHING
X-MEN

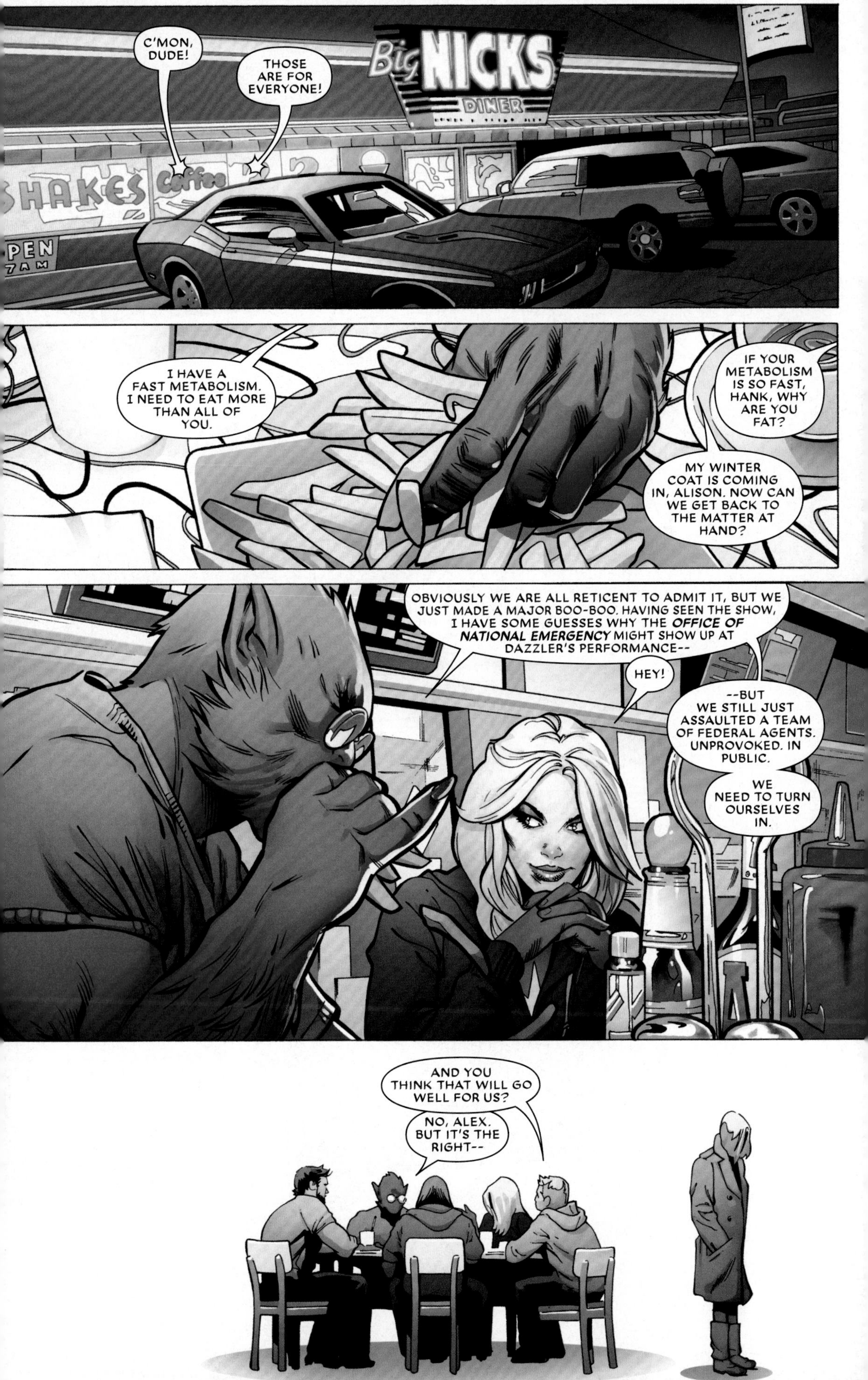
Big NICKS
DINER
SHAKES
Coffee
C'MON, DUDE!
THOSE ARE FOR EVERYONE!
I HAVE A FAST METABOLISM. I NEED TO EAT MORE THAN ALL OF YOU.
IF YOUR METABOLISM IS SO FAST, HANK, WHY ARE YOU FAT?
MY WINTER COAT IS COMING IN, ALISON. NOW CAN WE GET BACK TO THE MATTER AT HAND?
OBVIOUSLY WE ARE ALL RETICENT TO ADMIT IT, BUT WE JUST MADE A MAJOR BOO-BOO. HAVING SEEN THE SHOW, I HAVE SOME GUESSES WHY THE *OFFICE OF NATIONAL EMERGENCY* MIGHT SHOW UP AT DAZZLER'S PERFORMANCE--
HEY!
--BUT WE STILL JUST ASSAULTED A TEAM OF FEDERAL AGENTS. UNPROVOKED. IN PUBLIC.
WE NEED TO TURN OURSELVES IN.
AND YOU THINK THAT WILL GO WELL FOR US?
NO, ALEX. BUT IT'S THE RIGHT--

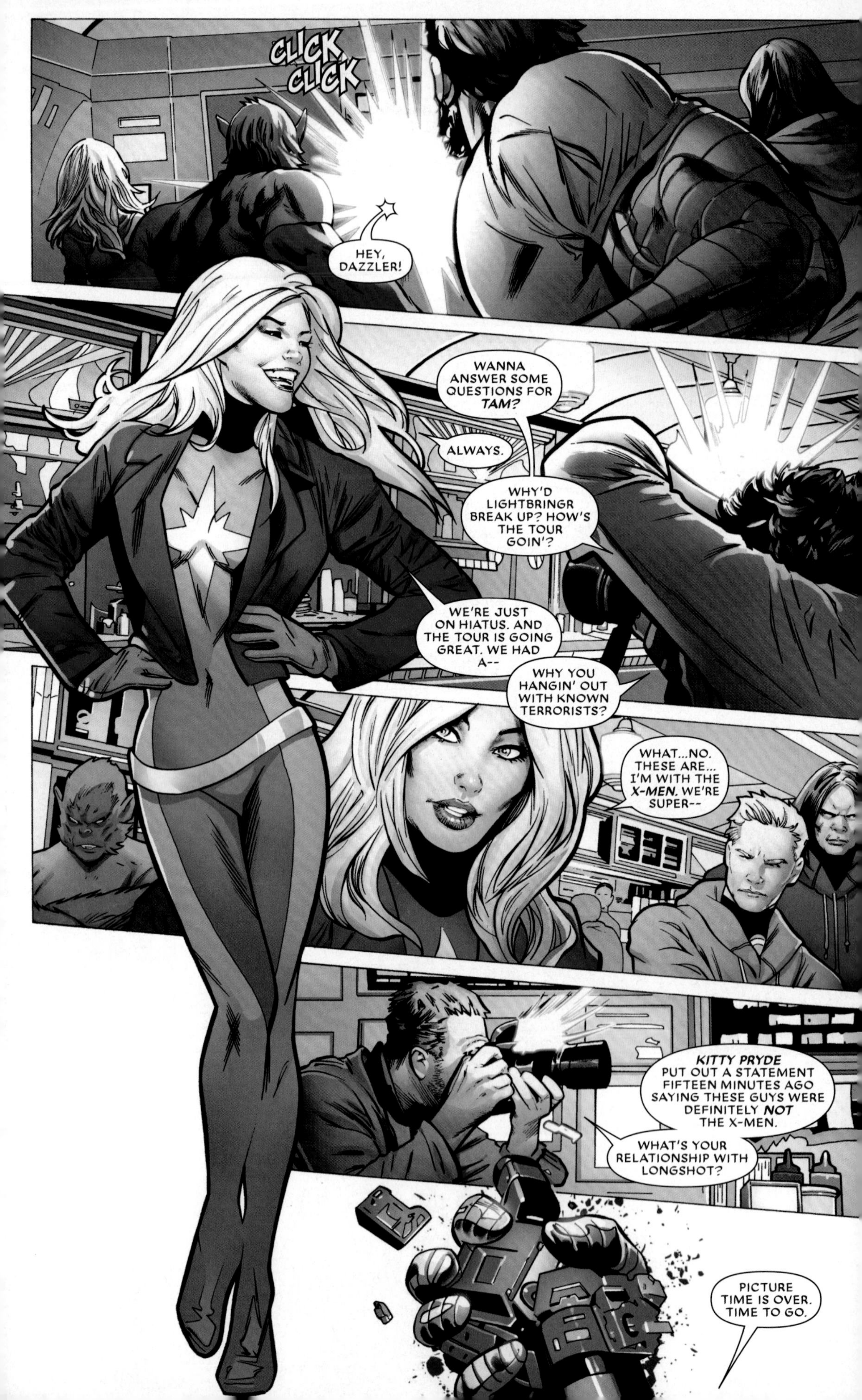
CLICK CLICK
HEY, DAZZLER!
WANNA ANSWER SOME QUESTIONS FOR TAM?
ALWAYS.
WHY'D LIGHTBRINGR BREAK UP? HOW'S THE TOUR GOIN'?
WE'RE JUST ON HIATUS. AND THE TOUR IS GOING GREAT. WE HAD A--
WHY YOU HANGIN' OUT WITH KNOWN TERRORISTS?
WHAT...NO. THESE ARE... I'M WITH THE X-MEN. WE'RE SUPER--
KITTY PRYDE PUT OUT A STATEMENT FIFTEEN MINUTES AGO SAYING THESE GUYS WERE DEFINITELY NOT THE X-MEN.
WHAT'S YOUR RELATIONSHIP WITH LONGSHOT?
PICTURE TIME IS OVER. TIME TO GO.

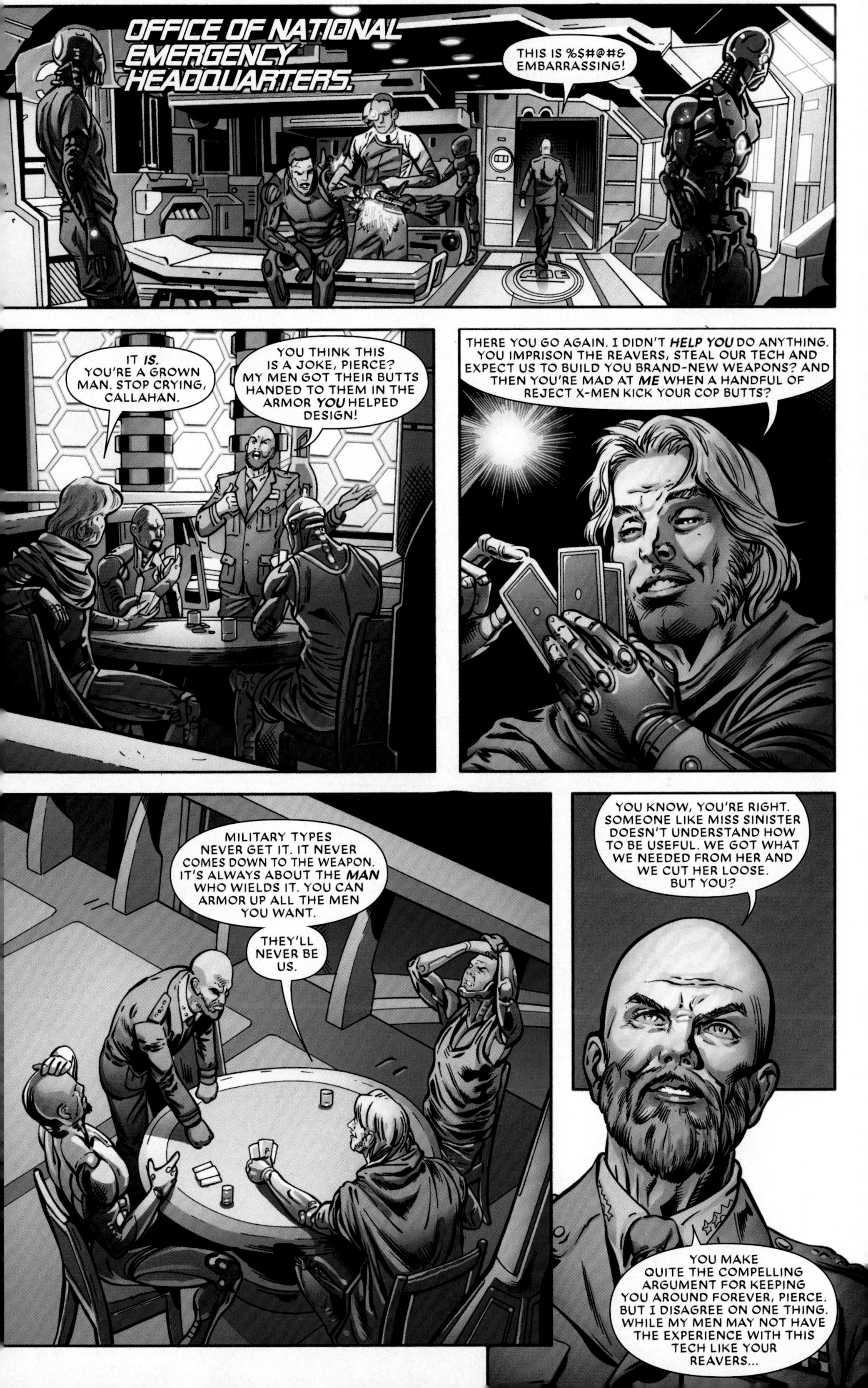
OFFICE OF NATIONAL EMERGENCY HEADQUARTERS.
THIS IS %$#@#& EMBARRASSING!
IT IS. YOU'RE A GROWN MAN. STOP CRYING, CALLAHAN.
YOU THINK THIS IS A JOKE, PIERCE? MY MEN GOT THEIR BUTTS HANDED TO THEM IN THE ARMOR YOU HELPED DESIGN!
THERE YOU GO AGAIN. I DIDN'T HELP YOU DO ANYTHING. YOU IMPRISON THE REAVERS, STEAL OUR TECH AND EXPECT US TO BUILD YOU BRAND-NEW WEAPONS? AND THEN YOU'RE MAD AT ME WHEN A HANDFUL OF REJECT X-MEN KICK YOUR COP BUTTS?
MILITARY TYPES NEVER GET IT. IT NEVER COMES DOWN TO THE WEAPON. IT'S ALWAYS ABOUT THE MAN WHO WIELDS IT. YOU CAN ARMOR UP ALL THE MEN YOU WANT.
THEY'LL NEVER BE US.
YOU KNOW, YOU'RE RIGHT. SOMEONE LIKE MISS SINISTER DOESN'T UNDERSTAND HOW TO BE USEFUL. WE GOT WHAT WE NEEDED FROM HER AND WE CUT HER LOOSE. BUT YOU?
YOU MAKE QUITE THE COMPELLING ARGUMENT FOR KEEPING YOU AROUND FOREVER, PIERCE. BUT I DISAGREE ON ONE THING. WHILE MY MEN MAY NOT HAVE THE EXPERIENCE WITH THIS TECH LIKE YOUR REAVERS...

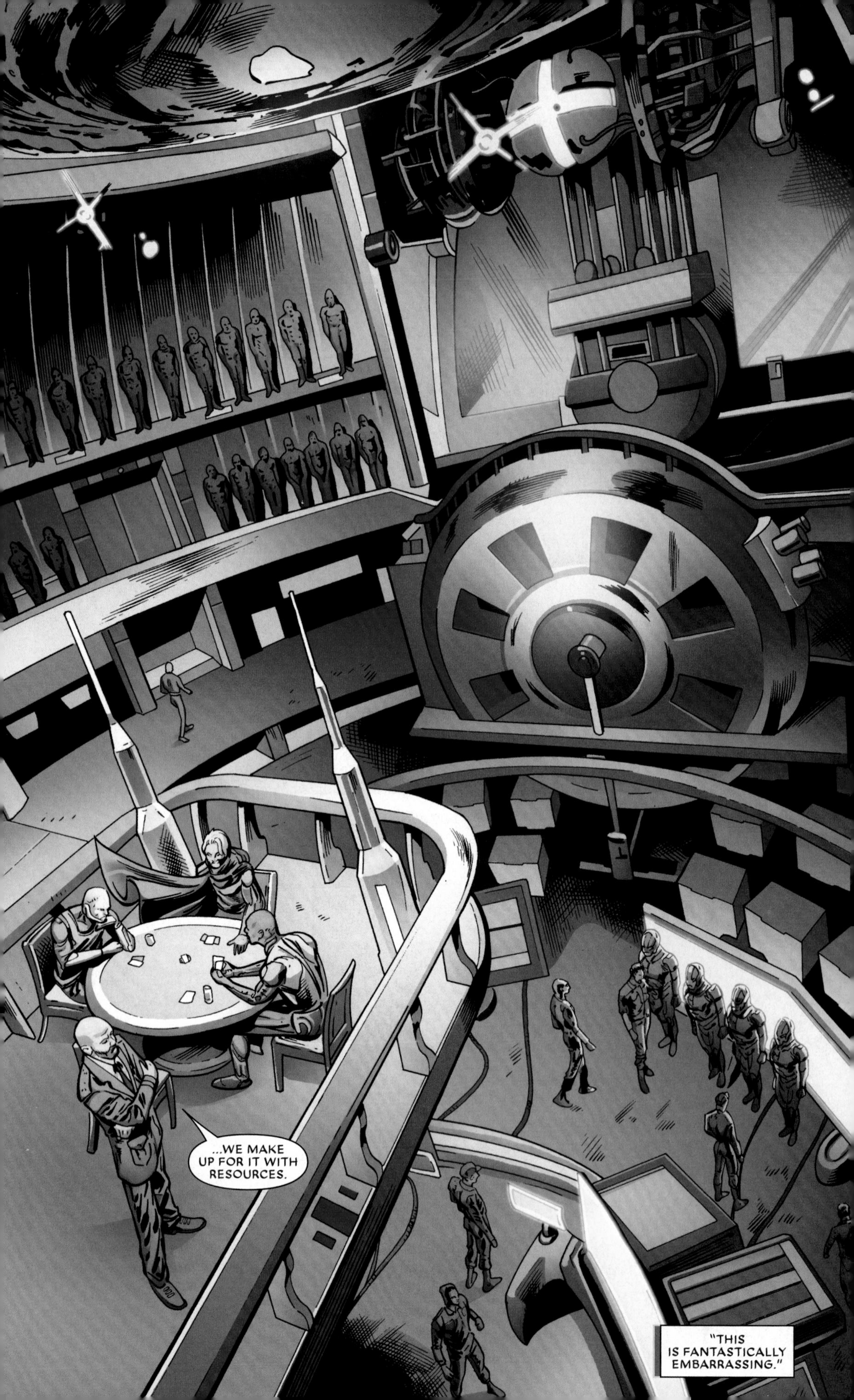
...WE MAKE UP FOR IT WITH RESOURCES.
"THIS IS FANTASTICALLY EMBARRASSING."

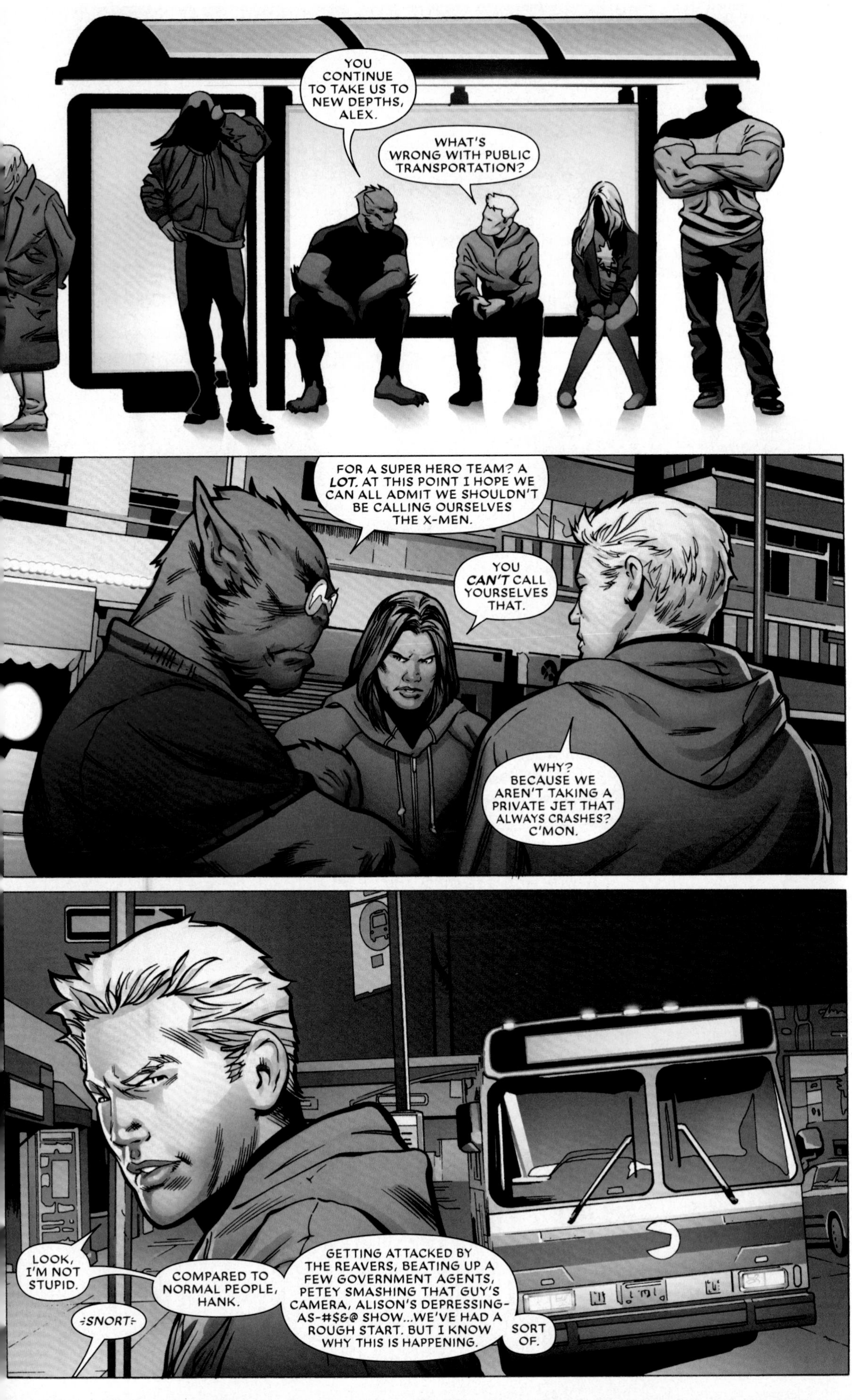
YOU CONTINUE TO TAKE US TO NEW DEPTHS, ALEX.
WHAT'S WRONG WITH PUBLIC TRANSPORTATION?
FOR A SUPER HERO TEAM? A *LOT.* AT THIS POINT I HOPE WE CAN ALL ADMIT WE SHOULDN'T BE CALLING OURSELVES THE X-MEN.
YOU ***CAN'T*** CALL YOURSELVES THAT.
WHY? BECAUSE WE AREN'T TAKING A PRIVATE JET THAT ALWAYS CRASHES? C'MON.
LOOK, I'M NOT STUPID.
COMPARED TO NORMAL PEOPLE, HANK.
÷SNORT÷
GETTING ATTACKED BY THE REAVERS, BEATING UP A FEW GOVERNMENT AGENTS, PETEY SMASHING THAT GUY'S CAMERA, ALISON'S DEPRESSING-AS-#$&@ SHOW...WE'VE HAD A ROUGH START. BUT I KNOW WHY THIS IS HAPPENING.
SORT OF.

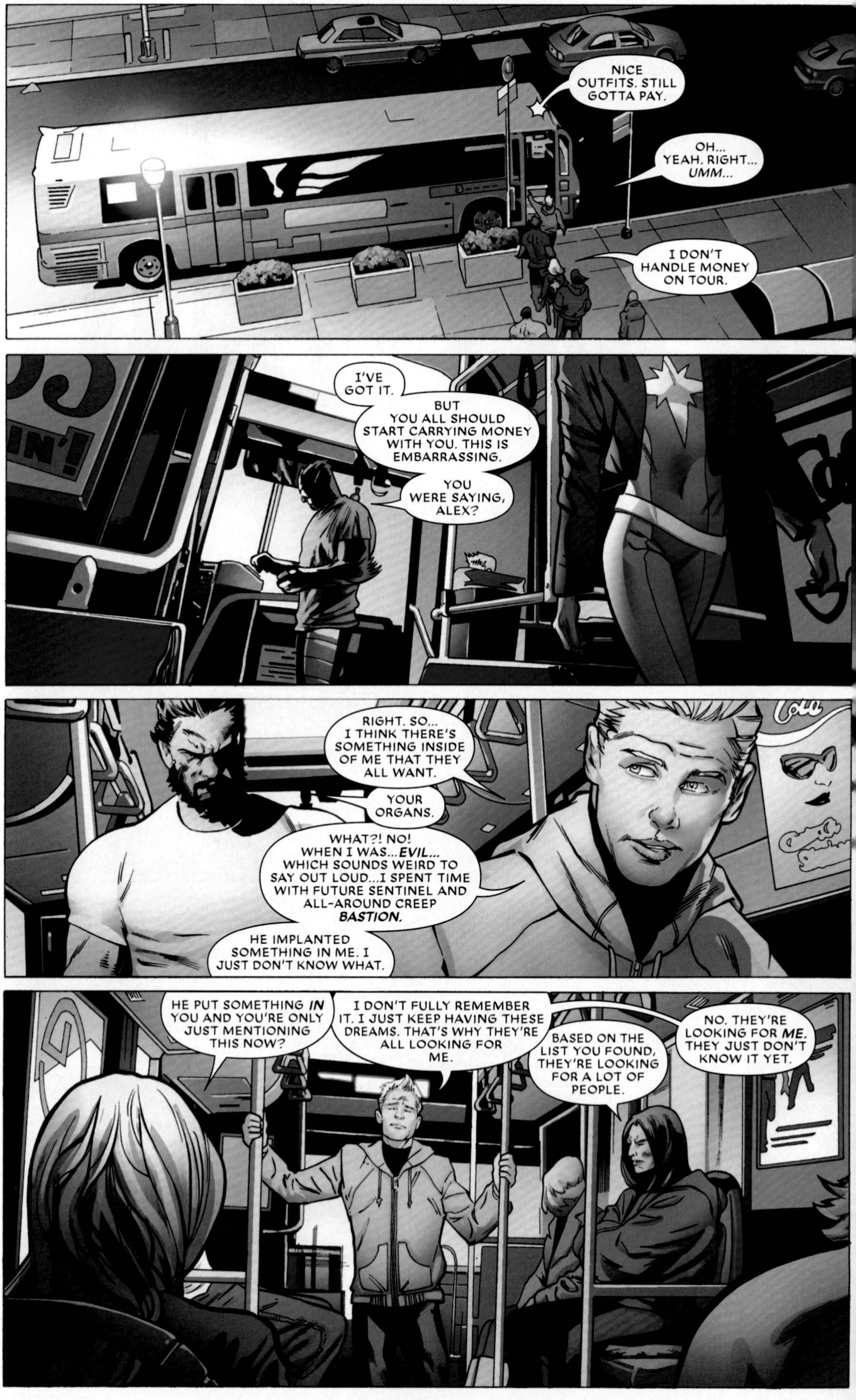
NICE OUTFITS. STILL GOTTA PAY.
OH... YEAH. RIGHT... *UMM*...
I DON'T HANDLE MONEY ON TOUR.
I'VE GOT IT.
BUT YOU ALL SHOULD START CARRYING MONEY WITH YOU. THIS IS EMBARRASSING.
YOU WERE SAYING, ALEX?
RIGHT. SO... I THINK THERE'S SOMETHING INSIDE OF ME THAT THEY ALL WANT.
YOUR ORGANS.
WHAT?! NO! WHEN I WAS...*EVIL*... WHICH SOUNDS WEIRD TO SAY OUT LOUD...I SPENT TIME WITH FUTURE SENTINEL AND ALL-AROUND CREEP **BASTION.**
HE IMPLANTED SOMETHING IN ME. I JUST DON'T KNOW WHAT.
HE PUT SOMETHING *IN* YOU AND YOU'RE ONLY JUST MENTIONING THIS NOW?
I DON'T FULLY REMEMBER IT. I JUST KEEP HAVING THESE DREAMS. THAT'S WHY THEY'RE ALL LOOKING FOR ME.
BASED ON THE LIST YOU FOUND, THEY'RE LOOKING FOR A LOT OF PEOPLE.
NO. THEY'RE LOOKING FOR *ME*. THEY JUST DON'T KNOW IT YET.

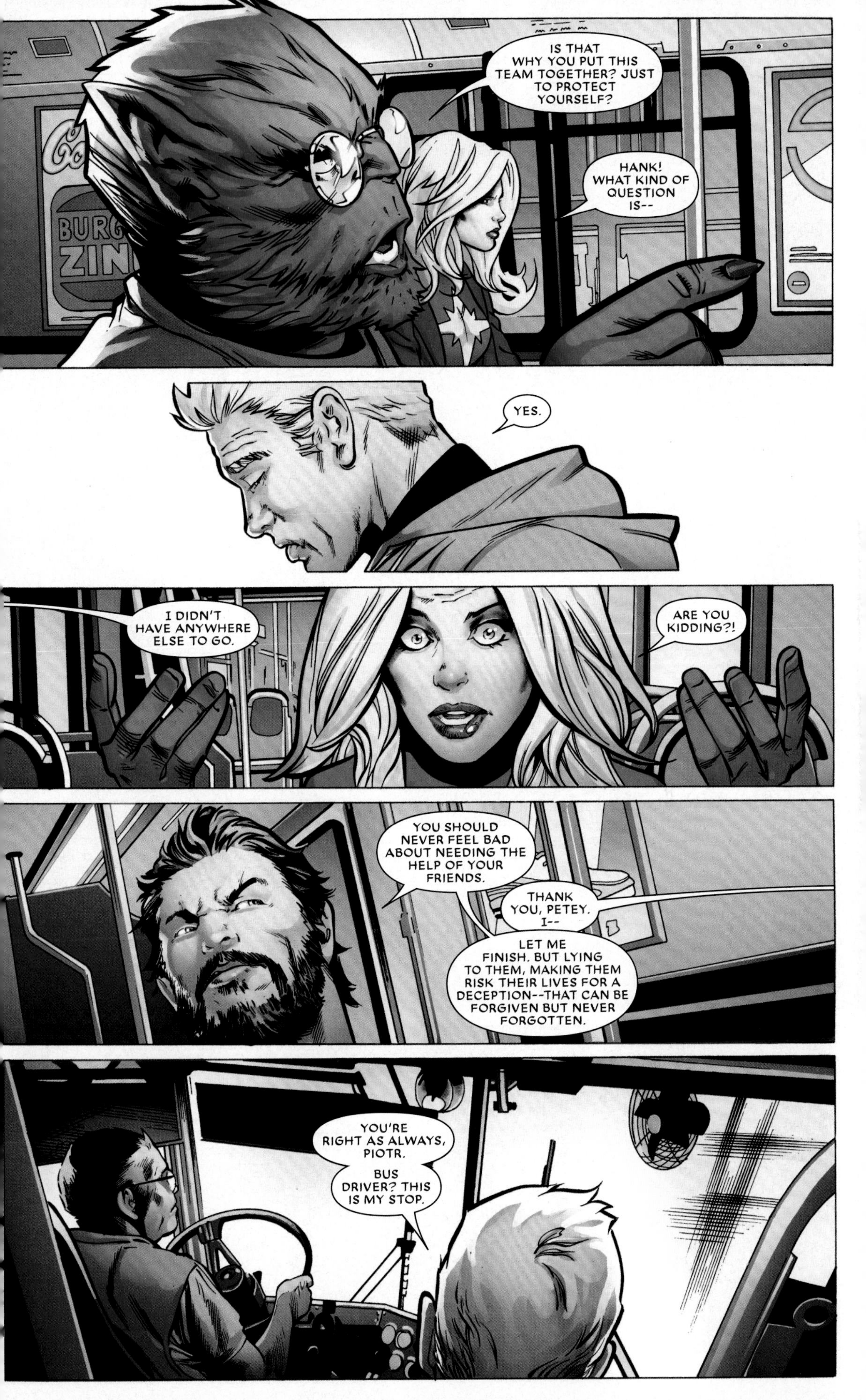
IS THAT WHY YOU PUT THIS TEAM TOGETHER? JUST TO PROTECT YOURSELF?
HANK! WHAT KIND OF QUESTION IS--
YES.
I DIDN'T HAVE ANYWHERE ELSE TO GO.
ARE YOU KIDDING?!
YOU SHOULD NEVER FEEL BAD ABOUT NEEDING THE HELP OF YOUR FRIENDS.
THANK YOU, PETEY. I--
LET ME FINISH. BUT LYING TO THEM, MAKING THEM RISK THEIR LIVES FOR A DECEPTION--THAT CAN BE FORGIVEN BUT NEVER FORGOTTEN.
YOU'RE RIGHT AS ALWAYS, PIOTR.
BUS DRIVER? THIS IS MY STOP.

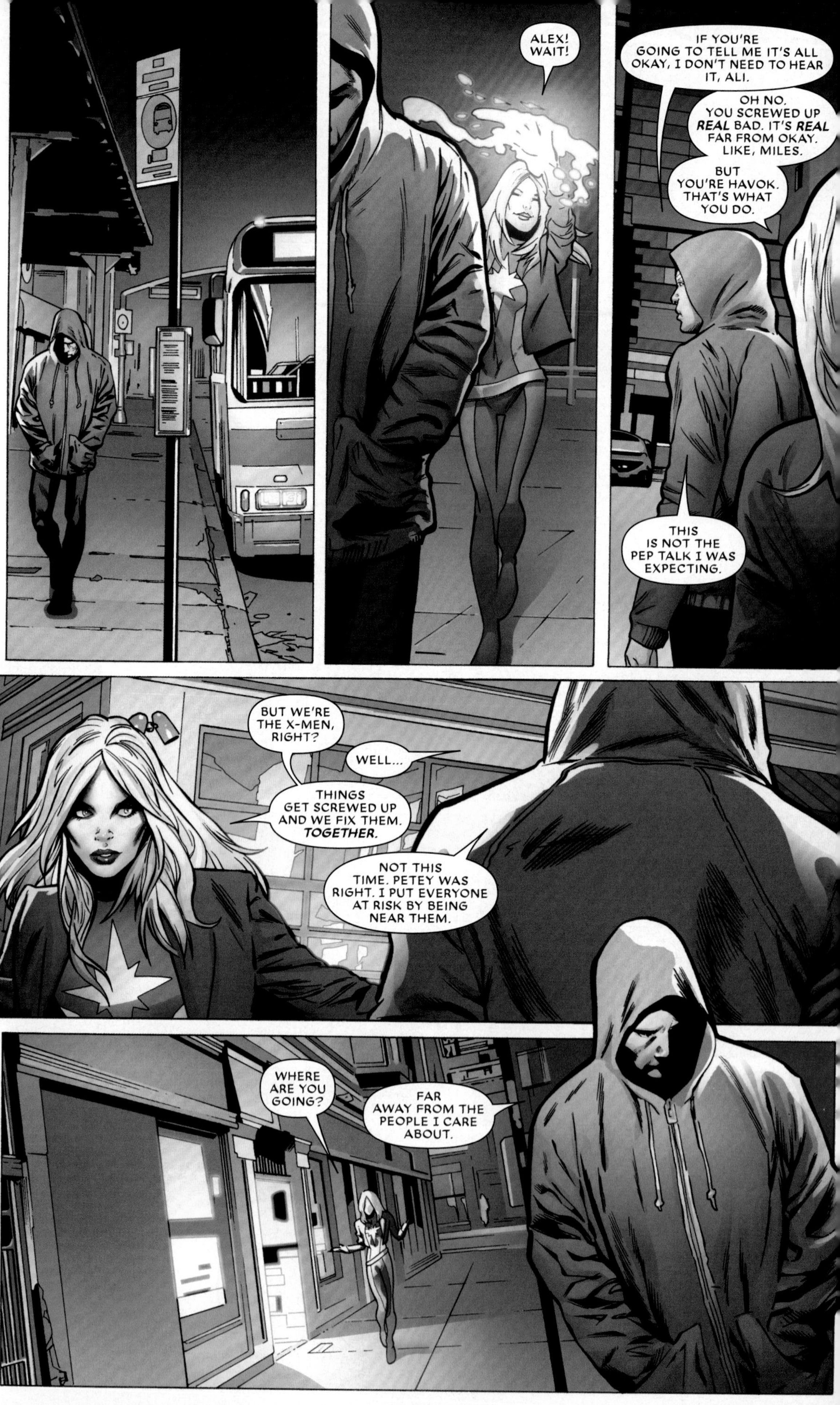
ALEX! WAIT!
IF YOU'RE GOING TO TELL ME IT'S ALL OKAY, I DON'T NEED TO HEAR IT, ALI.
OH NO. YOU SCREWED UP **REAL** BAD. IT'S **REAL** FAR FROM OKAY. LIKE, MILES.
BUT YOU'RE HAVOK. THAT'S WHAT YOU DO.
THIS IS NOT THE PEP TALK I WAS EXPECTING.
BUT WE'RE THE X-MEN, RIGHT?
WELL...
THINGS GET SCREWED UP AND WE FIX THEM. ***TOGETHER.***
NOT THIS TIME. PETEY WAS RIGHT. I PUT EVERYONE AT RISK BY BEING NEAR THEM.
WHERE ARE YOU GOING?
FAR AWAY FROM THE PEOPLE I CARE ABOUT.

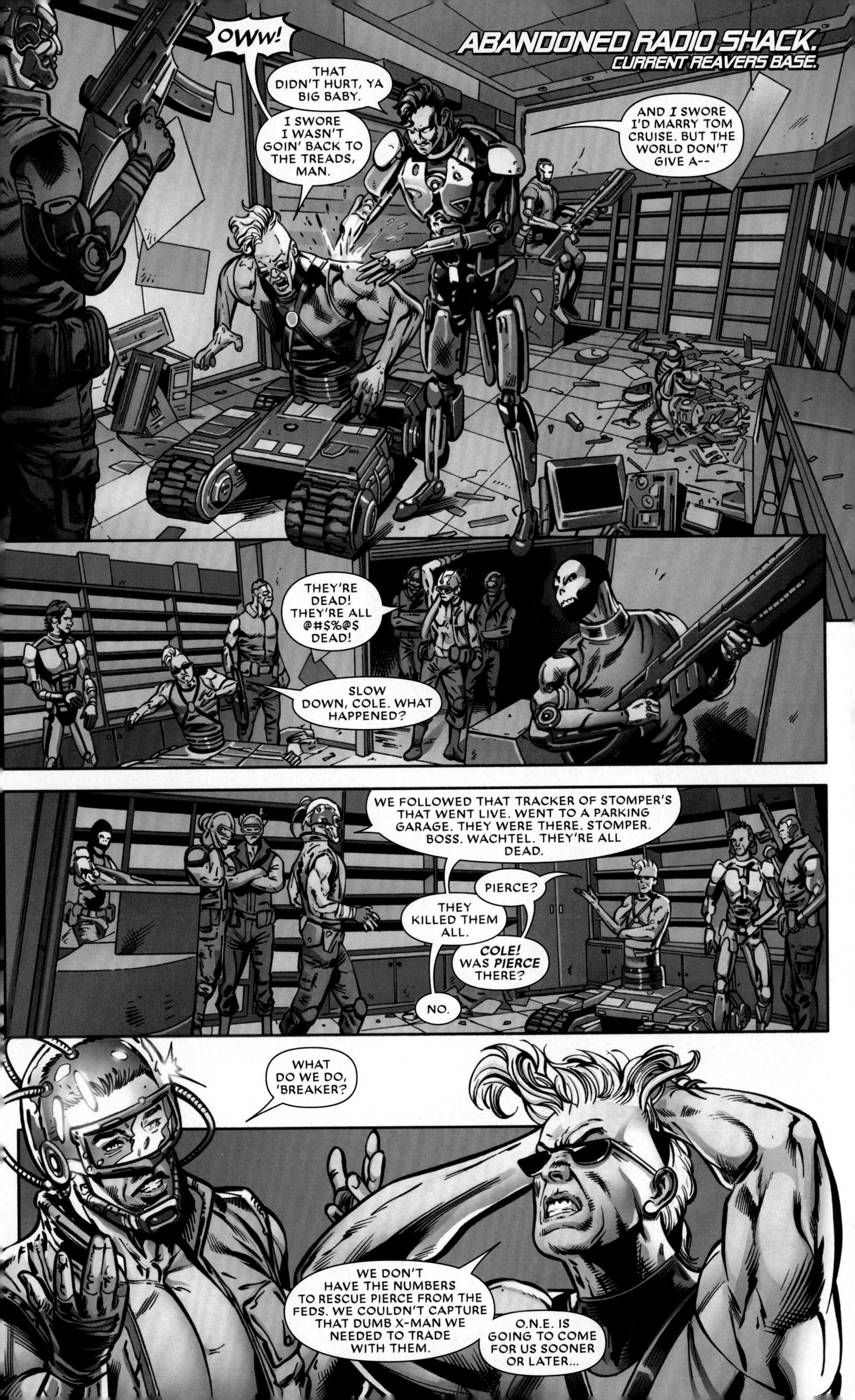
ABANDONED RADIO SHACK.
CURRENT REAVERS BASE.
OWW!
THAT DIDN'T HURT, YA BIG BABY.
I SWORE I WASN'T GOIN' BACK TO THE TREADS, MAN.
AND I SWORE I'D MARRY TOM CRUISE. BUT THE WORLD DON'T GIVE A--
THEY'RE DEAD! THEY'RE ALL @#$%@$ DEAD!
SLOW DOWN, COLE. WHAT HAPPENED?
WE FOLLOWED THAT TRACKER OF STOMPER'S THAT WENT LIVE. WENT TO A PARKING GARAGE. THEY WERE THERE. STOMPER. BOSS. WACHTEL. THEY'RE ALL DEAD.
PIERCE?
THEY KILLED THEM ALL.
COLE! WAS PIERCE THERE?
NO.
WHAT DO WE DO, 'BREAKER?
WE DON'T HAVE THE NUMBERS TO RESCUE PIERCE FROM THE FEDS. WE COULDN'T CAPTURE THAT DUMB X-MAN WE NEEDED TO TRADE WITH THEM.
O.N.E. IS GOING TO COME FOR US SOONER OR LATER...

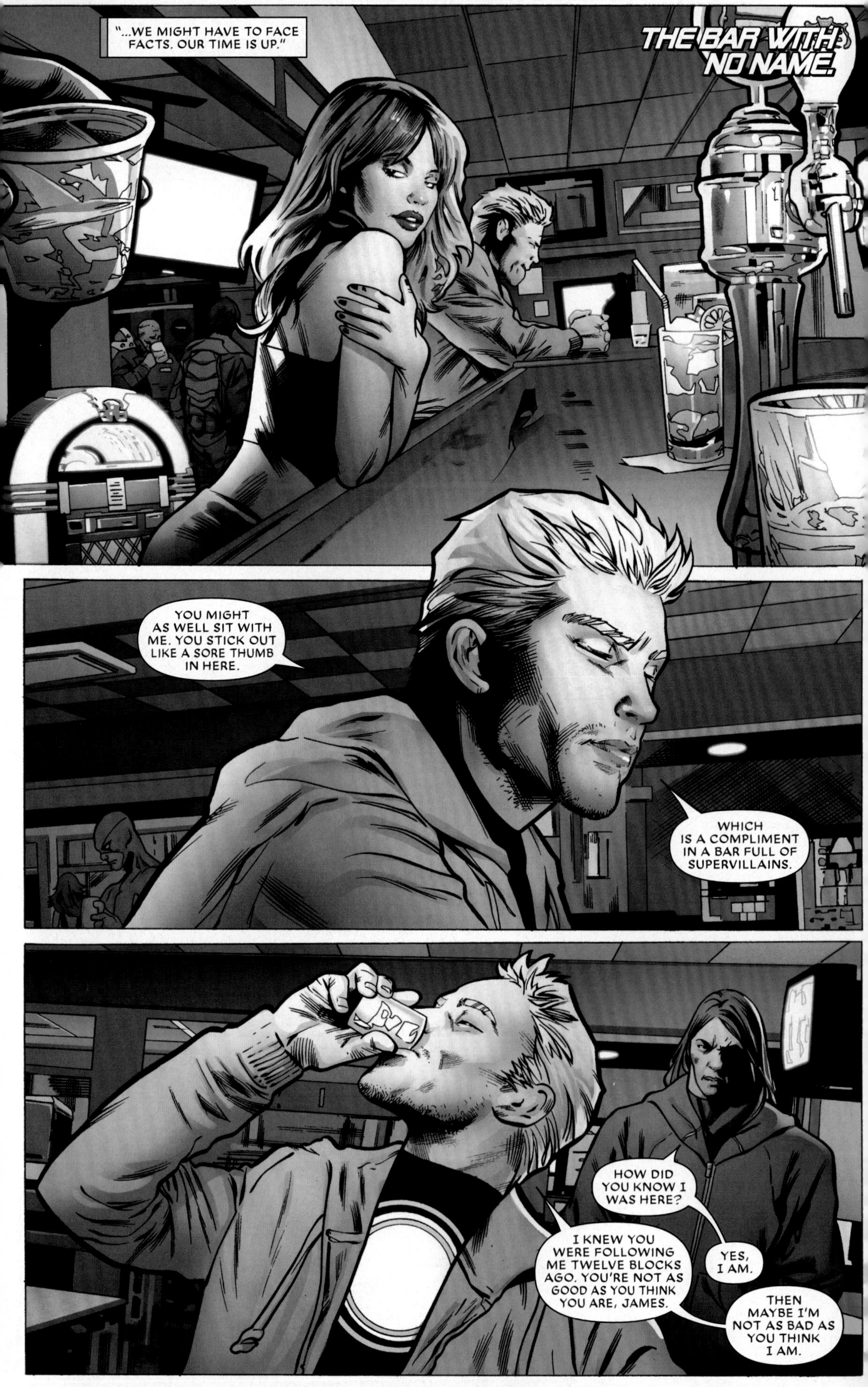
"...WE MIGHT HAVE TO FACE FACTS. OUR TIME IS UP."
THE BAR WITH NO NAME.
YOU MIGHT AS WELL SIT WITH ME. YOU STICK OUT LIKE A SORE THUMB IN HERE.
WHICH IS A COMPLIMENT IN A BAR FULL OF SUPERVILLAINS.
HOW DID YOU KNOW I WAS HERE?
I KNEW YOU WERE FOLLOWING ME TWELVE BLOCKS AGO. YOU'RE NOT AS GOOD AS YOU THINK YOU ARE, JAMES.
YES, I AM.
THEN MAYBE I'M NOT AS BAD AS YOU THINK I AM.

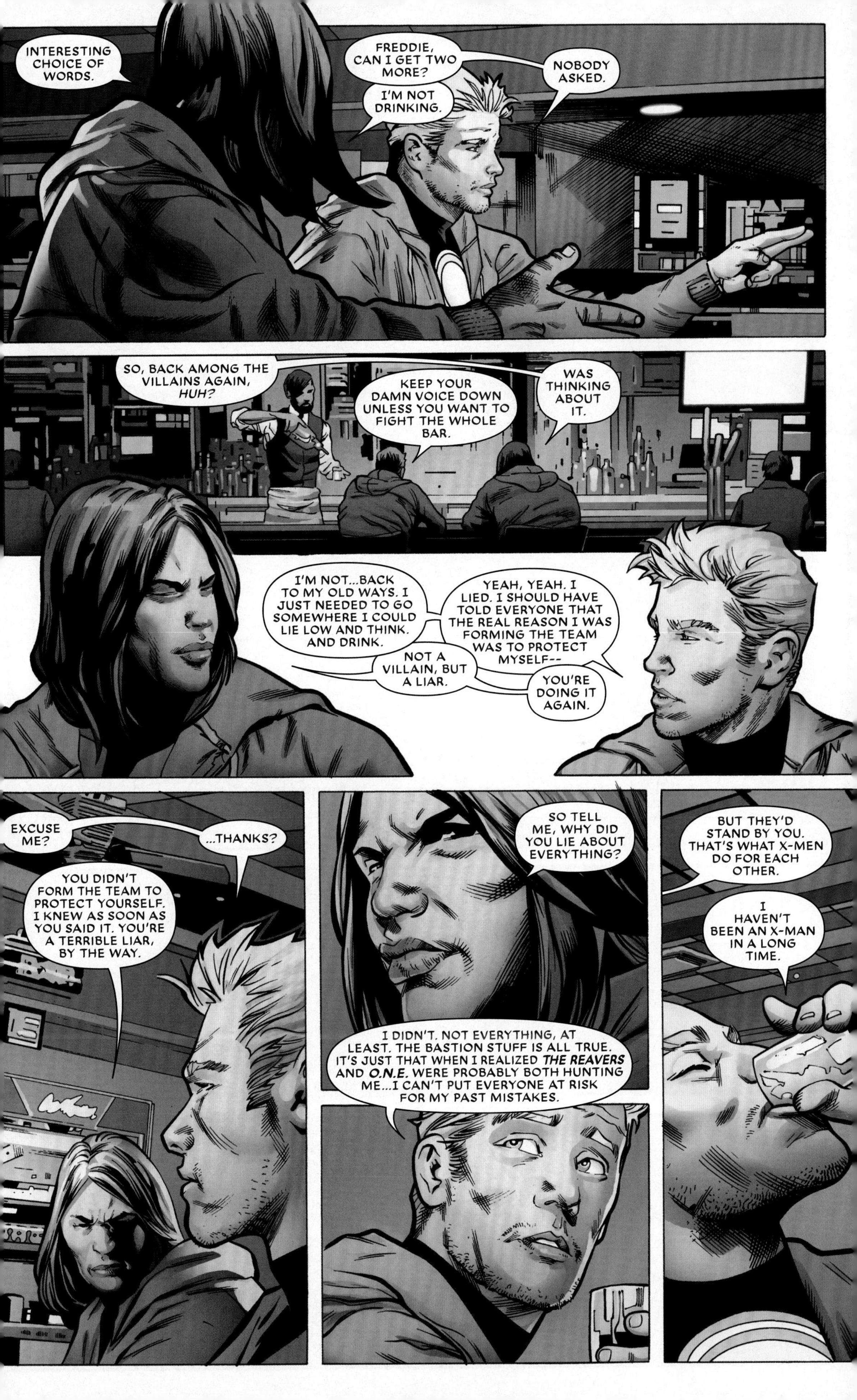

INTERESTING CHOICE OF WORDS.
FREDDIE, CAN I GET TWO MORE?
NOBODY ASKED.
I'M NOT DRINKING.
SO, BACK AMONG THE VILLAINS AGAIN, *HUH?*
WAS THINKING ABOUT IT.
KEEP YOUR DAMN VOICE DOWN UNLESS YOU WANT TO FIGHT THE WHOLE BAR.
I'M NOT...BACK TO MY OLD WAYS. I JUST NEEDED TO GO SOMEWHERE I COULD LIE LOW AND THINK. AND DRINK.
NOT A VILLAIN, BUT A LIAR.
YEAH, YEAH. I LIED. I SHOULD HAVE TOLD EVERYONE THAT THE REAL REASON I WAS FORMING THE TEAM WAS TO PROTECT MYSELF--
YOU'RE DOING IT AGAIN.
EXCUSE ME?
...THANKS?
YOU DIDN'T FORM THE TEAM TO PROTECT YOURSELF. I KNEW AS SOON AS YOU SAID IT. YOU'RE A TERRIBLE LIAR, BY THE WAY.
SO TELL ME, WHY DID YOU LIE ABOUT EVERYTHING?
I DIDN'T. NOT EVERYTHING, AT LEAST. THE BASTION STUFF IS ALL TRUE. IT'S JUST THAT WHEN I REALIZED *THE REAVERS* AND *O.N.E.* WERE PROBABLY BOTH HUNTING ME...I CAN'T PUT EVERYONE AT RISK FOR MY PAST MISTAKES.
BUT THEY'D STAND BY YOU. THAT'S WHAT X-MEN DO FOR EACH OTHER.
I HAVEN'T BEEN AN X-MAN IN A LONG TIME.

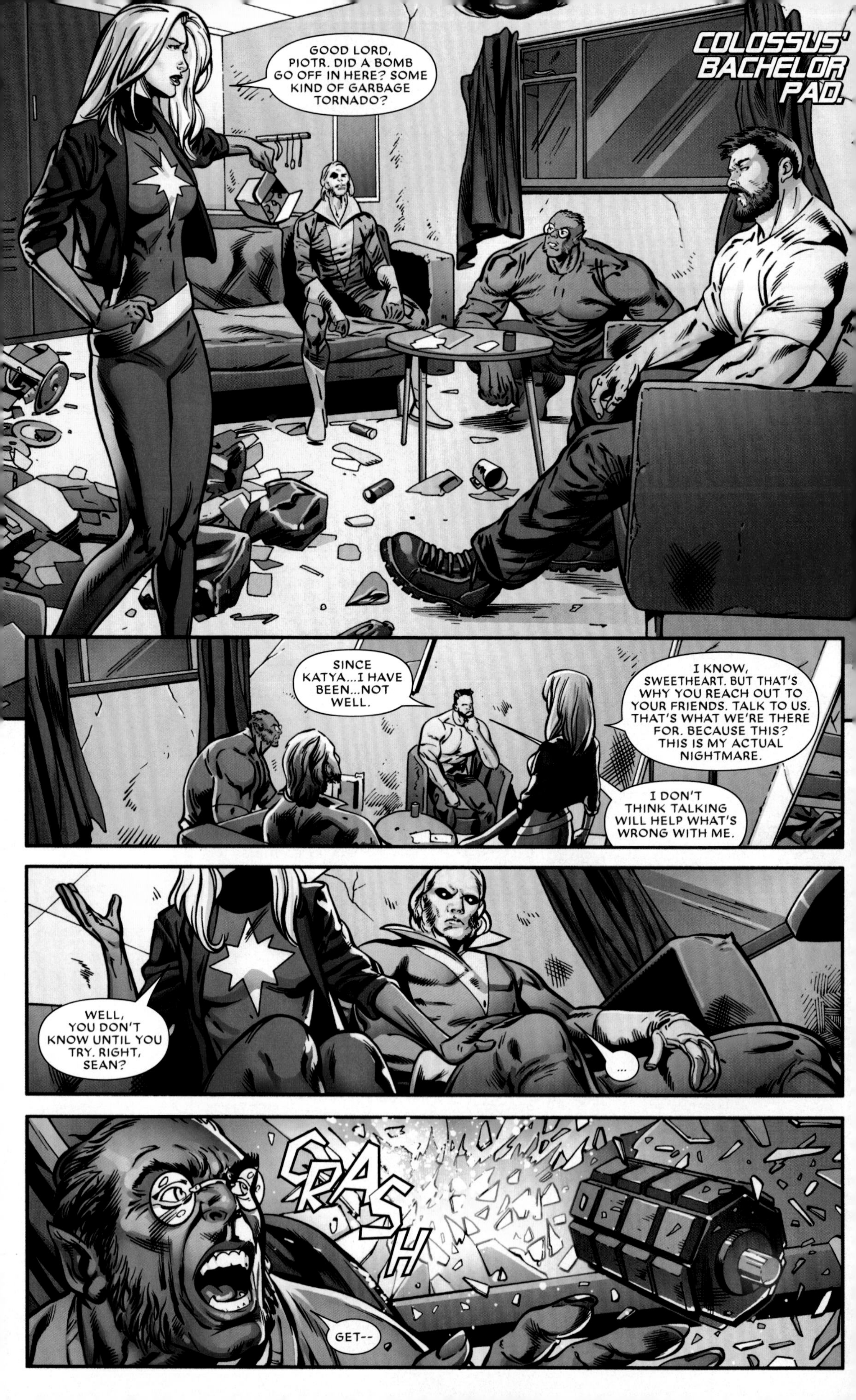
COLOSSUS' BACHELOR PAD.
GOOD LORD, PIOTR. DID A BOMB GO OFF IN HERE? SOME KIND OF GARBAGE TORNADO?
SINCE KATYA...I HAVE BEEN...NOT WELL.
I KNOW, SWEETHEART. BUT THAT'S WHY YOU REACH OUT TO YOUR FRIENDS. TALK TO US. THAT'S WHAT WE'RE THERE FOR. BECAUSE THIS? THIS IS MY ACTUAL NIGHTMARE.
I DON'T THINK TALKING WILL HELP WHAT'S WRONG WITH ME.
WELL, YOU DON'T KNOW UNTIL YOU TRY. RIGHT, SEAN?
...
CRASH
GET--

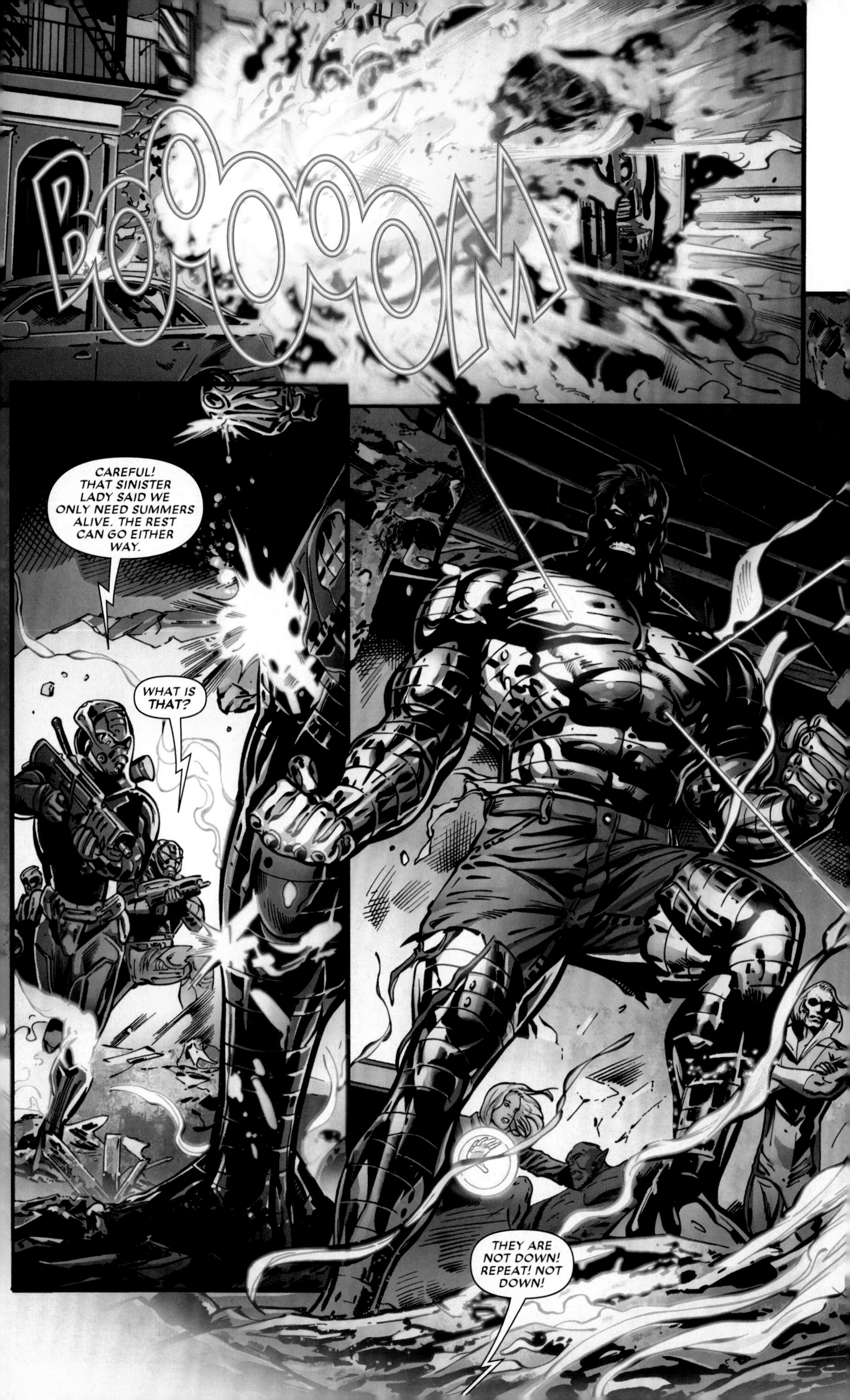
BOOOOOOM
CAREFUL! THAT SINISTER LADY SAID WE ONLY NEED SUMMERS ALIVE. THE REST CAN GO EITHER WAY.
WHAT IS THAT?
THEY ARE NOT DOWN! REPEAT! NOT DOWN!

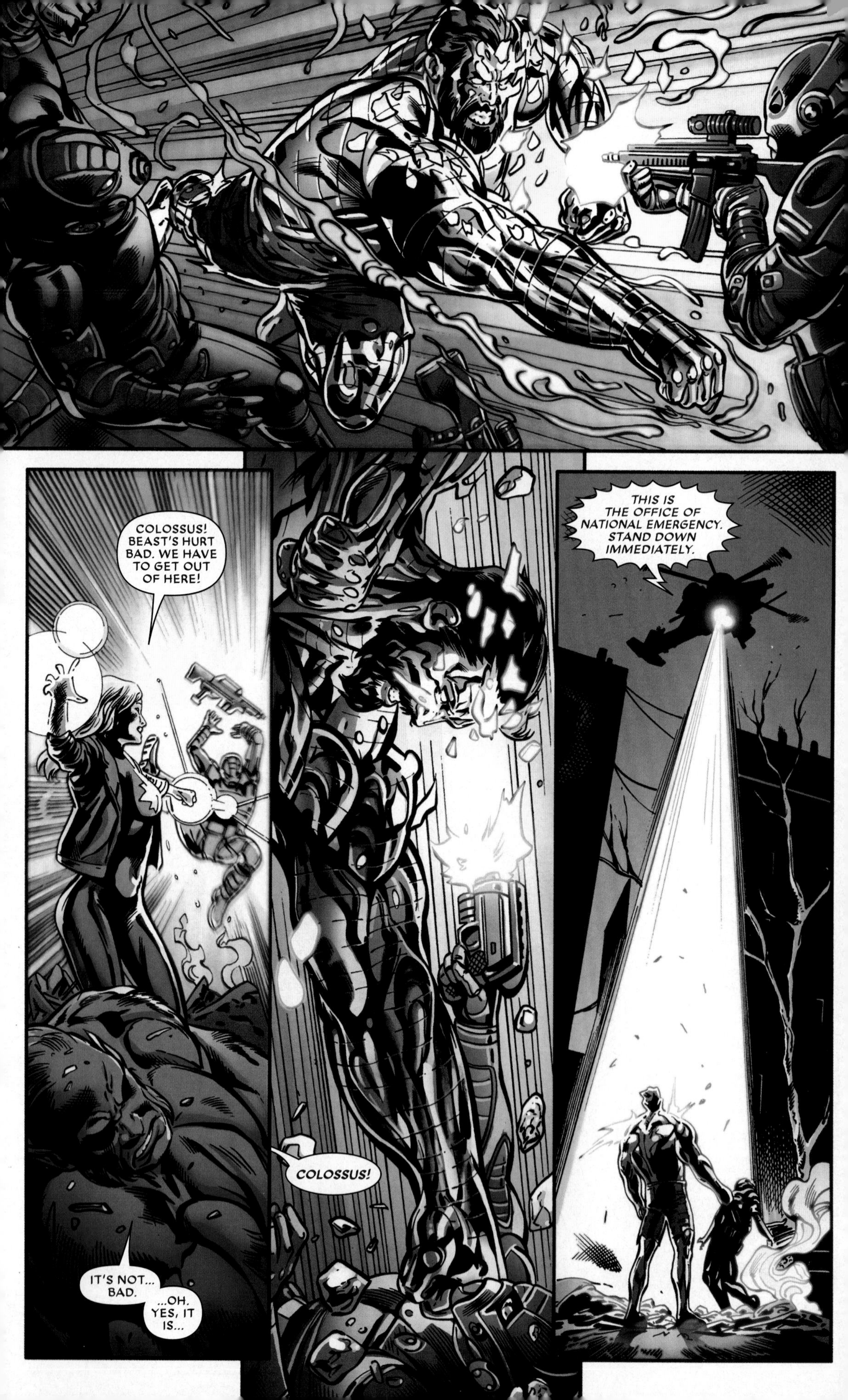
COLOSSUS! BEAST'S HURT BAD. WE HAVE TO GET OUT OF HERE!
IT'S NOT... BAD.
...OH. YES, IT IS...
COLOSSUS!
THIS IS THE OFFICE OF NATIONAL EMERGENCY. STAND DOWN IMMEDIATELY.

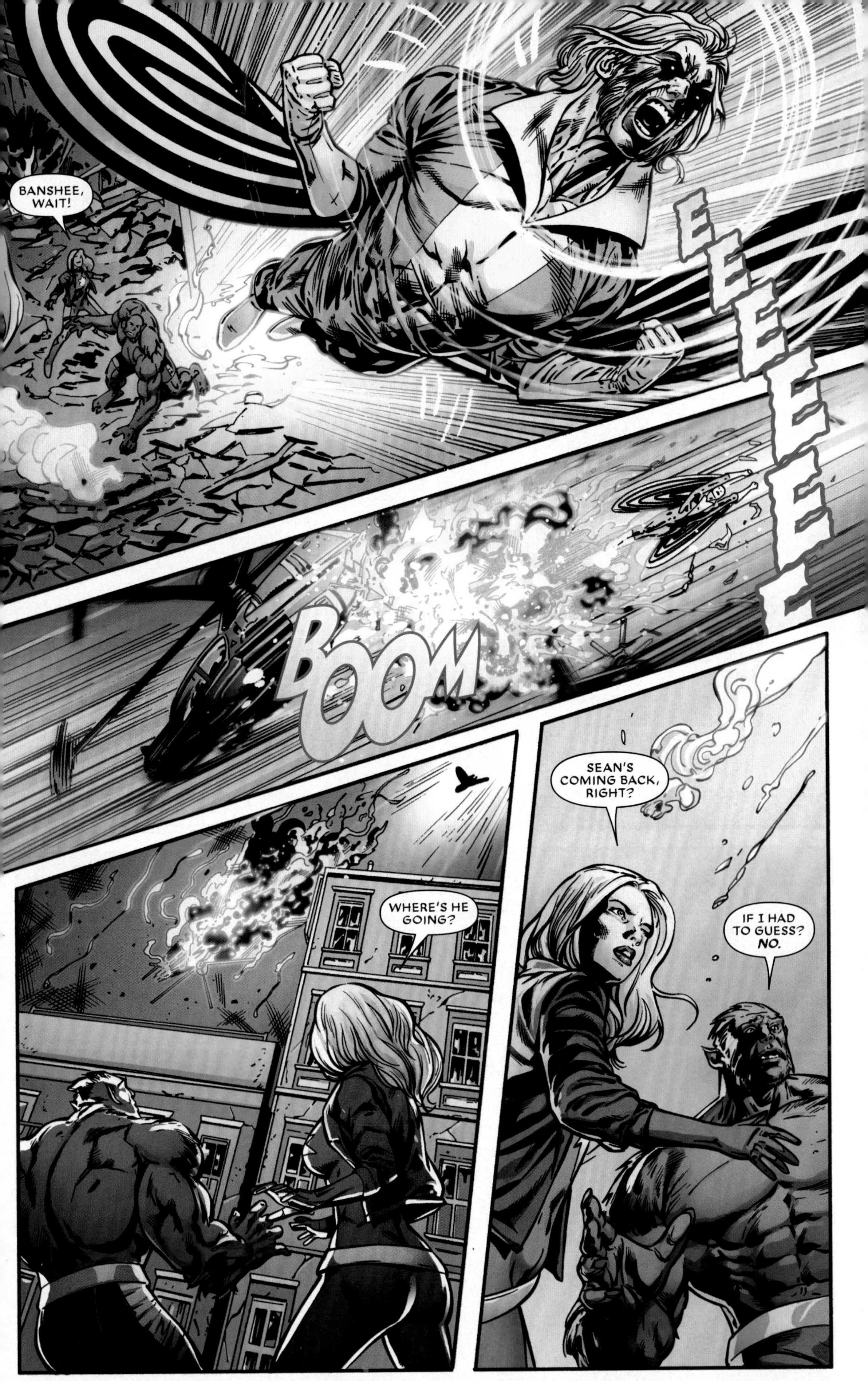
BANSHEE, WAIT!
EEEEEEEEE
BOOM
WHERE'S HE GOING?
SEAN'S COMING BACK, RIGHT?
IF I HAD TO GUESS? **NO.**

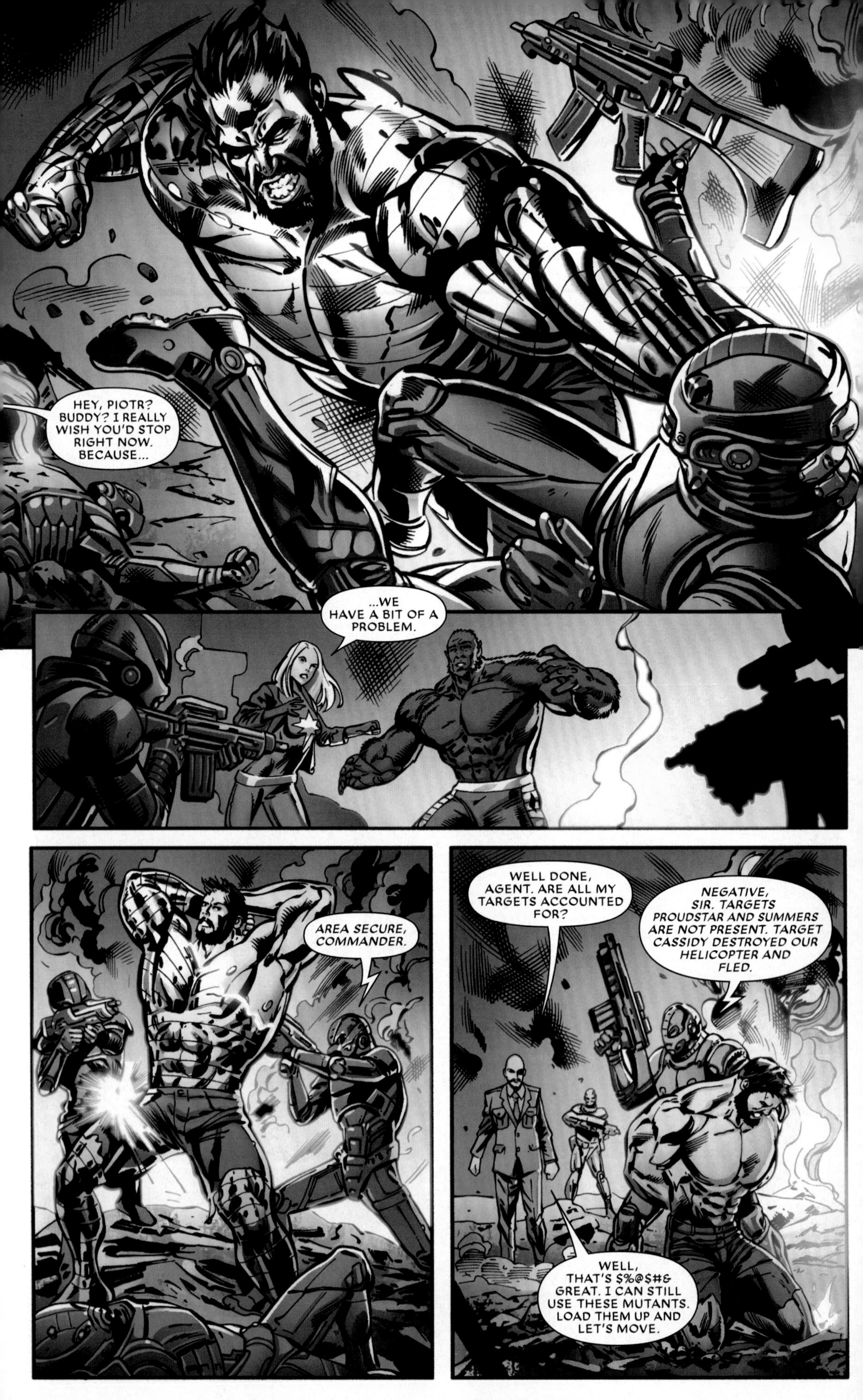
HEY, PIOTR? BUDDY? I REALLY WISH YOU'D STOP RIGHT NOW. BECAUSE...
...WE HAVE A BIT OF A PROBLEM.
AREA SECURE, COMMANDER.
WELL DONE, AGENT. ARE ALL MY TARGETS ACCOUNTED FOR?
NEGATIVE, SIR. TARGETS PROUDSTAR AND SUMMERS ARE NOT PRESENT. TARGET CASSIDY DESTROYED OUR HELICOPTER AND FLED.
WELL, THAT'S $%@$#& GREAT. I CAN STILL USE THESE MUTANTS. LOAD THEM UP AND LET'S MOVE.

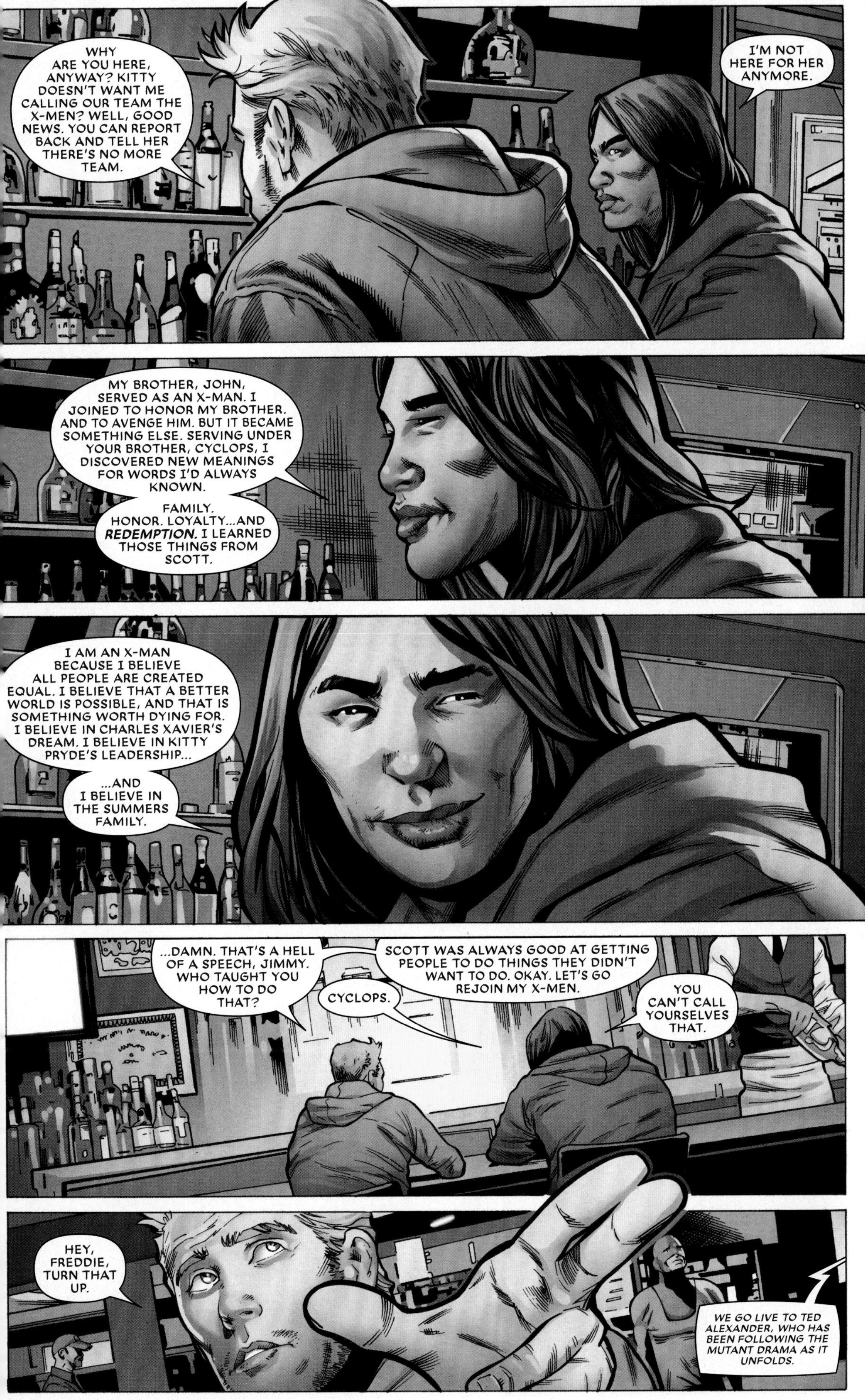
WHY ARE YOU HERE, ANYWAY? KITTY DOESN'T WANT ME CALLING OUR TEAM THE X-MEN? WELL, GOOD NEWS. YOU CAN REPORT BACK AND TELL HER THERE'S NO MORE TEAM.
I'M NOT HERE FOR HER ANYMORE.
MY BROTHER, JOHN, SERVED AS AN X-MAN. I JOINED TO HONOR MY BROTHER. AND TO AVENGE HIM. BUT IT BECAME SOMETHING ELSE. SERVING UNDER YOUR BROTHER, CYCLOPS, I DISCOVERED NEW MEANINGS FOR WORDS I'D ALWAYS KNOWN.
FAMILY. HONOR. LOYALTY...AND ***REDEMPTION.*** I LEARNED THOSE THINGS FROM SCOTT.
I AM AN X-MAN BECAUSE I BELIEVE ALL PEOPLE ARE CREATED EQUAL. I BELIEVE THAT A BETTER WORLD IS POSSIBLE, AND THAT IS SOMETHING WORTH DYING FOR. I BELIEVE IN CHARLES XAVIER'S DREAM. I BELIEVE IN KITTY PRYDE'S LEADERSHIP...
...AND I BELIEVE IN THE SUMMERS FAMILY.
...DAMN. THAT'S A HELL OF A SPEECH, JIMMY. WHO TAUGHT YOU HOW TO DO THAT?
CYCLOPS.
SCOTT WAS ALWAYS GOOD AT GETTING PEOPLE TO DO THINGS THEY DIDN'T WANT TO DO. OKAY. LET'S GO REJOIN MY X-MEN.
YOU CAN'T CALL YOURSELVES THAT.
HEY, FREDDIE, TURN THAT UP.
WE GO LIVE TO TED ALEXANDER, WHO HAS BEEN FOLLOWING THE MUTANT DRAMA AS IT UNFOLDS.

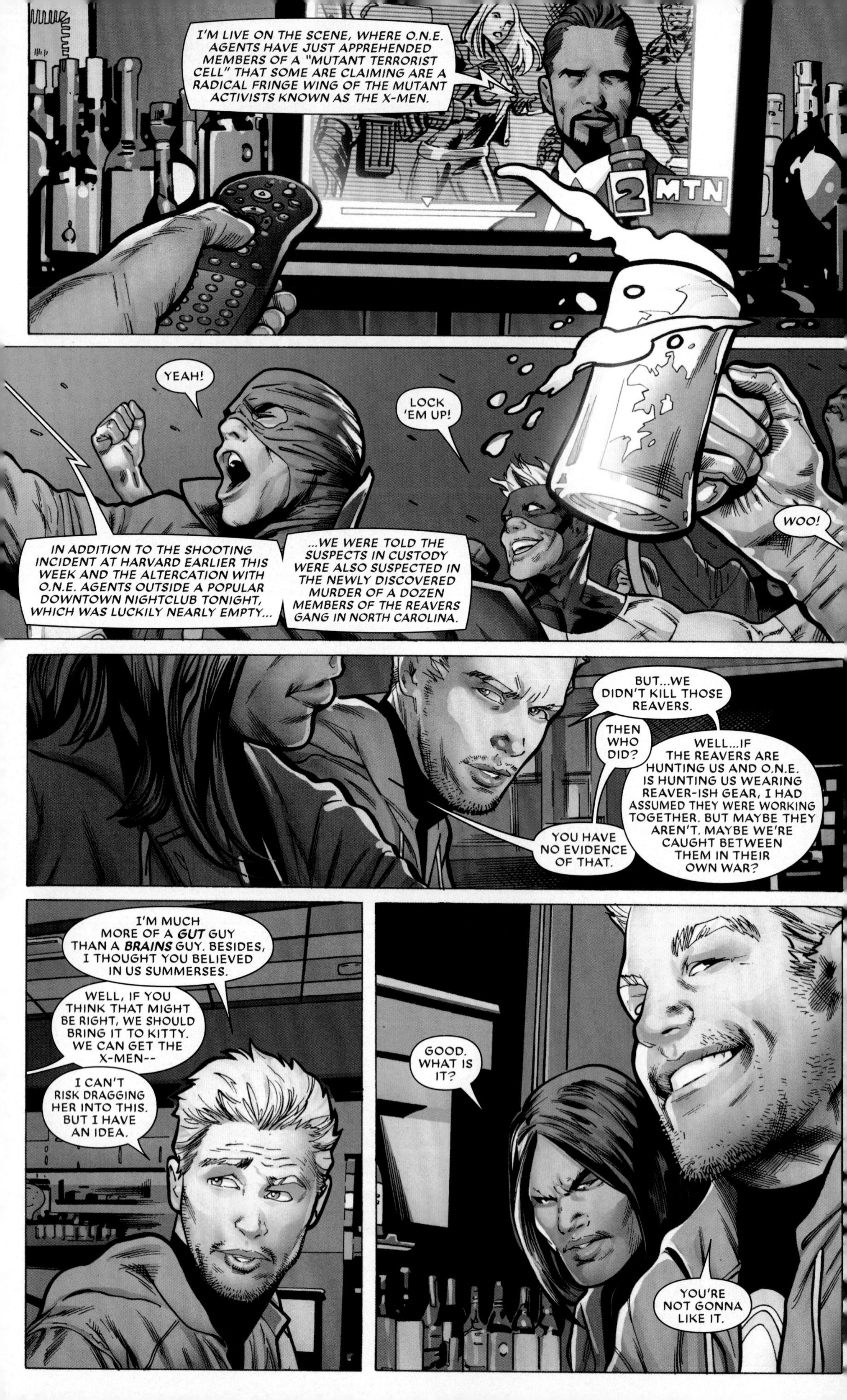
I'M LIVE ON THE SCENE, WHERE O.N.E. AGENTS HAVE JUST APPREHENDED MEMBERS OF A "MUTANT TERRORIST CELL" THAT SOME ARE CLAIMING ARE A RADICAL FRINGE WING OF THE MUTANT ACTIVISTS KNOWN AS THE X-MEN.
2 MTN
YEAH!
LOCK 'EM UP!
WOO!
IN ADDITION TO THE SHOOTING INCIDENT AT HARVARD EARLIER THIS WEEK AND THE ALTERCATION WITH O.N.E. AGENTS OUTSIDE A POPULAR DOWNTOWN NIGHTCLUB TONIGHT, WHICH WAS LUCKILY NEARLY EMPTY...
...WE WERE TOLD THE SUSPECTS IN CUSTODY WERE ALSO SUSPECTED IN THE NEWLY DISCOVERED MURDER OF A DOZEN MEMBERS OF THE REAVERS GANG IN NORTH CAROLINA.
BUT...WE DIDN'T KILL THOSE REAVERS.
THEN WHO DID?
WELL...IF THE REAVERS ARE HUNTING US AND O.N.E. IS HUNTING US WEARING REAVER-ISH GEAR, I HAD ASSUMED THEY WERE WORKING TOGETHER. BUT MAYBE THEY AREN'T. MAYBE WE'RE CAUGHT BETWEEN THEM IN THEIR OWN WAR?
YOU HAVE NO EVIDENCE OF THAT.
I'M MUCH MORE OF A GUT GUY THAN A BRAINS GUY. BESIDES, I THOUGHT YOU BELIEVED IN US SUMMERSES.
WELL, IF YOU THINK THAT MIGHT BE RIGHT, WE SHOULD BRING IT TO KITTY. WE CAN GET THE X-MEN--
I CAN'T RISK DRAGGING HER INTO THIS. BUT I HAVE AN IDEA.
GOOD. WHAT IS IT?
YOU'RE NOT GONNA LIKE IT.

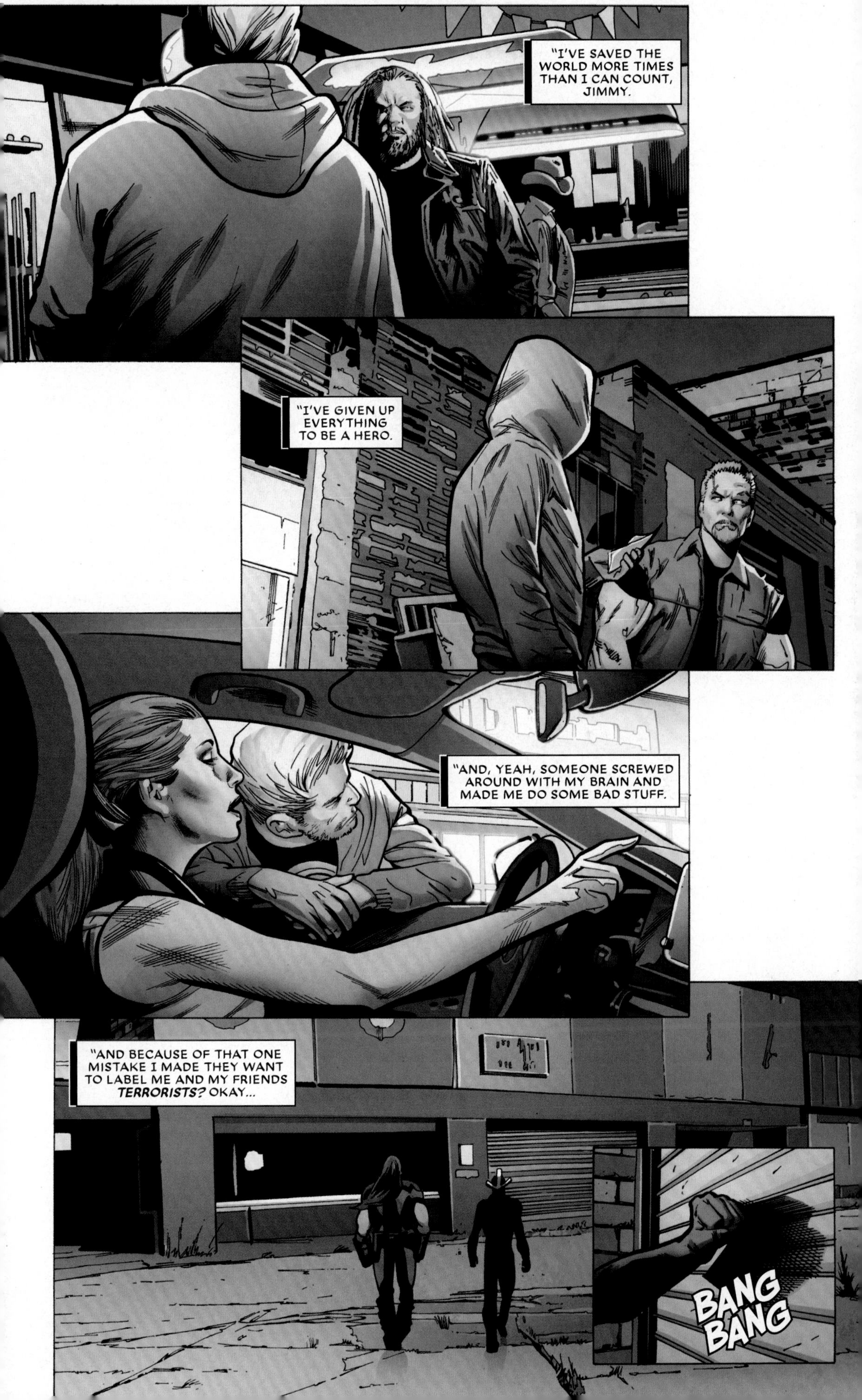
"I'VE SAVED THE WORLD MORE TIMES THAN I CAN COUNT, JIMMY.
"I'VE GIVEN UP EVERYTHING TO BE A HERO.
"AND, YEAH, SOMEONE SCREWED AROUND WITH MY BRAIN AND MADE ME DO SOME BAD STUFF.
"AND BECAUSE OF THAT ONE MISTAKE I MADE THEY WANT TO LABEL ME AND MY FRIENDS *TERRORISTS?* OKAY...
BANG BANG

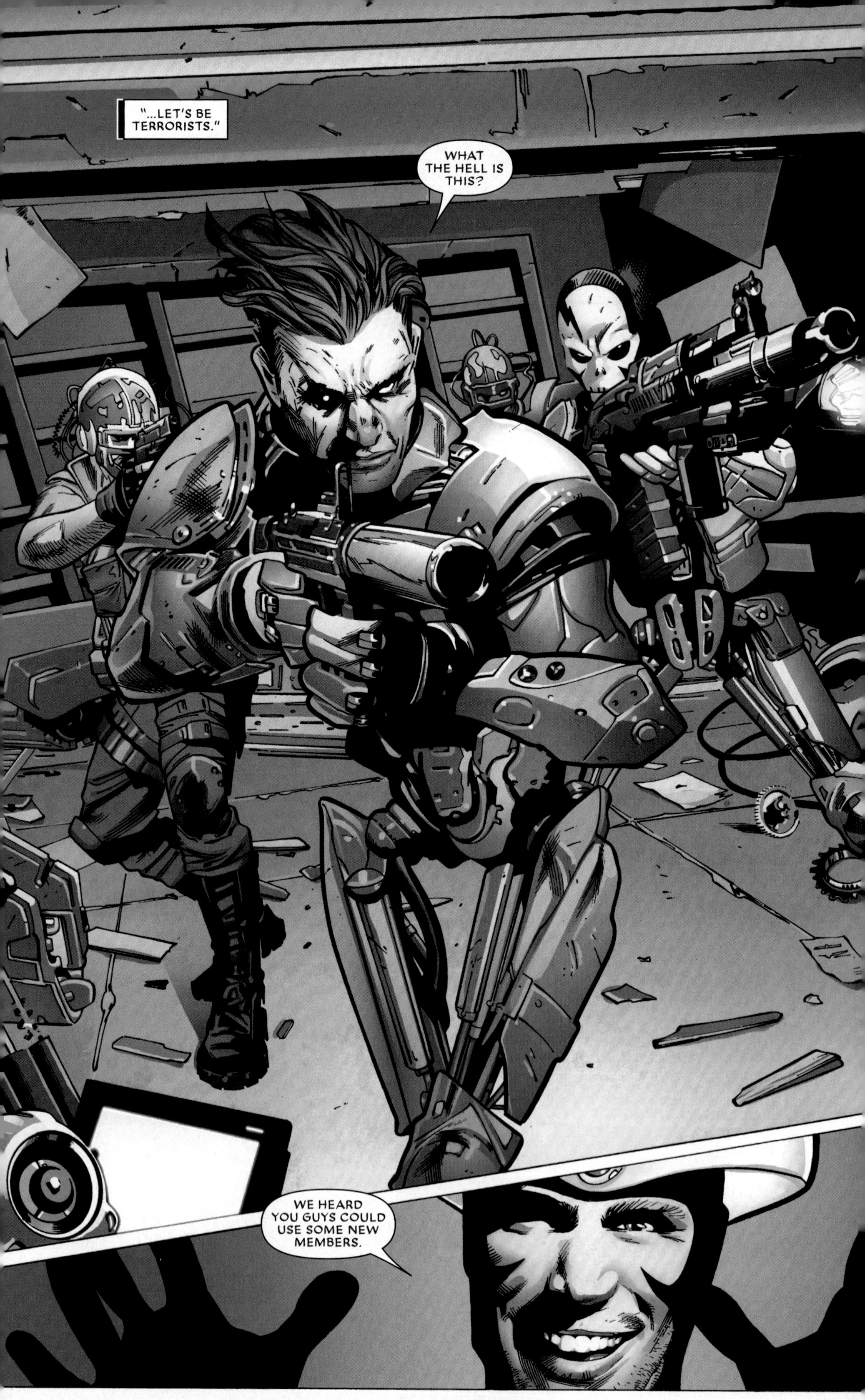
"...LET'S BE TERRORISTS."
WHAT THE HELL IS THIS?
WE HEARD YOU GUYS COULD USE SOME NEW MEMBERS.

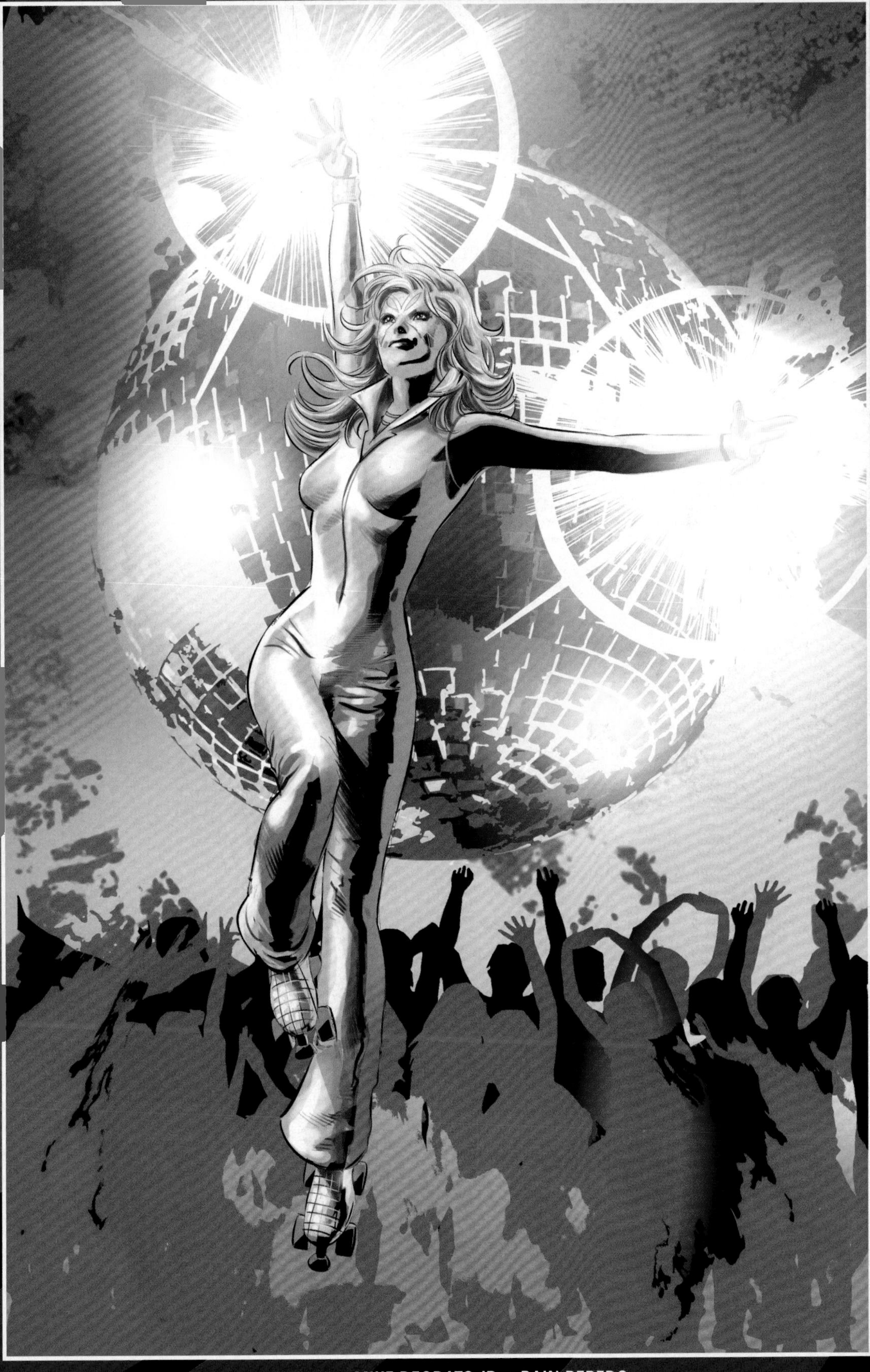

#13 VARIANT BY **MIKE DEODATO JR.** & **RAIN BEREDO**

16

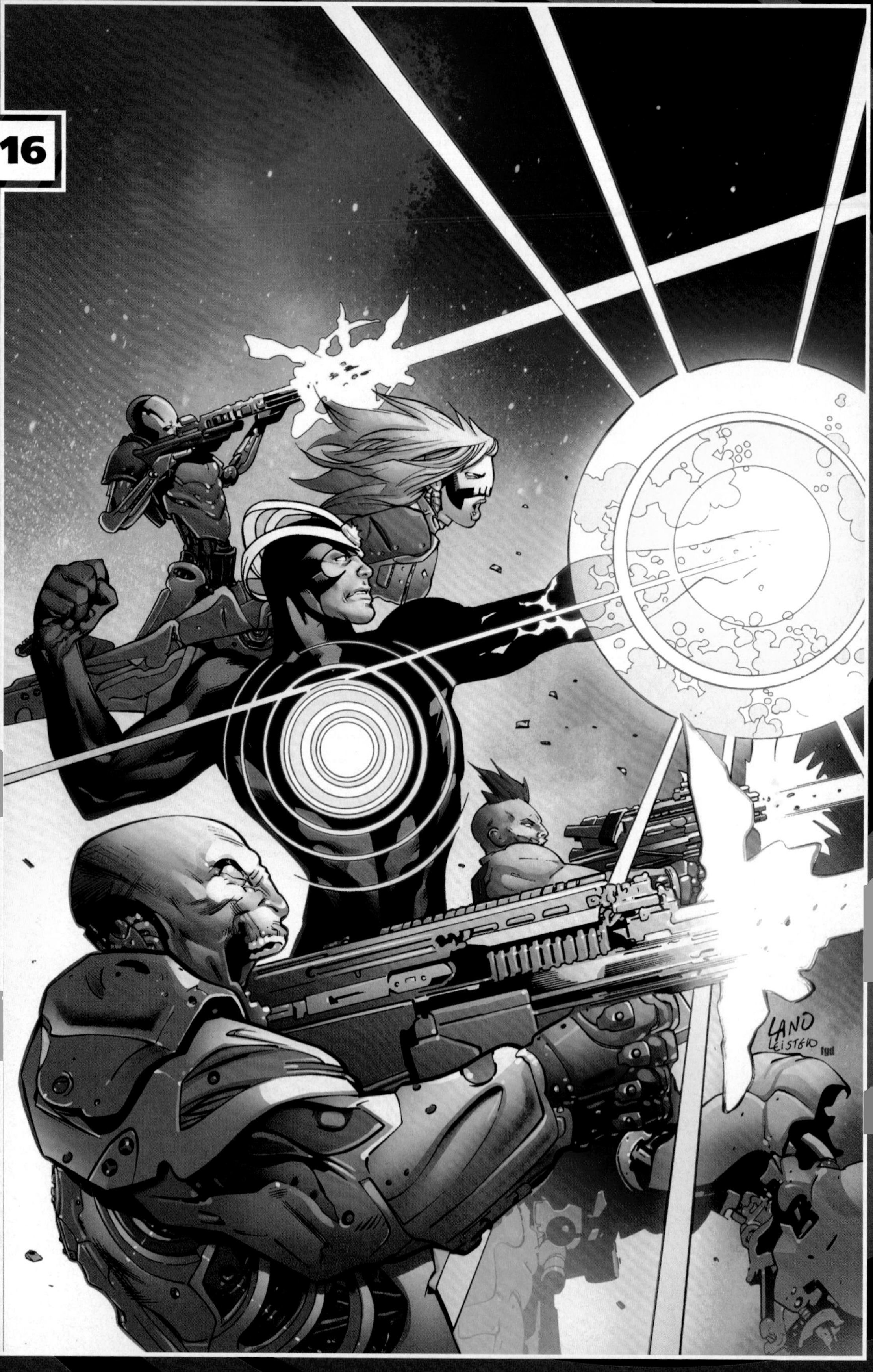

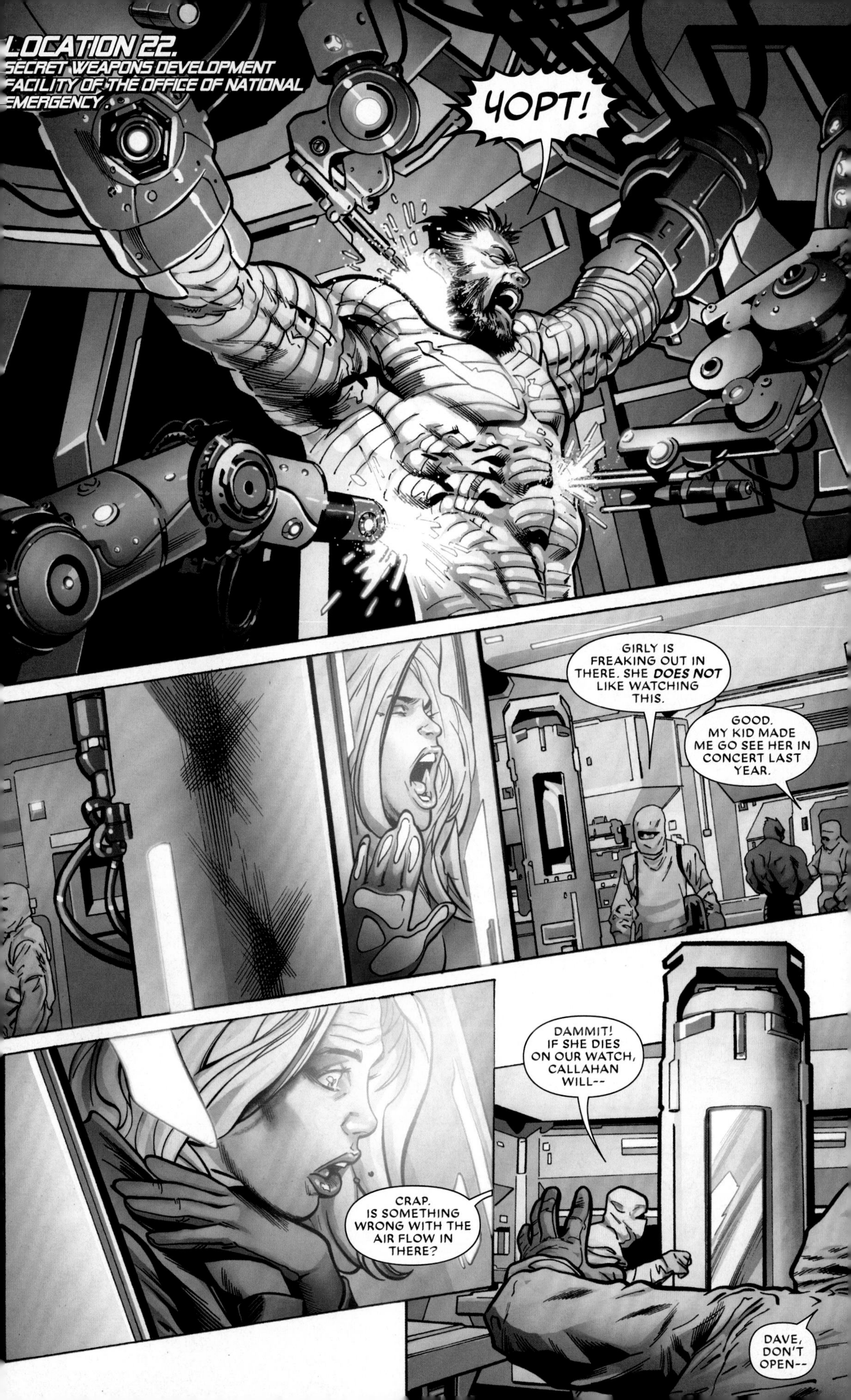
LOCATION 22.
SECRET WEAPONS DEVELOPMENT FACILITY OF THE OFFICE OF NATIONAL EMERGENCY.
ЧОРТ!
GIRLY IS FREAKING OUT IN THERE. SHE DOES NOT LIKE WATCHING THIS.
GOOD. MY KID MADE ME GO SEE HER IN CONCERT LAST YEAR.
DAMMIT! IF SHE DIES ON OUR WATCH, CALLAHAN WILL--
CRAP. IS SOMETHING WRONG WITH THE AIR FLOW IN THERE?
DAVE, DON'T OPEN--

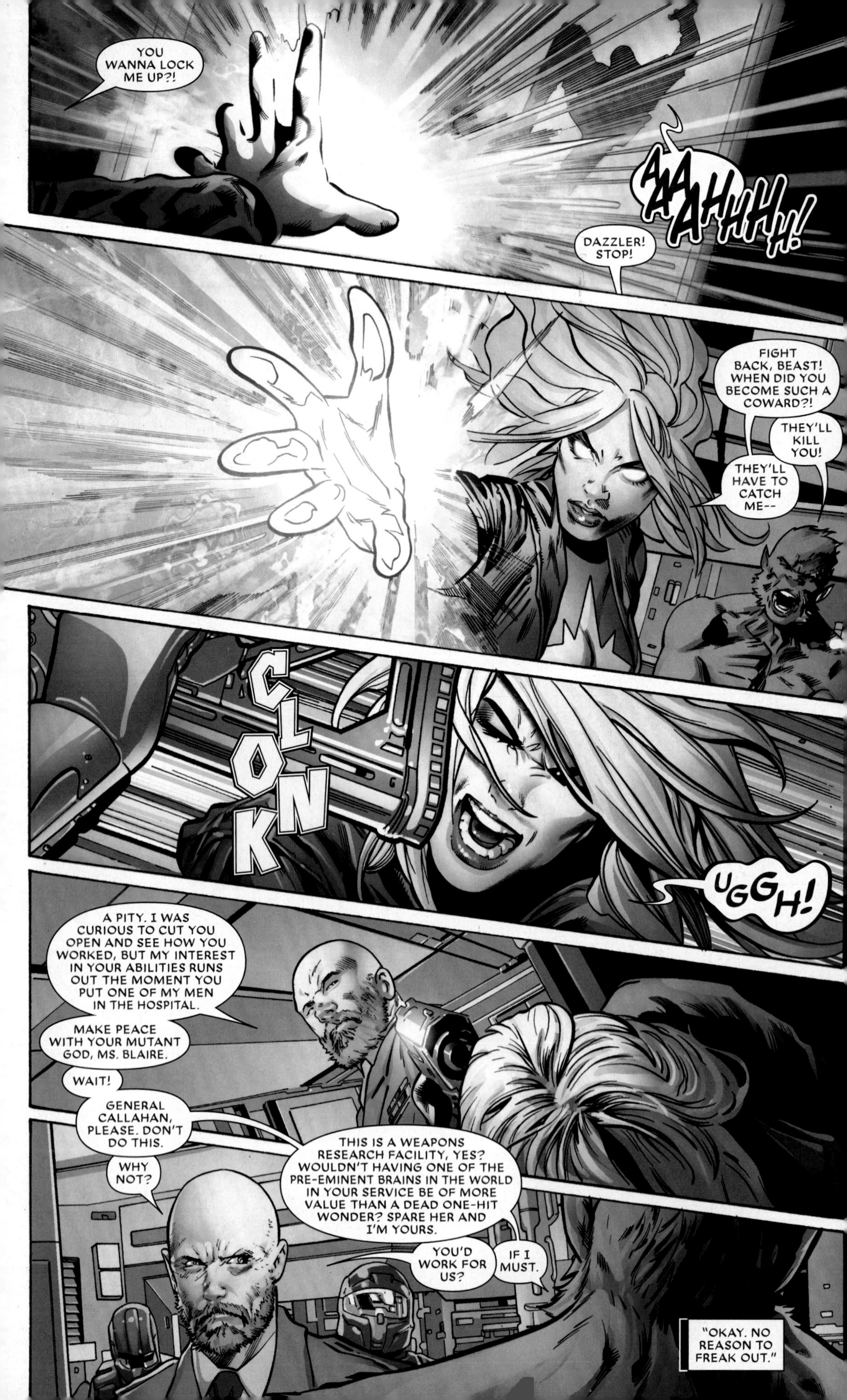
YOU WANNA LOCK ME UP?!
AAAAHHHH!
DAZZLER! STOP!
FIGHT BACK, BEAST! WHEN DID YOU BECOME SUCH A COWARD?!
THEY'LL KILL YOU!
THEY'LL HAVE TO CATCH ME--
CLONK
UGGH!
A PITY. I WAS CURIOUS TO CUT YOU OPEN AND SEE HOW YOU WORKED, BUT MY INTEREST IN YOUR ABILITIES RUNS OUT THE MOMENT YOU PUT ONE OF MY MEN IN THE HOSPITAL.
MAKE PEACE WITH YOUR MUTANT GOD, MS. BLAIRE.
WAIT!
GENERAL CALLAHAN, PLEASE. DON'T DO THIS.
WHY NOT?
THIS IS A WEAPONS RESEARCH FACILITY, YES? WOULDN'T HAVING ONE OF THE PRE-EMINENT BRAINS IN THE WORLD IN YOUR SERVICE BE OF MORE VALUE THAN A DEAD ONE-HIT WONDER? SPARE HER AND I'M YOURS.
YOU'D WORK FOR US?
IF I MUST.
"OKAY. NO REASON TO FREAK OUT."

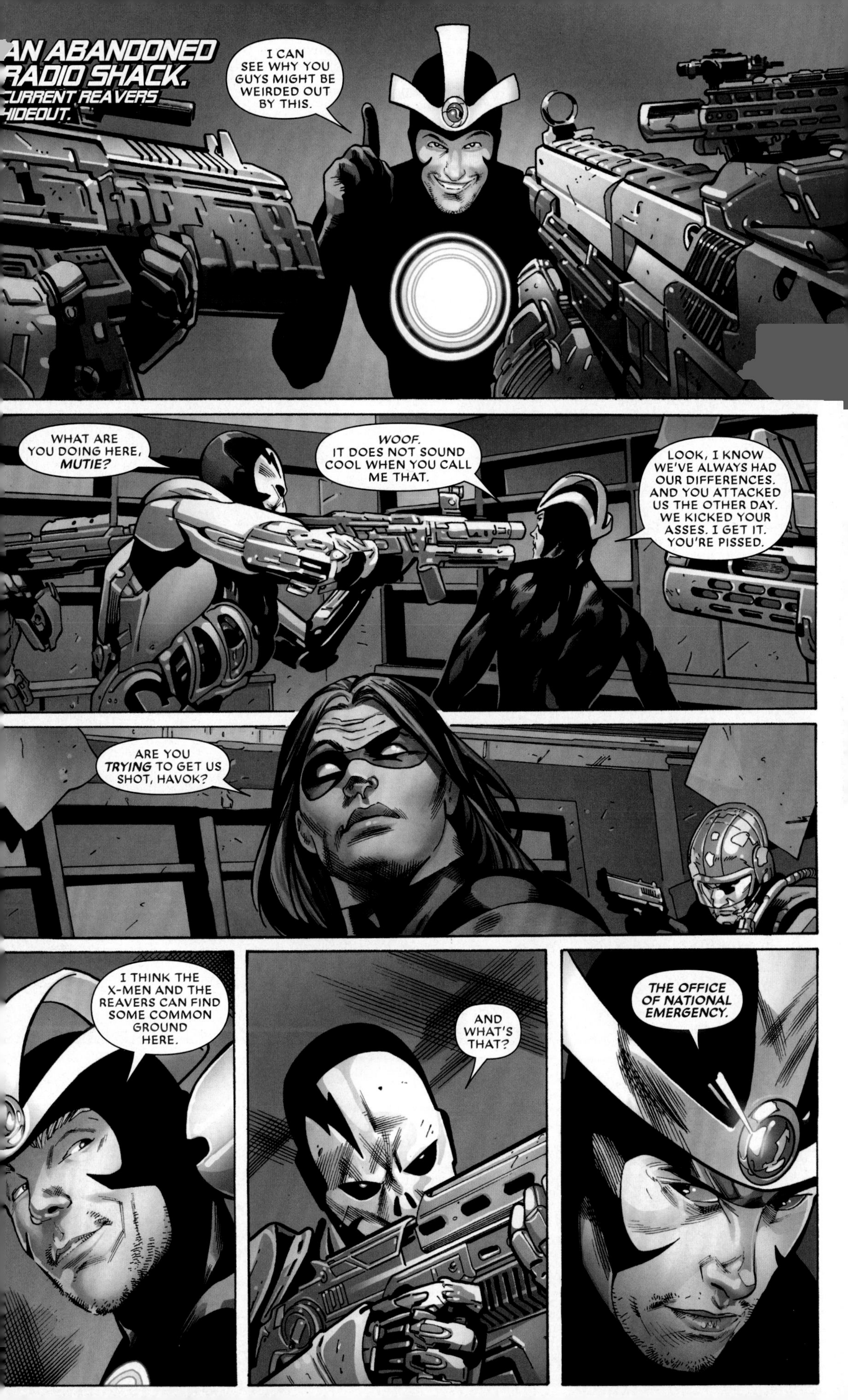
AN ABANDONED RADIO SHACK. CURRENT REAVERS HIDEOUT.
I CAN SEE WHY YOU GUYS MIGHT BE WEIRDED OUT BY THIS.
WHAT ARE YOU DOING HERE, MUTIE?
WOOF. IT DOES NOT SOUND COOL WHEN YOU CALL ME THAT.
LOOK, I KNOW WE'VE ALWAYS HAD OUR DIFFERENCES. AND YOU ATTACKED US THE OTHER DAY. WE KICKED YOUR ASSES. I GET IT. YOU'RE PISSED.
ARE YOU TRYING TO GET US SHOT, HAVOK?
I THINK THE X-MEN AND THE REAVERS CAN FIND SOME COMMON GROUND HERE.
AND WHAT'S THAT?
THE OFFICE OF NATIONAL EMERGENCY.

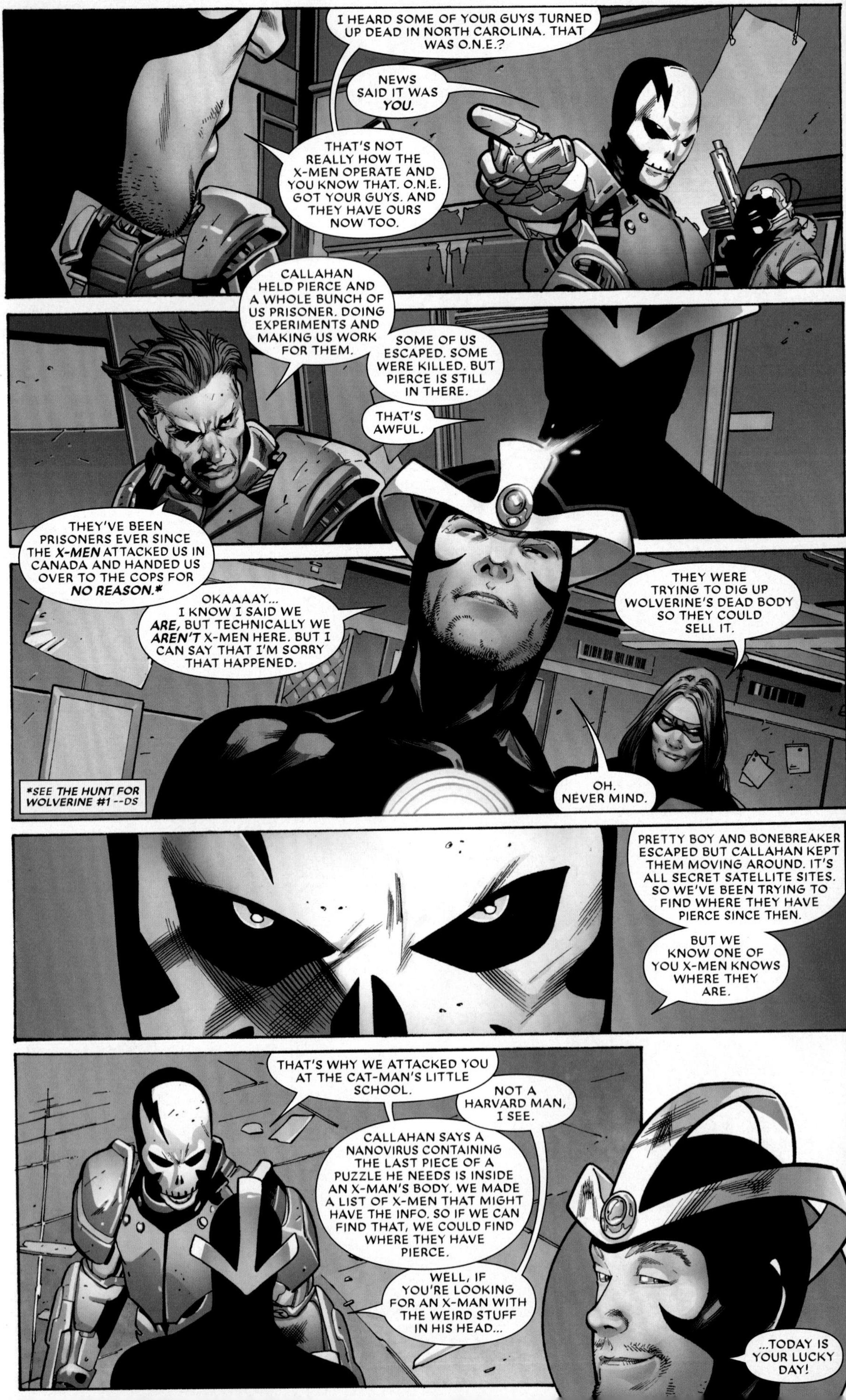
I HEARD SOME OF YOUR GUYS TURNED UP DEAD IN NORTH CAROLINA. THAT WAS O.N.E.?
NEWS SAID IT WAS YOU.
THAT'S NOT REALLY HOW THE X-MEN OPERATE AND YOU KNOW THAT. O.N.E. GOT YOUR GUYS. AND THEY HAVE OURS NOW TOO.
CALLAHAN HELD PIERCE AND A WHOLE BUNCH OF US PRISONER. DOING EXPERIMENTS AND MAKING US WORK FOR THEM.
SOME OF US ESCAPED. SOME WERE KILLED. BUT PIERCE IS STILL IN THERE.
THAT'S AWFUL.
THEY'VE BEEN PRISONERS EVER SINCE THE X-MEN ATTACKED US IN CANADA AND HANDED US OVER TO THE COPS FOR NO REASON.*
OKAAAAY... I KNOW I SAID WE ARE, BUT TECHNICALLY WE AREN'T X-MEN HERE. BUT I CAN SAY THAT I'M SORRY THAT HAPPENED.
THEY WERE TRYING TO DIG UP WOLVERINE'S DEAD BODY SO THEY COULD SELL IT.
OH. NEVER MIND.
*SEE THE HUNT FOR WOLVERINE #1 --DS
PRETTY BOY AND BONEBREAKER ESCAPED BUT CALLAHAN KEPT THEM MOVING AROUND. IT'S ALL SECRET SATELLITE SITES. SO WE'VE BEEN TRYING TO FIND WHERE THEY HAVE PIERCE SINCE THEN.
BUT WE KNOW ONE OF YOU X-MEN KNOWS WHERE THEY ARE.
THAT'S WHY WE ATTACKED YOU AT THE CAT-MAN'S LITTLE SCHOOL.
NOT A HARVARD MAN, I SEE.
CALLAHAN SAYS A NANOVIRUS CONTAINING THE LAST PIECE OF A PUZZLE HE NEEDS IS INSIDE AN X-MAN'S BODY. WE MADE A LIST OF X-MEN THAT MIGHT HAVE THE INFO. SO IF WE CAN FIND THAT, WE COULD FIND WHERE THEY HAVE PIERCE.
WELL, IF YOU'RE LOOKING FOR AN X-MAN WITH THE WEIRD STUFF IN HIS HEAD...
...TODAY IS YOUR LUCKY DAY!

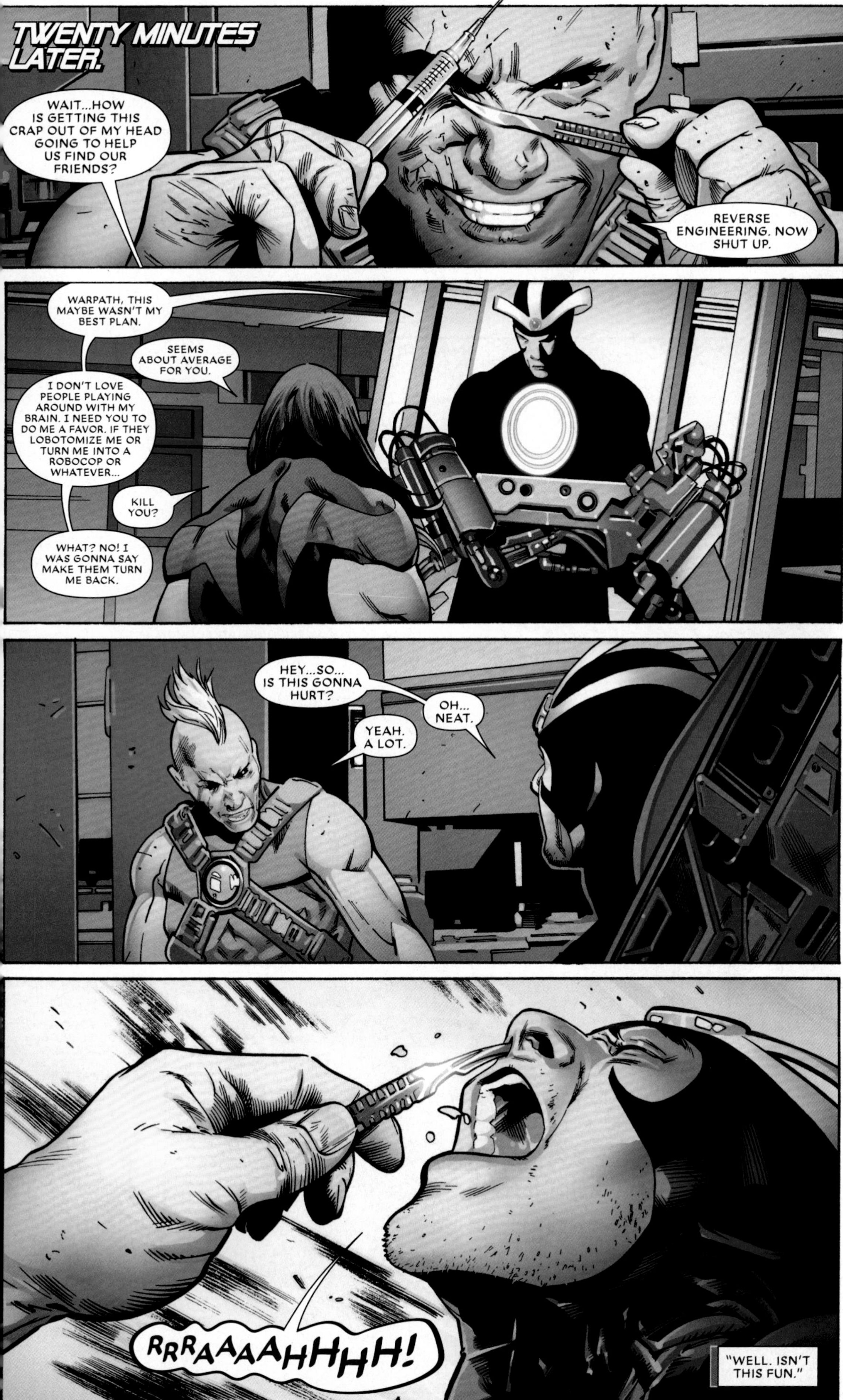
TWENTY MINUTES LATER.
WAIT...HOW IS GETTING THIS CRAP OUT OF MY HEAD GOING TO HELP US FIND OUR FRIENDS?
REVERSE ENGINEERING. NOW SHUT UP.
WARPATH, THIS MAYBE WASN'T MY BEST PLAN.
SEEMS ABOUT AVERAGE FOR YOU.
I DON'T LOVE PEOPLE PLAYING AROUND WITH MY BRAIN. I NEED YOU TO DO ME A FAVOR. IF THEY LOBOTOMIZE ME OR TURN ME INTO A ROBOCOP OR WHATEVER...
KILL YOU?
WHAT? NO! I WAS GONNA SAY MAKE THEM TURN ME BACK.
HEY...SO... IS THIS GONNA HURT?
YEAH. A LOT.
OH... NEAT.
RRRAAAAHHHH!
"WELL. ISN'T THIS FUN."

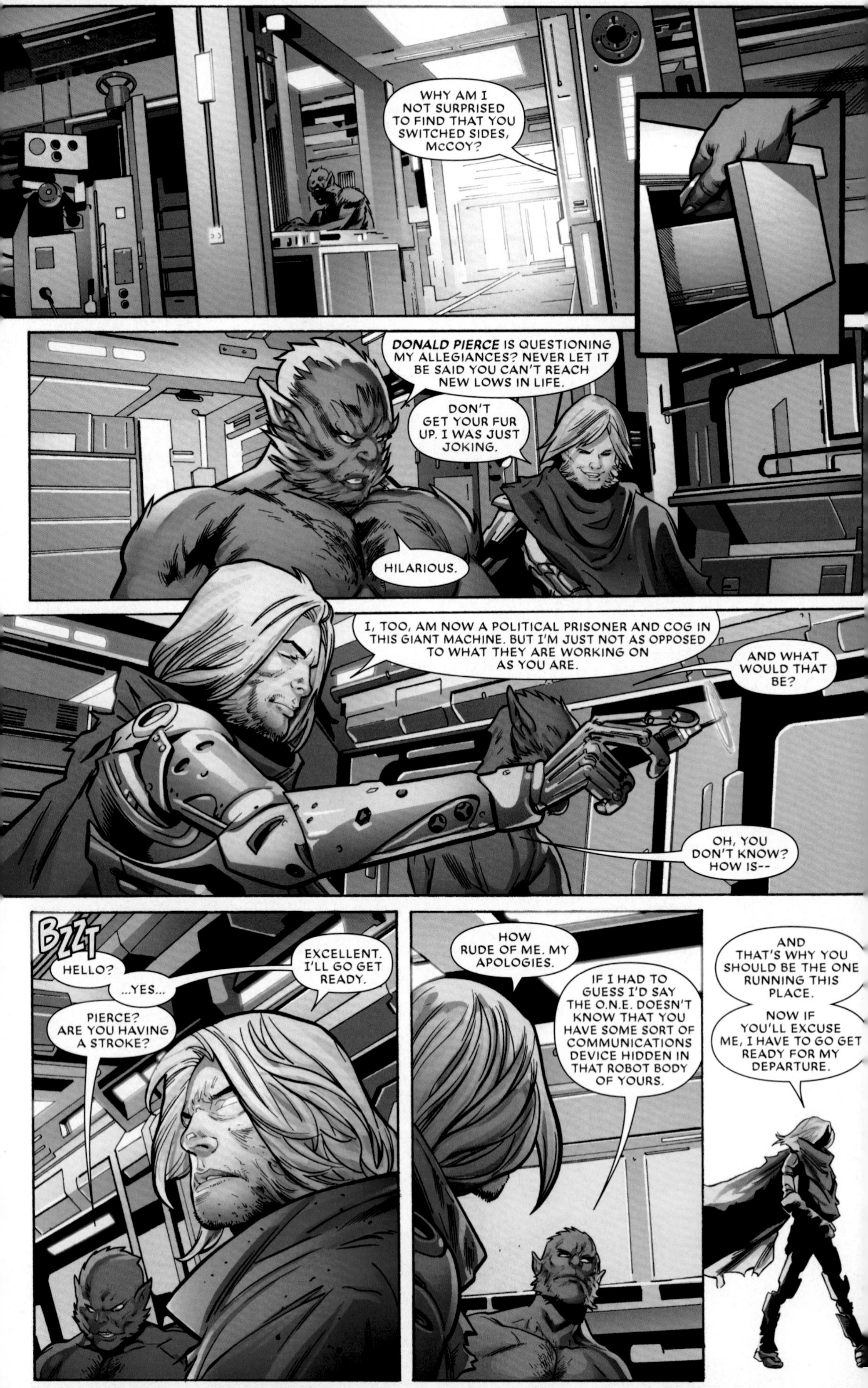
WHY AM I NOT SURPRISED TO FIND THAT YOU SWITCHED SIDES, McCOY?
DONALD PIERCE IS QUESTIONING MY ALLEGIANCES? NEVER LET IT BE SAID YOU CAN'T REACH NEW LOWS IN LIFE.
DON'T GET YOUR FUR UP. I WAS JUST JOKING.
HILARIOUS.
I, TOO, AM NOW A POLITICAL PRISONER AND COG IN THIS GIANT MACHINE. BUT I'M JUST NOT AS OPPOSED TO WHAT THEY ARE WORKING ON AS YOU ARE.
AND WHAT WOULD THAT BE?
OH, YOU DON'T KNOW? HOW IS--
BZZT
HELLO?
...YES...
EXCELLENT. I'LL GO GET READY.
PIERCE? ARE YOU HAVING A STROKE?
HOW RUDE OF ME. MY APOLOGIES.
IF I HAD TO GUESS I'D SAY THE O.N.E. DOESN'T KNOW THAT YOU HAVE SOME SORT OF COMMUNICATIONS DEVICE HIDDEN IN THAT ROBOT BODY OF YOURS.
AND THAT'S WHY YOU SHOULD BE THE ONE RUNNING THIS PLACE.
NOW IF YOU'LL EXCUSE ME, I HAVE TO GO GET READY FOR MY DEPARTURE.

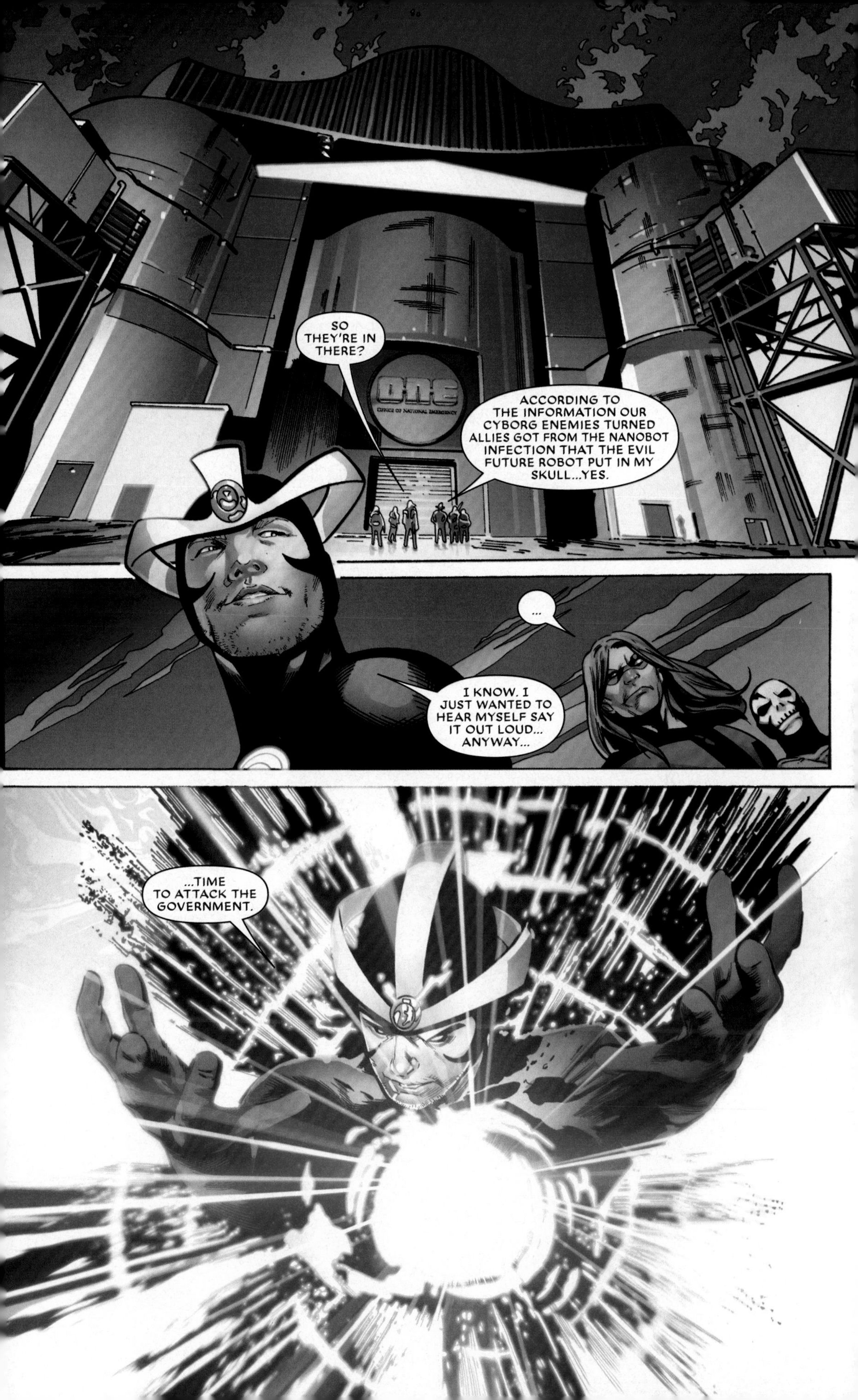
SO THEY'RE IN THERE?
ONE
OFFICE OF NATIONAL EMERGENCY
ACCORDING TO THE INFORMATION OUR CYBORG ENEMIES TURNED ALLIES GOT FROM THE NANOBOT INFECTION THAT THE EVIL FUTURE ROBOT PUT IN MY SKULL...YES.
...
I KNOW. I JUST WANTED TO HEAR MYSELF SAY IT OUT LOUD... ANYWAY...
...TIME TO ATTACK THE GOVERNMENT.

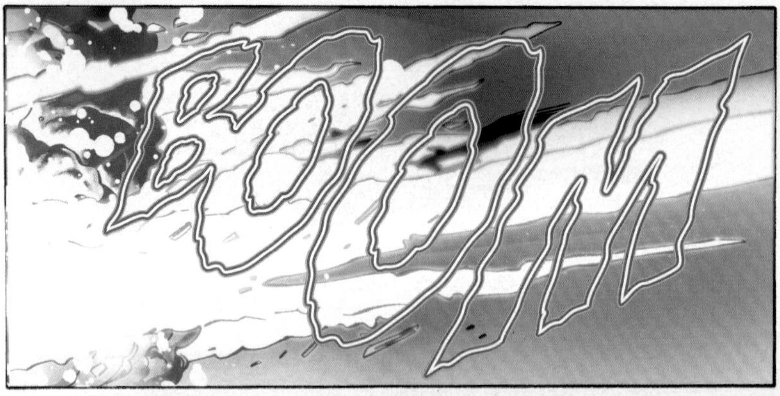
BOOOM

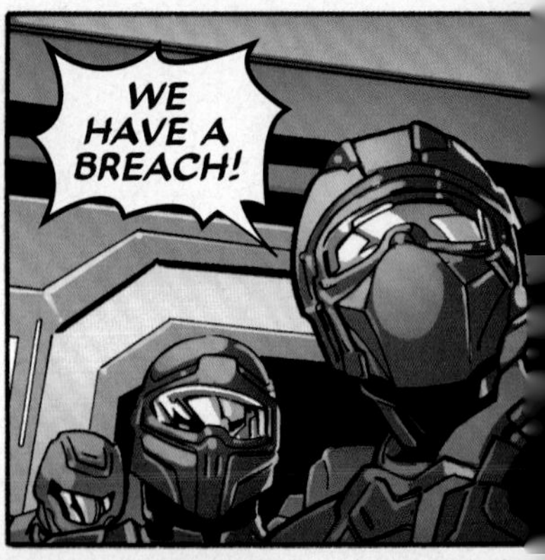
WE HAVE A BREACH!

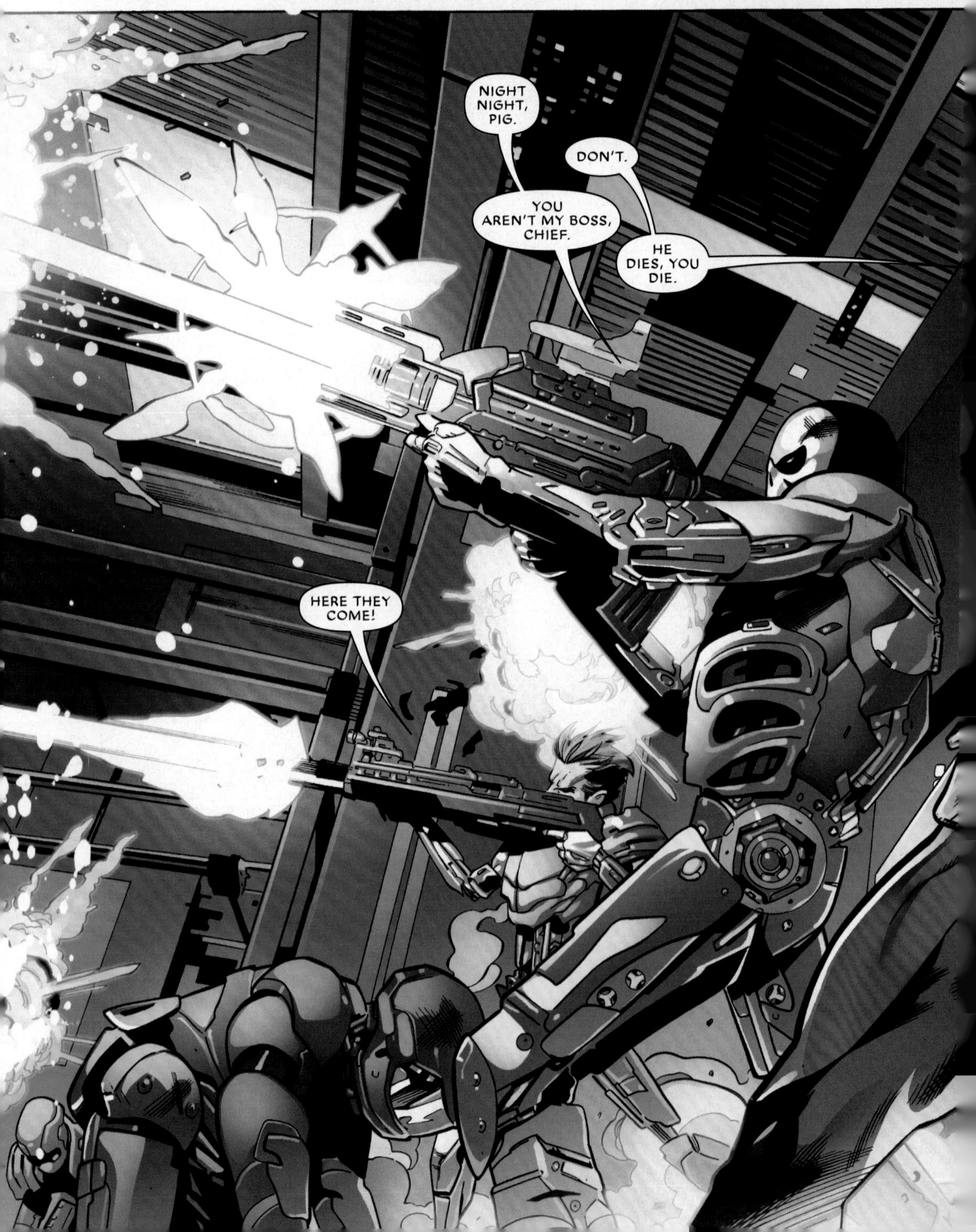
NIGHT NIGHT, PIG.
DON'T.
YOU AREN'T MY BOSS, CHIEF.
HE DIES, YOU DIE.
HERE THEY COME!

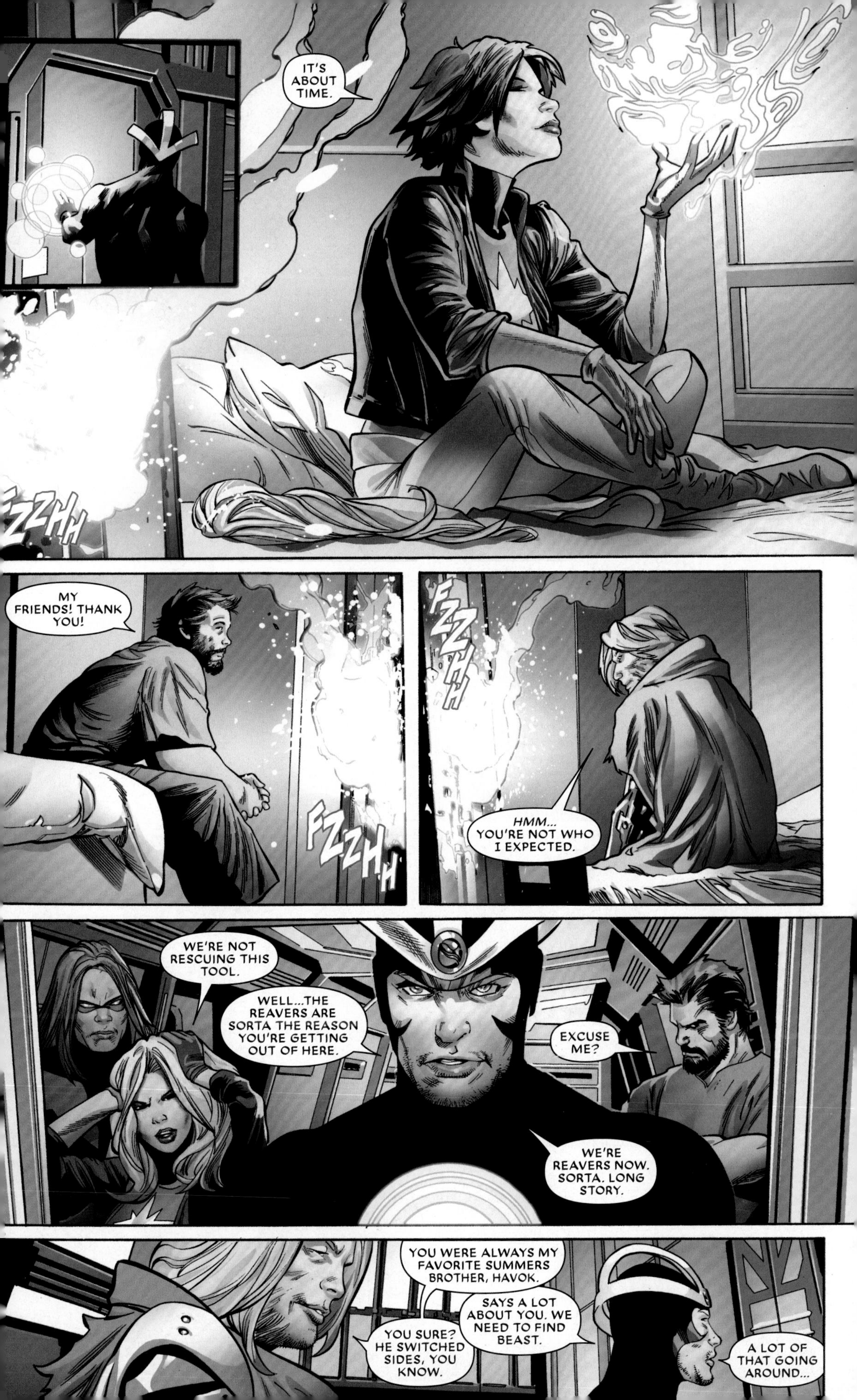
IT'S ABOUT TIME.
FZZHH
MY FRIENDS! THANK YOU!
FZZHH
FZZHH
HMM... YOU'RE NOT WHO I EXPECTED.
WE'RE NOT RESCUING THIS TOOL.
WELL...THE REAVERS ARE SORTA THE REASON YOU'RE GETTING OUT OF HERE.
EXCUSE ME?
WE'RE REAVERS NOW. SORTA. LONG STORY.
YOU WERE ALWAYS MY FAVORITE SUMMERS BROTHER, HAVOK.
YOU SURE? HE SWITCHED SIDES, YOU KNOW.
SAYS A LOT ABOUT YOU. WE NEED TO FIND BEAST.
A LOT OF THAT GOING AROUND...

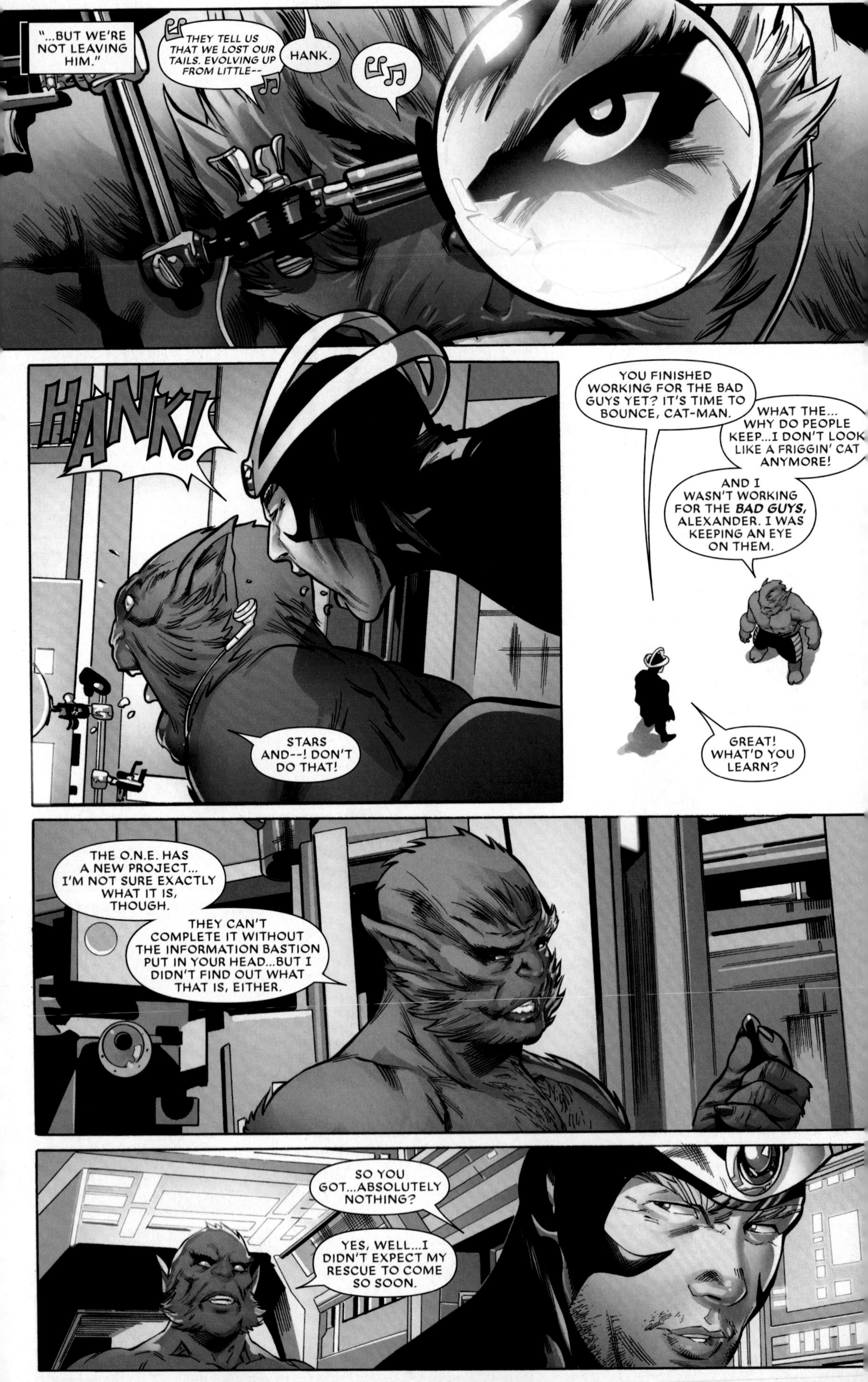
"...BUT WE'RE NOT LEAVING HIM."
THEY TELL US THAT WE LOST OUR TAILS. EVOLVING UP FROM LITTLE--
HANK.
HANK!
YOU FINISHED WORKING FOR THE BAD GUYS YET? IT'S TIME TO BOUNCE, CAT-MAN.
WHAT THE... WHY DO PEOPLE KEEP...I DON'T LOOK LIKE A FRIGGIN' CAT ANYMORE!
AND I WASN'T WORKING FOR THE *BAD GUYS,* ALEXANDER. I WAS KEEPING AN EYE ON THEM.
STARS AND--! DON'T DO THAT!
GREAT! WHAT'D YOU LEARN?
THE O.N.E. HAS A NEW PROJECT... I'M NOT SURE EXACTLY WHAT IT IS, THOUGH.
THEY CAN'T COMPLETE IT WITHOUT THE INFORMATION BASTION PUT IN YOUR HEAD...BUT I DIDN'T FIND OUT WHAT THAT IS, EITHER.
SO YOU GOT...ABSOLUTELY NOTHING?
YES, WELL...I DIDN'T EXPECT MY RESCUE TO COME SO SOON.

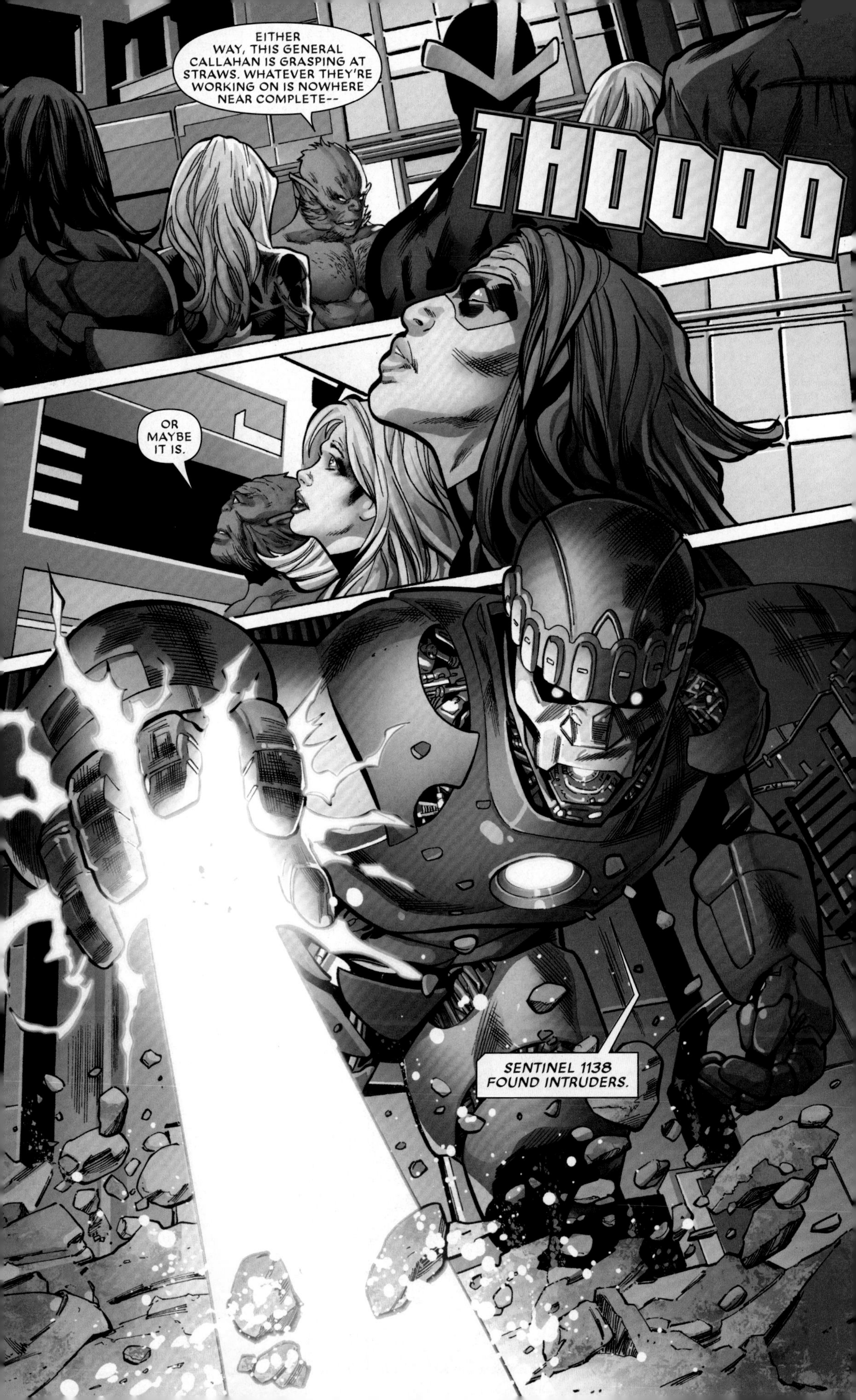
EITHER WAY, THIS GENERAL CALLAHAN IS GRASPING AT STRAWS. WHATEVER THEY'RE WORKING ON IS NOWHERE NEAR COMPLETE--
THOOOD
OR MAYBE IT IS.
SENTINEL 1138 FOUND INTRUDERS.

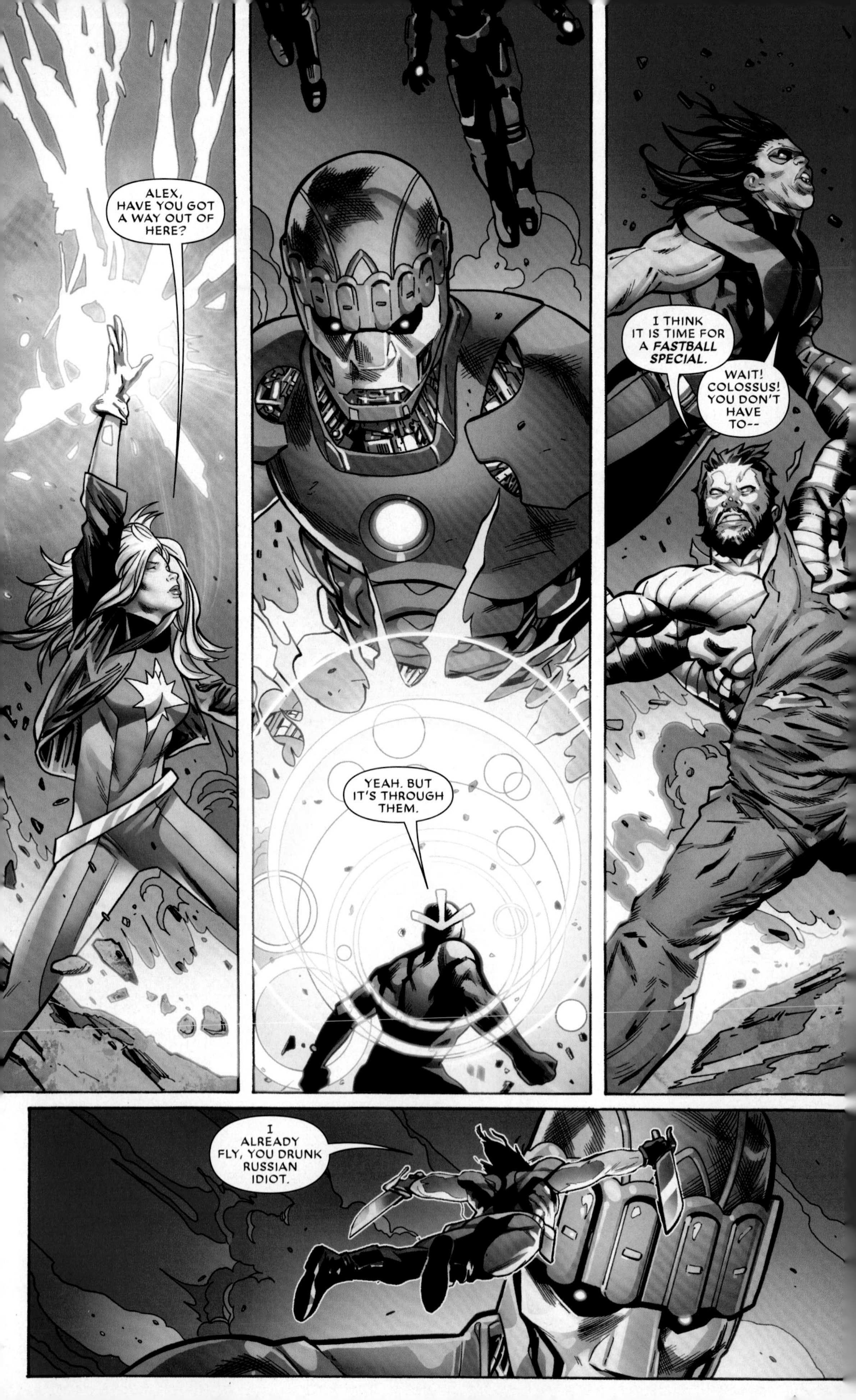
ALEX, HAVE YOU GOT A WAY OUT OF HERE?
YEAH. BUT IT'S THROUGH THEM.
I THINK IT IS TIME FOR A FASTBALL SPECIAL.
WAIT! COLOSSUS! YOU DON'T HAVE TO--
I ALREADY FLY, YOU DRUNK RUSSIAN IDIOT.

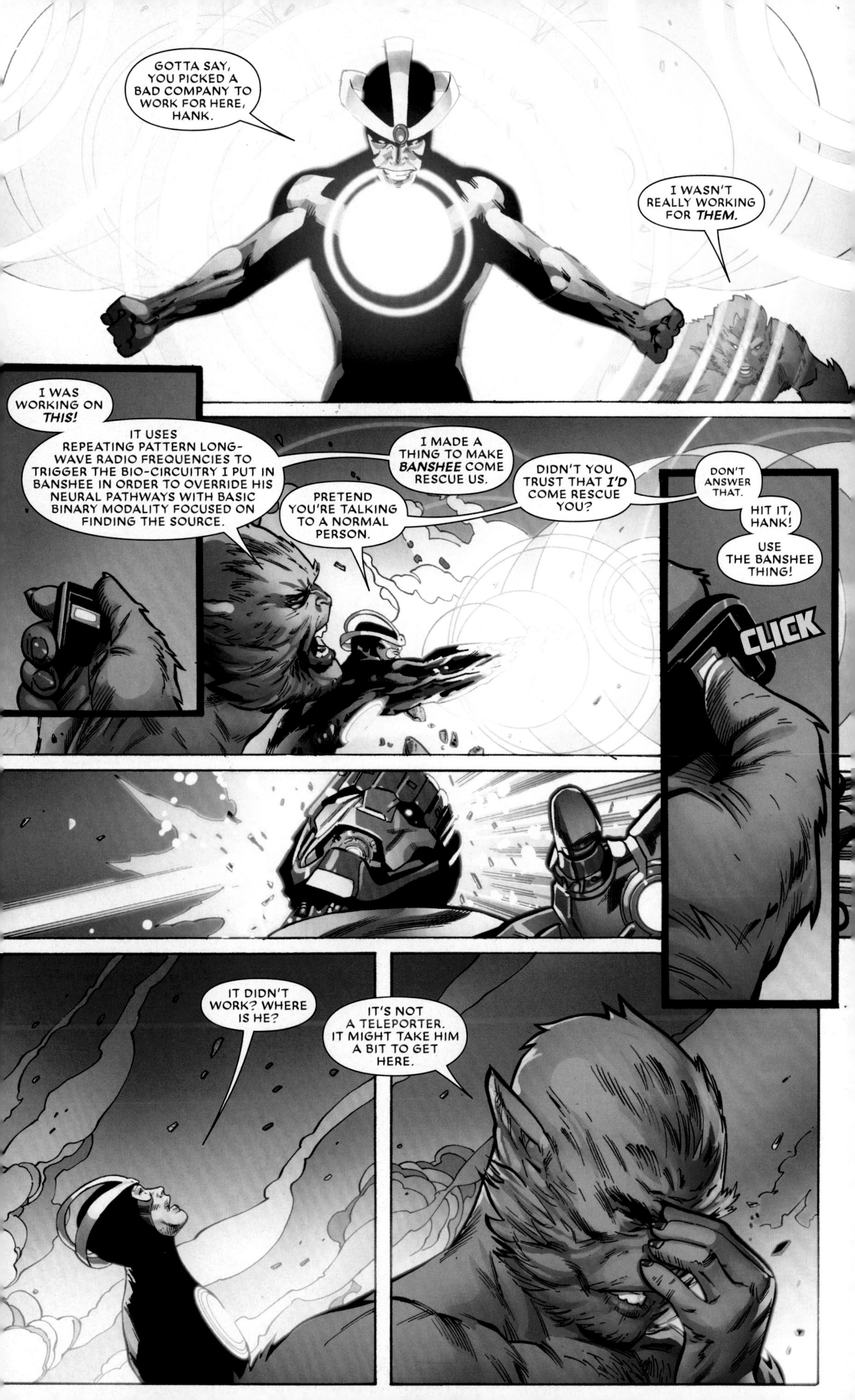

GOTTA SAY, YOU PICKED A BAD COMPANY TO WORK FOR HERE, HANK.
I WASN'T REALLY WORKING FOR *THEM.*
I WAS WORKING ON *THIS!*
IT USES REPEATING PATTERN LONG-WAVE RADIO FREQUENCIES TO TRIGGER THE BIO-CIRCUITRY I PUT IN BANSHEE IN ORDER TO OVERRIDE HIS NEURAL PATHWAYS WITH BASIC BINARY MODALITY FOCUSED ON FINDING THE SOURCE.
PRETEND YOU'RE TALKING TO A NORMAL PERSON.
I MADE A THING TO MAKE *BANSHEE* COME RESCUE US.
DIDN'T YOU TRUST THAT *I'D* COME RESCUE YOU?
DON'T ANSWER THAT.
HIT IT, HANK!
USE THE BANSHEE THING!
CLICK
IT DIDN'T WORK? WHERE IS HE?
IT'S NOT A TELEPORTER. IT MIGHT TAKE HIM A BIT TO GET HERE.

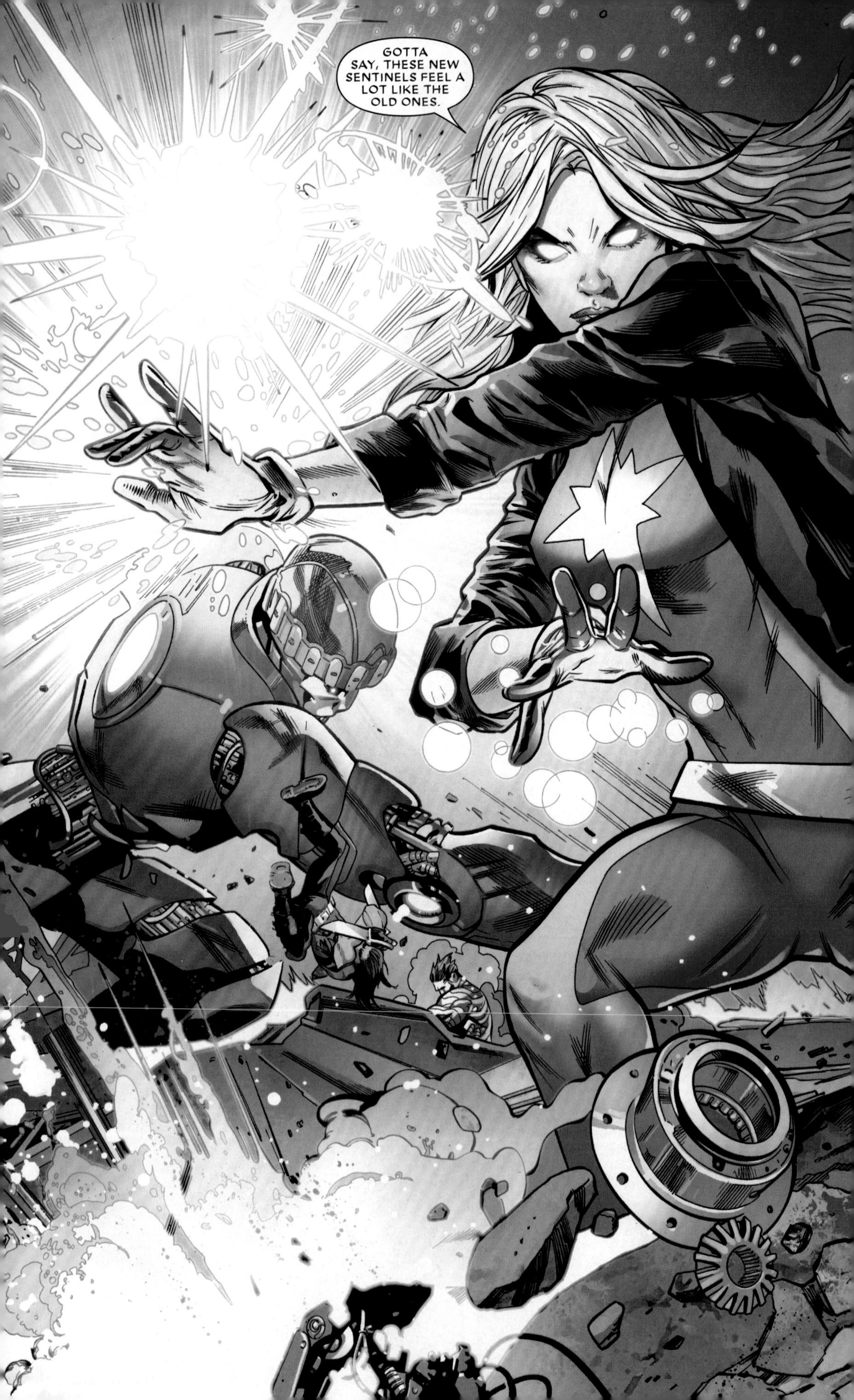
GOTTA SAY, THESE NEW SENTINELS FEEL A LOT LIKE THE OLD ONES.

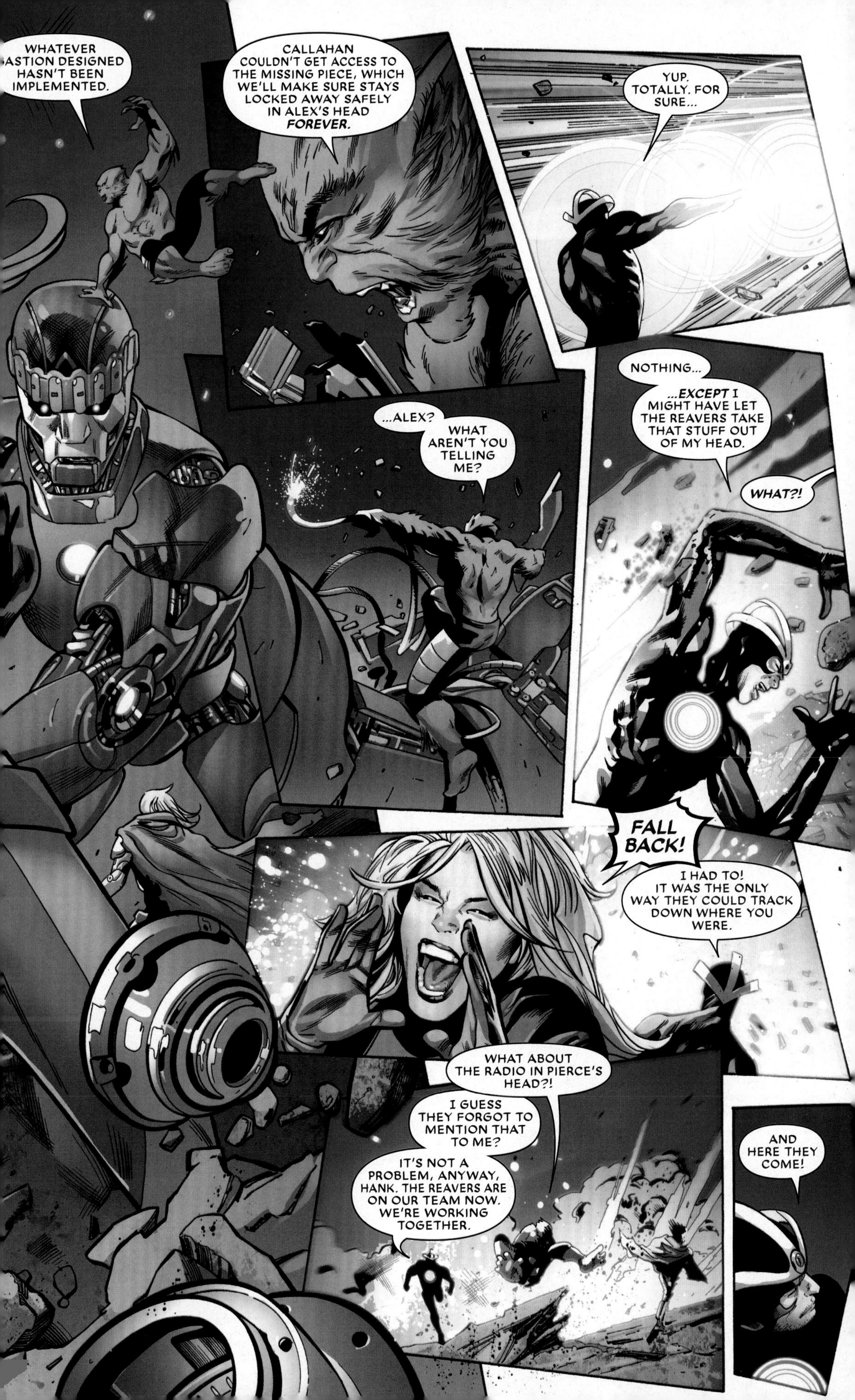
WHATEVER BASTION DESIGNED HASN'T BEEN IMPLEMENTED.
CALLAHAN COULDN'T GET ACCESS TO THE MISSING PIECE, WHICH WE'LL MAKE SURE STAYS LOCKED AWAY SAFELY IN ALEX'S HEAD *FOREVER.*
YUP. TOTALLY. FOR SURE...
...ALEX?
WHAT AREN'T YOU TELLING ME?
NOTHING...
...*EXCEPT* I MIGHT HAVE LET THE REAVERS TAKE THAT STUFF OUT OF MY HEAD.
WHAT?!
FALL BACK!
I HAD TO! IT WAS THE ONLY WAY THEY COULD TRACK DOWN WHERE YOU WERE.
WHAT ABOUT THE RADIO IN PIERCE'S HEAD?!
I GUESS THEY FORGOT TO MENTION THAT TO ME?
IT'S NOT A PROBLEM, ANYWAY, HANK. THE REAVERS ARE ON OUR TEAM NOW. WE'RE WORKING TOGETHER.
AND HERE THEY COME!

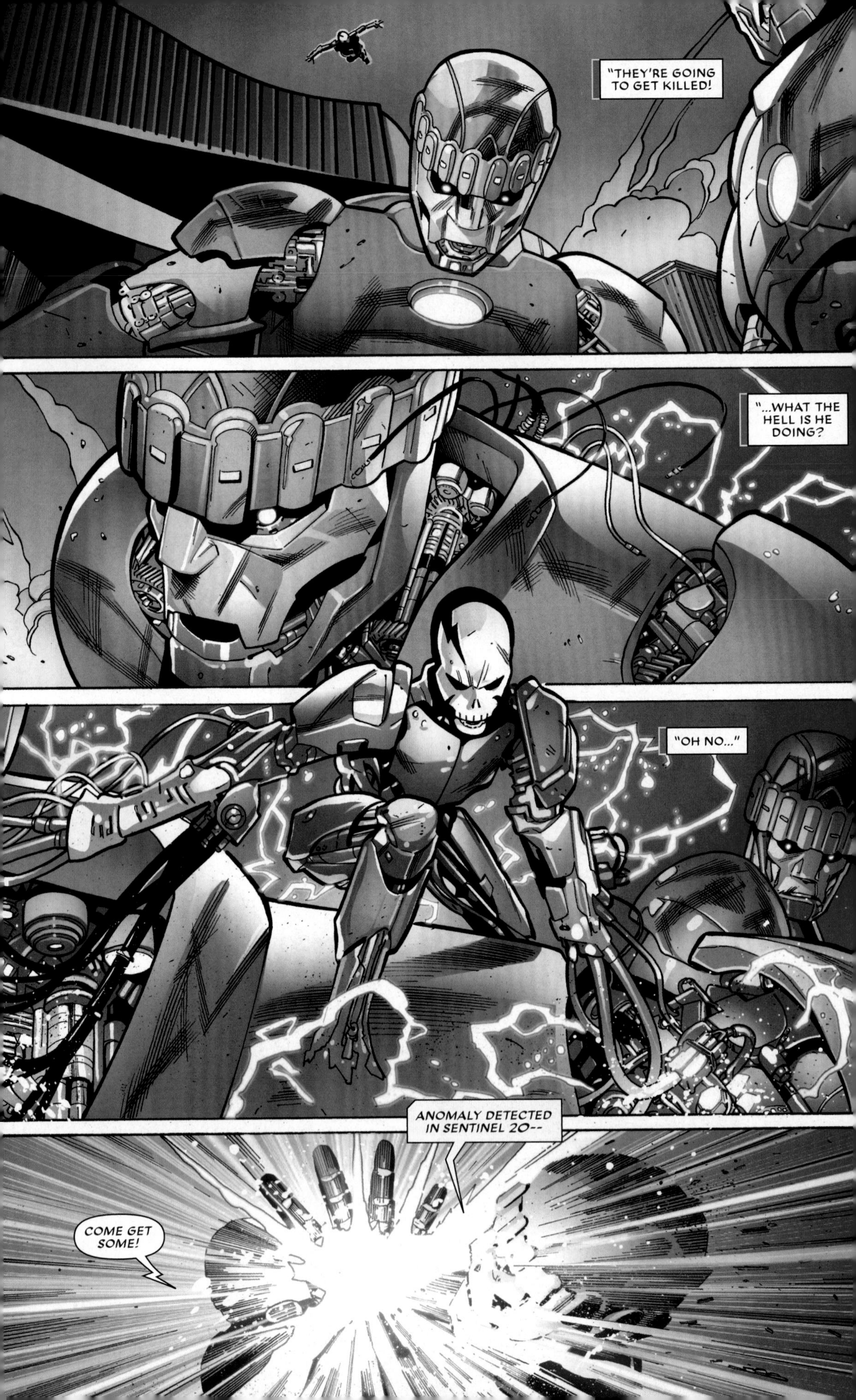
"THEY'RE GOING TO GET KILLED!
"...WHAT THE HELL IS HE DOING?
"OH NO..."
ANOMALY DETECTED IN SENTINEL 20--
COME GET SOME!

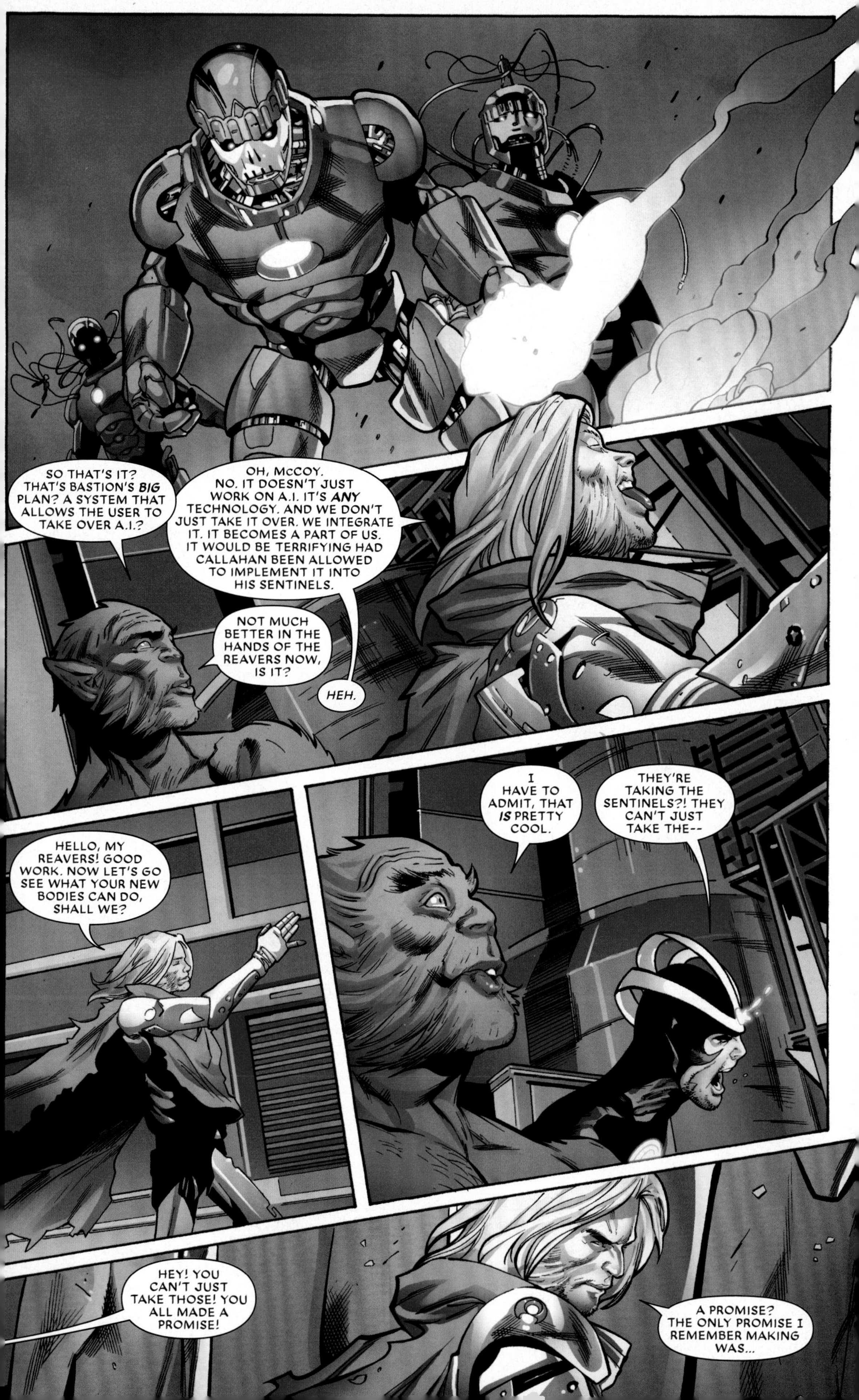
SO THAT'S IT? THAT'S BASTION'S BIG PLAN? A SYSTEM THAT ALLOWS THE USER TO TAKE OVER A.I.?
OH, McCOY. NO. IT DOESN'T JUST WORK ON A.I. IT'S ANY TECHNOLOGY. AND WE DON'T JUST TAKE IT OVER. WE INTEGRATE IT. IT BECOMES A PART OF US. IT WOULD BE TERRIFYING HAD CALLAHAN BEEN ALLOWED TO IMPLEMENT IT INTO HIS SENTINELS.
NOT MUCH BETTER IN THE HANDS OF THE REAVERS NOW, IS IT?
HEH.
HELLO, MY REAVERS! GOOD WORK. NOW LET'S GO SEE WHAT YOUR NEW BODIES CAN DO, SHALL WE?
I HAVE TO ADMIT, THAT IS PRETTY COOL.
THEY'RE TAKING THE SENTINELS?! THEY CAN'T JUST TAKE THE--
HEY! YOU CAN'T JUST TAKE THOSE! YOU ALL MADE A PROMISE!
A PROMISE? THE ONLY PROMISE I REMEMBER MAKING WAS...

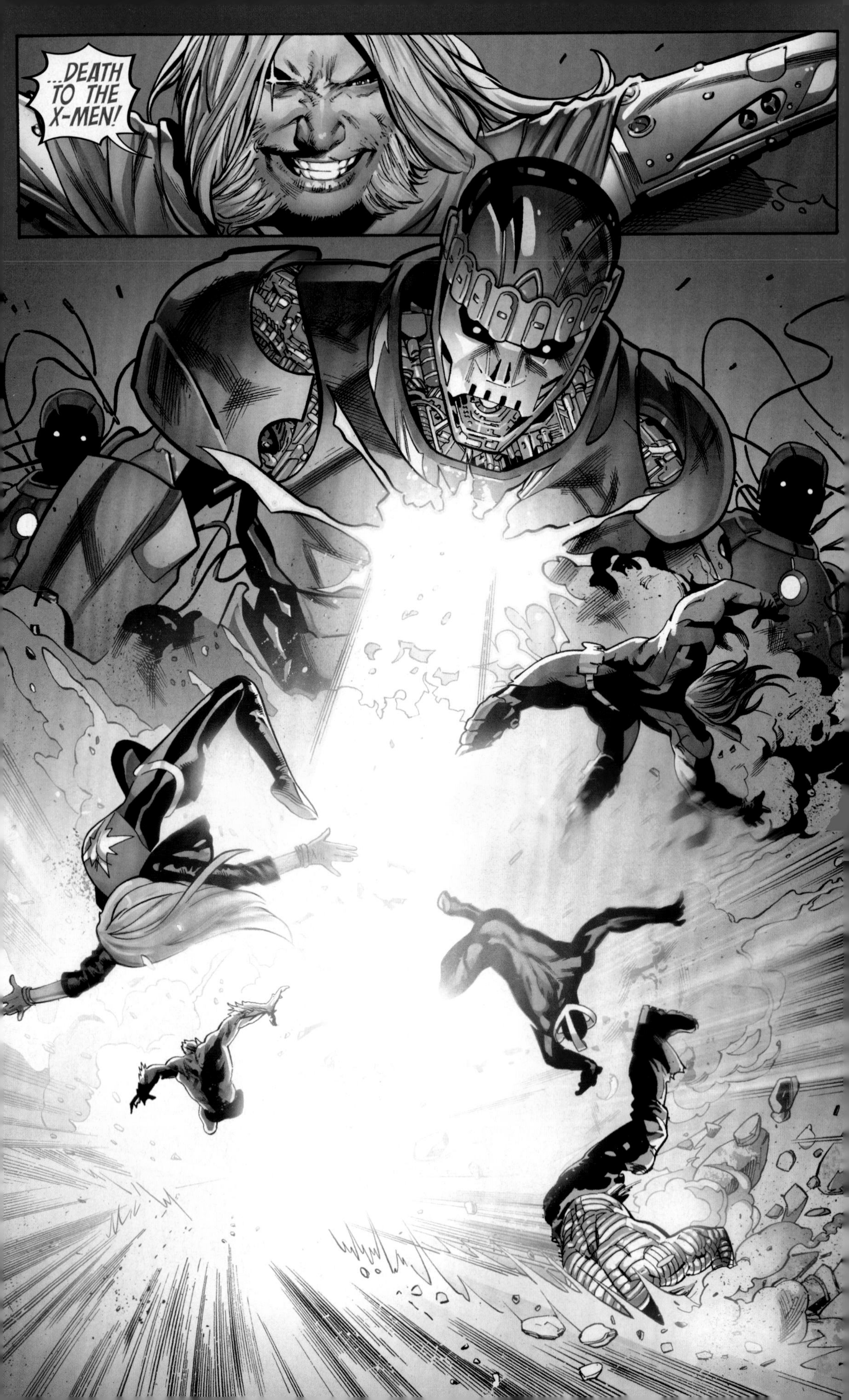
...DEATH TO THE X-MEN!

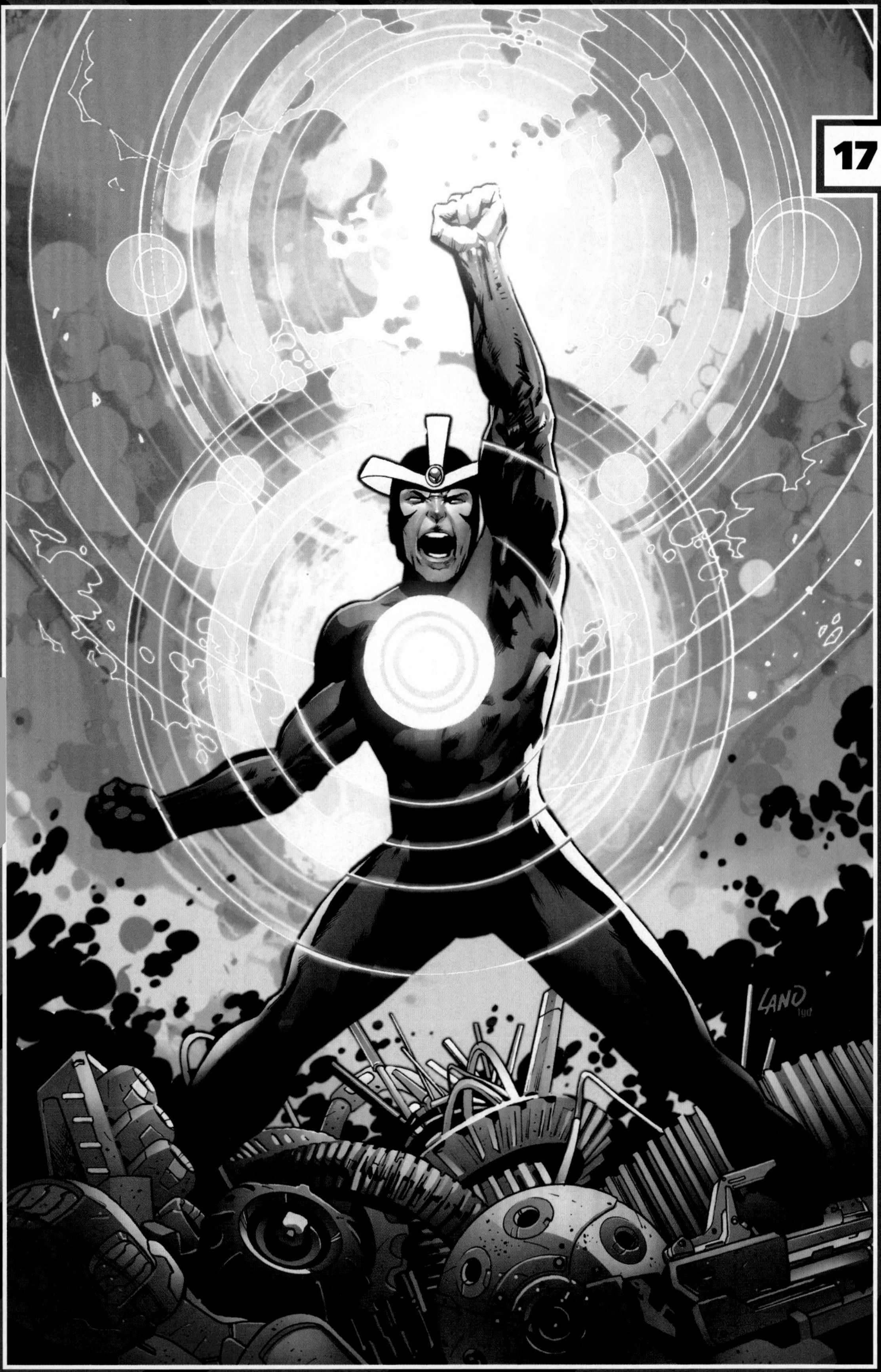
LAND

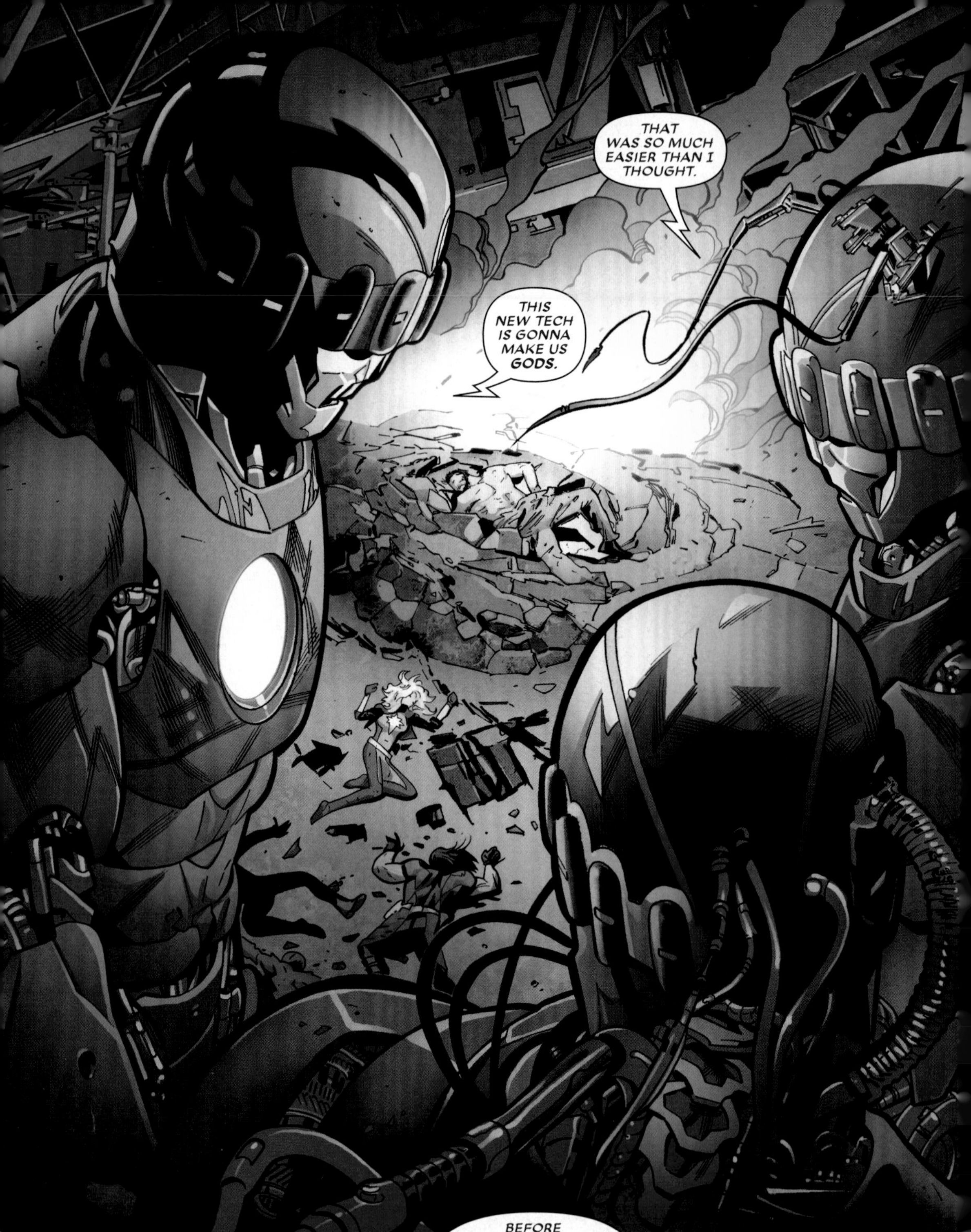
THAT WAS SO MUCH EASIER THAN I THOUGHT.
THIS NEW TECH IS GONNA MAKE US GODS.

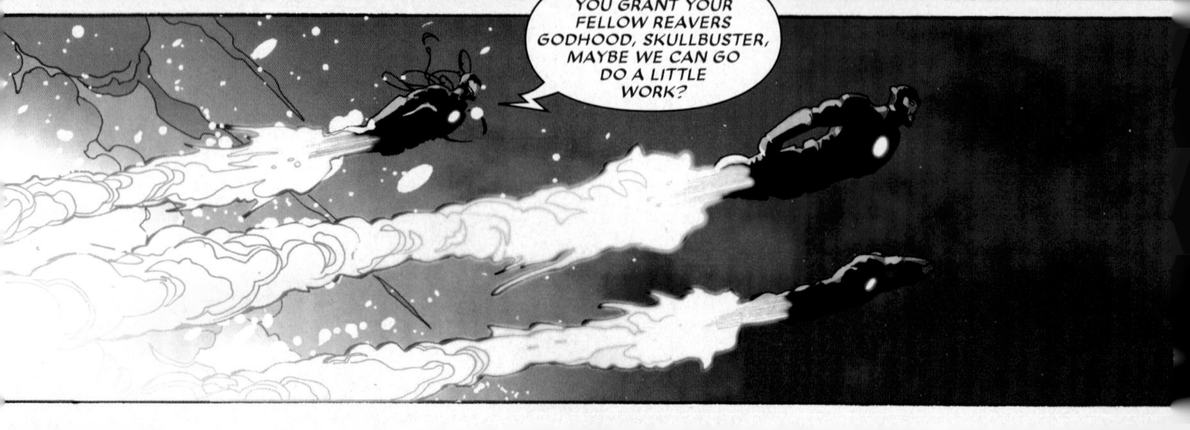
BEFORE YOU GRANT YOUR FELLOW REAVERS GODHOOD, SKULLBUSTER, MAYBE WE CAN GO DO A LITTLE WORK?

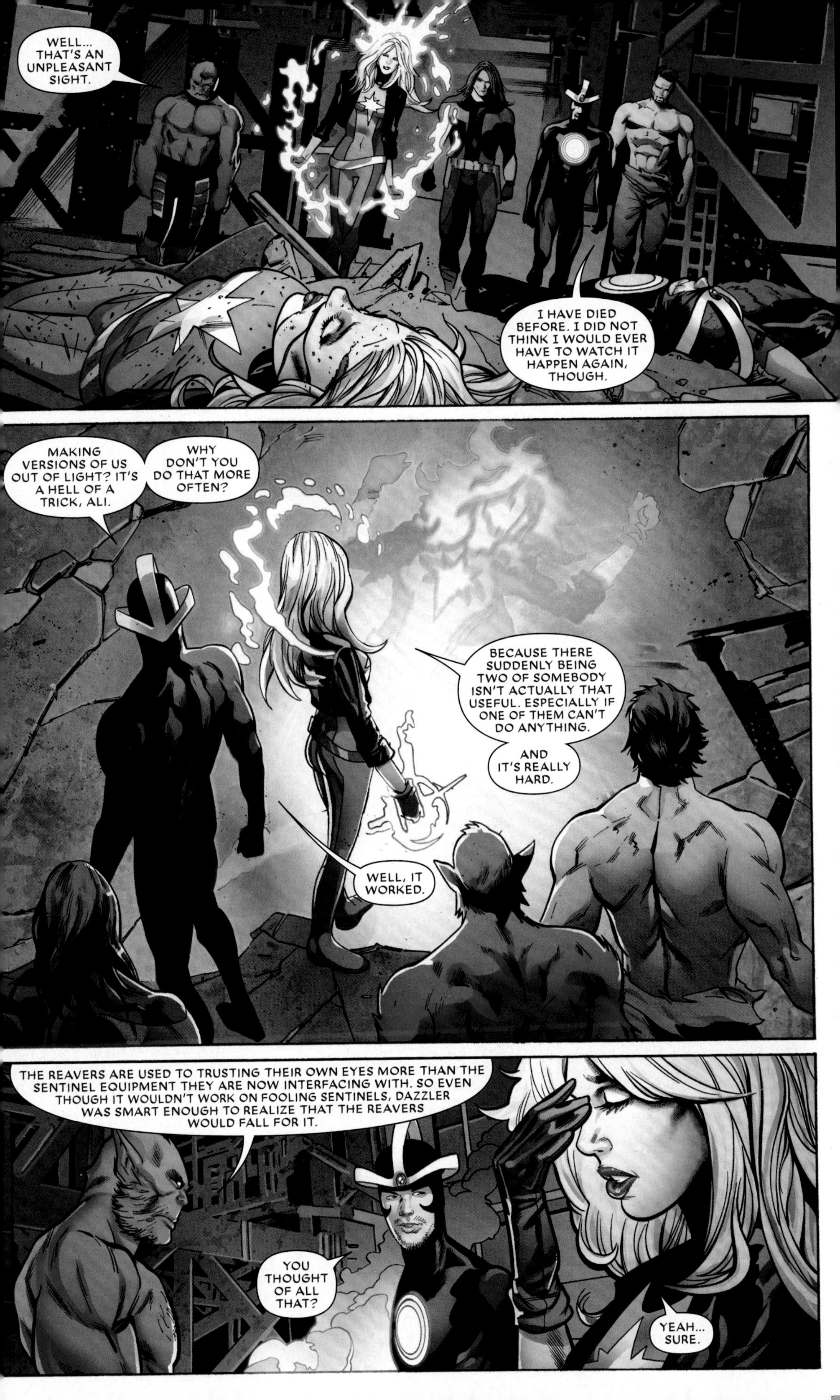
WELL... THAT'S AN UNPLEASANT SIGHT.
I HAVE DIED BEFORE. I DID NOT THINK I WOULD EVER HAVE TO WATCH IT HAPPEN AGAIN, THOUGH.
MAKING VERSIONS OF US OUT OF LIGHT? IT'S A HELL OF A TRICK, ALI.
WHY DON'T YOU DO THAT MORE OFTEN?
BECAUSE THERE SUDDENLY BEING TWO OF SOMEBODY ISN'T ACTUALLY THAT USEFUL. ESPECIALLY IF ONE OF THEM CAN'T DO ANYTHING.
AND IT'S REALLY HARD.
WELL, IT WORKED.
THE REAVERS ARE USED TO TRUSTING THEIR OWN EYES MORE THAN THE SENTINEL EQUIPMENT THEY ARE NOW INTERFACING WITH. SO EVEN THOUGH IT WOULDN'T WORK ON FOOLING SENTINELS, DAZZLER WAS SMART ENOUGH TO REALIZE THAT THE REAVERS WOULD FALL FOR IT.
YOU THOUGHT OF ALL THAT?
YEAH... SURE.

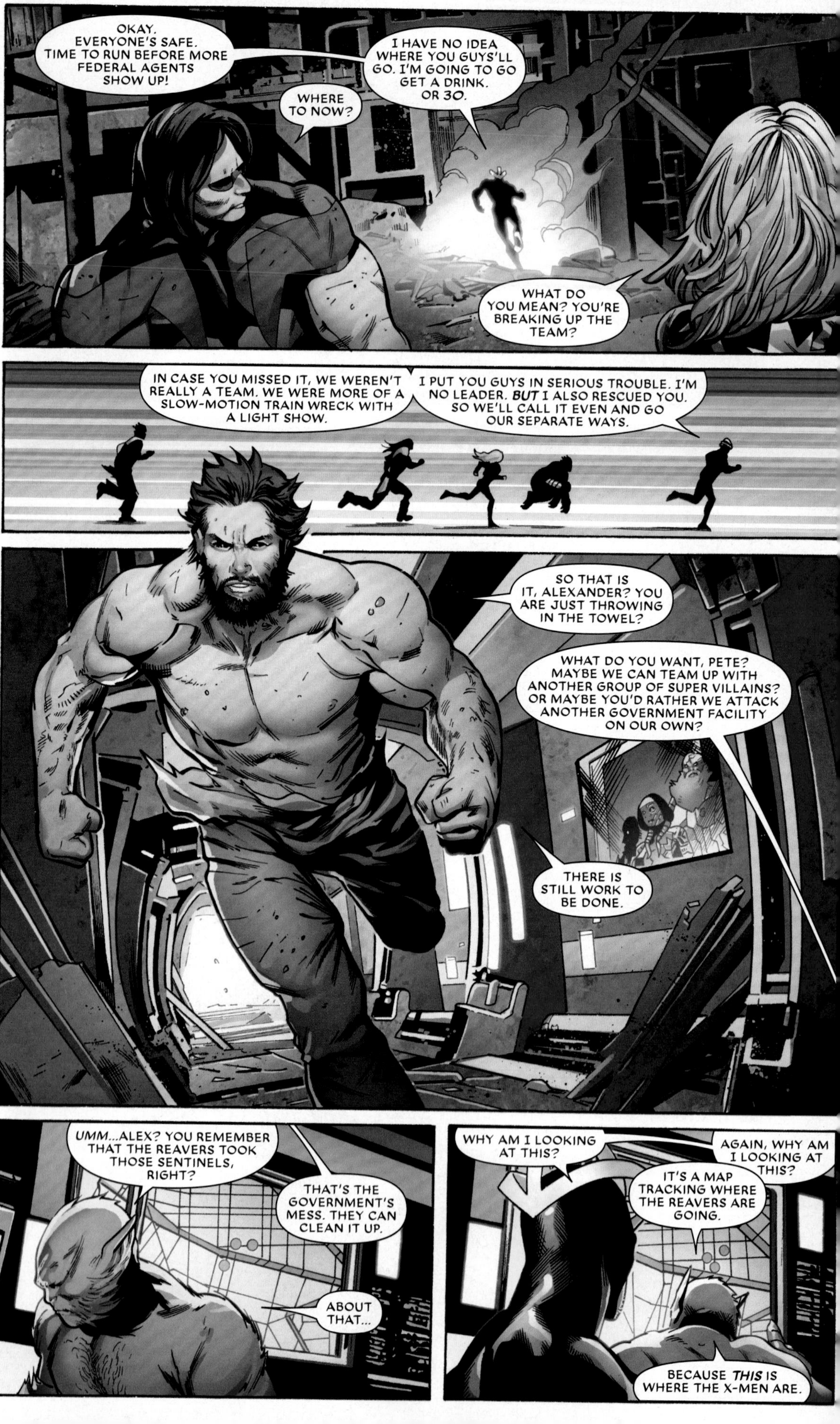

OKAY. EVERYONE'S SAFE. TIME TO RUN BEFORE MORE FEDERAL AGENTS SHOW UP!
WHERE TO NOW?
I HAVE NO IDEA WHERE YOU GUYS'LL GO. I'M GOING TO GO GET A DRINK. OR 30.
WHAT DO YOU MEAN? YOU'RE BREAKING UP THE TEAM?
IN CASE YOU MISSED IT, WE WEREN'T REALLY A TEAM. WE WERE MORE OF A SLOW-MOTION TRAIN WRECK WITH A LIGHT SHOW.
I PUT YOU GUYS IN SERIOUS TROUBLE. I'M NO LEADER. *BUT* I ALSO RESCUED YOU. SO WE'LL CALL IT EVEN AND GO OUR SEPARATE WAYS.
SO THAT IS IT, ALEXANDER? YOU ARE JUST THROWING IN THE TOWEL?
WHAT DO YOU WANT, PETE? MAYBE WE CAN TEAM UP WITH ANOTHER GROUP OF SUPER VILLAINS? OR MAYBE YOU'D RATHER WE ATTACK ANOTHER GOVERNMENT FACILITY ON OUR OWN?
THERE IS STILL WORK TO BE DONE.
UMM...ALEX? YOU REMEMBER THAT THE REAVERS TOOK THOSE SENTINELS, RIGHT?
THAT'S THE GOVERNMENT'S MESS. THEY CAN CLEAN IT UP.
ABOUT THAT...
WHY AM I LOOKING AT THIS?
IT'S A MAP TRACKING WHERE THE REAVERS ARE GOING.
AGAIN, WHY AM I LOOKING AT THIS?
BECAUSE *THIS* IS WHERE THE X-MEN ARE.

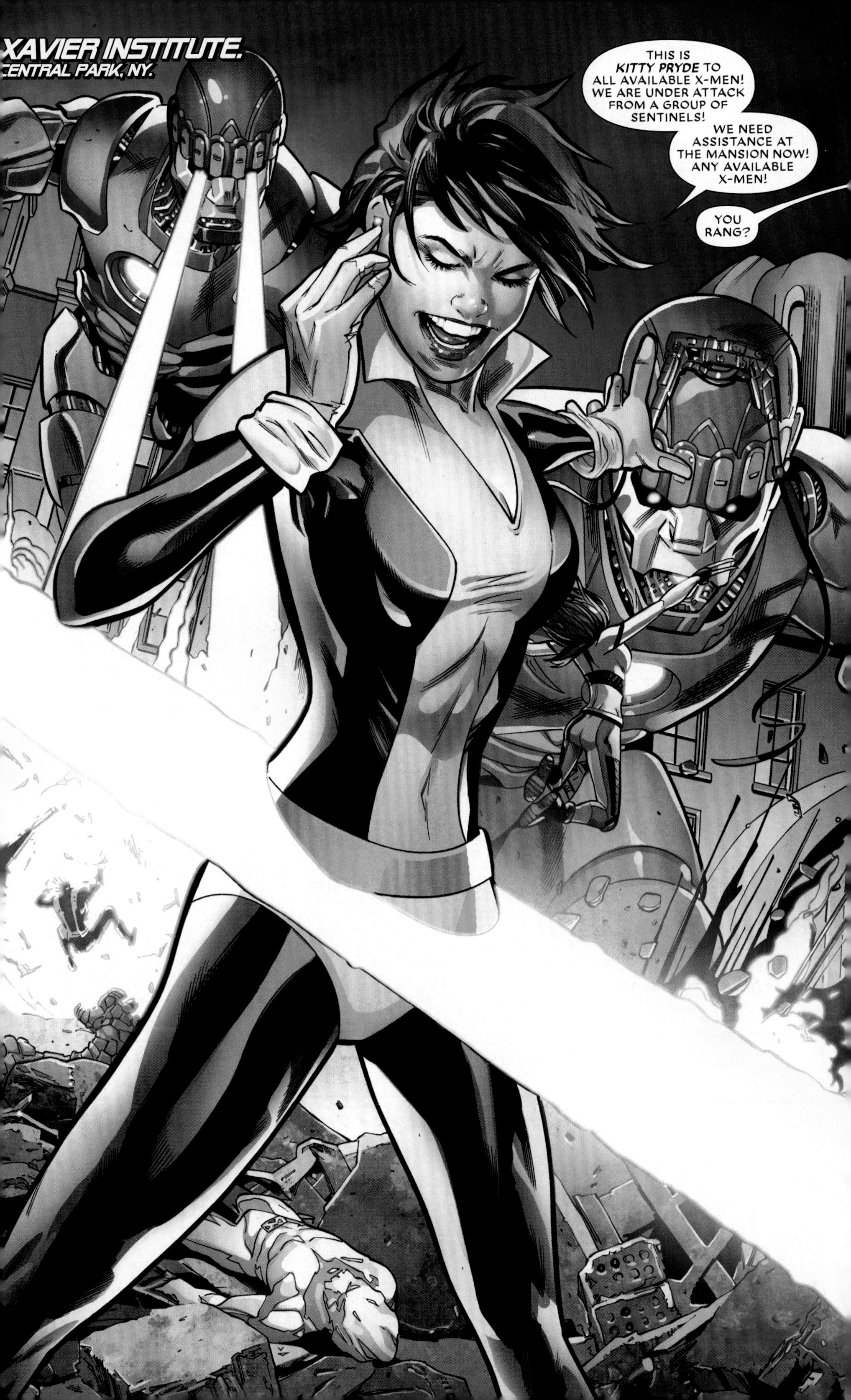

XAVIER INSTITUTE.
CENTRAL PARK, NY.
THIS IS KITTY PRYDE TO ALL AVAILABLE X-MEN! WE ARE UNDER ATTACK FROM A GROUP OF SENTINELS!
WE NEED ASSISTANCE AT THE MANSION NOW! ANY AVAILABLE X-MEN!
YOU RANG?

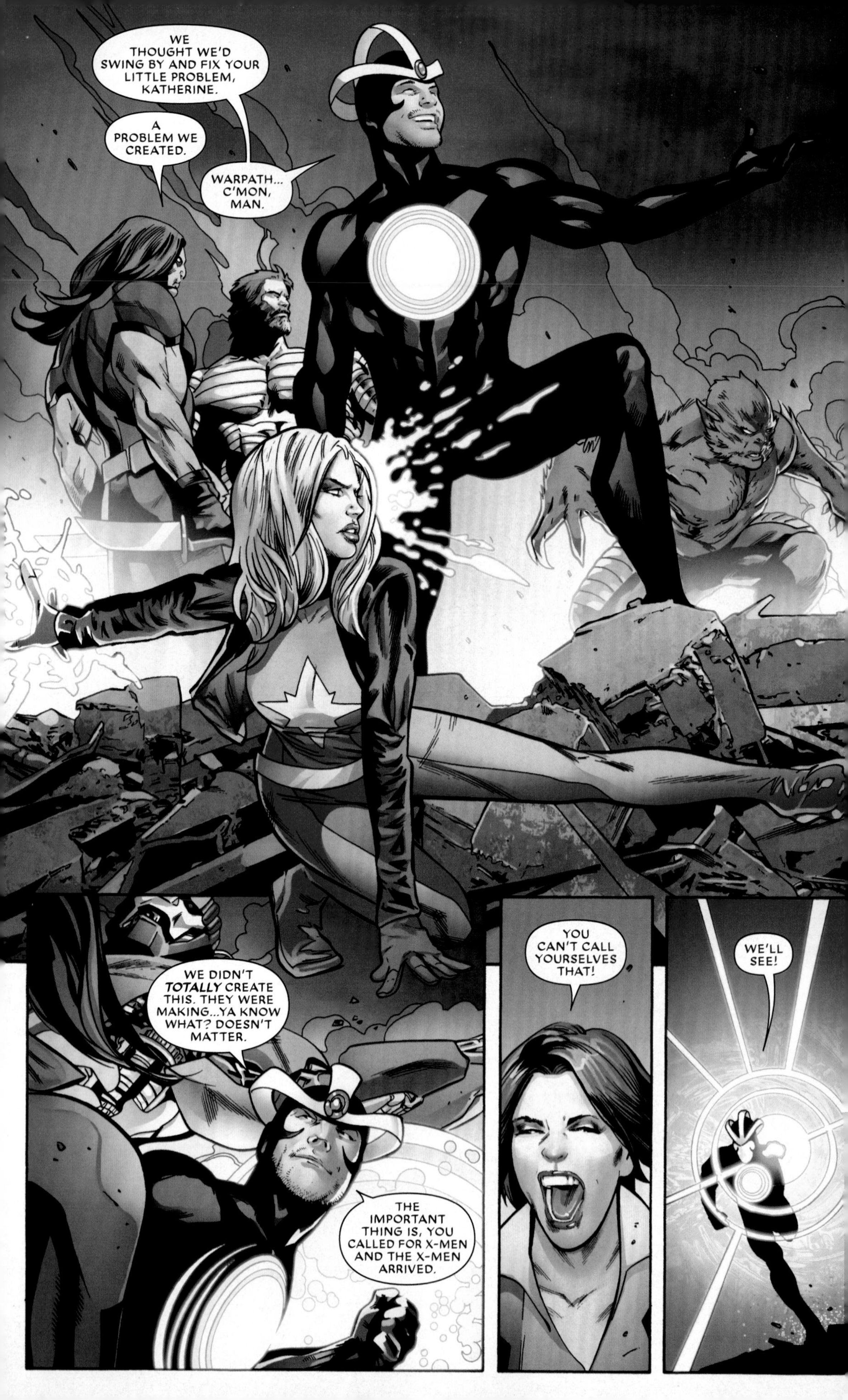
WE THOUGHT WE'D SWING BY AND FIX YOUR LITTLE PROBLEM, KATHERINE.
A PROBLEM WE CREATED.
WARPATH... C'MON, MAN.
WE DIDN'T *TOTALLY* CREATE THIS. THEY WERE MAKING...YA KNOW WHAT? DOESN'T MATTER.
THE IMPORTANT THING IS, YOU CALLED FOR X-MEN AND THE X-MEN ARRIVED.
YOU CAN'T CALL YOURSELVES THAT!
WE'LL SEE!

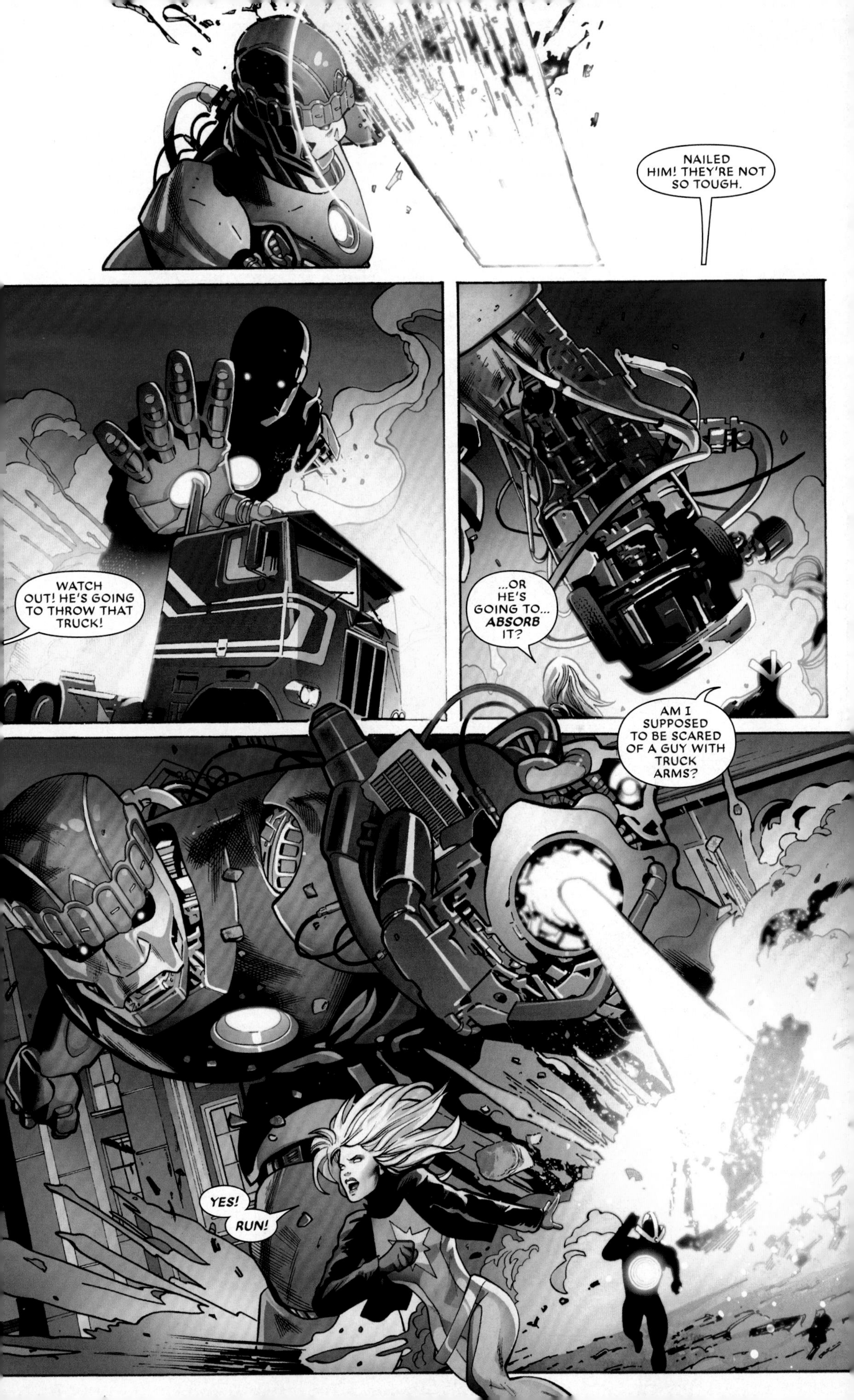
NAILED HIM! THEY'RE NOT SO TOUGH.
WATCH OUT! HE'S GOING TO THROW THAT TRUCK!
...OR HE'S GOING TO... ABSORB IT?
AM I SUPPOSED TO BE SCARED OF A GUY WITH TRUCK ARMS?
YES!
RUN!

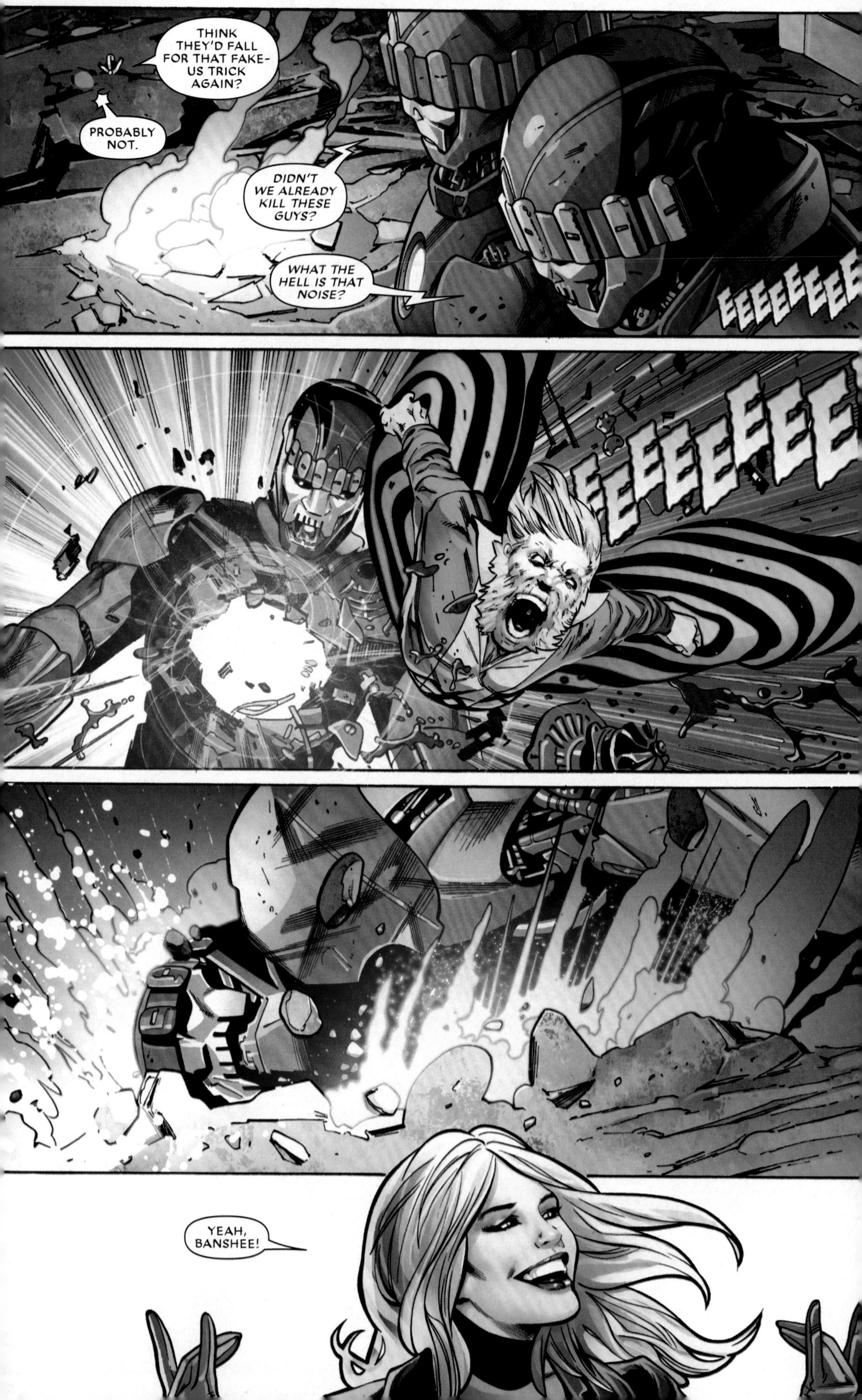
THINK THEY'D FALL FOR THAT FAKE-US TRICK AGAIN?
PROBABLY NOT.
DIDN'T WE ALREADY KILL THESE GUYS?
WHAT THE HELL IS THAT NOISE?
EEEEEEEE
EEEEEEEEEE
YEAH, BANSHEE!

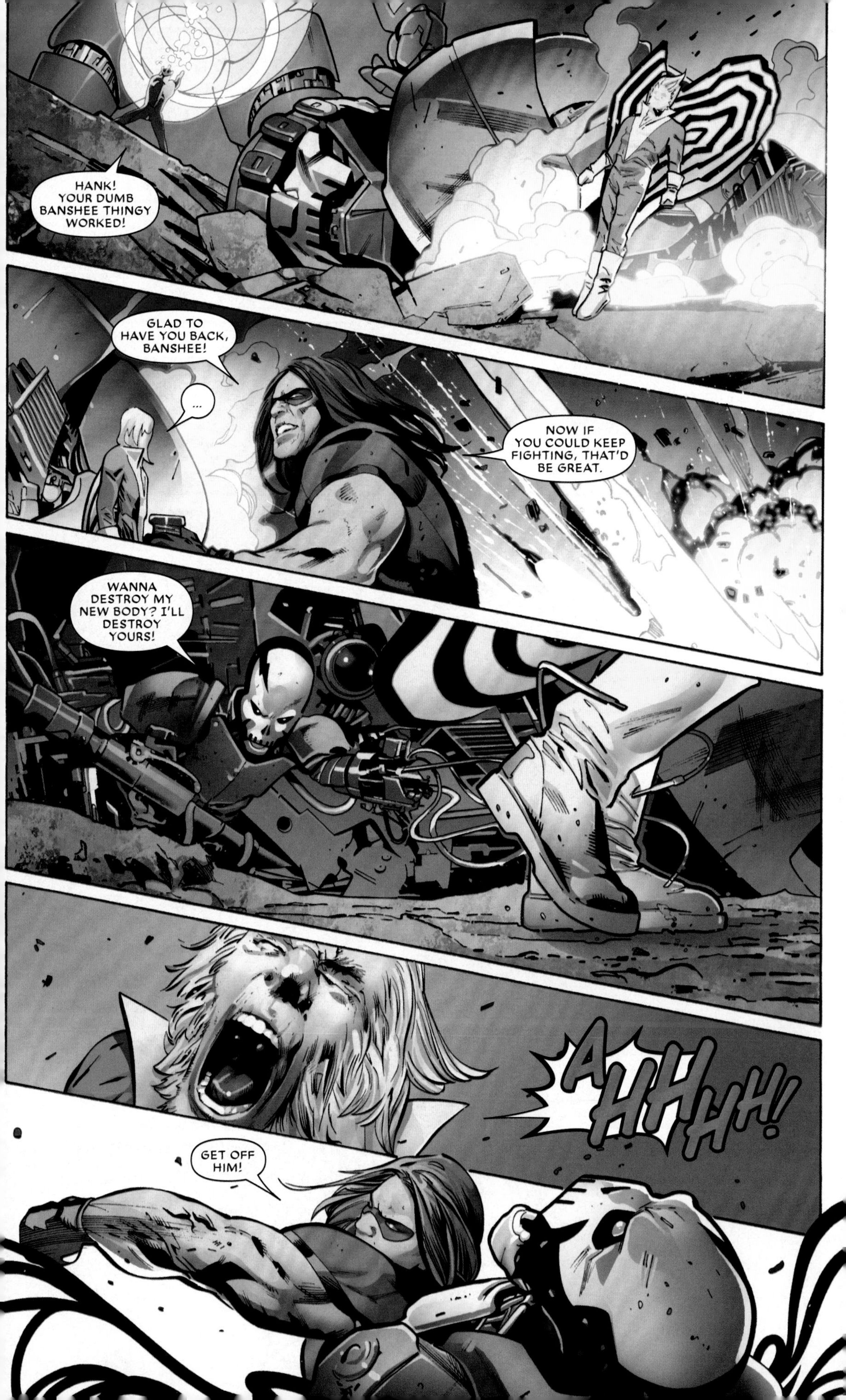
HANK! YOUR DUMB BANSHEE THINGY WORKED!
GLAD TO HAVE YOU BACK, BANSHEE!
...
NOW IF YOU COULD KEEP FIGHTING, THAT'D BE GREAT.
WANNA DESTROY MY NEW BODY? I'LL DESTROY YOURS!
AHHHH!
GET OFF HIM!

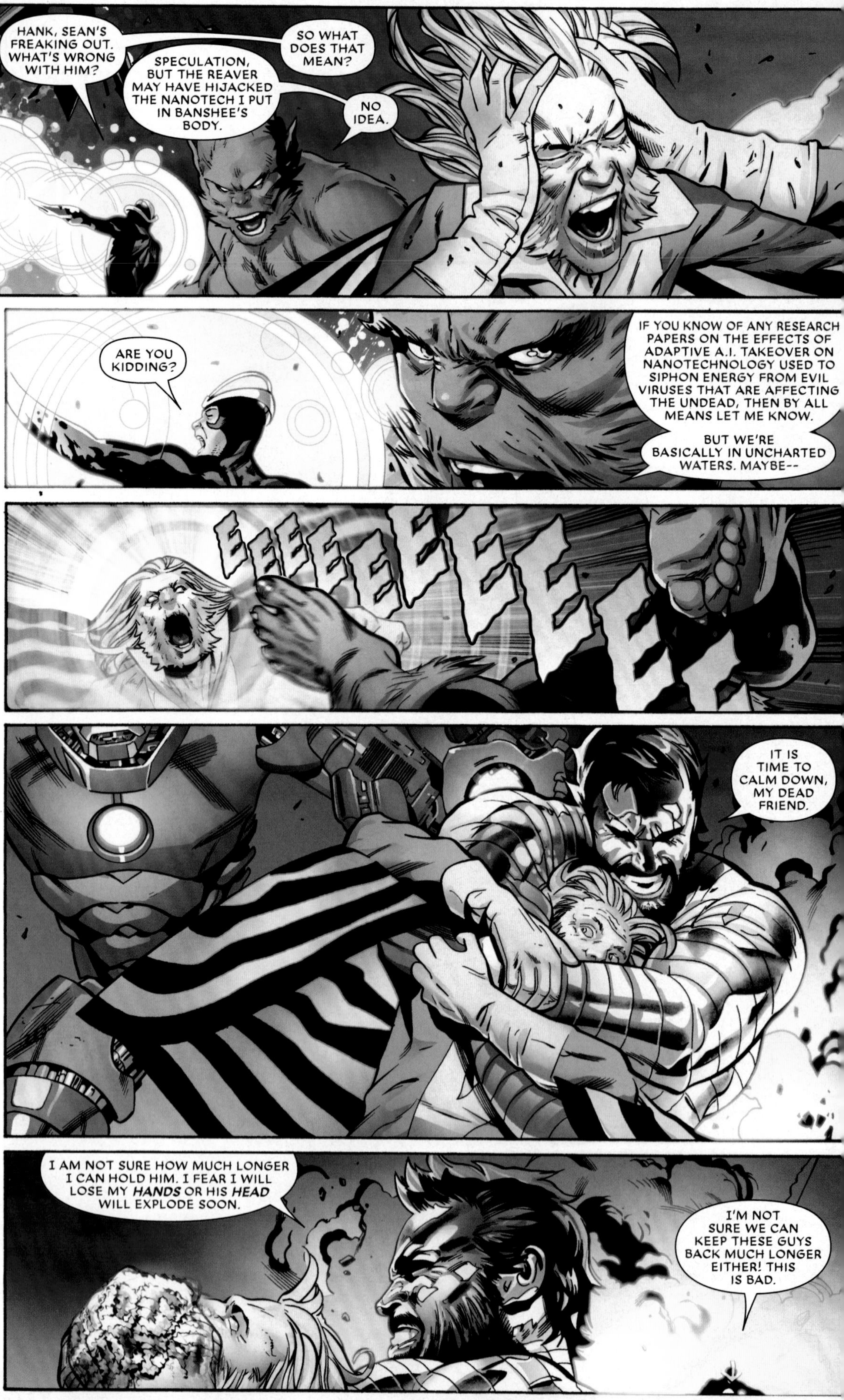
HANK, SEAN'S FREAKING OUT. WHAT'S WRONG WITH HIM?
SPECULATION, BUT THE REAVER MAY HAVE HIJACKED THE NANOTECH I PUT IN BANSHEE'S BODY.
SO WHAT DOES THAT MEAN?
NO IDEA.
ARE YOU KIDDING?
IF YOU KNOW OF ANY RESEARCH PAPERS ON THE EFFECTS OF ADAPTIVE A.I. TAKEOVER ON NANOTECHNOLOGY USED TO SIPHON ENERGY FROM EVIL VIRUSES THAT ARE AFFECTING THE UNDEAD, THEN BY ALL MEANS LET ME KNOW.
BUT WE'RE BASICALLY IN UNCHARTED WATERS. MAYBE--
EEEEEEEEEE
IT IS TIME TO CALM DOWN, MY DEAD FRIEND.
I AM NOT SURE HOW MUCH LONGER I CAN HOLD HIM. I FEAR I WILL LOSE MY *HANDS* OR HIS *HEAD* WILL EXPLODE SOON.
I'M NOT SURE WE CAN KEEP THESE GUYS BACK MUCH LONGER EITHER! THIS IS BAD.

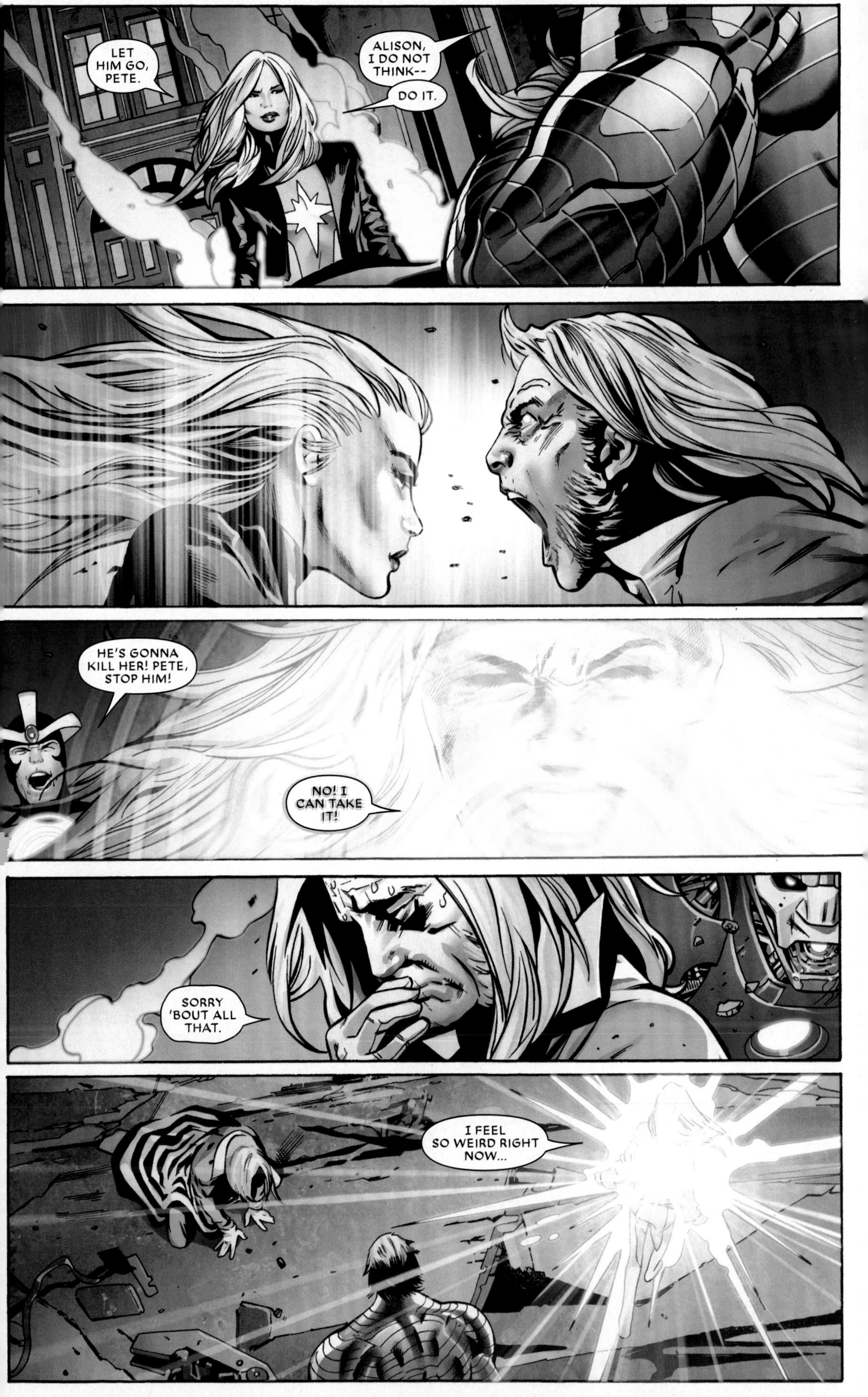
LET HIM GO, PETE.
ALISON, I DO NOT THINK--
DO IT.
HE'S GONNA KILL HER! PETE, STOP HIM!
NO! I CAN TAKE IT!
SORRY 'BOUT ALL THAT.
I FEEL SO WEIRD RIGHT NOW...

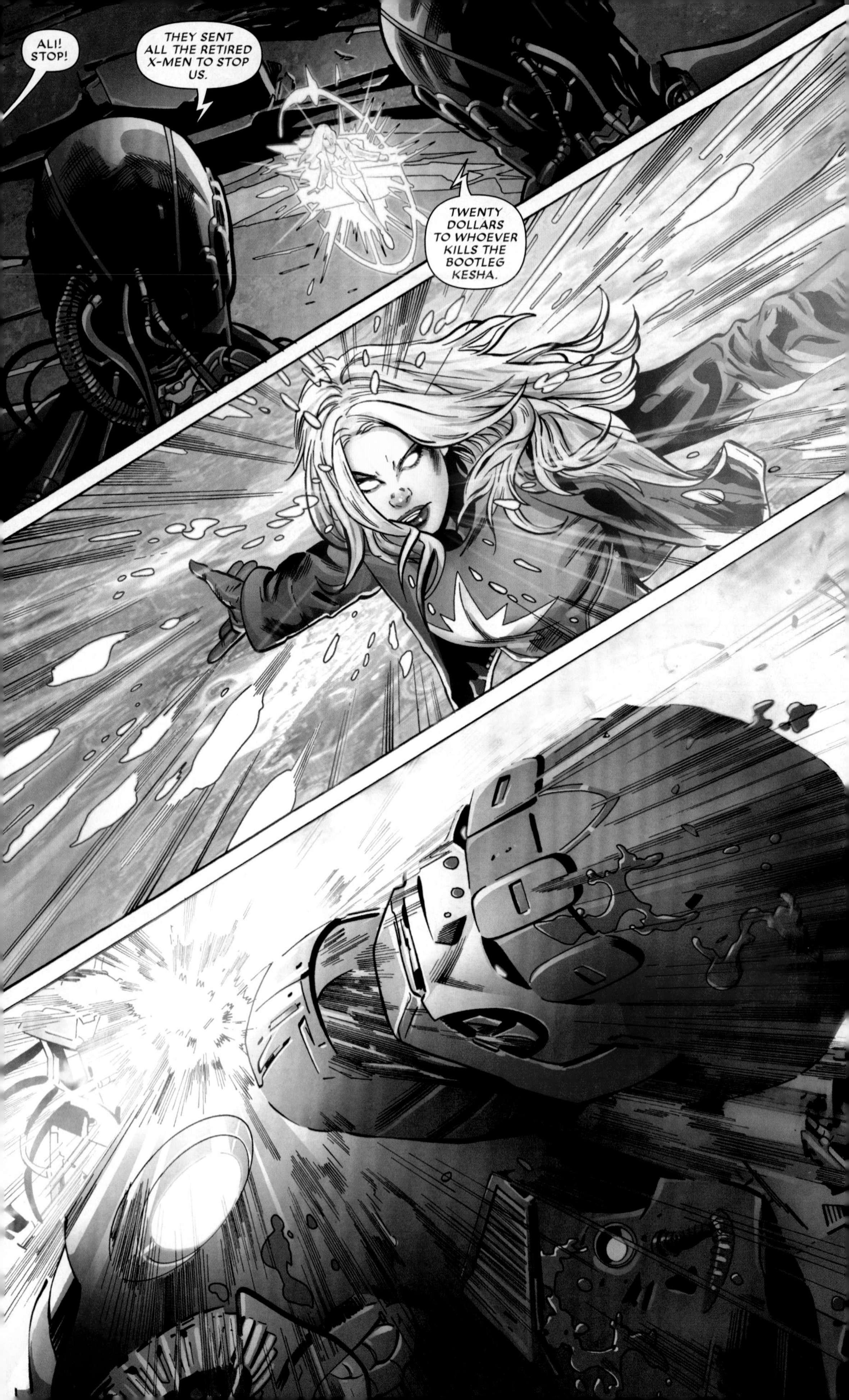
ALI! STOP!
THEY SENT ALL THE RETIRED X-MEN TO STOP US.
TWENTY DOLLARS TO WHOEVER KILLS THE BOOTLEG KESHA.

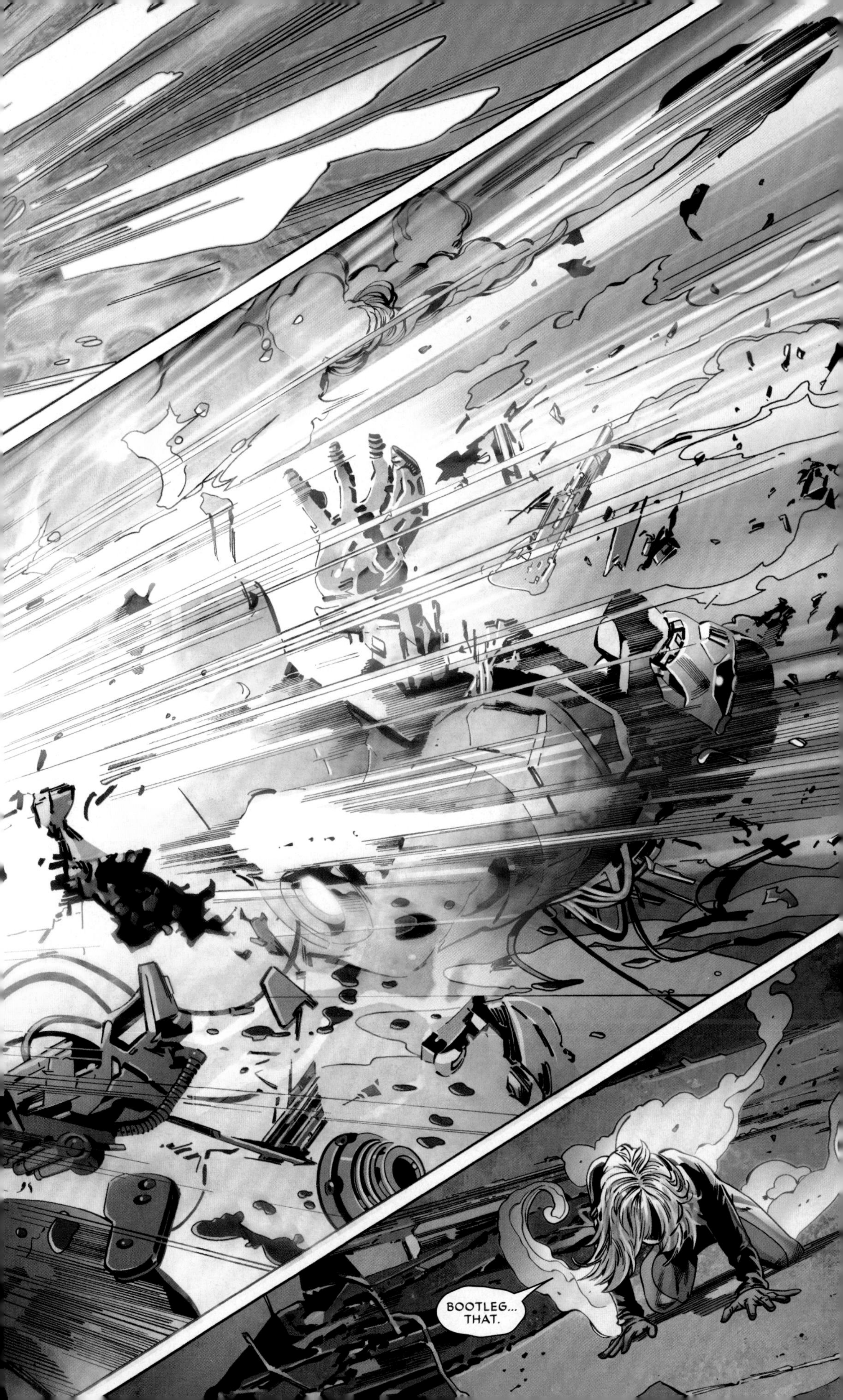
BOOTLEG... THAT.

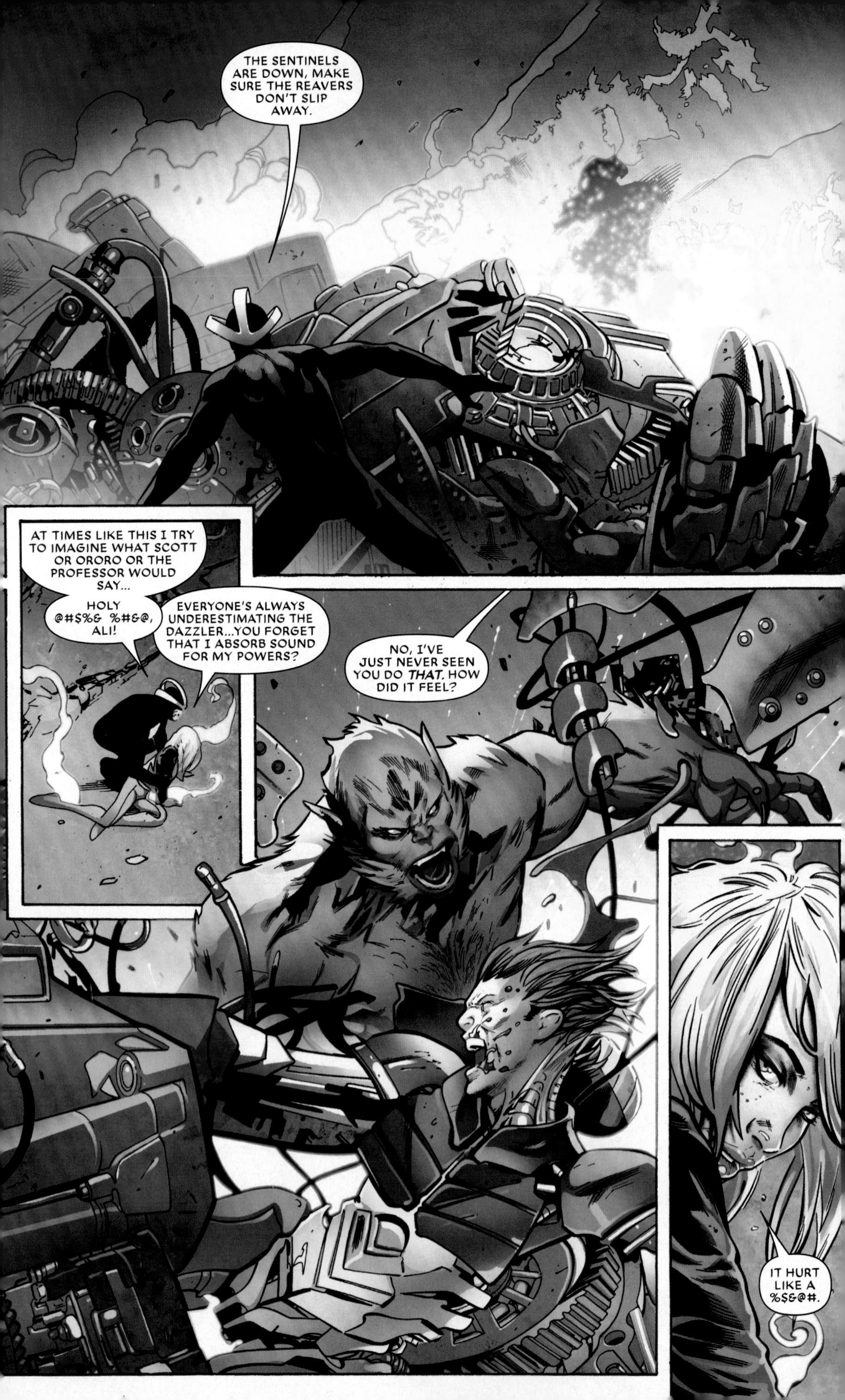
THE SENTINELS ARE DOWN, MAKE SURE THE REAVERS DON'T SLIP AWAY.
AT TIMES LIKE THIS I TRY TO IMAGINE WHAT SCOTT OR ORORO OR THE PROFESSOR WOULD SAY...
HOLY @#$%& %#&@, ALI!
EVERYONE'S ALWAYS UNDERESTIMATING THE DAZZLER...YOU FORGET THAT I ABSORB SOUND FOR MY POWERS?
NO, I'VE JUST NEVER SEEN YOU DO *THAT.* HOW DID IT FEEL?
IT HURT LIKE A %$&@#.

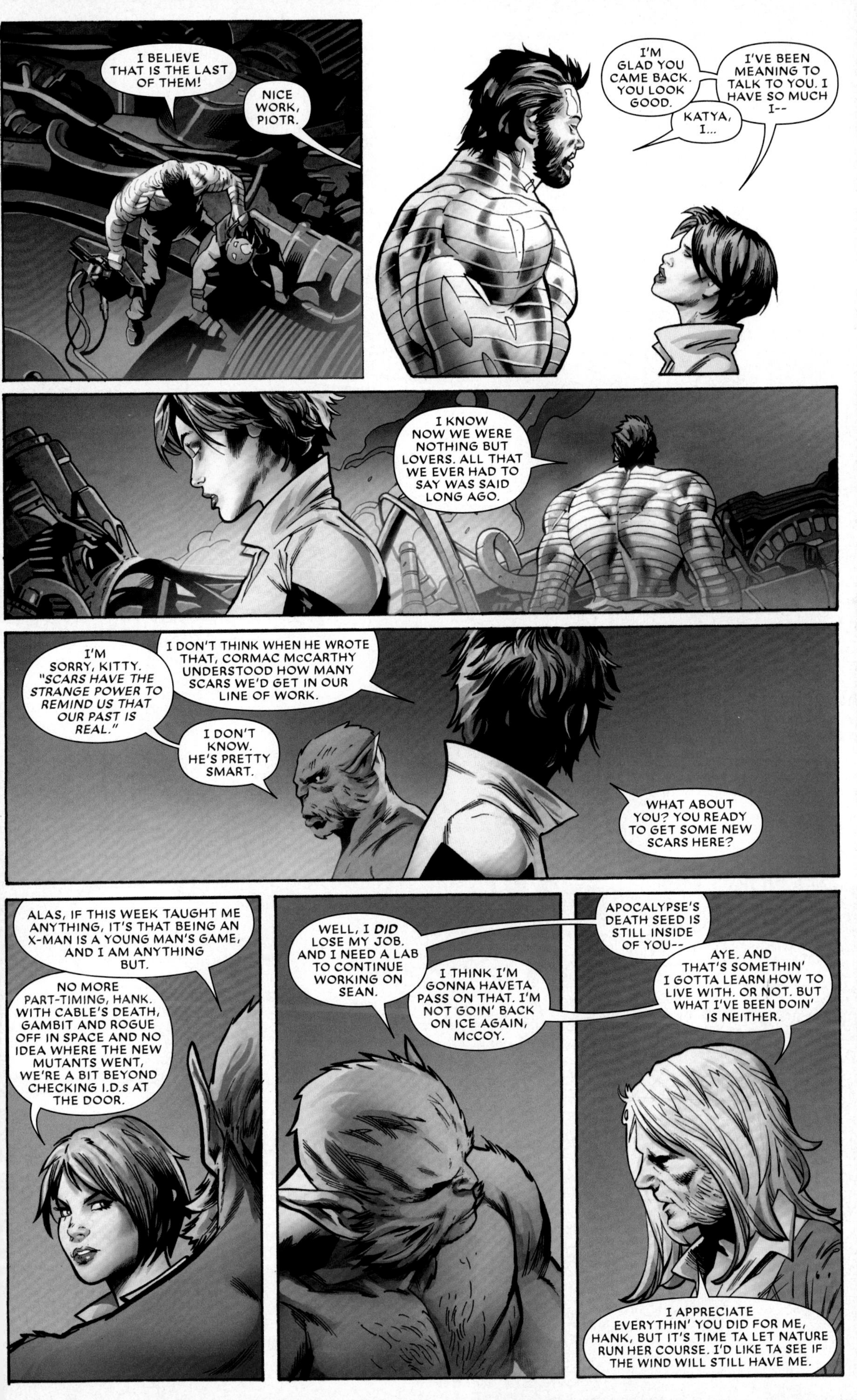
I BELIEVE THAT IS THE LAST OF THEM!
NICE WORK, PIOTR.
I'M GLAD YOU CAME BACK. YOU LOOK GOOD.
KATYA, I...
I'VE BEEN MEANING TO TALK TO YOU. I HAVE SO MUCH I--
I KNOW NOW WE WERE NOTHING BUT LOVERS. ALL THAT WE EVER HAD TO SAY WAS SAID LONG AGO.
I'M SORRY, KITTY. "SCARS HAVE THE STRANGE POWER TO REMIND US THAT OUR PAST IS REAL."
I DON'T THINK WHEN HE WROTE THAT, CORMAC McCARTHY UNDERSTOOD HOW MANY SCARS WE'D GET IN OUR LINE OF WORK.
I DON'T KNOW. HE'S PRETTY SMART.
WHAT ABOUT YOU? YOU READY TO GET SOME NEW SCARS HERE?
ALAS, IF THIS WEEK TAUGHT ME ANYTHING, IT'S THAT BEING AN X-MAN IS A YOUNG MAN'S GAME, AND I AM ANYTHING BUT.
NO MORE PART-TIMING, HANK. WITH CABLE'S DEATH, GAMBIT AND ROGUE OFF IN SPACE AND NO IDEA WHERE THE NEW MUTANTS WENT, WE'RE A BIT BEYOND CHECKING I.D.s AT THE DOOR.
WELL, I DID LOSE MY JOB. AND I NEED A LAB TO CONTINUE WORKING ON SEAN.
I THINK I'M GONNA HAVETA PASS ON THAT. I'M NOT GOIN' BACK ON ICE AGAIN, McCOY.
APOCALYPSE'S DEATH SEED IS STILL INSIDE OF YOU--
AYE. AND THAT'S SOMETHIN' I GOTTA LEARN HOW TO LIVE WITH. OR NOT. BUT WHAT I'VE BEEN DOIN' IS NEITHER.
I APPRECIATE EVERYTHIN' YOU DID FOR ME, HANK, BUT IT'S TIME TA LET NATURE RUN HER COURSE. I'D LIKE TA SEE IF THE WIND WILL STILL HAVE ME.

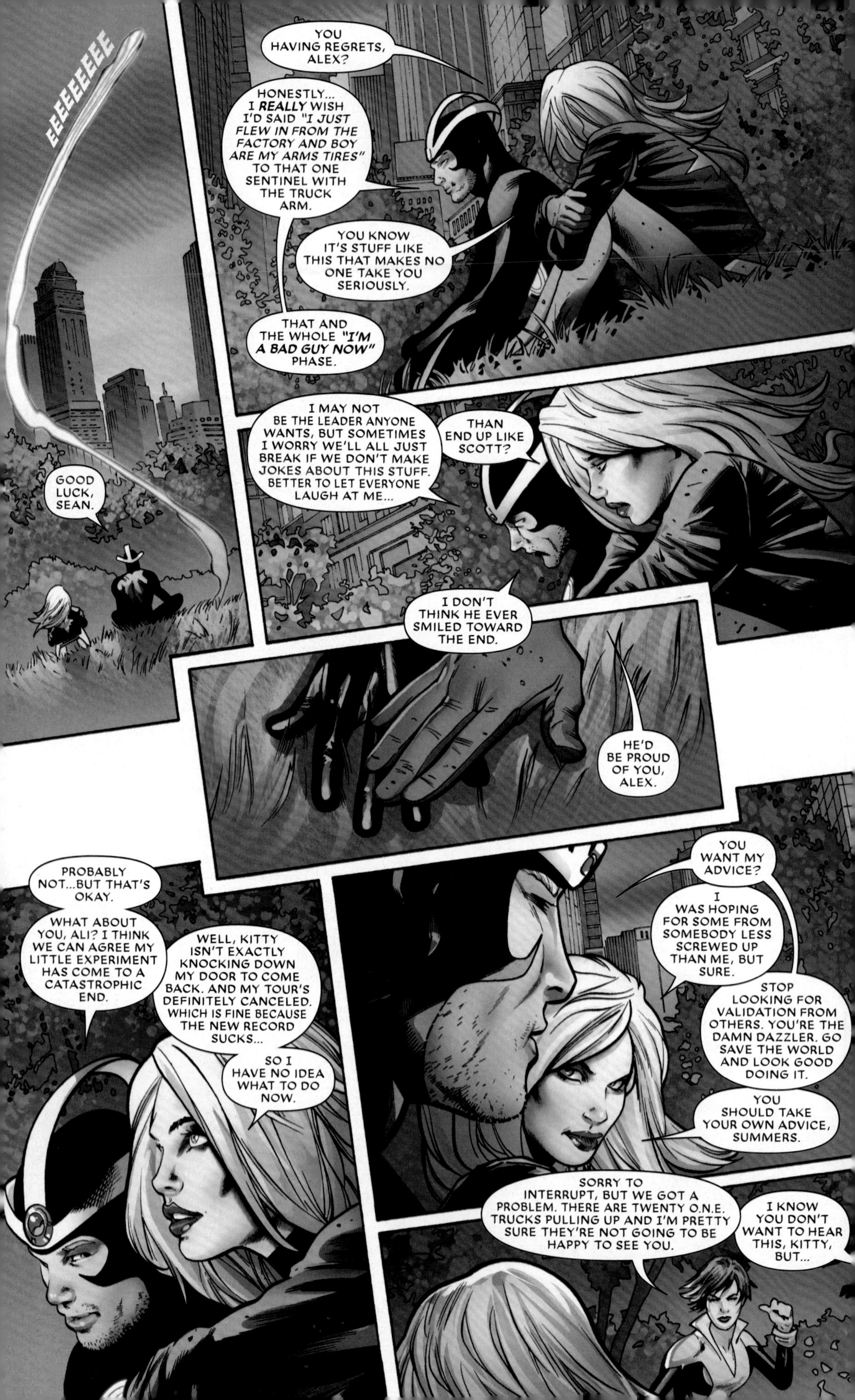
EEEEEEEE
GOOD LUCK, SEAN.
YOU HAVING REGRETS, ALEX?
HONESTLY... I REALLY WISH I'D SAID "I JUST FLEW IN FROM THE FACTORY AND BOY ARE MY ARMS TIRES" TO THAT ONE SENTINEL WITH THE TRUCK ARM.
YOU KNOW IT'S STUFF LIKE THIS THAT MAKES NO ONE TAKE YOU SERIOUSLY.
THAT AND THE WHOLE "I'M A BAD GUY NOW" PHASE.
I MAY NOT BE THE LEADER ANYONE WANTS, BUT SOMETIMES I WORRY WE'LL ALL JUST BREAK IF WE DON'T MAKE JOKES ABOUT THIS STUFF. BETTER TO LET EVERYONE LAUGH AT ME...
THAN END UP LIKE SCOTT?
I DON'T THINK HE EVER SMILED TOWARD THE END.
HE'D BE PROUD OF YOU, ALEX.
PROBABLY NOT...BUT THAT'S OKAY.
WHAT ABOUT YOU, ALI? I THINK WE CAN AGREE MY LITTLE EXPERIMENT HAS COME TO A CATASTROPHIC END.
WELL, KITTY ISN'T EXACTLY KNOCKING DOWN MY DOOR TO COME BACK. AND MY TOUR'S DEFINITELY CANCELED. WHICH IS FINE BECAUSE THE NEW RECORD SUCKS...
SO I HAVE NO IDEA WHAT TO DO NOW.
YOU WANT MY ADVICE?
I WAS HOPING FOR SOME FROM SOMEBODY LESS SCREWED UP THAN ME, BUT SURE.
STOP LOOKING FOR VALIDATION FROM OTHERS. YOU'RE THE DAMN DAZZLER. GO SAVE THE WORLD AND LOOK GOOD DOING IT.
YOU SHOULD TAKE YOUR OWN ADVICE, SUMMERS.
SORRY TO INTERRUPT, BUT WE GOT A PROBLEM. THERE ARE TWENTY O.N.E. TRUCKS PULLING UP AND I'M PRETTY SURE THEY'RE NOT GOING TO BE HAPPY TO SEE YOU.
I KNOW YOU DON'T WANT TO HEAR THIS, KITTY, BUT...

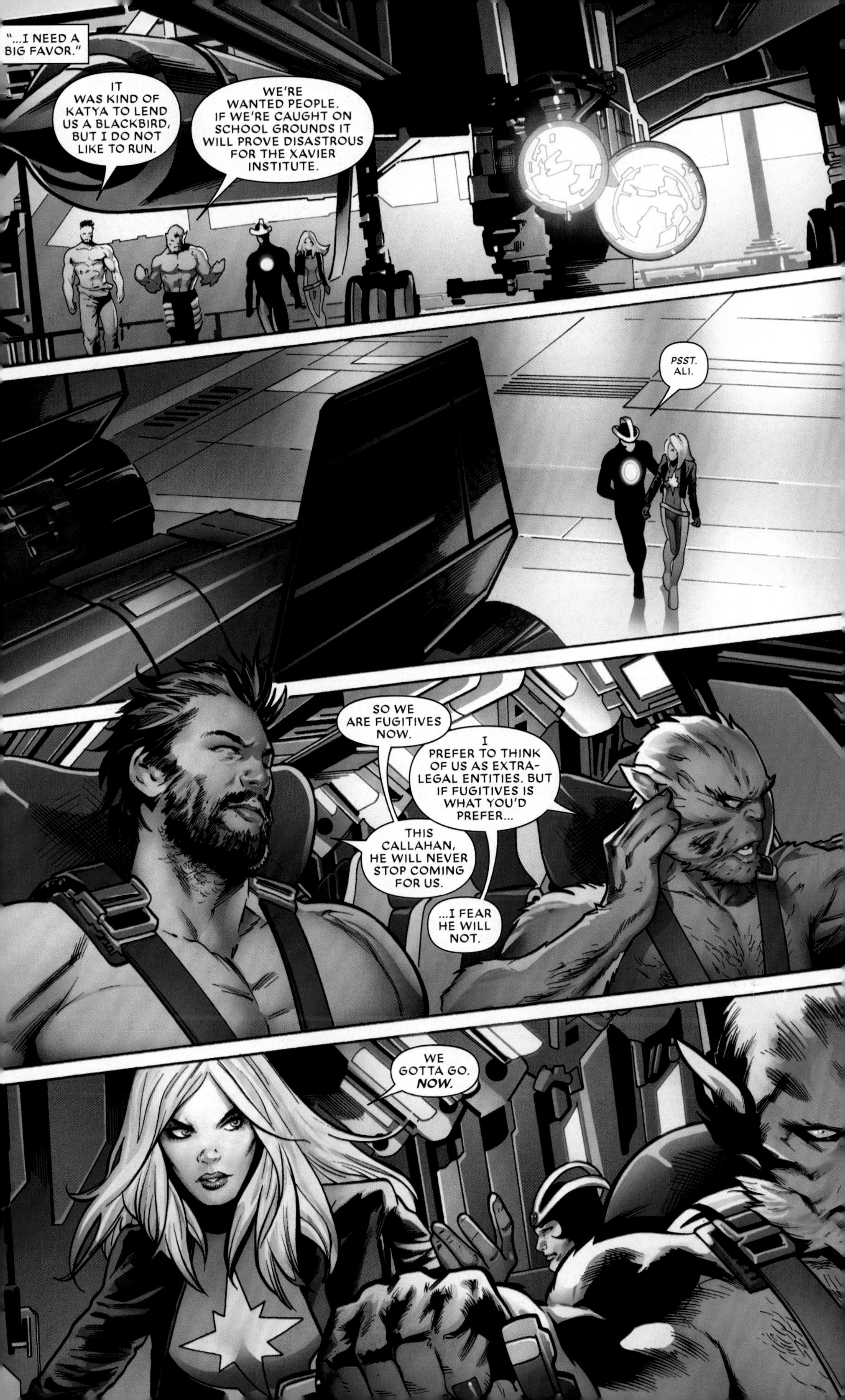
"...I NEED A BIG FAVOR."
IT WAS KIND OF KATYA TO LEND US A BLACKBIRD, BUT I DO NOT LIKE TO RUN.
WE'RE WANTED PEOPLE. IF WE'RE CAUGHT ON SCHOOL GROUNDS IT WILL PROVE DISASTROUS FOR THE XAVIER INSTITUTE.
PSST. ALI.
SO WE ARE FUGITIVES NOW.
I PREFER TO THINK OF US AS EXTRA-LEGAL ENTITIES. BUT IF FUGITIVES IS WHAT YOU'D PREFER...
THIS CALLAHAN, HE WILL NEVER STOP COMING FOR US.
...I FEAR HE WILL NOT.
WE GOTTA GO. NOW.

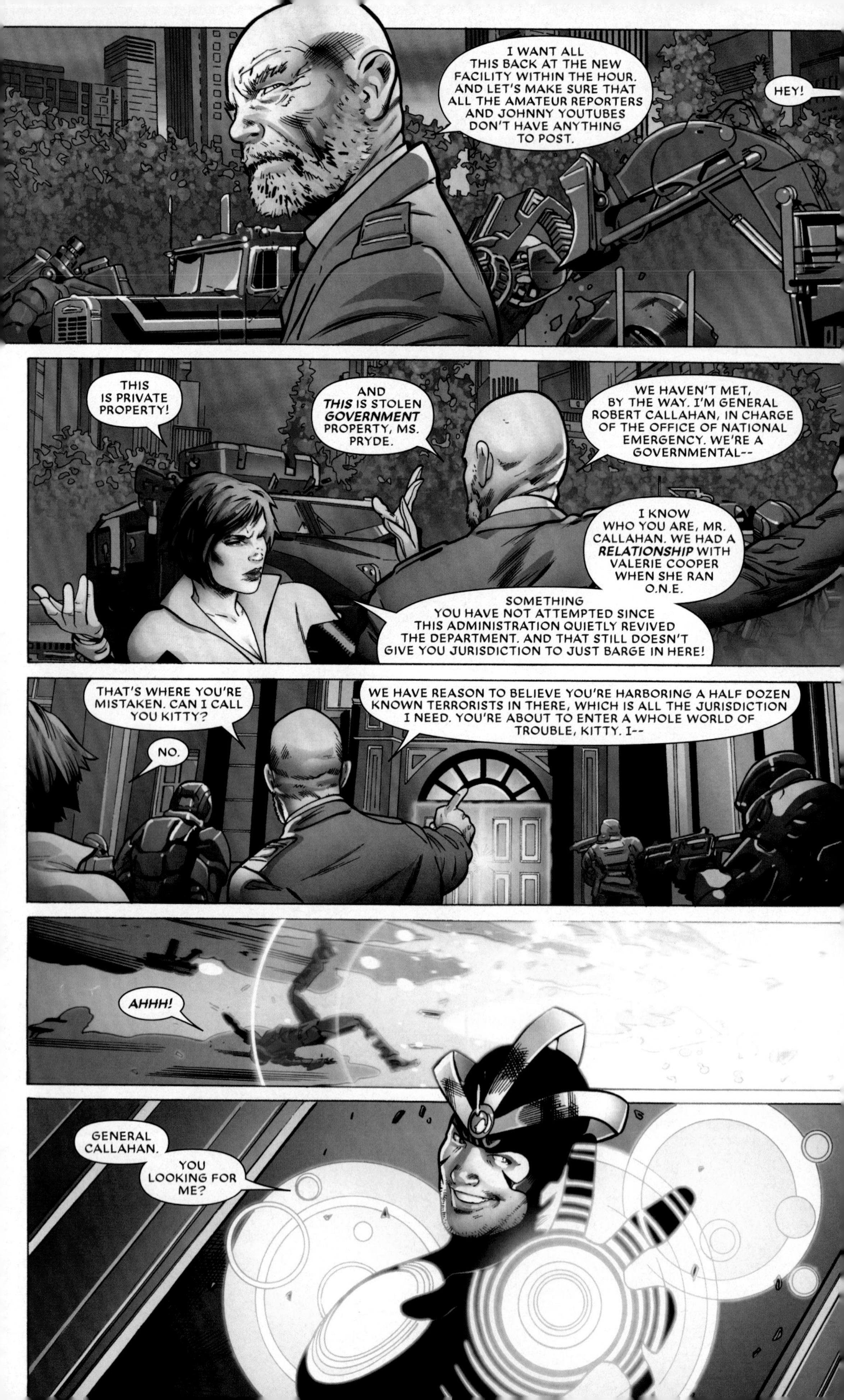
I WANT ALL THIS BACK AT THE NEW FACILITY WITHIN THE HOUR. AND LET'S MAKE SURE THAT ALL THE AMATEUR REPORTERS AND JOHNNY YOUTUBES DON'T HAVE ANYTHING TO POST.
HEY!
THIS IS PRIVATE PROPERTY!
AND *THIS* IS STOLEN *GOVERNMENT* PROPERTY, MS. PRYDE.
WE HAVEN'T MET, BY THE WAY. I'M GENERAL ROBERT CALLAHAN, IN CHARGE OF THE OFFICE OF NATIONAL EMERGENCY. WE'RE A GOVERNMENTAL--
I KNOW WHO YOU ARE, MR. CALLAHAN. WE HAD A *RELATIONSHIP* WITH VALERIE COOPER WHEN SHE RAN O.N.E.
SOMETHING YOU HAVE NOT ATTEMPTED SINCE THIS ADMINISTRATION QUIETLY REVIVED THE DEPARTMENT. AND THAT STILL DOESN'T GIVE YOU JURISDICTION TO JUST BARGE IN HERE!
THAT'S WHERE YOU'RE MISTAKEN. CAN I CALL YOU KITTY?
NO.
WE HAVE REASON TO BELIEVE YOU'RE HARBORING A HALF DOZEN KNOWN TERRORISTS IN THERE, WHICH IS ALL THE JURISDICTION I NEED. YOU'RE ABOUT TO ENTER A WHOLE WORLD OF TROUBLE, KITTY. I--
AHHH!
GENERAL CALLAHAN.
YOU LOOKING FOR ME?

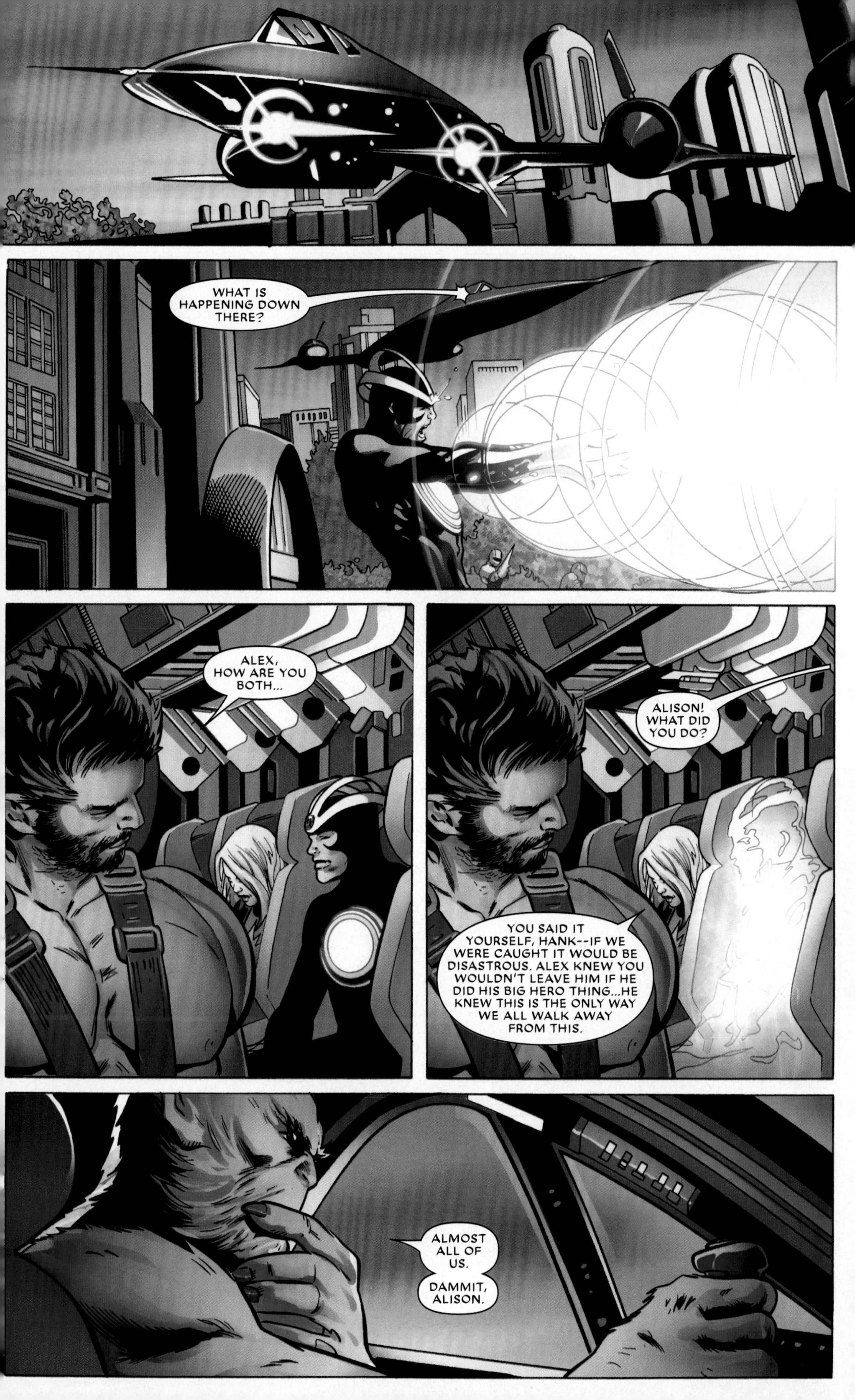
WHAT IS HAPPENING DOWN THERE?
ALEX, HOW ARE YOU BOTH...
ALISON! WHAT DID YOU DO?
YOU SAID IT YOURSELF, HANK--IF WE WERE CAUGHT IT WOULD BE DISASTROUS. ALEX KNEW YOU WOULDN'T LEAVE HIM IF HE DID HIS BIG HERO THING...HE KNEW THIS IS THE ONLY WAY WE ALL WALK AWAY FROM THIS.
ALMOST ALL OF US.
DAMMIT, ALISON.

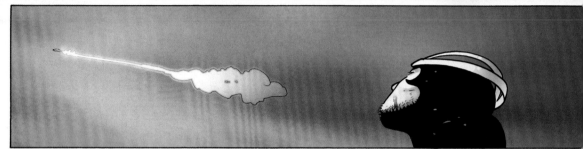

OKAY, CALLAHAN! HOW ABOUT WE MAKE A LITTLE DEAL?

YOU ADMIT IT WAS *JUST* ME WITH THE REAVERS THAT ATTACKED YOUR BASE AND LEAVE THE X-MEN ALONE.

IN EXCHANGE, I SURRENDER PEACEFULLY...

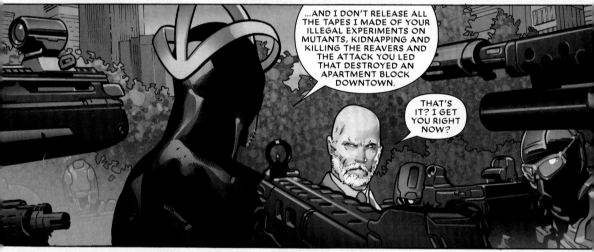

...AND I DON'T RELEASE ALL THE TAPES I MADE OF YOUR ILLEGAL EXPERIMENTS ON MUTANTS, KIDNAPPING AND KILLING THE REAVERS AND THE ATTACK YOU LED THAT DESTROYED AN APARTMENT BLOCK DOWNTOWN.

THAT'S IT? I GET YOU RIGHT NOW?

THAT'S IT. BUT IF YOU EVER GO AFTER MY TEAM OR THE X-MEN AGAIN, I PROMISE YOU YOUR FACE WILL BE ON THE FRONT PAGE OF EVERY NEWSPAPER IN THE COUNTRY...

DEAL... CUFF HIM!

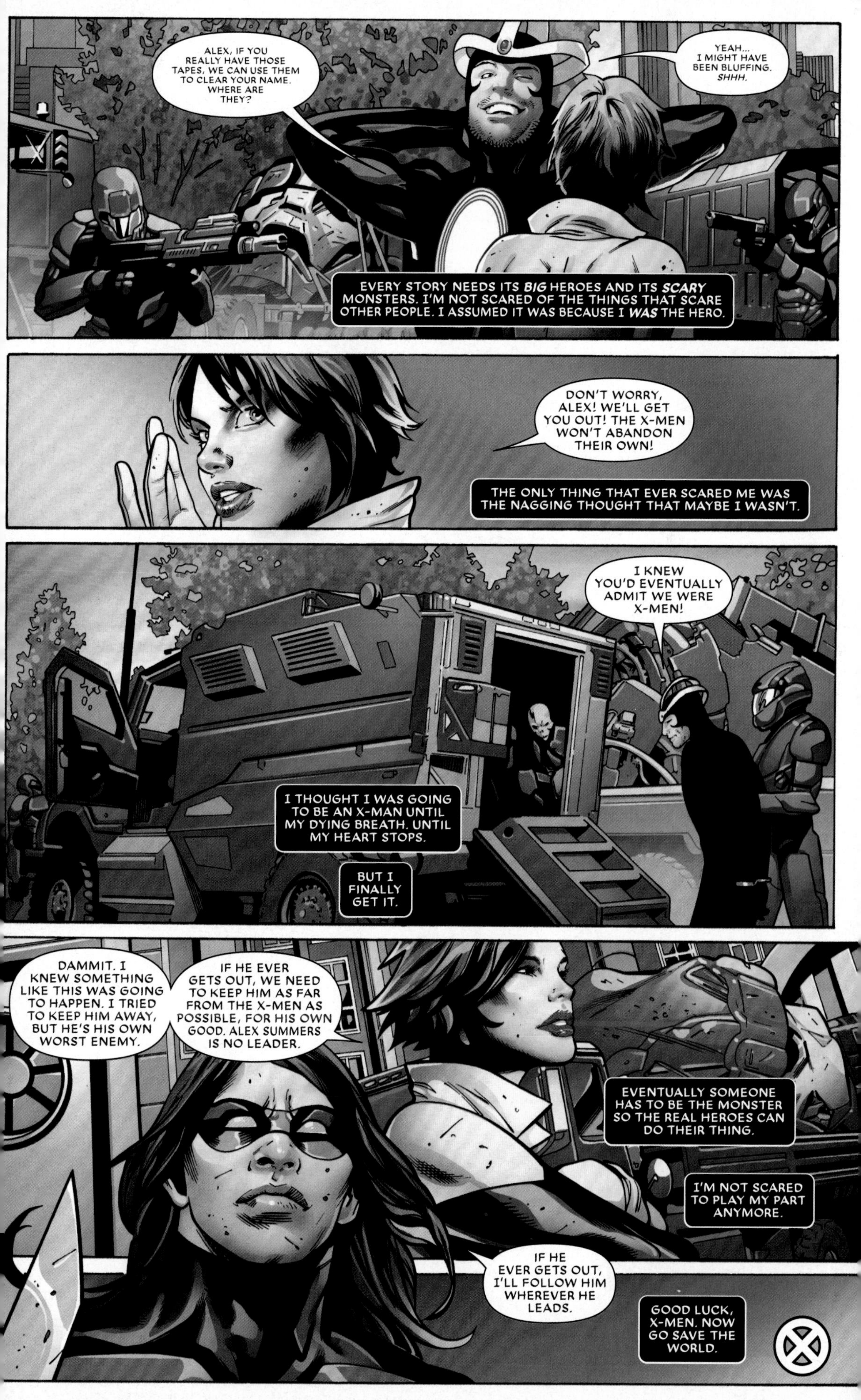
ALEX, IF YOU REALLY HAVE THOSE TAPES, WE CAN USE THEM TO CLEAR YOUR NAME. WHERE ARE THEY?
YEAH... I MIGHT HAVE BEEN BLUFFING. SHHH.
EVERY STORY NEEDS ITS BIG HEROES AND ITS SCARY MONSTERS. I'M NOT SCARED OF THE THINGS THAT SCARE OTHER PEOPLE. I ASSUMED IT WAS BECAUSE I WAS THE HERO.
DON'T WORRY, ALEX! WE'LL GET YOU OUT! THE X-MEN WON'T ABANDON THEIR OWN!
THE ONLY THING THAT EVER SCARED ME WAS THE NAGGING THOUGHT THAT MAYBE I WASN'T.
I KNEW YOU'D EVENTUALLY ADMIT WE WERE X-MEN!
I THOUGHT I WAS GOING TO BE AN X-MAN UNTIL MY DYING BREATH. UNTIL MY HEART STOPS.
BUT I FINALLY GET IT.
DAMMIT. I KNEW SOMETHING LIKE THIS WAS GOING TO HAPPEN. I TRIED TO KEEP HIM AWAY, BUT HE'S HIS OWN WORST ENEMY.
IF HE EVER GETS OUT, WE NEED TO KEEP HIM AS FAR FROM THE X-MEN AS POSSIBLE, FOR HIS OWN GOOD. ALEX SUMMERS IS NO LEADER.
EVENTUALLY SOMEONE HAS TO BE THE MONSTER SO THE REAL HEROES CAN DO THEIR THING.
I'M NOT SCARED TO PLAY MY PART ANYMORE.
IF HE EVER GETS OUT, I'LL FOLLOW HIM WHEREVER HE LEADS.
GOOD LUCK, X-MEN. NOW GO SAVE THE WORLD.

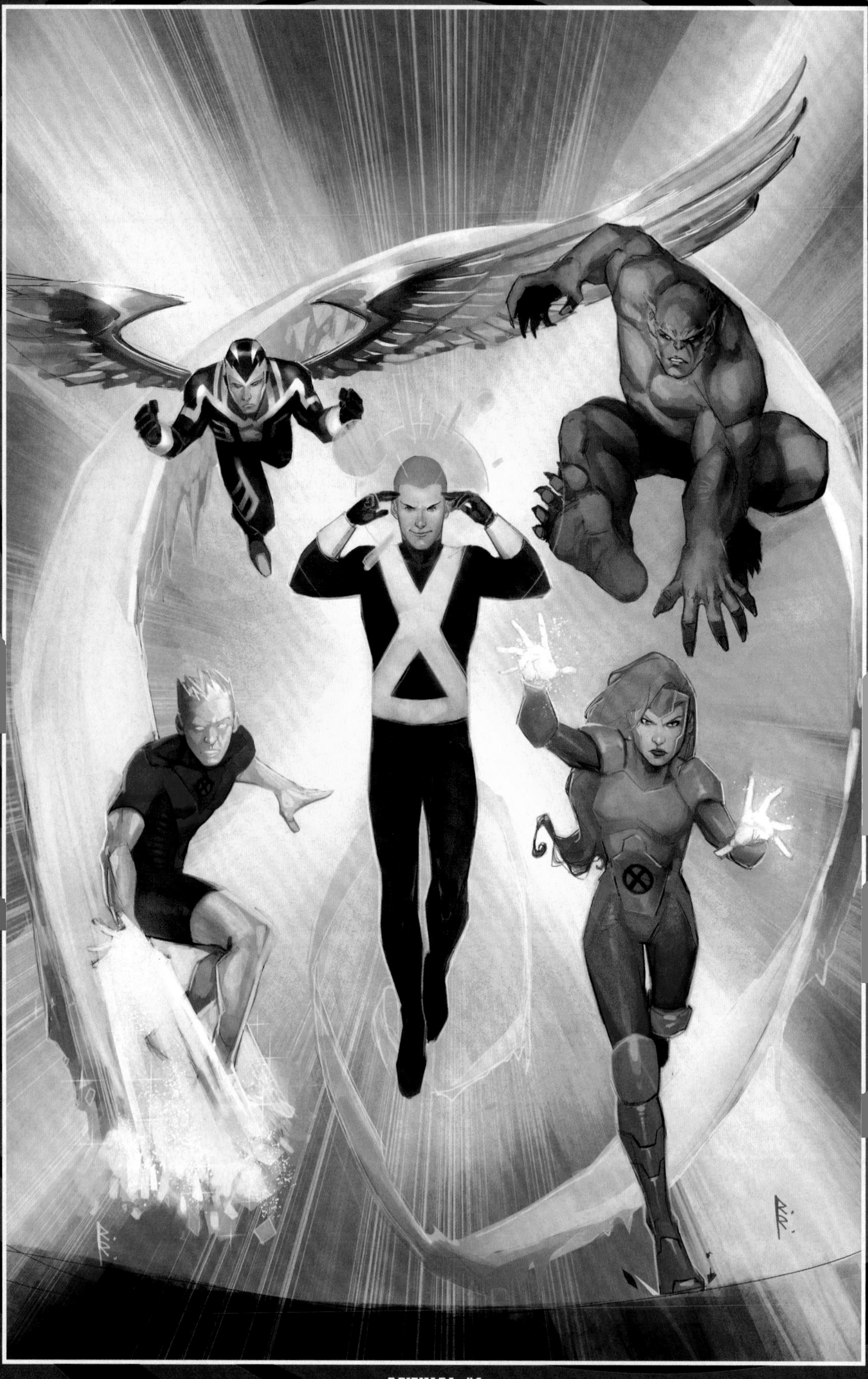

ANNUAL #1

PROFESSOR CHARLES XAVIER, FOUNDER AND LEADER OF THE X-MEN, WAS DEAD. KILLED BY A PHOENIX-POSSESSED CYCLOPS, XAVIER'S ABSENCE IS STILL FELT TO THIS DAY. IN REALITY, HE WAS TRAPPED IN A BRUTAL, PROLONGED DUEL WITH THE SHADOW KING IN THE ASTRAL PLANE. WITH THE HELP OF A TEAM OF X-MEN, CHARLES' CONSCIOUSNESS ESCAPED INTO THE BODY OF FANTOMEX. HE THEN ERASED THE TEAM'S MEMORIES OF HIS NEWFOUND EXISTENCE. CHARLES, NOW CALLING HIMSELF "X," IS EMBRACING A NEW DESTINY...

JEAN GREY, ONE OF THE ORIGINAL X-MEN AND HOST OF THE PHOENIX FORCE, WAS DEAD — KILLED IN BATTLE BY ONE OF THEIR GREATEST FOES. JEAN'S DEATH LEFT A CLOUD OVER THE X-MEN THAT NEVER PASSED. RECENTLY, THE X-MEN DISCOVERED THAT JEAN HAD BEEN REVIVED BY THE PHOENIX. NOW, SHE BEGINS A NEW CHAPTER IN HER LIFE, ONE IN WHICH HER HUSBAND, CYCLOPS, IS NO LONGER ALIVE...

HELLO, I'M MEETING A FRIEND.

AH, YES. WELCOME TO THE GRAND--

MONDAY.
THE GRAND SALON.
NEW YORK CITY.

OH, MY... HELLO THERE. ARE YOU SURE YOU'RE IN THE RIGHT PLACE?

YES. YES, I AM.

UNFORTUNATELY, SIR, WE HAVE A DRESS CODE AT THIS ESTABLISHMENT AND YOU DON'T QUITE FIT--

I'M WELL AWARE OF YOUR DRESS CODE. I CHOSE NOT TO ABIDE BY IT.

AS I'M SURE YOU ARE AWARE, IN WEATHER LIKE THIS, HOW INCONSIDERATE IT IS TOWARD PEOPLE OF THE FURRY PERSUASION.

AS A PROFESSOR OF BOTH HARVARD *AND* CAMBRIDGE UNIVERSITY, A MacARTHUR FELLOWSHIP RECIPIENT, A NOBEL PRIZE WINNER, A NINE-TIME RECIPIENT OF THE PRESIDENTIAL MEDAL OF FREEDOM...

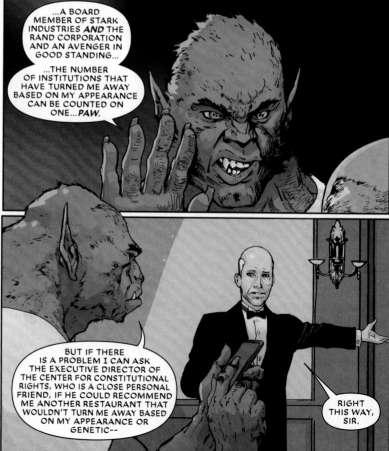

...A BOARD MEMBER OF STARK INDUSTRIES *AND* THE RAND CORPORATION AND AN AVENGER IN GOOD STANDING...

...THE NUMBER OF INSTITUTIONS THAT HAVE TURNED ME AWAY BASED ON MY APPEARANCE CAN BE COUNTED ON ONE... *PAW.*

BUT IF THERE IS A PROBLEM I CAN ASK THE EXECUTIVE DIRECTOR OF THE CENTER FOR CONSTITUTIONAL RIGHTS, WHO IS A CLOSE PERSONAL FRIEND, IF HE COULD RECOMMEND ME ANOTHER RESTAURANT THAT WOULDN'T TURN ME AWAY BASED ON MY APPEARANCE OR GENETIC--

RIGHT THIS WAY, SIR.

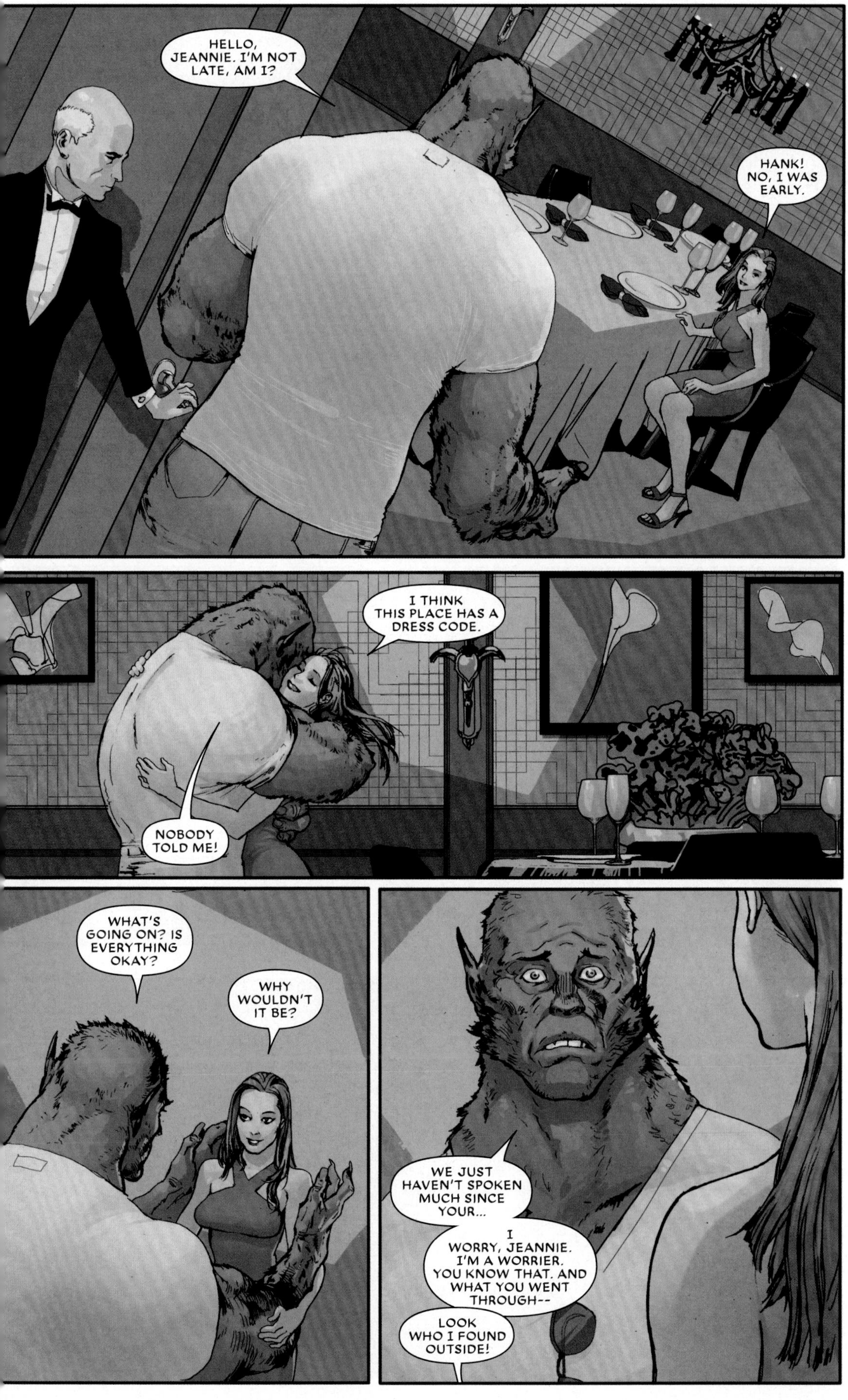
HELLO, JEANNIE. I'M NOT LATE, AM I?
HANK! NO, I WAS EARLY.
I THINK THIS PLACE HAS A DRESS CODE.
NOBODY TOLD ME!
WHAT'S GOING ON? IS EVERYTHING OKAY?
WHY WOULDN'T IT BE?
WE JUST HAVEN'T SPOKEN MUCH SINCE YOUR...
I WORRY, JEANNIE. I'M A WORRIER. YOU KNOW THAT. AND WHAT YOU WENT THROUGH--
LOOK WHO I FOUND OUTSIDE!

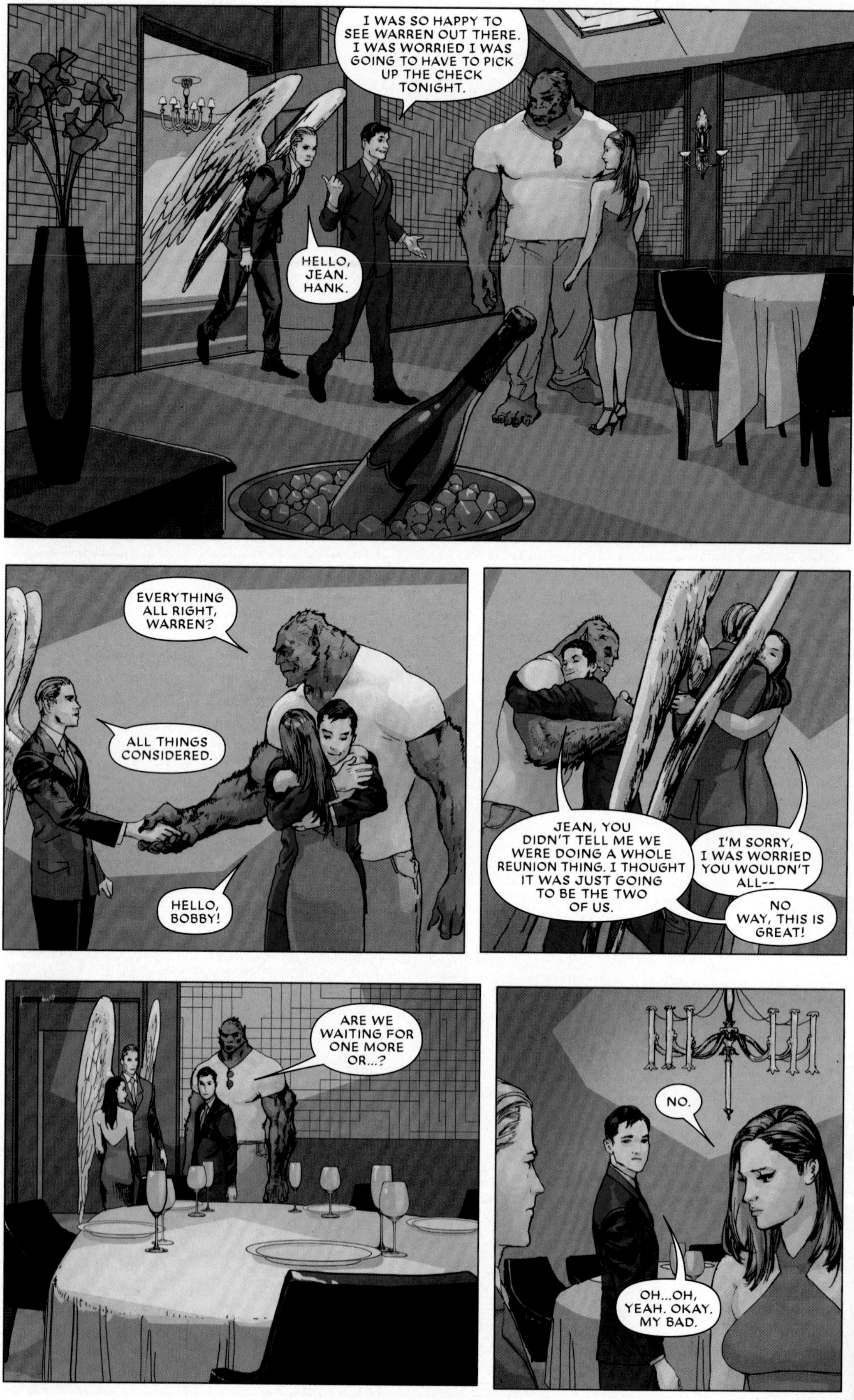
I WAS SO HAPPY TO SEE WARREN OUT THERE. I WAS WORRIED I WAS GOING TO HAVE TO PICK UP THE CHECK TONIGHT.
HELLO, JEAN. HANK.
EVERYTHING ALL RIGHT, WARREN?
ALL THINGS CONSIDERED.
HELLO, BOBBY!
JEAN, YOU DIDN'T TELL ME WE WERE DOING A WHOLE REUNION THING. I THOUGHT IT WAS JUST GOING TO BE THE TWO OF US.
I'M SORRY, I WAS WORRIED YOU WOULDN'T ALL--
NO WAY, THIS IS GREAT!
ARE WE WAITING FOR ONE MORE OR...?
NO.
OH...OH, YEAH. OKAY. MY BAD.

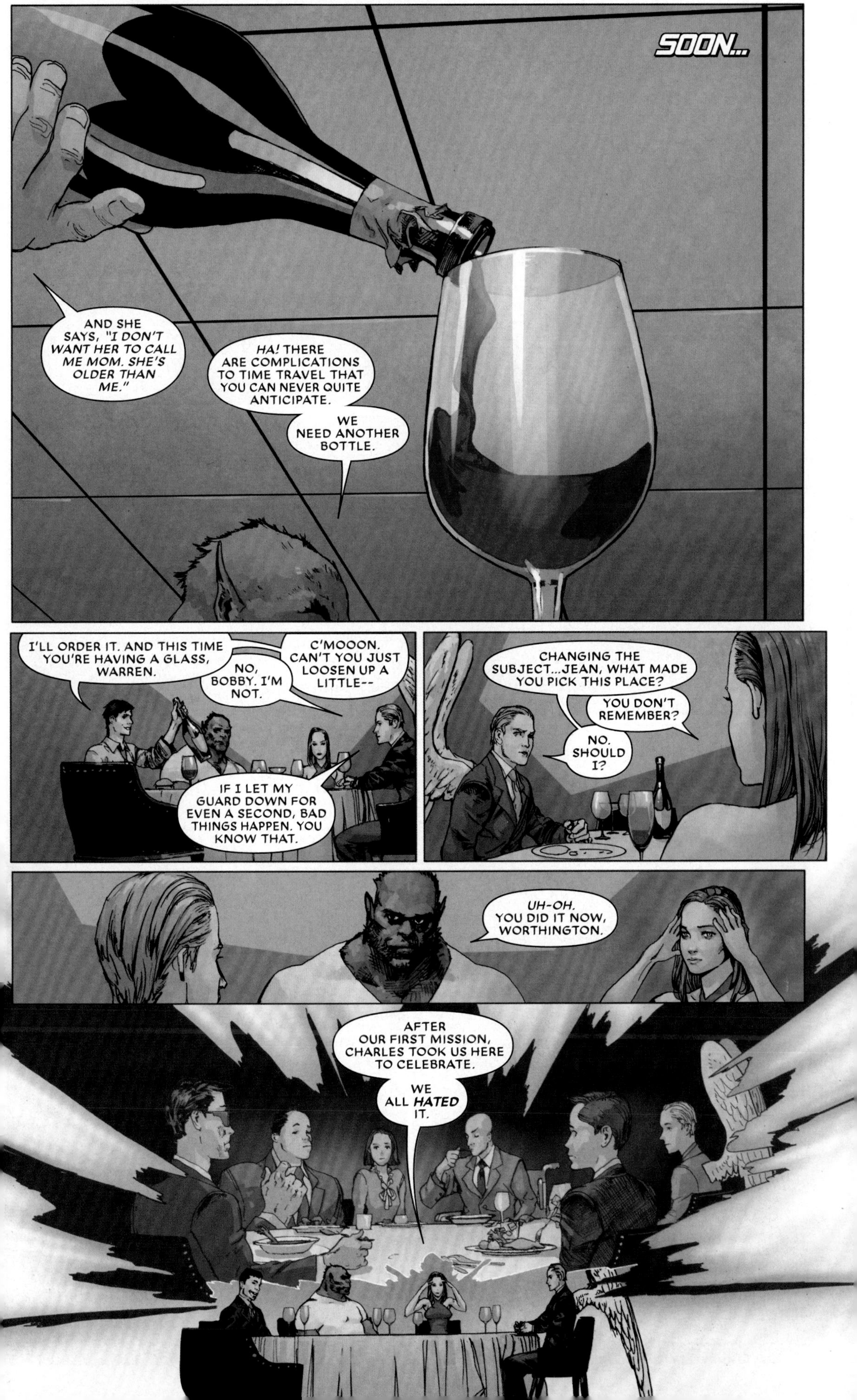
SOON...
AND SHE SAYS, "I DON'T WANT HER TO CALL ME MOM. SHE'S OLDER THAN ME."
HA! THERE ARE COMPLICATIONS TO TIME TRAVEL THAT YOU CAN NEVER QUITE ANTICIPATE.
WE NEED ANOTHER BOTTLE.
I'LL ORDER IT. AND THIS TIME YOU'RE HAVING A GLASS, WARREN.
NO, BOBBY. I'M NOT.
C'MOOON. CAN'T YOU JUST LOOSEN UP A LITTLE--
IF I LET MY GUARD DOWN FOR EVEN A SECOND, BAD THINGS HAPPEN. YOU KNOW THAT.
CHANGING THE SUBJECT...JEAN, WHAT MADE YOU PICK THIS PLACE?
YOU DON'T REMEMBER?
NO. SHOULD I?
UH-OH. YOU DID IT NOW, WORTHINGTON.
AFTER OUR FIRST MISSION, CHARLES TOOK US HERE TO CELEBRATE.
WE ALL HATED IT.

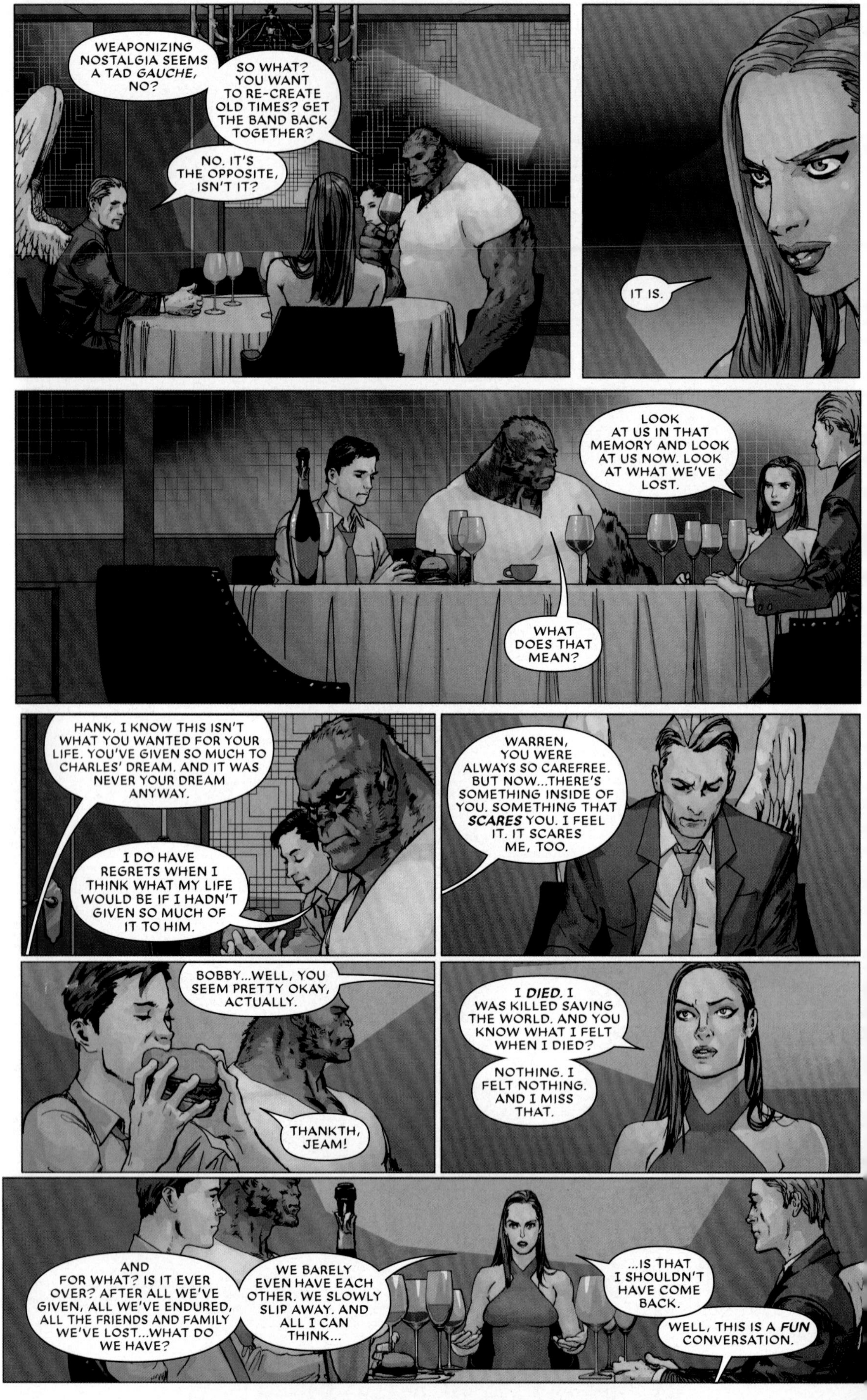
WEAPONIZING NOSTALGIA SEEMS A TAD *GAUCHE*, NO?
SO WHAT? YOU WANT TO RE-CREATE OLD TIMES? GET THE BAND BACK TOGETHER?
NO. IT'S THE OPPOSITE, ISN'T IT?
IT IS.
LOOK AT US IN THAT MEMORY AND LOOK AT US NOW. LOOK AT WHAT WE'VE LOST.
WHAT DOES THAT MEAN?
HANK, I KNOW THIS ISN'T WHAT YOU WANTED FOR YOUR LIFE. YOU'VE GIVEN SO MUCH TO CHARLES' DREAM. AND IT WAS NEVER YOUR DREAM ANYWAY.
I DO HAVE REGRETS WHEN I THINK WHAT MY LIFE WOULD BE IF I HADN'T GIVEN SO MUCH OF IT TO HIM.
WARREN, YOU WERE ALWAYS SO CAREFREE. BUT NOW...THERE'S SOMETHING INSIDE OF YOU. SOMETHING THAT ***SCARES*** YOU. I FEEL IT. IT SCARES ME, TOO.
BOBBY...WELL, YOU SEEM PRETTY OKAY, ACTUALLY.
THANKTH, JEAM!
I ***DIED.*** I WAS KILLED SAVING THE WORLD. AND YOU KNOW WHAT I FELT WHEN I DIED?
NOTHING. I FELT NOTHING. AND I MISS THAT.
AND FOR WHAT? IS IT EVER OVER? AFTER ALL WE'VE GIVEN, ALL WE'VE ENDURED, ALL THE FRIENDS AND FAMILY WE'VE LOST...WHAT DO WE HAVE?
WE BARELY EVEN HAVE EACH OTHER. WE SLOWLY SLIP AWAY. AND ALL I CAN THINK...
...IS THAT I SHOULDN'T HAVE COME BACK.
WELL, THIS IS A *FUN* CONVERSATION.

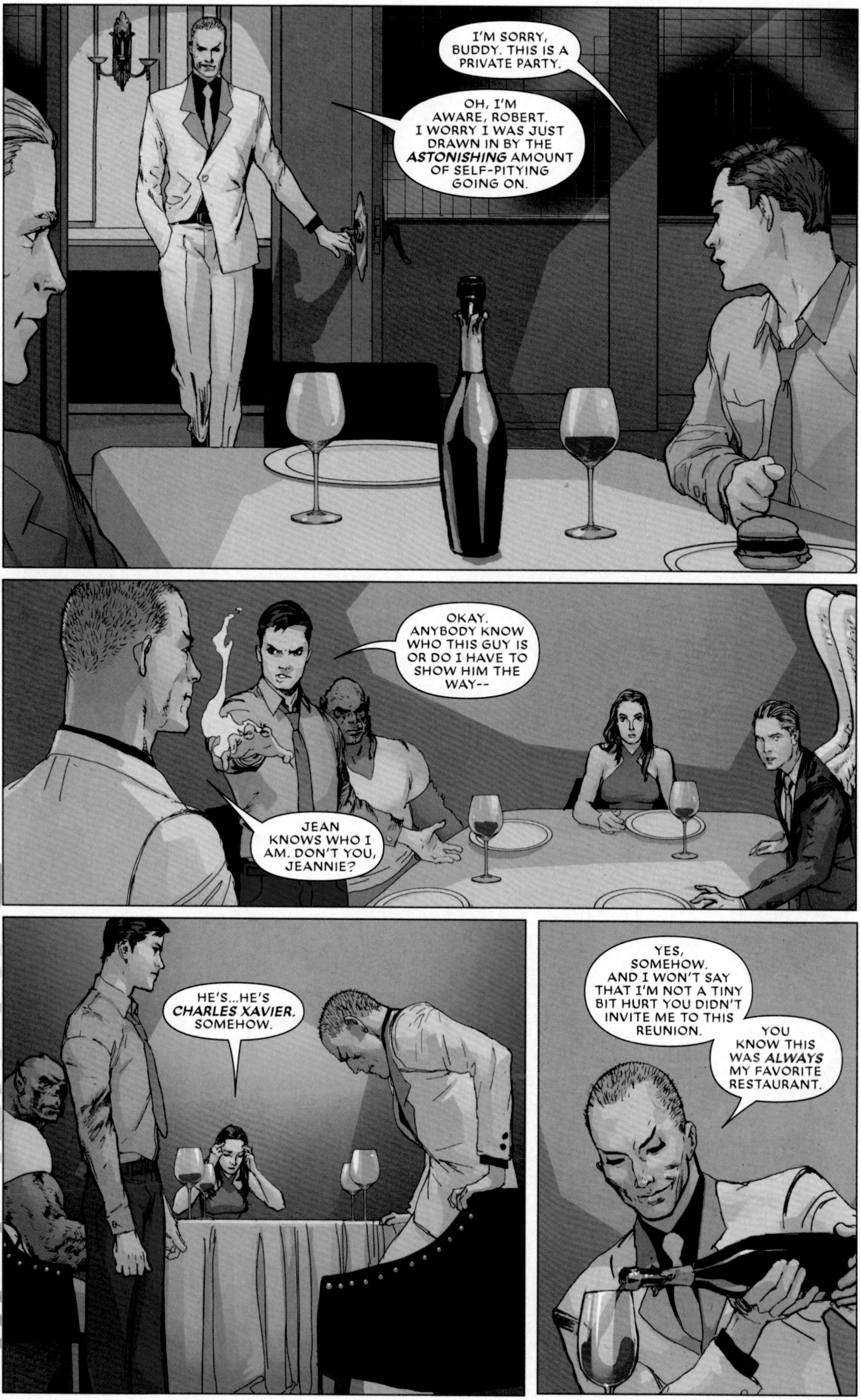
I'M SORRY, BUDDY. THIS IS A PRIVATE PARTY.
OH, I'M AWARE, ROBERT. I WORRY I WAS JUST DRAWN IN BY THE ***ASTONISHING*** AMOUNT OF SELF-PITYING GOING ON.
OKAY. ANYBODY KNOW WHO THIS GUY IS OR DO I HAVE TO SHOW HIM THE WAY--
JEAN KNOWS WHO I AM. DON'T YOU, JEANNIE?
HE'S...HE'S ***CHARLES XAVIER.*** SOMEHOW.
YES, SOMEHOW. AND I WON'T SAY THAT I'M NOT A TINY BIT HURT YOU DIDN'T INVITE ME TO THIS REUNION.
YOU KNOW THIS WAS ***ALWAYS*** MY FAVORITE RESTAURANT.

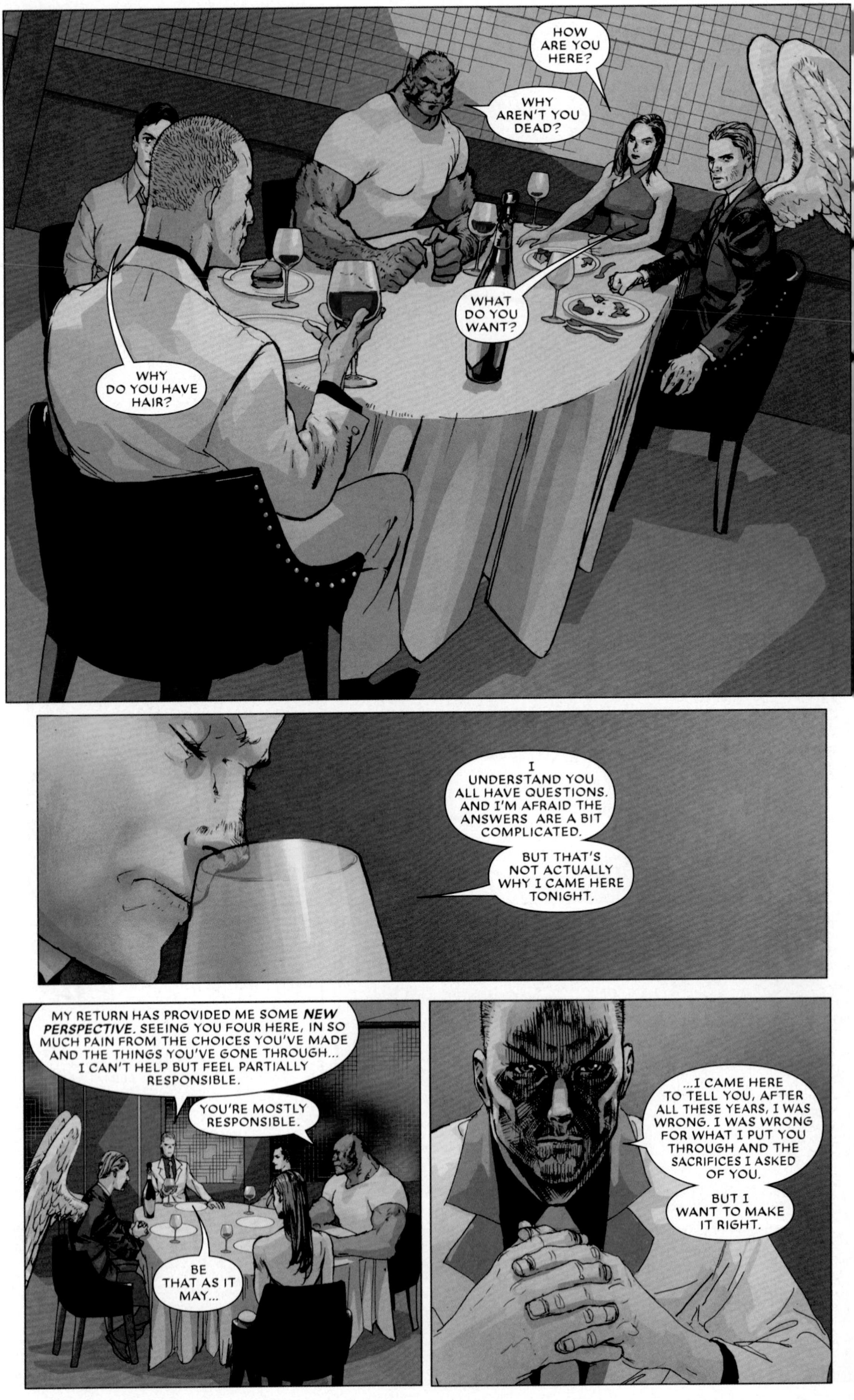
HOW ARE YOU HERE?
WHY AREN'T YOU DEAD?
WHAT DO YOU WANT?
WHY DO YOU HAVE HAIR?
I UNDERSTAND YOU ALL HAVE QUESTIONS. AND I'M AFRAID THE ANSWERS ARE A BIT COMPLICATED.
BUT THAT'S NOT ACTUALLY WHY I CAME HERE TONIGHT.
MY RETURN HAS PROVIDED ME SOME NEW PERSPECTIVE. SEEING YOU FOUR HERE, IN SO MUCH PAIN FROM THE CHOICES YOU'VE MADE AND THE THINGS YOU'VE GONE THROUGH... I CAN'T HELP BUT FEEL PARTIALLY RESPONSIBLE.
YOU'RE MOSTLY RESPONSIBLE.
BE THAT AS IT MAY...
...I CAME HERE TO TELL YOU, AFTER ALL THESE YEARS, I WAS WRONG. I WAS WRONG FOR WHAT I PUT YOU THROUGH AND THE SACRIFICES I ASKED OF YOU.
BUT I WANT TO MAKE IT RIGHT.

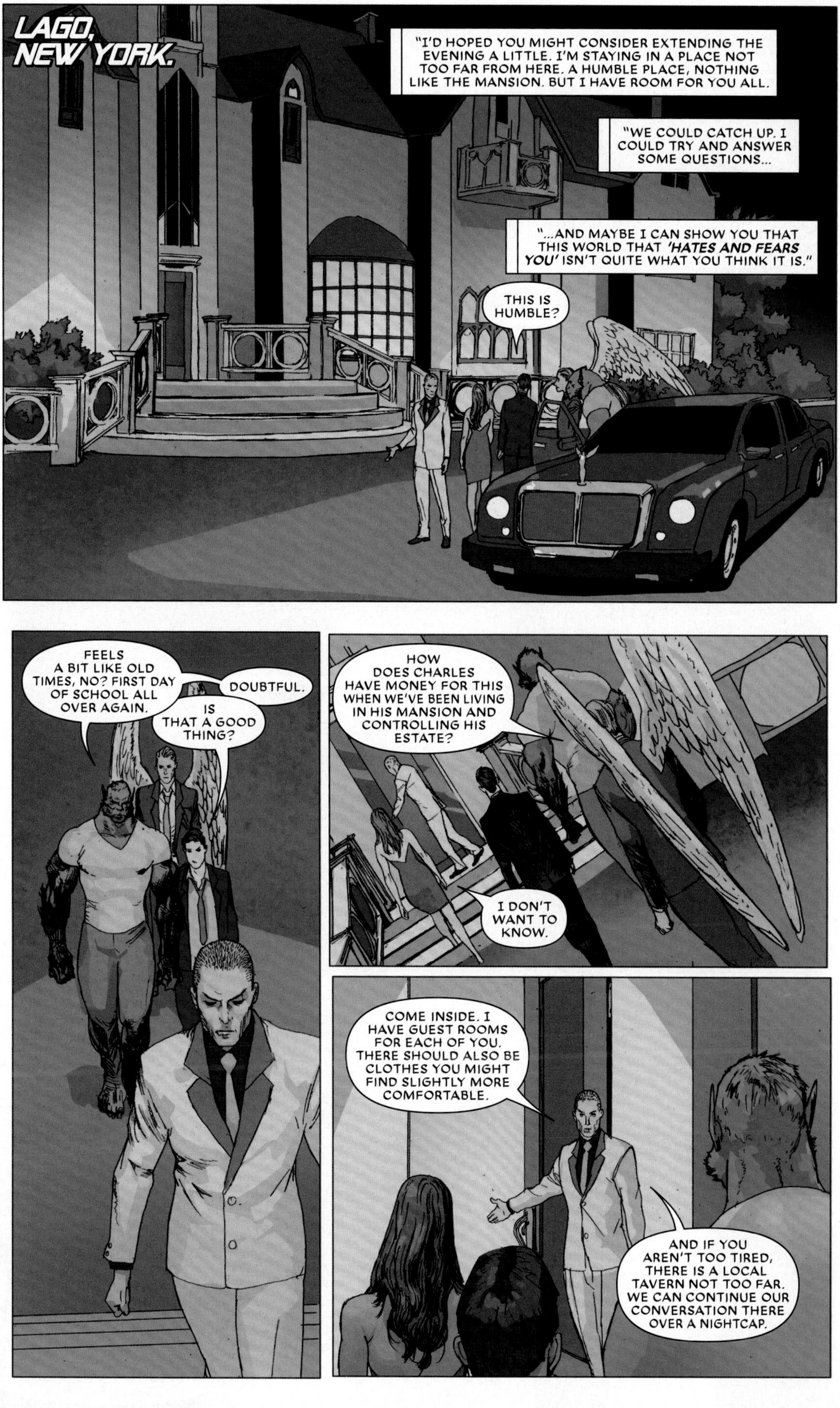
LAGO, NEW YORK.
"I'D HOPED YOU MIGHT CONSIDER EXTENDING THE EVENING A LITTLE. I'M STAYING IN A PLACE NOT TOO FAR FROM HERE. A HUMBLE PLACE, NOTHING LIKE THE MANSION. BUT I HAVE ROOM FOR YOU ALL.
"WE COULD CATCH UP. I COULD TRY AND ANSWER SOME QUESTIONS...
"...AND MAYBE I CAN SHOW YOU THAT THIS WORLD THAT *'HATES AND FEARS YOU'* ISN'T QUITE WHAT YOU THINK IT IS."
THIS IS HUMBLE?
FEELS A BIT LIKE OLD TIMES, NO? FIRST DAY OF SCHOOL ALL OVER AGAIN.
DOUBTFUL.
IS THAT A GOOD THING?
HOW DOES CHARLES HAVE MONEY FOR THIS WHEN WE'VE BEEN LIVING IN HIS MANSION AND CONTROLLING HIS ESTATE?
I DON'T WANT TO KNOW.
COME INSIDE. I HAVE GUEST ROOMS FOR EACH OF YOU. THERE SHOULD ALSO BE CLOTHES YOU MIGHT FIND SLIGHTLY MORE COMFORTABLE.
AND IF YOU AREN'T TOO TIRED, THERE IS A LOCAL TAVERN NOT TOO FAR. WE CAN CONTINUE OUR CONVERSATION THERE OVER A NIGHTCAP.

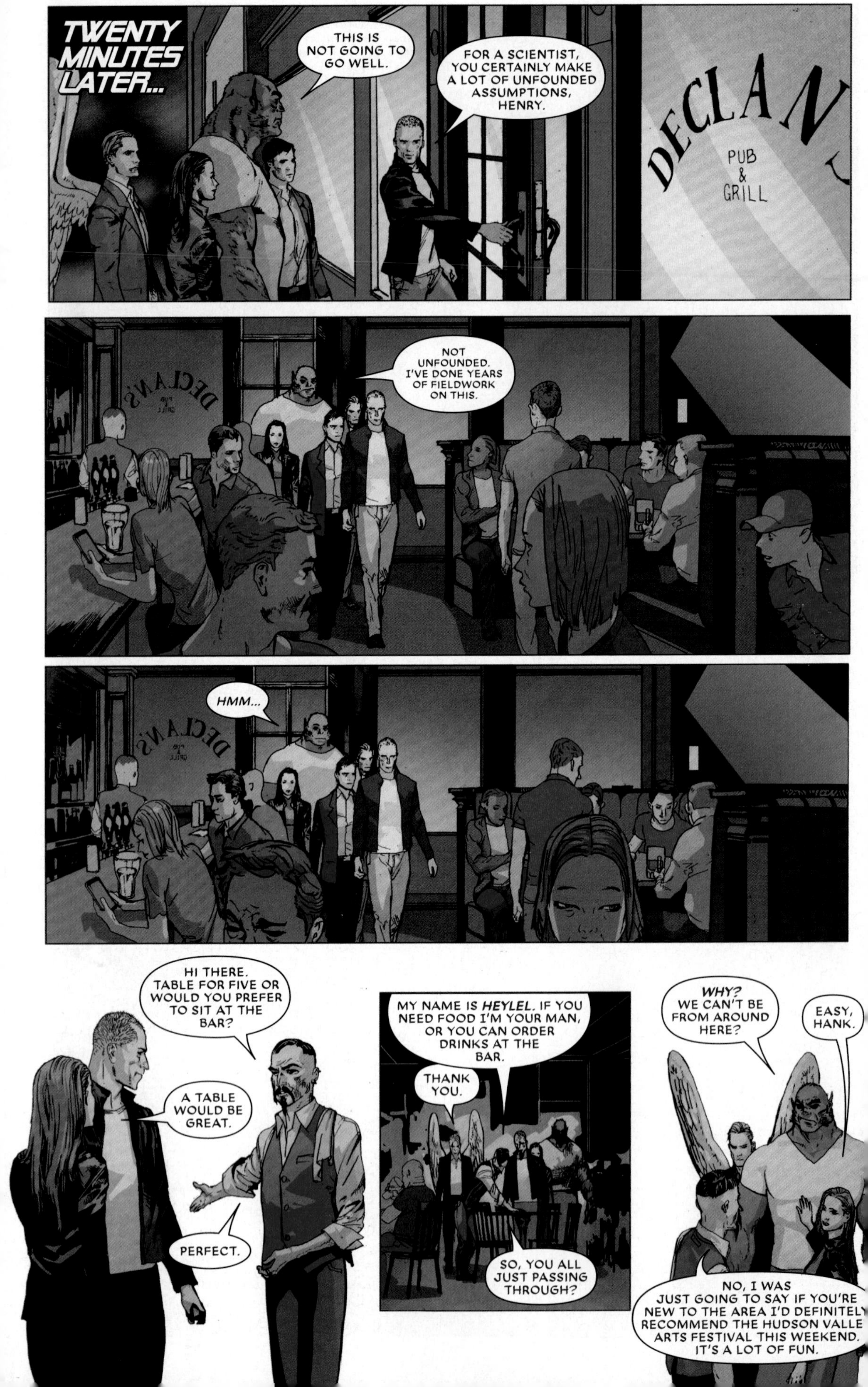
TWENTY MINUTES LATER...
THIS IS NOT GOING TO GO WELL.
FOR A SCIENTIST, YOU CERTAINLY MAKE A LOT OF UNFOUNDED ASSUMPTIONS, HENRY.
DECLAN
PUB & GRILL
NOT UNFOUNDED. I'VE DONE YEARS OF FIELDWORK ON THIS.
DECLAN'S PUB & GRILL
HMM...
DECLAN'S PUB & GRILL
HI THERE. TABLE FOR FIVE OR WOULD YOU PREFER TO SIT AT THE BAR?
A TABLE WOULD BE GREAT.
PERFECT.
MY NAME IS HEYLEL. IF YOU NEED FOOD I'M YOUR MAN, OR YOU CAN ORDER DRINKS AT THE BAR.
THANK YOU.
SO, YOU ALL JUST PASSING THROUGH?
WHY? WE CAN'T BE FROM AROUND HERE?
EASY, HANK.
NO, I WAS JUST GOING TO SAY IF YOU'RE NEW TO THE AREA I'D DEFINITELY RECOMMEND THE HUDSON VALLE ARTS FESTIVAL THIS WEEKEND. IT'S A LOT OF FUN.

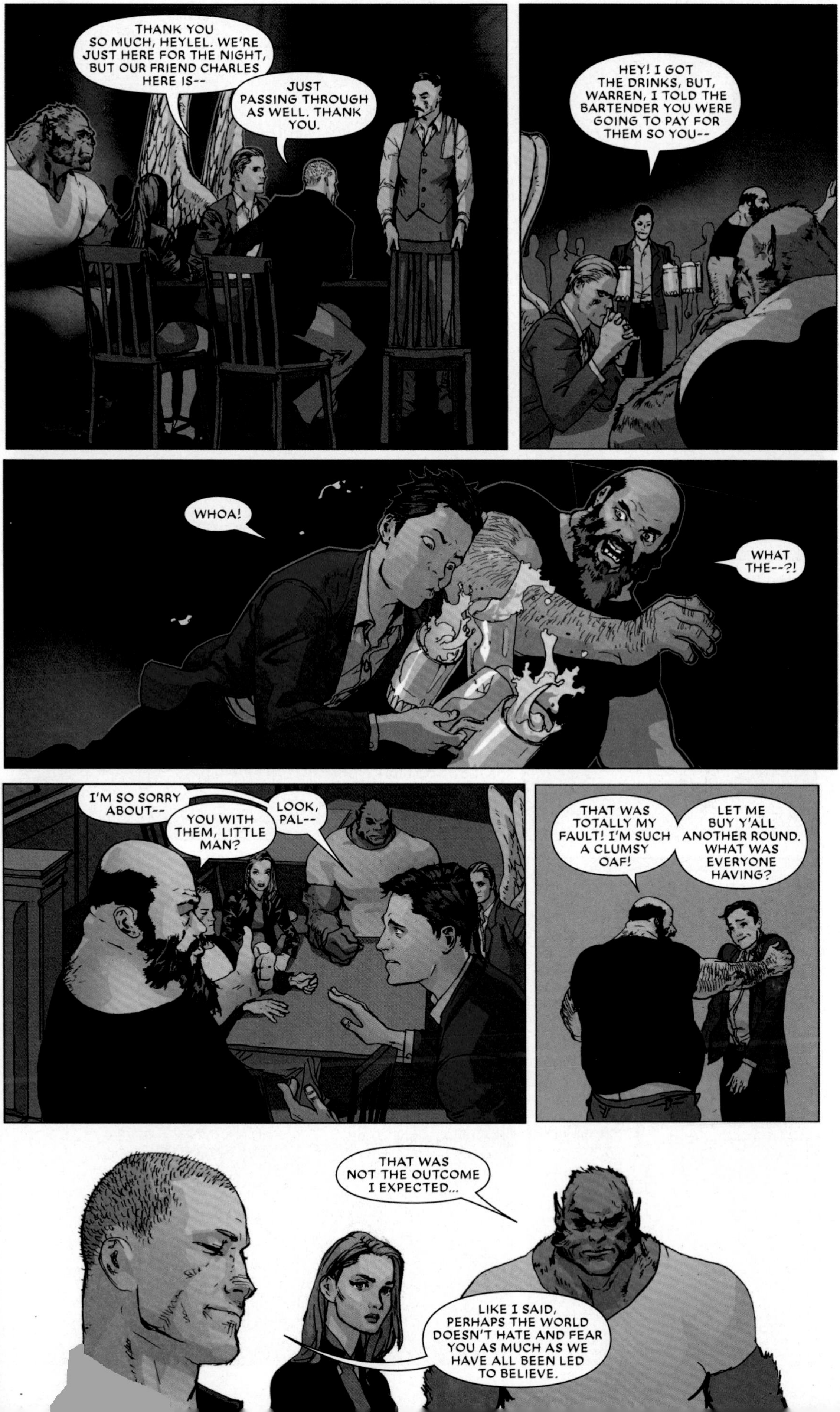
THANK YOU SO MUCH, HEYLEL. WE'RE JUST HERE FOR THE NIGHT, BUT OUR FRIEND CHARLES HERE IS--
JUST PASSING THROUGH AS WELL. THANK YOU.
HEY! I GOT THE DRINKS, BUT, WARREN, I TOLD THE BARTENDER YOU WERE GOING TO PAY FOR THEM SO YOU--
WHOA!
WHAT THE--?!
I'M SO SORRY ABOUT--
LOOK, PAL--
YOU WITH THEM, LITTLE MAN?
THAT WAS TOTALLY MY FAULT! I'M SUCH A CLUMSY OAF!
LET ME BUY Y'ALL ANOTHER ROUND. WHAT WAS EVERYONE HAVING?
THAT WAS NOT THE OUTCOME I EXPECTED...
LIKE I SAID, PERHAPS THE WORLD DOESN'T HATE AND FEAR YOU AS MUCH AS WE HAVE ALL BEEN LED TO BELIEVE.

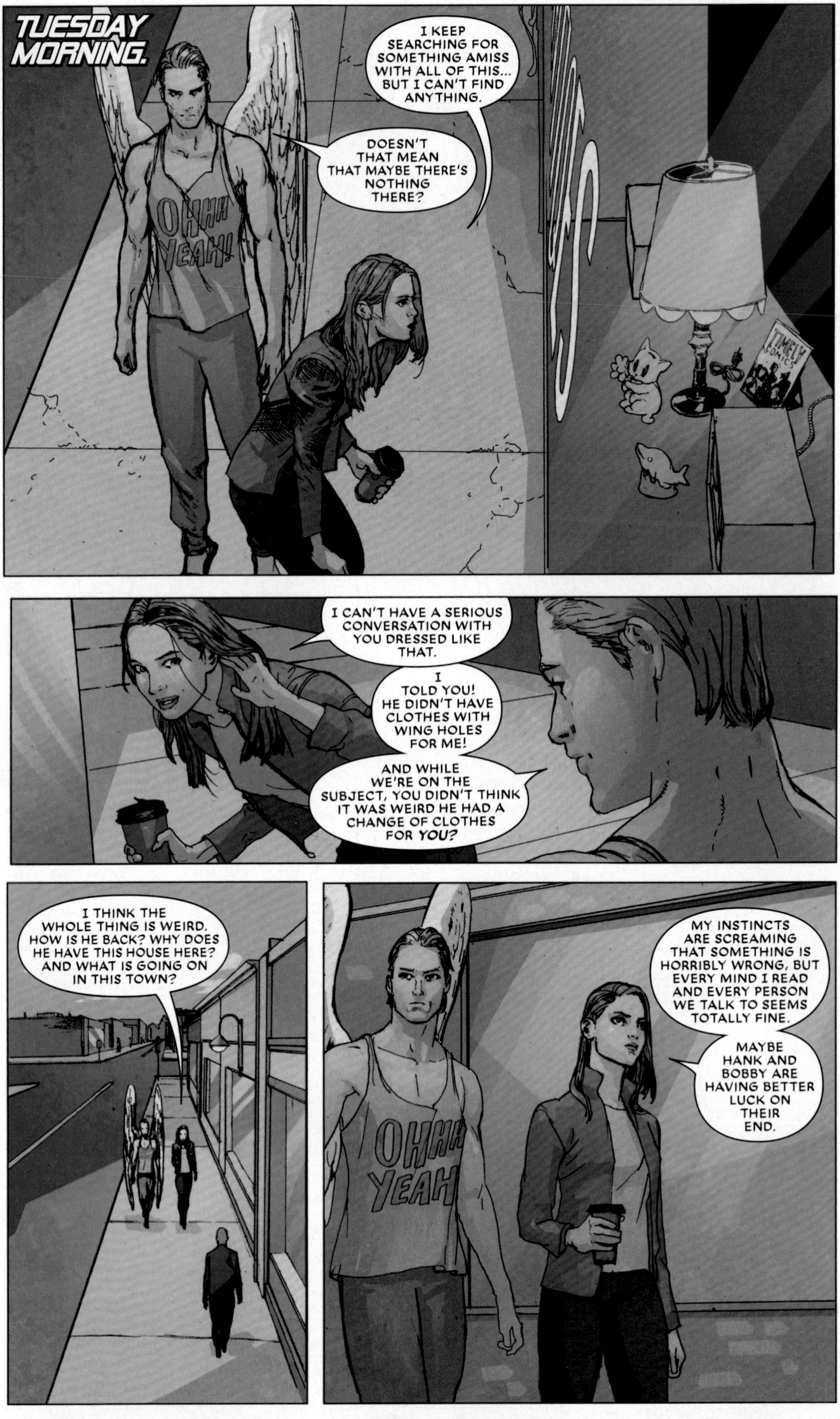
TUESDAY MORNING.
I KEEP SEARCHING FOR SOMETHING AMISS WITH ALL OF THIS... BUT I CAN'T FIND ANYTHING.
DOESN'T THAT MEAN THAT MAYBE THERE'S NOTHING THERE?
OHHH YEAH!
TIMELY COMICS
I CAN'T HAVE A SERIOUS CONVERSATION WITH YOU DRESSED LIKE THAT.
I TOLD YOU! HE DIDN'T HAVE CLOTHES WITH WING HOLES FOR ME!
AND WHILE WE'RE ON THE SUBJECT, YOU DIDN'T THINK IT WAS WEIRD HE HAD A CHANGE OF CLOTHES FOR *YOU?*
I THINK THE WHOLE THING IS WEIRD. HOW IS HE BACK? WHY DOES HE HAVE THIS HOUSE HERE? AND WHAT IS GOING ON IN THIS TOWN?
OHHH YEAH
MY INSTINCTS ARE SCREAMING THAT SOMETHING IS HORRIBLY WRONG, BUT EVERY MIND I READ AND EVERY PERSON WE TALK TO SEEMS TOTALLY FINE.
MAYBE HANK AND BOBBY ARE HAVING BETTER LUCK ON THEIR END.

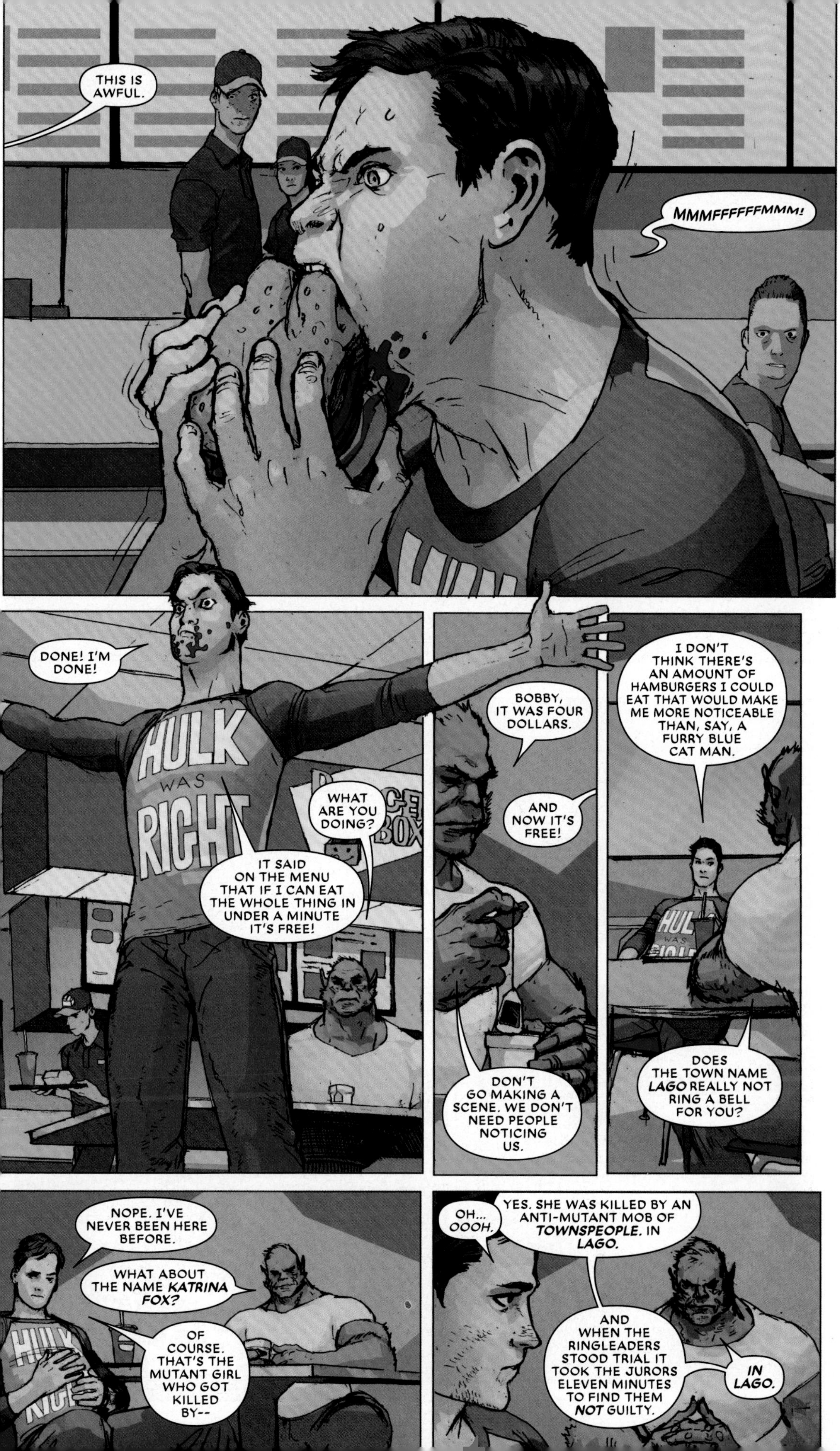
THIS IS AWFUL.
MMMFFFFFFMMM!
HULK
DONE! I'M DONE!
HULK WAS RIGHT
WHAT ARE YOU DOING?
IT SAID ON THE MENU THAT IF I CAN EAT THE WHOLE THING IN UNDER A MINUTE IT'S FREE!
BOBBY, IT WAS FOUR DOLLARS.
AND NOW IT'S FREE!
DON'T GO MAKING A SCENE. WE DON'T NEED PEOPLE NOTICING US.
I DON'T THINK THERE'S AN AMOUNT OF HAMBURGERS I COULD EAT THAT WOULD MAKE ME MORE NOTICEABLE THAN, SAY, A FURRY BLUE CAT MAN.
DOES THE TOWN NAME LAGO REALLY NOT RING A BELL FOR YOU?
NOPE. I'VE NEVER BEEN HERE BEFORE.
WHAT ABOUT THE NAME KATRINA FOX?
OF COURSE. THAT'S THE MUTANT GIRL WHO GOT KILLED BY--
OH... OOOH.
YES. SHE WAS KILLED BY AN ANTI-MUTANT MOB OF TOWNSPEOPLE. IN LAGO.
AND WHEN THE RINGLEADERS STOOD TRIAL IT TOOK THE JURORS ELEVEN MINUTES TO FIND THEM NOT GUILTY.
IN LAGO.

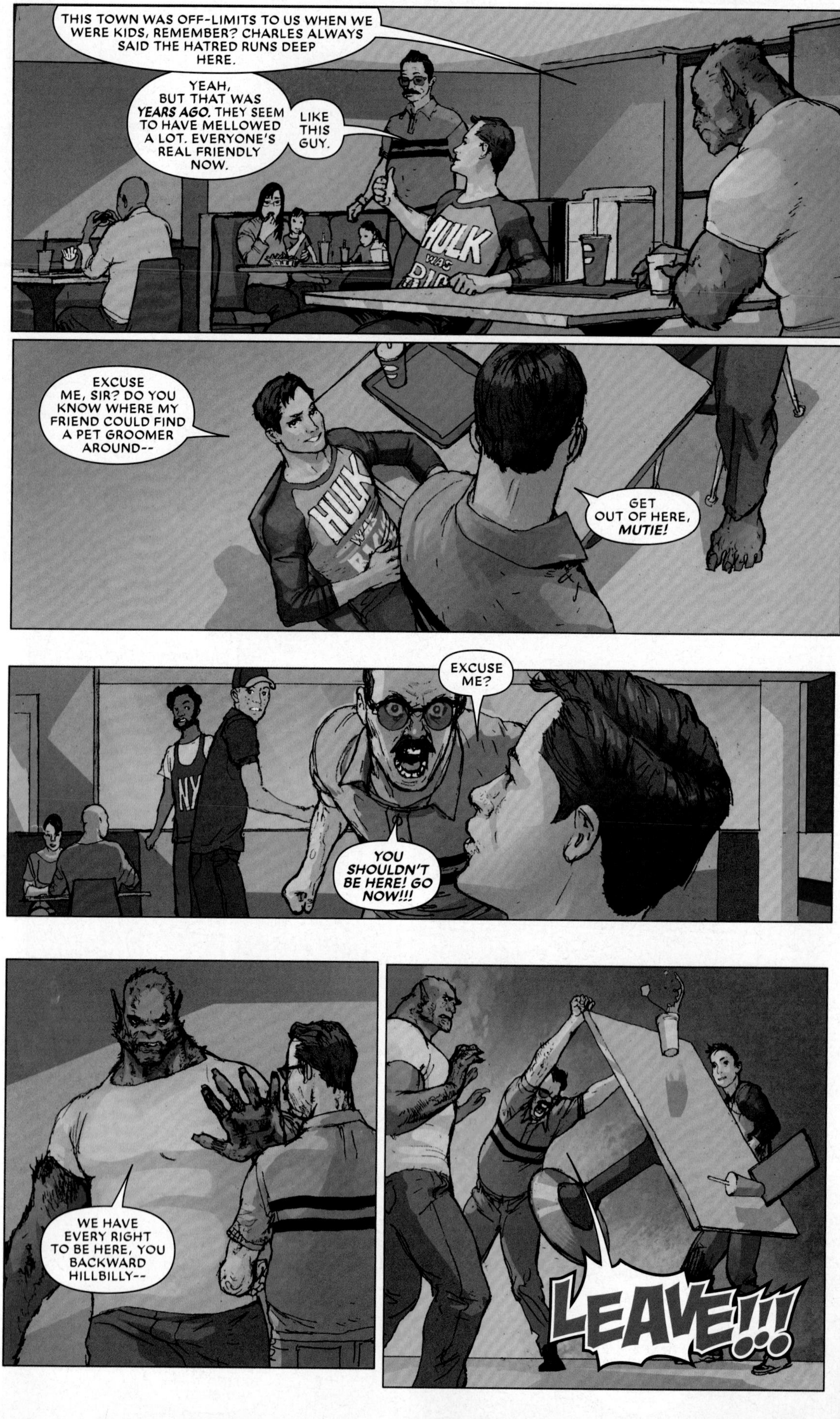
THIS TOWN WAS OFF-LIMITS TO US WHEN WE WERE KIDS, REMEMBER? CHARLES ALWAYS SAID THE HATRED RUNS DEEP HERE.
YEAH, BUT THAT WAS *YEARS AGO.* THEY SEEM TO HAVE MELLOWED A LOT. EVERYONE'S REAL FRIENDLY NOW.
LIKE THIS GUY.
HULK WAS
EXCUSE ME, SIR? DO YOU KNOW WHERE MY FRIEND COULD FIND A PET GROOMER AROUND--
GET OUT OF HERE, *MUTIE!*
EXCUSE ME?
YOU SHOULDN'T BE HERE! GO NOW!!!
WE HAVE EVERY RIGHT TO BE HERE, YOU BACKWARD HILLBILLY--
LEAVE!!!

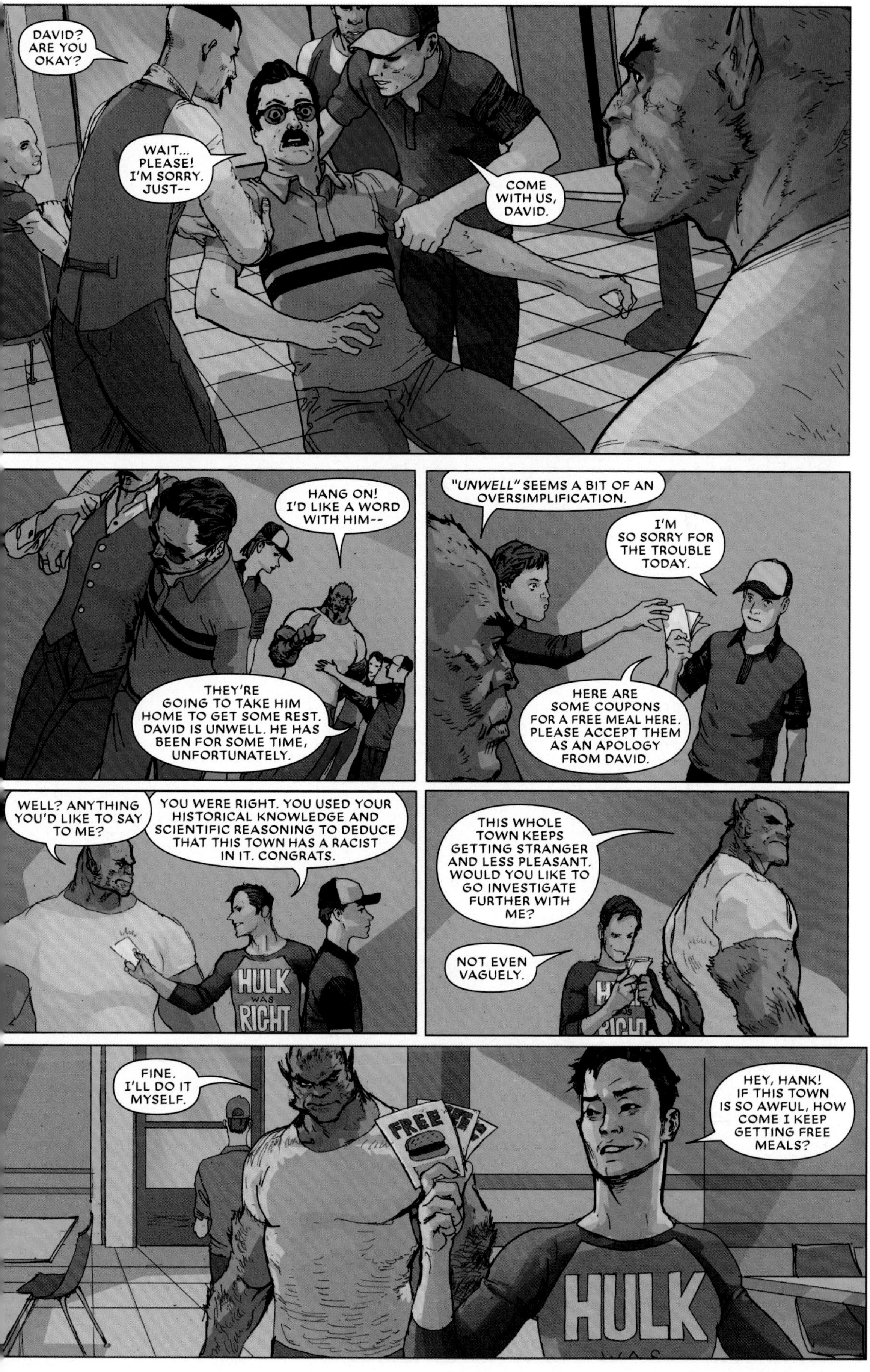
DAVID? ARE YOU OKAY?
WAIT... PLEASE! I'M SORRY. JUST--
COME WITH US, DAVID.
HANG ON! I'D LIKE A WORD WITH HIM--
THEY'RE GOING TO TAKE HIM HOME TO GET SOME REST. DAVID IS UNWELL. HE HAS BEEN FOR SOME TIME, UNFORTUNATELY.
"UNWELL" SEEMS A BIT OF AN OVERSIMPLIFICATION.
I'M SO SORRY FOR THE TROUBLE TODAY.
HERE ARE SOME COUPONS FOR A FREE MEAL HERE. PLEASE ACCEPT THEM AS AN APOLOGY FROM DAVID.
WELL? ANYTHING YOU'D LIKE TO SAY TO ME?
YOU WERE RIGHT. YOU USED YOUR HISTORICAL KNOWLEDGE AND SCIENTIFIC REASONING TO DEDUCE THAT THIS TOWN HAS A RACIST IN IT. CONGRATS.
HULK WAS RIGHT
THIS WHOLE TOWN KEEPS GETTING STRANGER AND LESS PLEASANT. WOULD YOU LIKE TO GO INVESTIGATE FURTHER WITH ME?
NOT EVEN VAGUELY.
FINE. I'LL DO IT MYSELF.
FREE
HEY, HANK! IF THIS TOWN IS SO AWFUL, HOW COME I KEEP GETTING FREE MEALS?
HULK

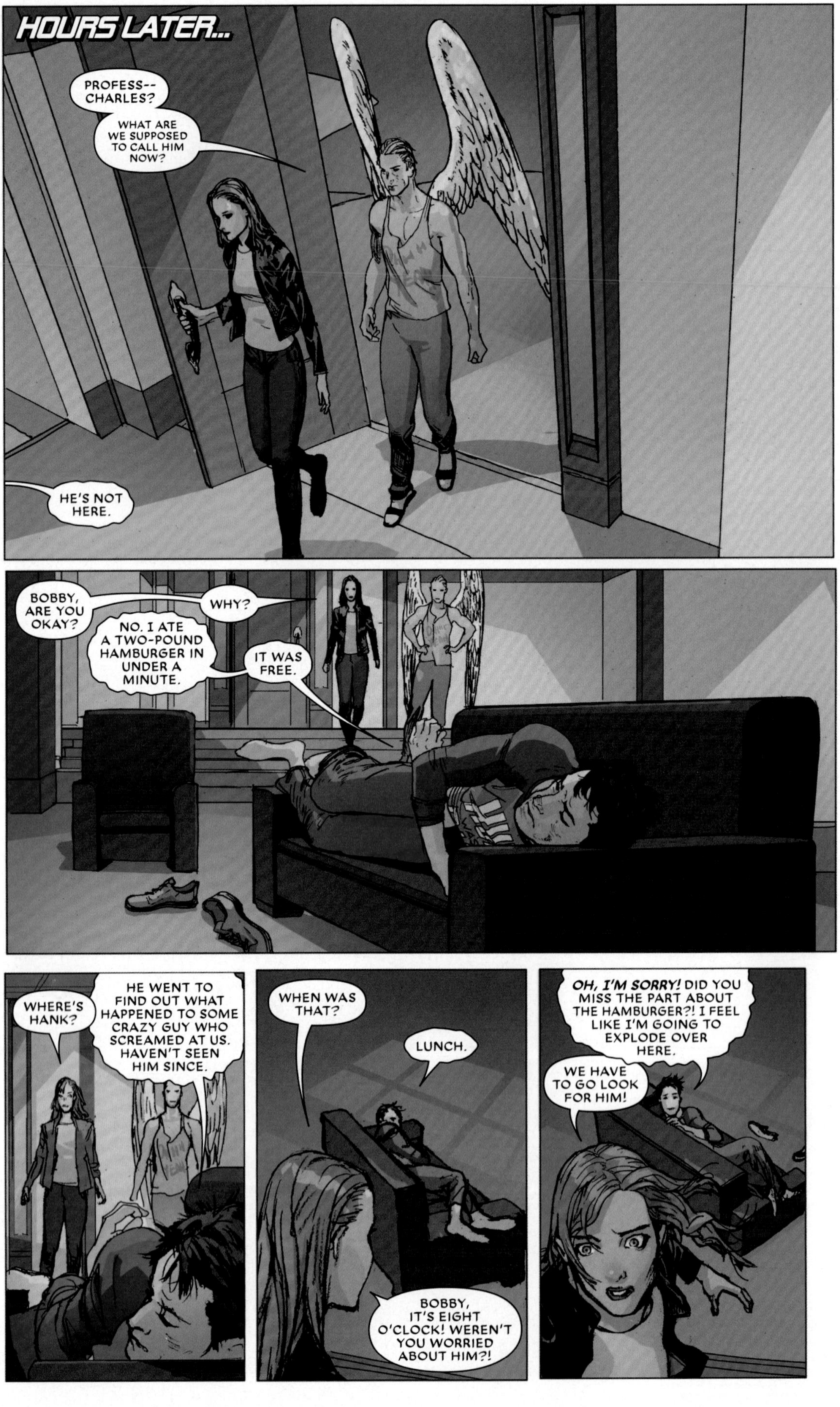
HOURS LATER...
PROFESS--CHARLES?
WHAT ARE WE SUPPOSED TO CALL HIM NOW?
HE'S NOT HERE.
BOBBY, ARE YOU OKAY?
WHY?
NO. I ATE A TWO-POUND HAMBURGER IN UNDER A MINUTE.
IT WAS FREE.
WHERE'S HANK?
HE WENT TO FIND OUT WHAT HAPPENED TO SOME CRAZY GUY WHO SCREAMED AT US. HAVEN'T SEEN HIM SINCE.
WHEN WAS THAT?
LUNCH.
BOBBY, IT'S EIGHT O'CLOCK! WEREN'T YOU WORRIED ABOUT HIM?!
OH, I'M SORRY! DID YOU MISS THE PART ABOUT THE HAMBURGER?! I FEEL LIKE I'M GOING TO EXPLODE OVER HERE.
WE HAVE TO GO LOOK FOR HIM!

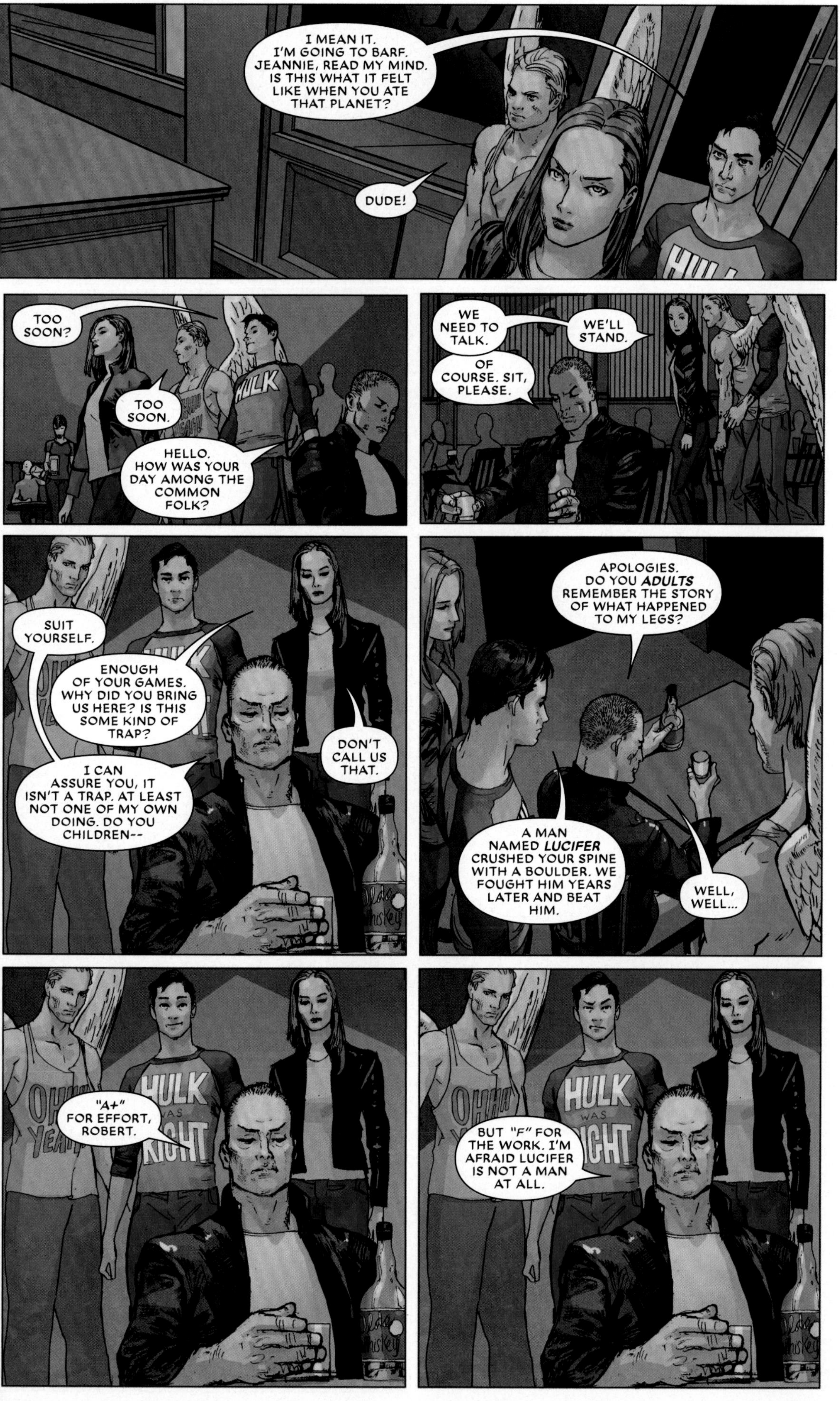
I MEAN IT. I'M GOING TO BARF. JEANNIE, READ MY MIND. IS THIS WHAT IT FELT LIKE WHEN YOU ATE THAT PLANET?
DUDE!
TOO SOON?
TOO SOON.
HELLO. HOW WAS YOUR DAY AMONG THE COMMON FOLK?
WE NEED TO TALK.
WE'LL STAND.
OF COURSE. SIT, PLEASE.
SUIT YOURSELF.
ENOUGH OF YOUR GAMES. WHY DID YOU BRING US HERE? IS THIS SOME KIND OF TRAP?
DON'T CALL US THAT.
I CAN ASSURE YOU, IT ISN'T A TRAP. AT LEAST NOT ONE OF MY OWN DOING. DO YOU CHILDREN--
APOLOGIES. DO YOU *ADULTS* REMEMBER THE STORY OF WHAT HAPPENED TO MY LEGS?
A MAN NAMED *LUCIFER* CRUSHED YOUR SPINE WITH A BOULDER. WE FOUGHT HIM YEARS LATER AND BEAT HIM.
WELL, WELL...
"A+" FOR EFFORT, ROBERT.
BUT *"F"* FOR THE WORK. I'M AFRAID LUCIFER IS NOT A MAN AT ALL.

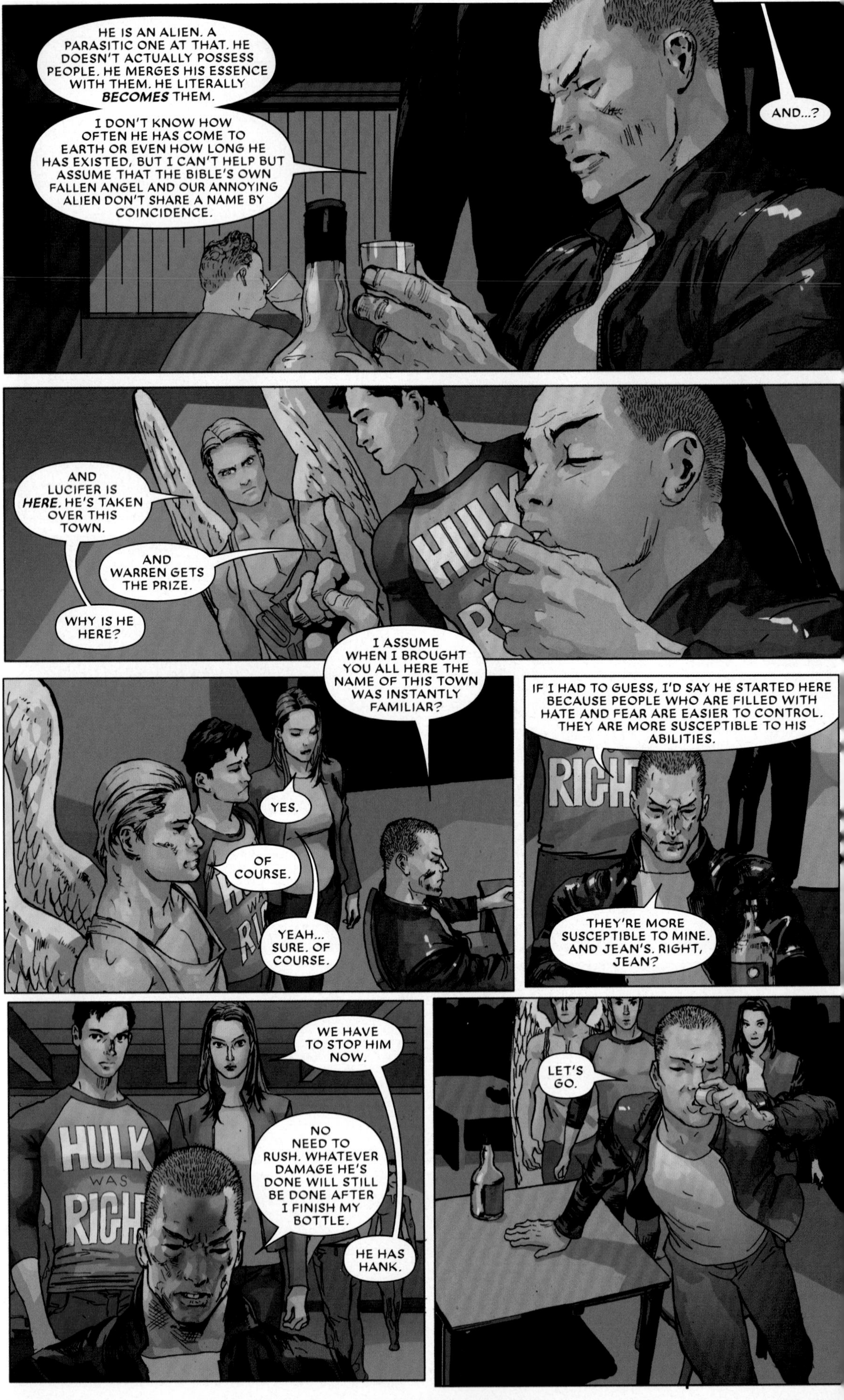
HE IS AN ALIEN. A PARASITIC ONE AT THAT. HE DOESN'T ACTUALLY POSSESS PEOPLE. HE MERGES HIS ESSENCE WITH THEM. HE LITERALLY *BECOMES* THEM.
I DON'T KNOW HOW OFTEN HE HAS COME TO EARTH OR EVEN HOW LONG HE HAS EXISTED, BUT I CAN'T HELP BUT ASSUME THAT THE BIBLE'S OWN FALLEN ANGEL AND OUR ANNOYING ALIEN DON'T SHARE A NAME BY COINCIDENCE.
AND...?
AND LUCIFER IS *HERE.* HE'S TAKEN OVER THIS TOWN.
AND WARREN GETS THE PRIZE.
WHY IS HE HERE?
I ASSUME WHEN I BROUGHT YOU ALL HERE THE NAME OF THIS TOWN WAS INSTANTLY FAMILIAR?
YES.
OF COURSE.
YEAH... SURE. OF COURSE.
IF I HAD TO GUESS, I'D SAY HE STARTED HERE BECAUSE PEOPLE WHO ARE FILLED WITH HATE AND FEAR ARE EASIER TO CONTROL. THEY ARE MORE SUSCEPTIBLE TO HIS ABILITIES.
THEY'RE MORE SUSCEPTIBLE TO MINE. AND JEAN'S. RIGHT, JEAN?
WE HAVE TO STOP HIM NOW.
NO NEED TO RUSH. WHATEVER DAMAGE HE'S DONE WILL STILL BE DONE AFTER I FINISH MY BOTTLE.
HE HAS HANK.
LET'S GO.

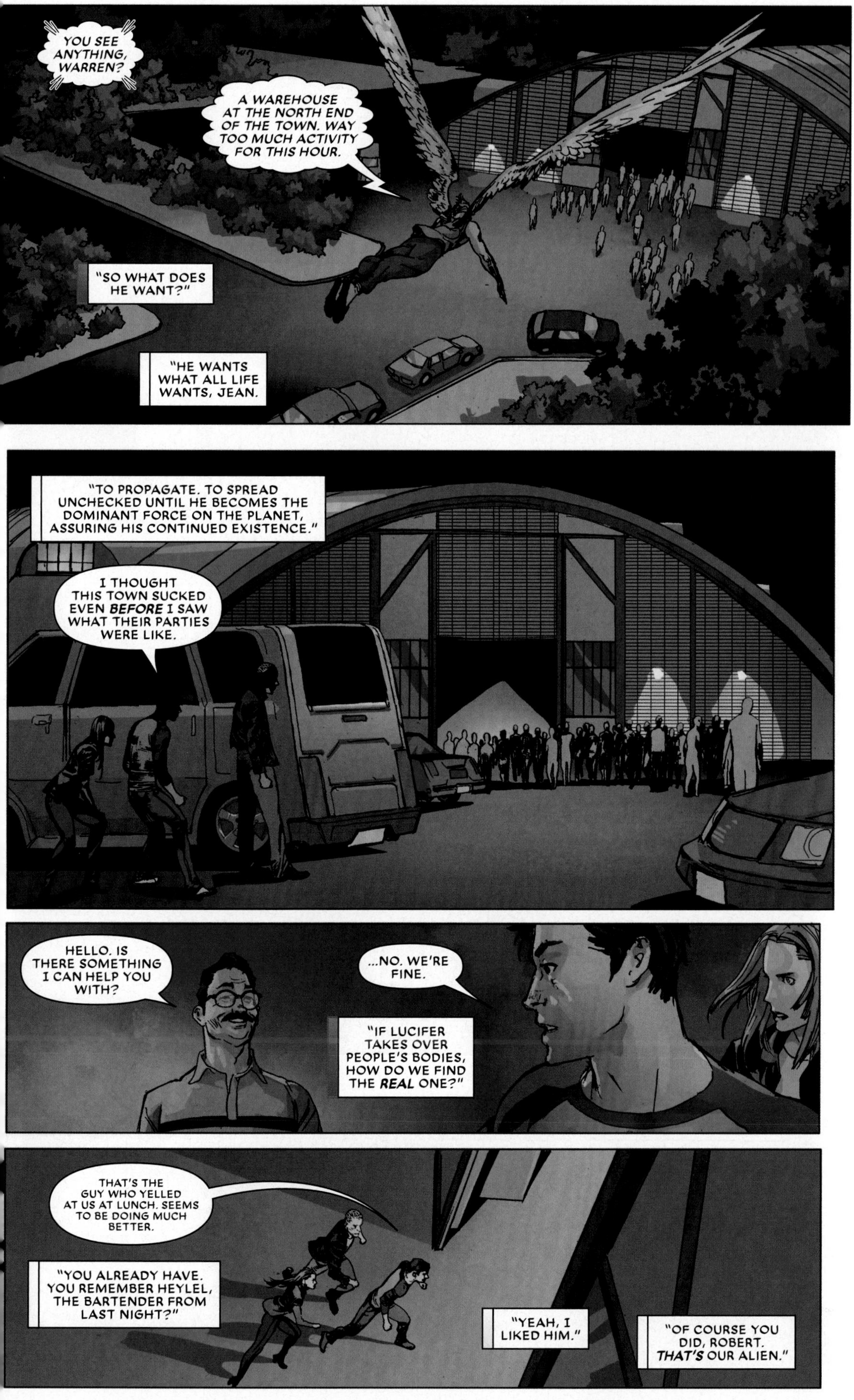
YOU SEE ANYTHING, WARREN?
A WAREHOUSE AT THE NORTH END OF THE TOWN. WAY TOO MUCH ACTIVITY FOR THIS HOUR.
"SO WHAT DOES HE WANT?"
"HE WANTS WHAT ALL LIFE WANTS, JEAN.
"TO PROPAGATE. TO SPREAD UNCHECKED UNTIL HE BECOMES THE DOMINANT FORCE ON THE PLANET, ASSURING HIS CONTINUED EXISTENCE."
I THOUGHT THIS TOWN SUCKED EVEN BEFORE I SAW WHAT THEIR PARTIES WERE LIKE.
HELLO. IS THERE SOMETHING I CAN HELP YOU WITH?
...NO. WE'RE FINE.
"IF LUCIFER TAKES OVER PEOPLE'S BODIES, HOW DO WE FIND THE REAL ONE?"
THAT'S THE GUY WHO YELLED AT US AT LUNCH. SEEMS TO BE DOING MUCH BETTER.
"YOU ALREADY HAVE. YOU REMEMBER HEYLEL, THE BARTENDER FROM LAST NIGHT?"
"YEAH, I LIKED HIM."
"OF COURSE YOU DID, ROBERT. THAT'S OUR ALIEN."

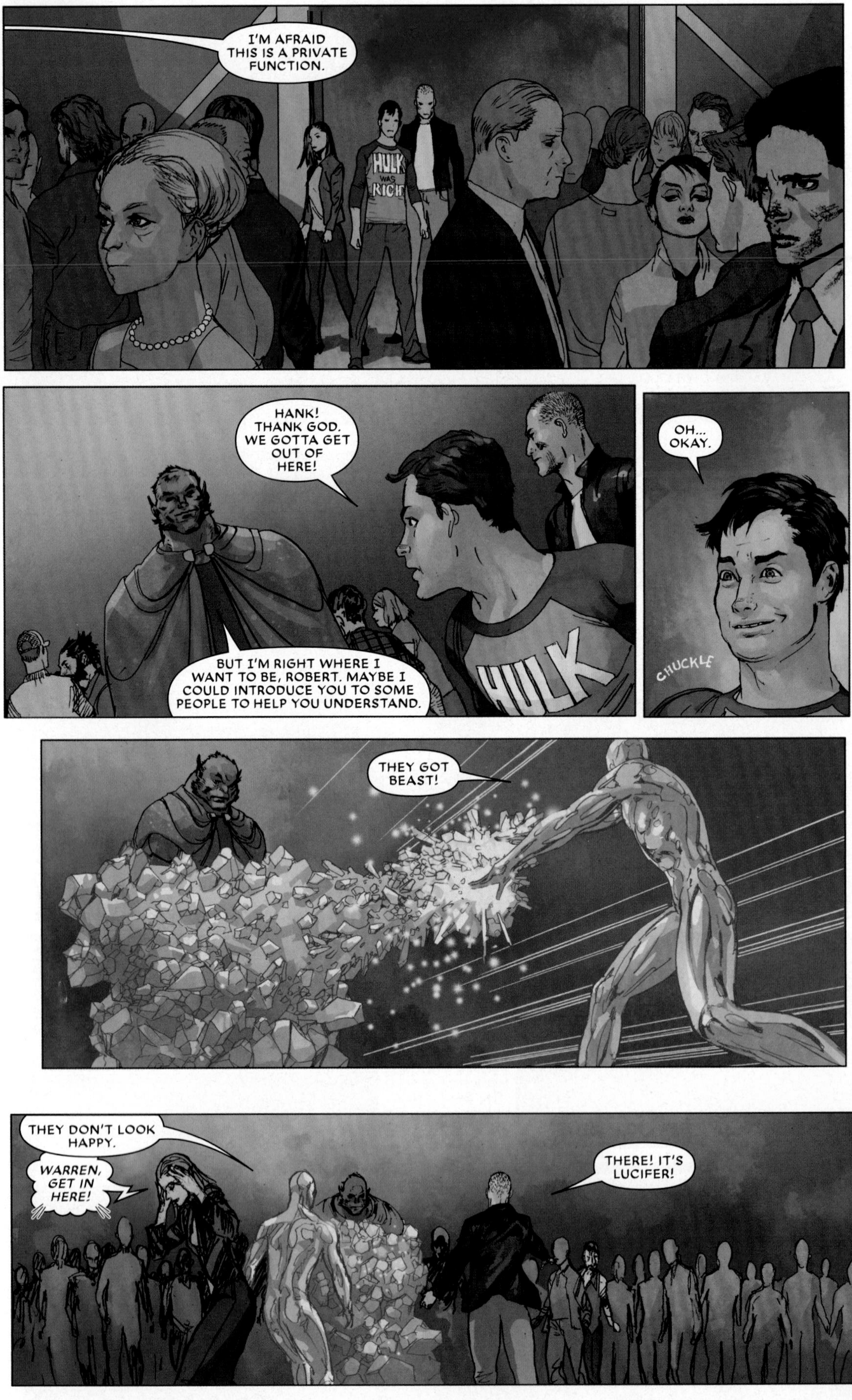
I'M AFRAID THIS IS A PRIVATE FUNCTION.
HULK WAS RIGHT
HANK! THANK GOD. WE GOTTA GET OUT OF HERE!
BUT I'M RIGHT WHERE I WANT TO BE, ROBERT. MAYBE I COULD INTRODUCE YOU TO SOME PEOPLE TO HELP YOU UNDERSTAND.
HULK
OH... OKAY.
CHUCKLE
THEY GOT BEAST!
THEY DON'T LOOK HAPPY.
WARREN, GET IN HERE!
THERE! IT'S LUCIFER!

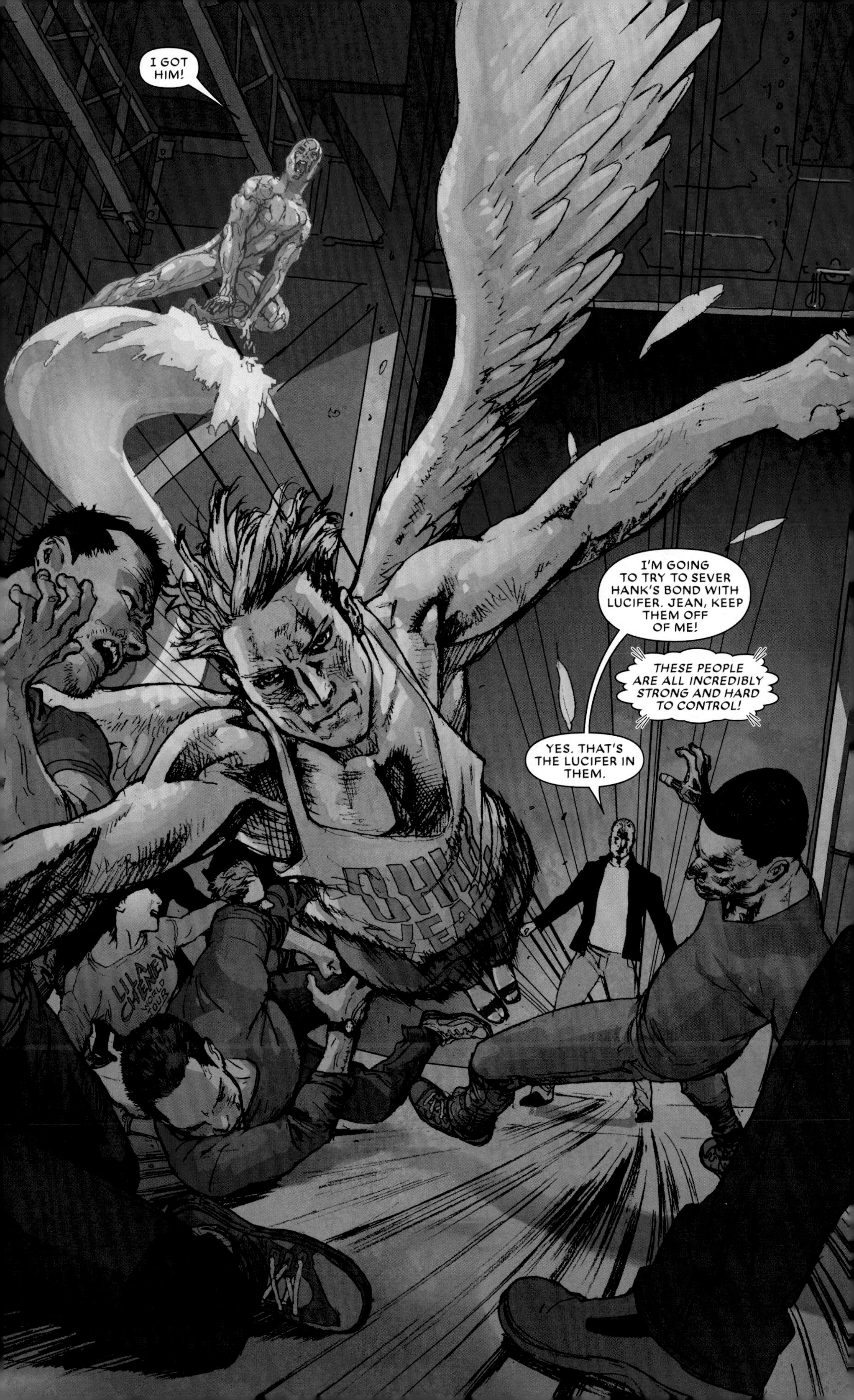
I GOT HIM!
I'M GOING TO TRY TO SEVER HANK'S BOND WITH LUCIFER. JEAN, KEEP THEM OFF OF ME!
THESE PEOPLE ARE ALL INCREDIBLY STRONG AND HARD TO CONTROL!
YES. THAT'S THE LUCIFER IN THEM.

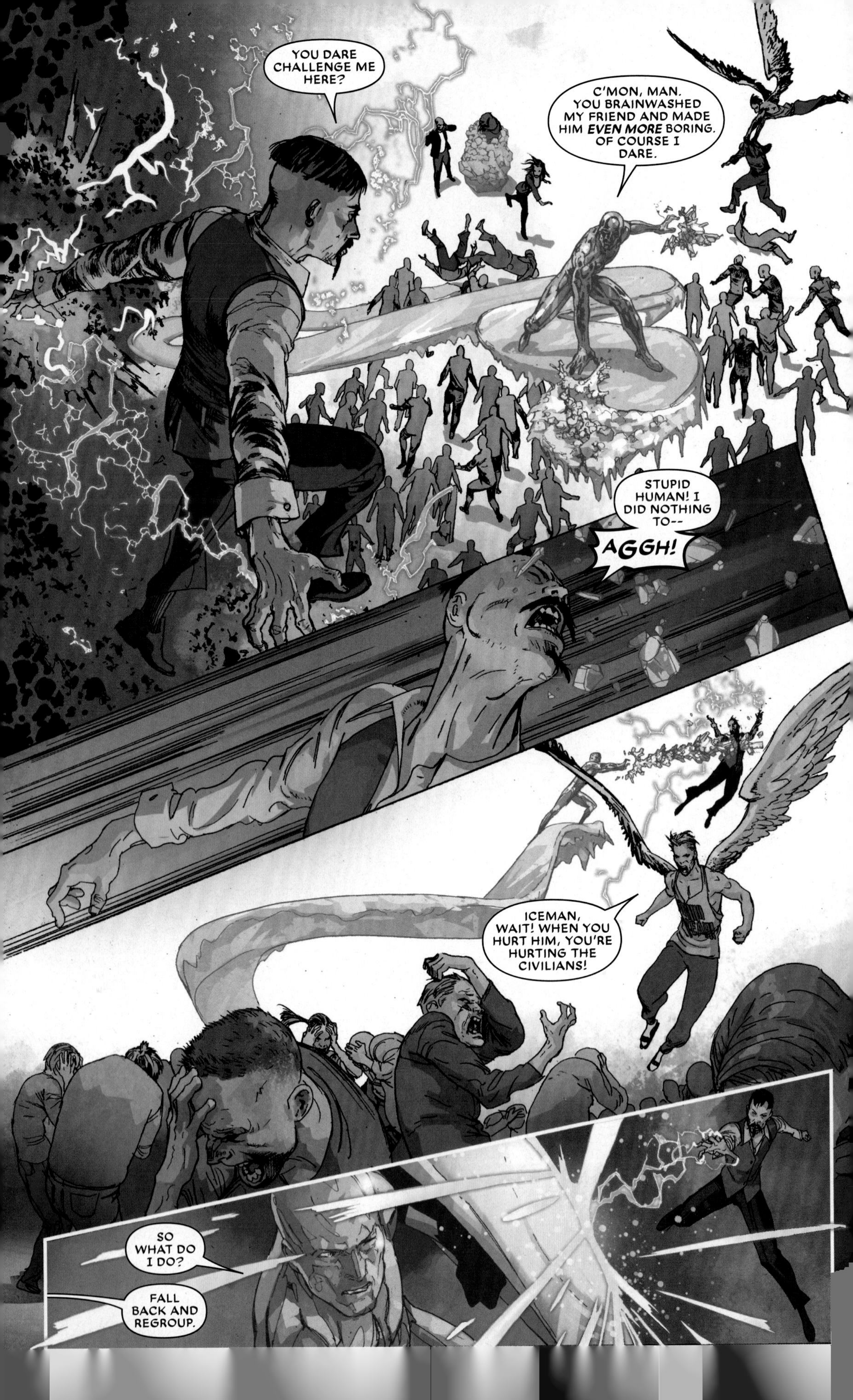
YOU DARE CHALLENGE ME HERE?
C'MON, MAN. YOU BRAINWASHED MY FRIEND AND MADE HIM *EVEN MORE* BORING. OF COURSE I DARE.
STUPID HUMAN! I DID NOTHING TO--
AGGH!
ICEMAN, WAIT! WHEN YOU HURT HIM, YOU'RE HURTING THE CIVILIANS!
SO WHAT DO I DO?
FALL BACK AND REGROUP.

HOW WE DOING HERE?

THIS ISN'T LIKE FLIPPING A SWITCH. I HAVE TO REROUTE HIS BRAIN FUNCTIONS AROUND THE PART LUCIFER TOOK.

LUCKILY, HE HAS JUST BEEN TURNED, SO IT'S EASY TO RECOGNIZE WHAT IS HANK'S AND WHAT ISN'T.

GRRAARGG!

HEADS UP! HE'S LOOSE!

WAIT...

?

...IT'S ALL RIGHT. HE'S BACK TO NORMAL.

HANK? YOU OKAY?

JEANNIE... WHAT DID YOU DO TO ME?

NO, IT WAS LUCIFER. HE--

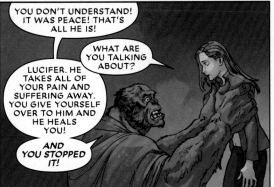

YOU DON'T UNDERSTAND! IT WAS PEACE! THAT'S ALL HE IS!

WHAT ARE YOU TALKING ABOUT?

LUCIFER. HE TAKES ALL OF YOUR PAIN AND SUFFERING AWAY. YOU GIVE YOURSELF OVER TO HIM AND HE HEALS YOU!

AND YOU STOPPED IT!

NO, YOU'RE JUST CONFUSED. IT'S GOING TO BE OKAY.

I GAVE UP A LITTLE BIT OF MYSELF TO HIM AND FOR A MOMENT I FELT GOOD. AND YOU TOOK IT FROM ME.

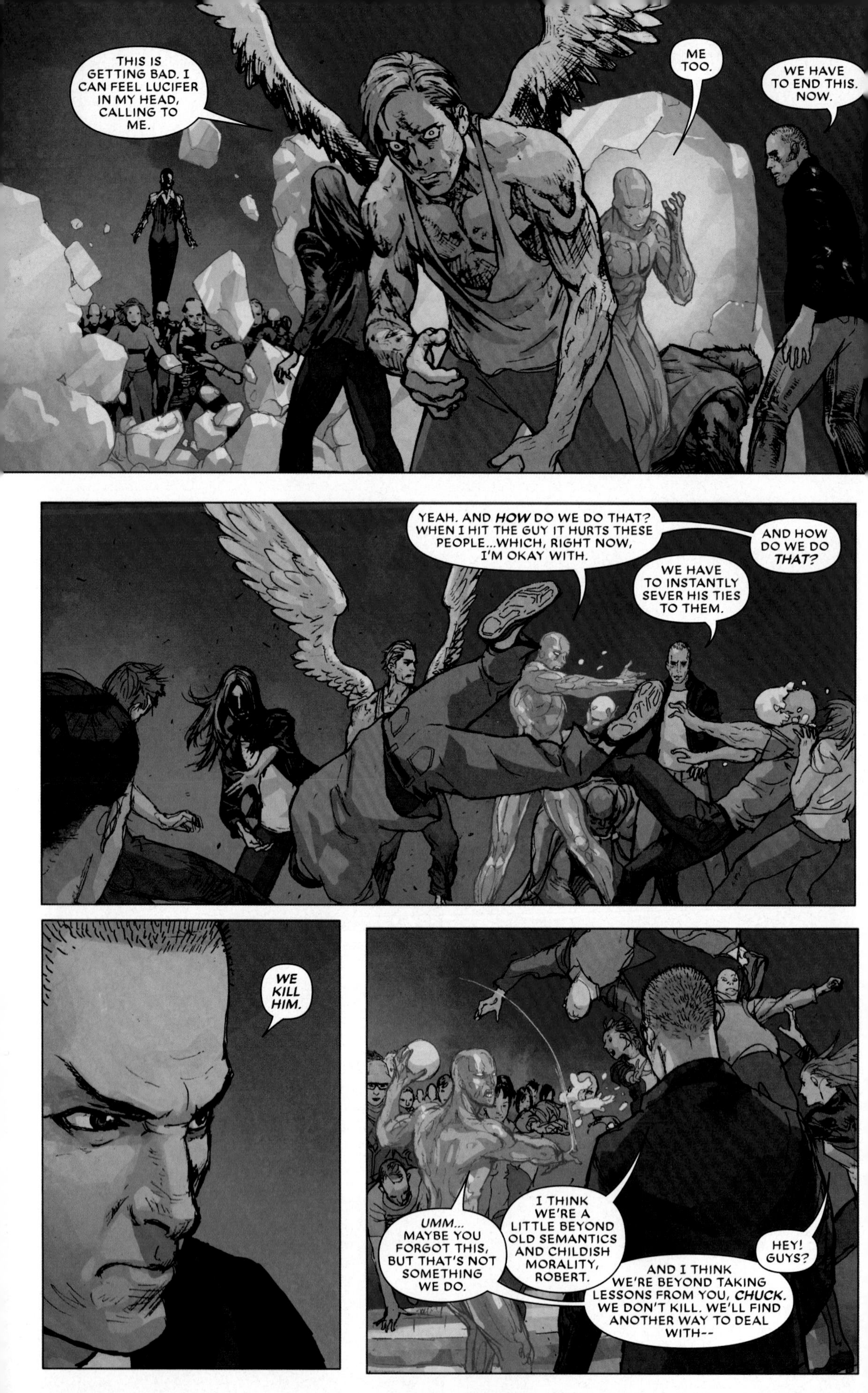
THIS IS GETTING BAD. I CAN FEEL LUCIFER IN MY HEAD, CALLING TO ME.
ME TOO.
WE HAVE TO END THIS. NOW.
YEAH. AND HOW DO WE DO THAT? WHEN I HIT THE GUY IT HURTS THESE PEOPLE...WHICH, RIGHT NOW, I'M OKAY WITH.
WE HAVE TO INSTANTLY SEVER HIS TIES TO THEM.
AND HOW DO WE DO THAT?
WE KILL HIM.
UMM... MAYBE YOU FORGOT THIS, BUT THAT'S NOT SOMETHING WE DO.
I THINK WE'RE A LITTLE BEYOND OLD SEMANTICS AND CHILDISH MORALITY, ROBERT.
HEY! GUYS?
AND I THINK WE'RE BEYOND TAKING LESSONS FROM YOU, CHUCK. WE DON'T KILL. WE'LL FIND ANOTHER WAY TO DEAL WITH--

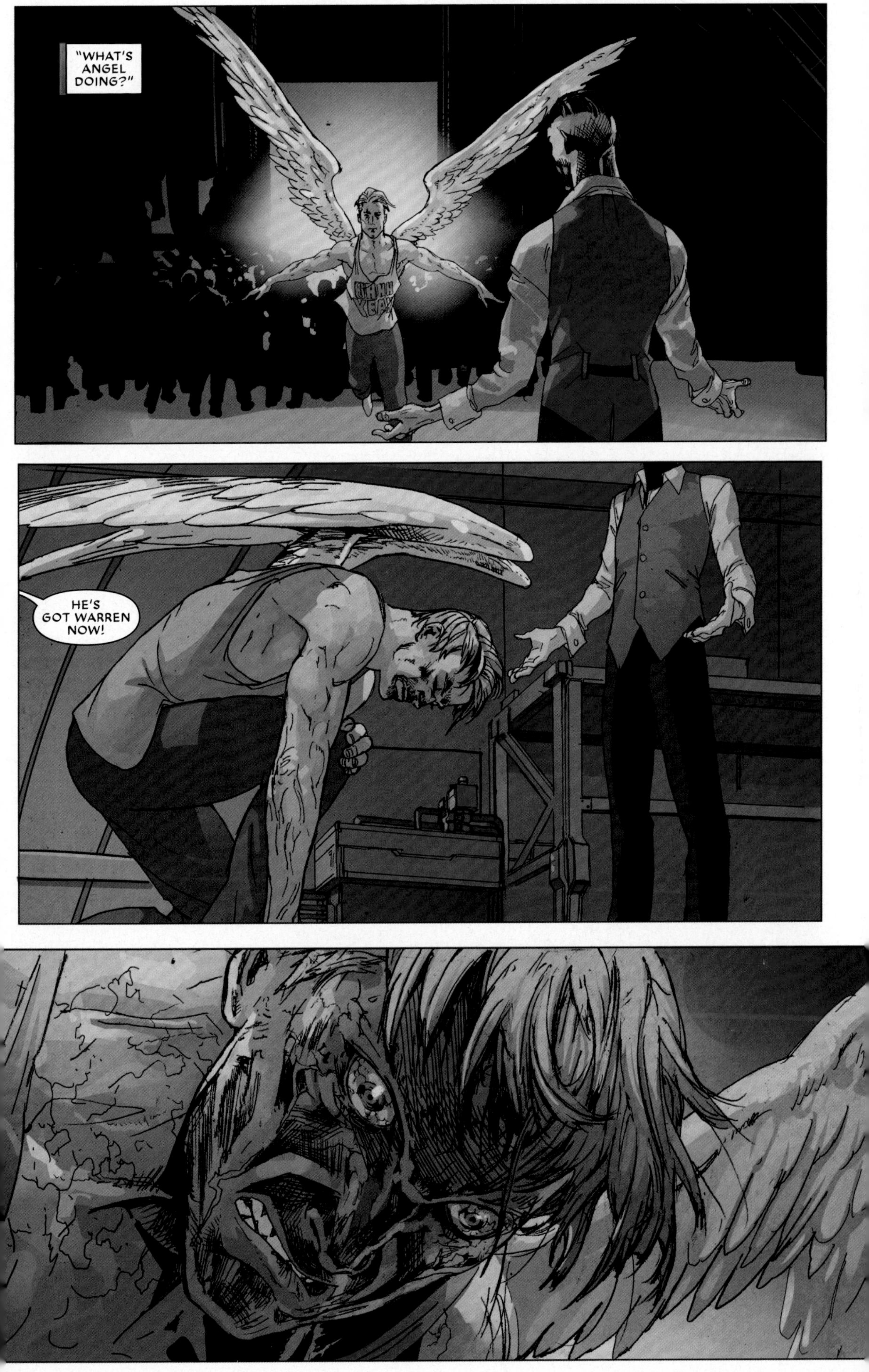
"WHAT'S ANGEL DOING?"
HE'S GOT WARREN NOW!

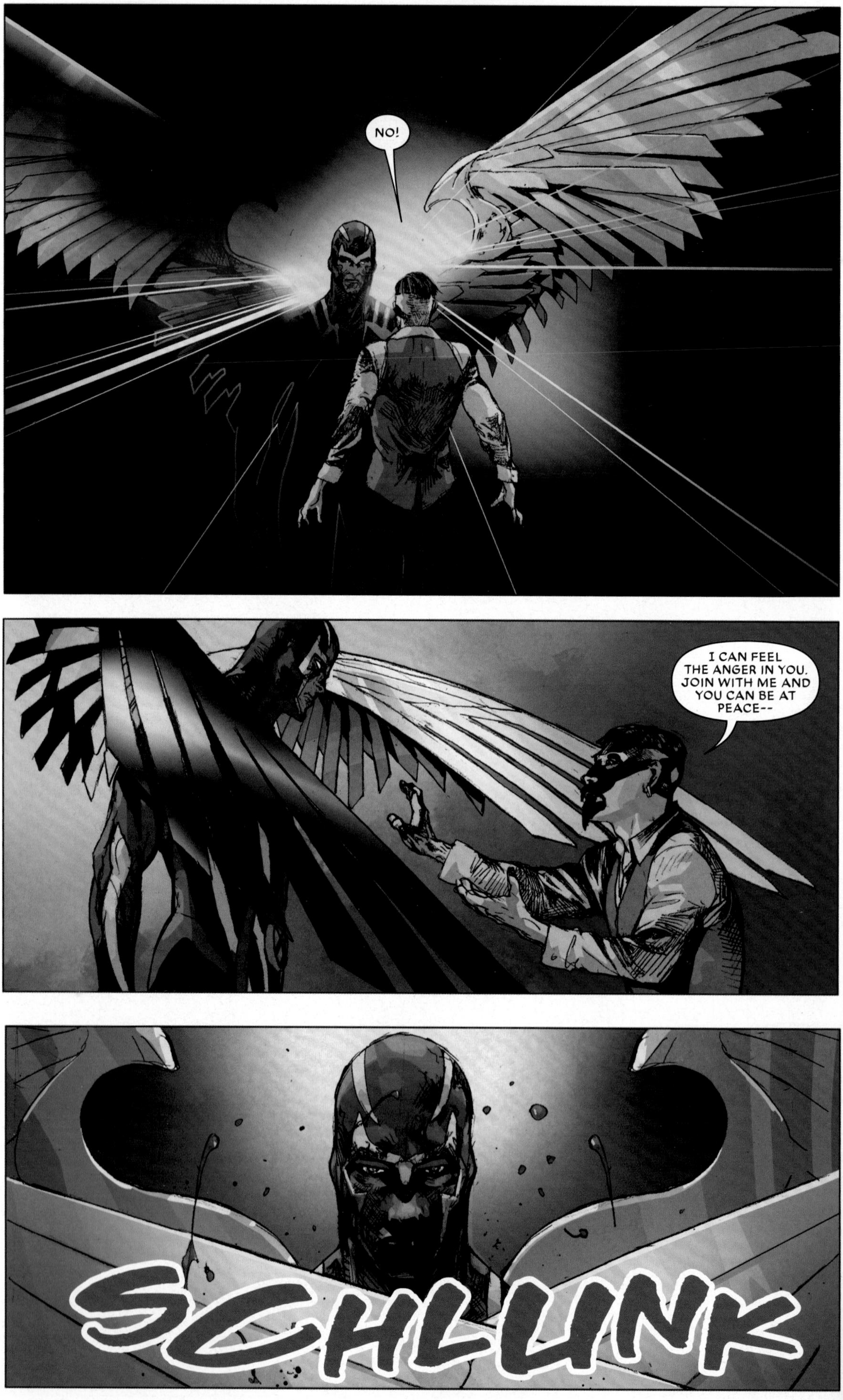
NO!
I CAN FEEL THE ANGER IN YOU. JOIN WITH ME AND YOU CAN BE AT PEACE--
SCHLUNK

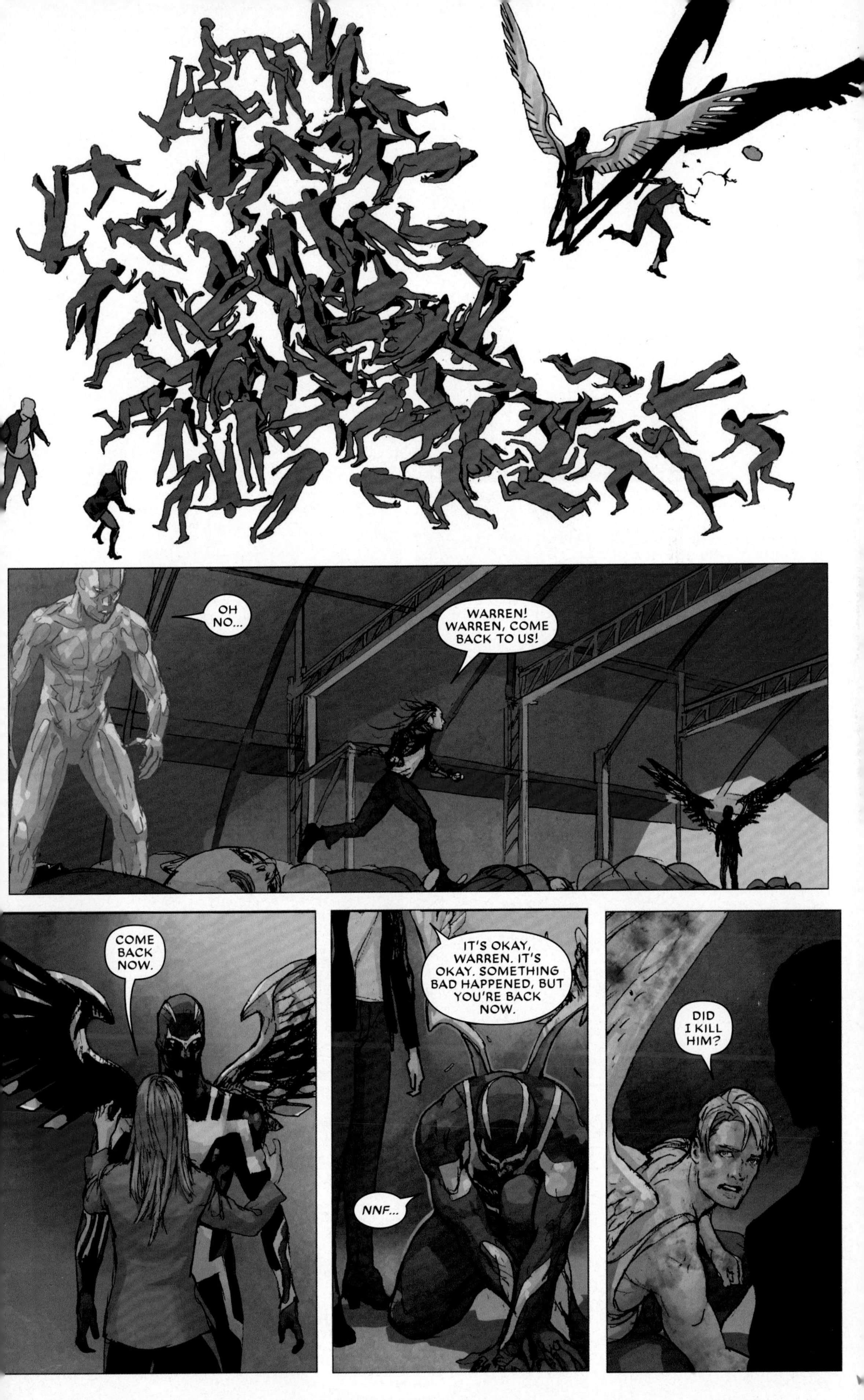
OH NO...
WARREN! WARREN, COME BACK TO US!
COME BACK NOW.
IT'S OKAY, WARREN. IT'S OKAY. SOMETHING BAD HAPPENED, BUT YOU'RE BACK NOW.
NNF...
DID I KILL HIM?

YES. WERE YOU... TRYING TO?

CHARLES WAS RIGHT. HE HAD TO BE STOPPED. HE WAS TOO POWERFUL.

I COULD FEEL HIM IN MY SKULL. TELLING ME THAT EVERYTHING WAS FINE. MAKING ME FEEL LIKE NOTHING WAS GOING WRONG. THE PULL OF SOMETHING LIKE THAT... A LIFE WITHOUT TROUBLE.

THE WORLD WOULD FALL TO HIM WITHOUT EVER FIRING A SHOT.

THE TOWNSPEOPLE... THEY'RE ALL DEAD.

OH GOD. HANK?

I'M ALIVE. IT FEELS LIKE SOMETHING WAS JUST RIPPED OUT OF MY SKULL, BUT I'M ALIVE.

YOU! YOU MADE WARREN DO THIS!

MADE HIM? NO. I DIDN'T MAKE HIM DO ANYTHING.

BUT YOU KNEW IT WOULD HAPPEN. THESE PEOPLE'S BLOOD IS ON YOUR HANDS. NOT WARREN'S.

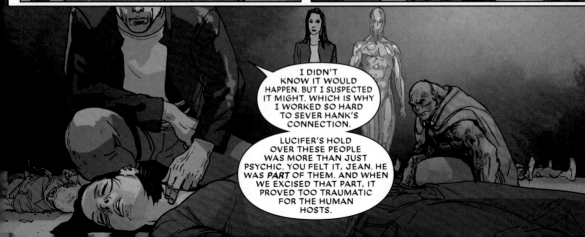

I DIDN'T KNOW IT WOULD HAPPEN. BUT I SUSPECTED IT MIGHT. WHICH IS WHY I WORKED SO HARD TO SEVER HANK'S CONNECTION.

LUCIFER'S HOLD OVER THESE PEOPLE WAS MORE THAN JUST PSYCHIC. YOU FELT IT, JEAN. HE WAS PART OF THEM. AND WHEN WE EXCISED THAT PART, IT PROVED TOO TRAUMATIC FOR THE HUMAN HOSTS.

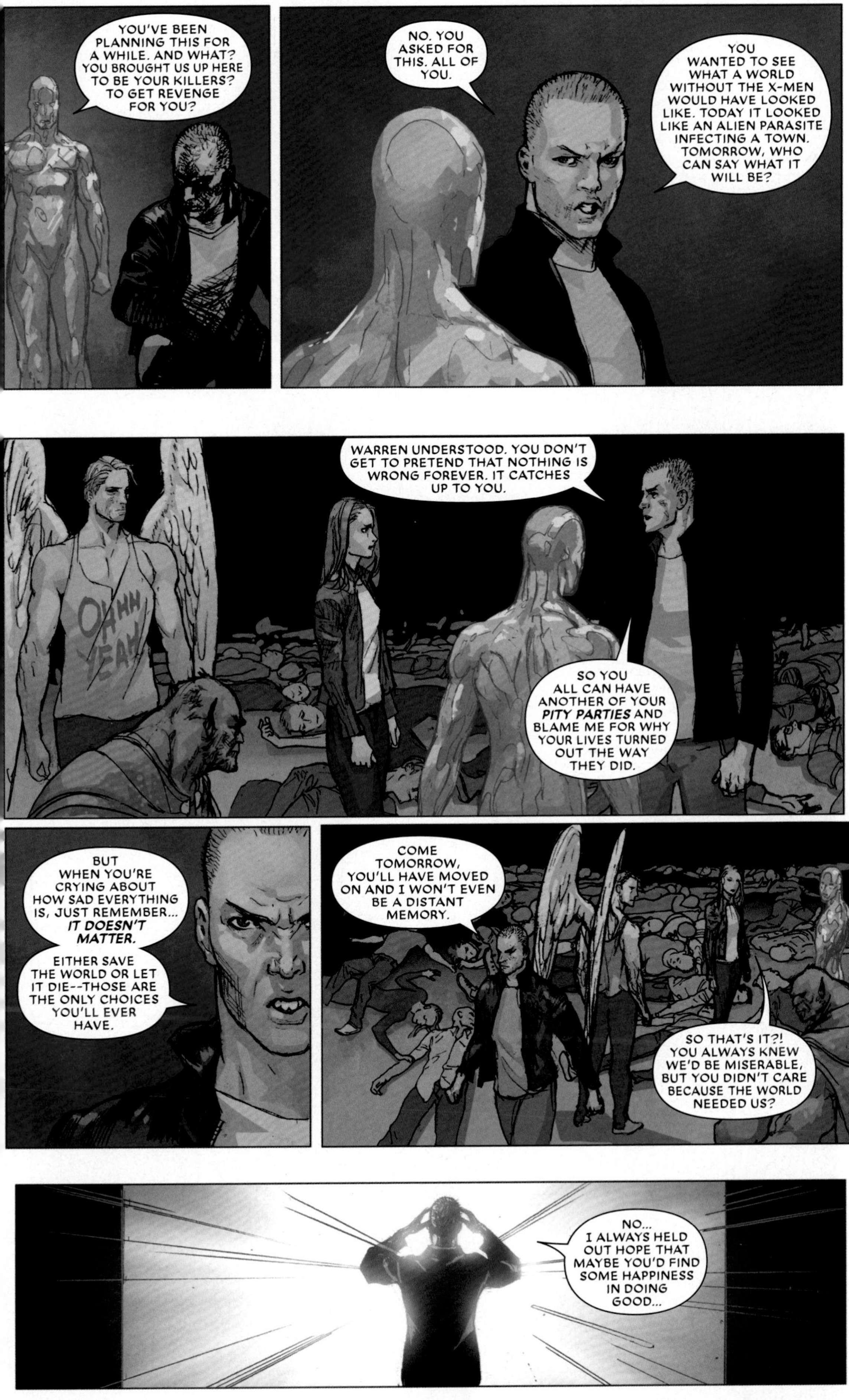
YOU'VE BEEN PLANNING THIS FOR A WHILE. AND WHAT? YOU BROUGHT US UP HERE TO BE YOUR KILLERS? TO GET REVENGE FOR YOU?
NO. YOU ASKED FOR THIS. ALL OF YOU.
YOU WANTED TO SEE WHAT A WORLD WITHOUT THE X-MEN WOULD HAVE LOOKED LIKE. TODAY IT LOOKED LIKE AN ALIEN PARASITE INFECTING A TOWN. TOMORROW, WHO CAN SAY WHAT IT WILL BE?
WARREN UNDERSTOOD. YOU DON'T GET TO PRETEND THAT NOTHING IS WRONG FOREVER. IT CATCHES UP TO YOU.
OHHH YEAH
SO YOU ALL CAN HAVE ANOTHER OF YOUR *PITY PARTIES* AND BLAME ME FOR WHY YOUR LIVES TURNED OUT THE WAY THEY DID.
BUT WHEN YOU'RE CRYING ABOUT HOW SAD EVERYTHING IS, JUST REMEMBER... ***IT DOESN'T MATTER.***
EITHER SAVE THE WORLD OR LET IT DIE--THOSE ARE THE ONLY CHOICES YOU'LL EVER HAVE.
COME TOMORROW, YOU'LL HAVE MOVED ON AND I WON'T EVEN BE A DISTANT MEMORY.
SO THAT'S IT?! YOU ALWAYS KNEW WE'D BE MISERABLE, BUT YOU DIDN'T CARE BECAUSE THE WORLD NEEDED US?
NO... I ALWAYS HELD OUT HOPE THAT MAYBE YOU'D FIND SOME HAPPINESS IN DOING GOOD...

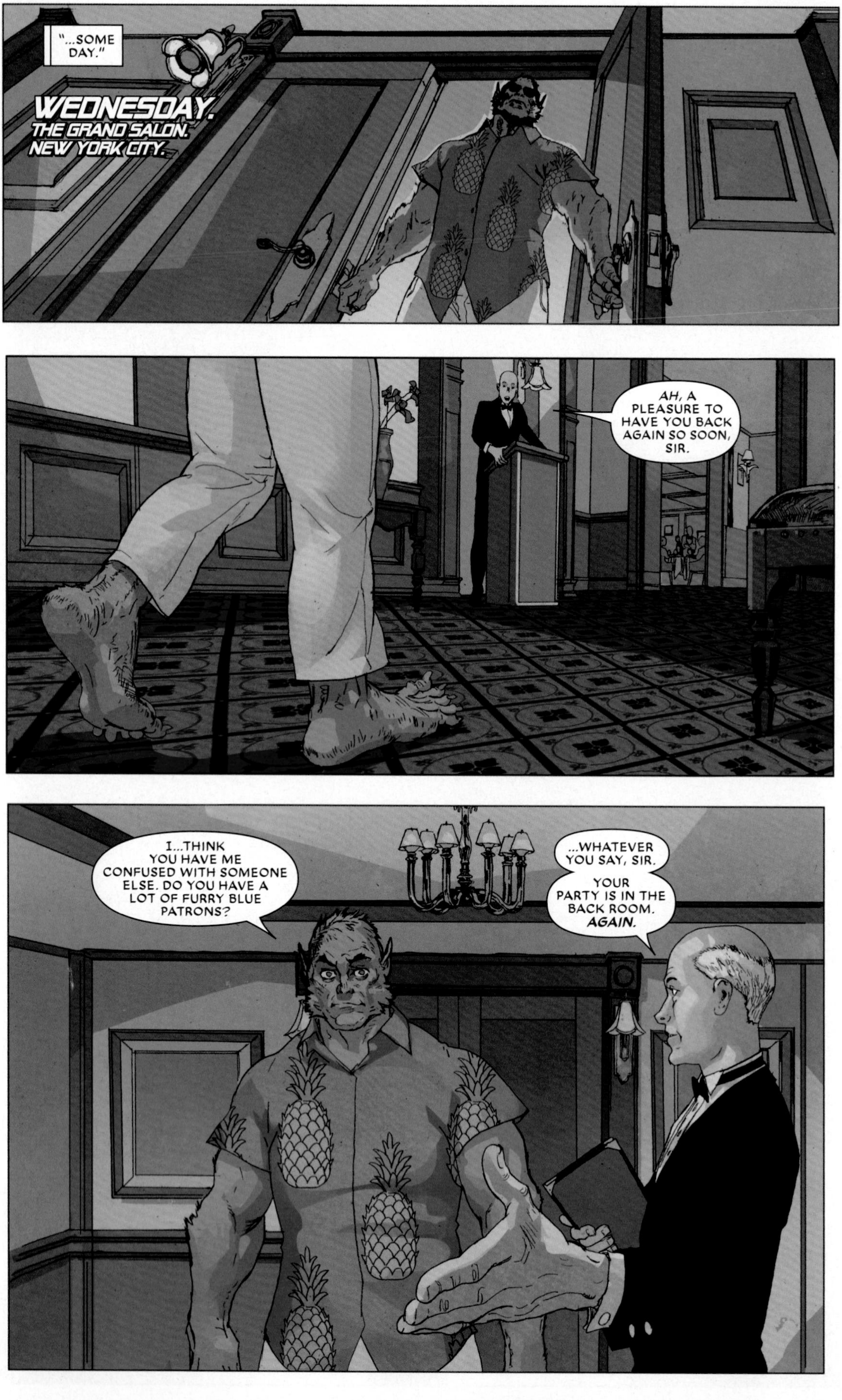
"...SOME DAY."
WEDNESDAY. THE GRAND SALON. NEW YORK CITY.
AH, A PLEASURE TO HAVE YOU BACK AGAIN SO SOON, SIR.
I...THINK YOU HAVE ME CONFUSED WITH SOMEONE ELSE. DO YOU HAVE A LOT OF FURRY BLUE PATRONS?
...WHATEVER YOU SAY, SIR.
YOUR PARTY IS IN THE BACK ROOM. AGAIN.

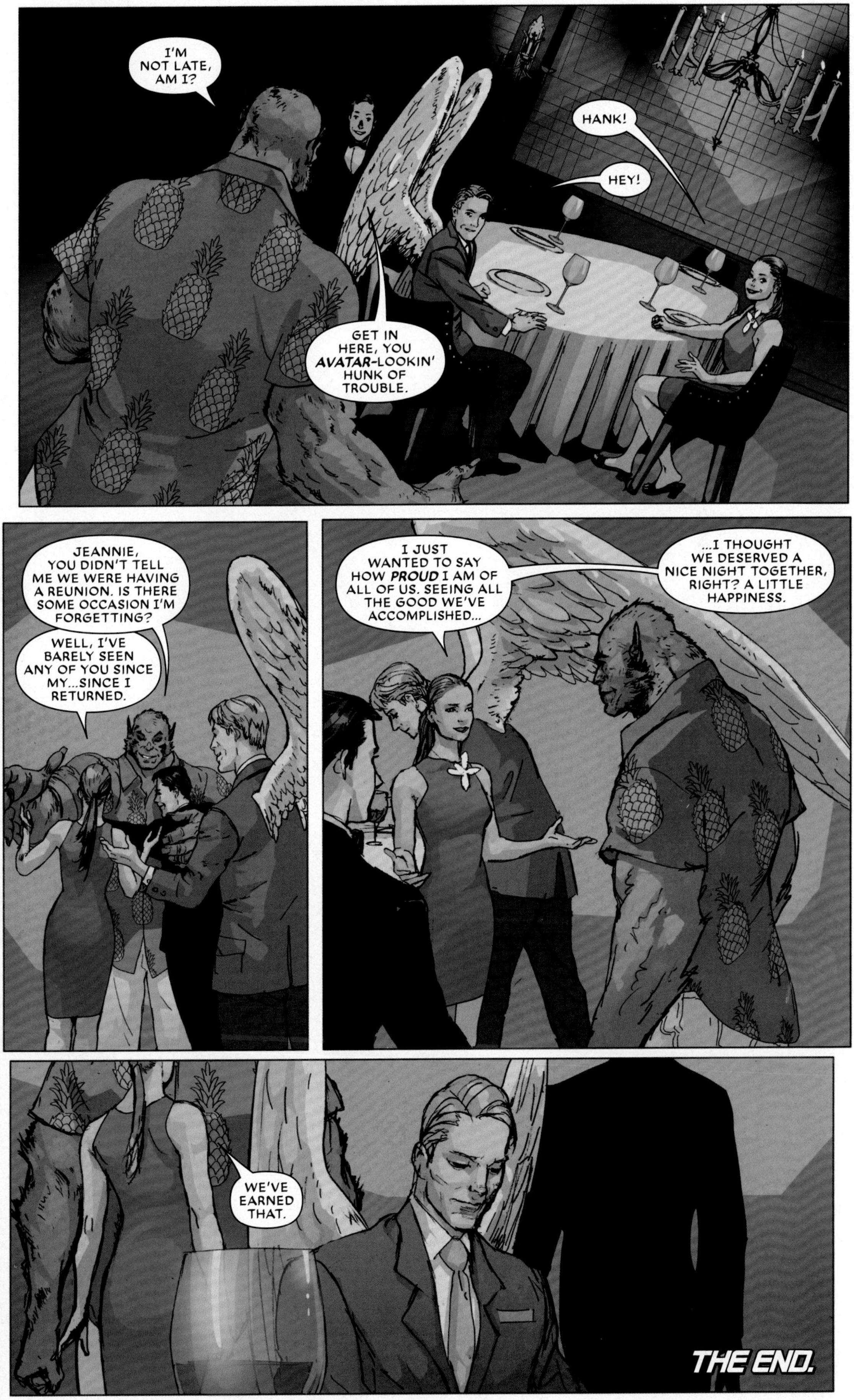
I'M NOT LATE, AM I?
HANK!
HEY!
GET IN HERE, YOU AVATAR-LOOKIN' HUNK OF TROUBLE.
JEANNIE, YOU DIDN'T TELL ME WE WERE HAVING A REUNION. IS THERE SOME OCCASION I'M FORGETTING?
WELL, I'VE BARELY SEEN ANY OF YOU SINCE MY...SINCE I RETURNED.
I JUST WANTED TO SAY HOW PROUD I AM OF ALL OF US. SEEING ALL THE GOOD WE'VE ACCOMPLISHED...
...I THOUGHT WE DESERVED A NICE NIGHT TOGETHER, RIGHT? A LITTLE HAPPINESS.
WE'VE EARNED THAT.
THE END.

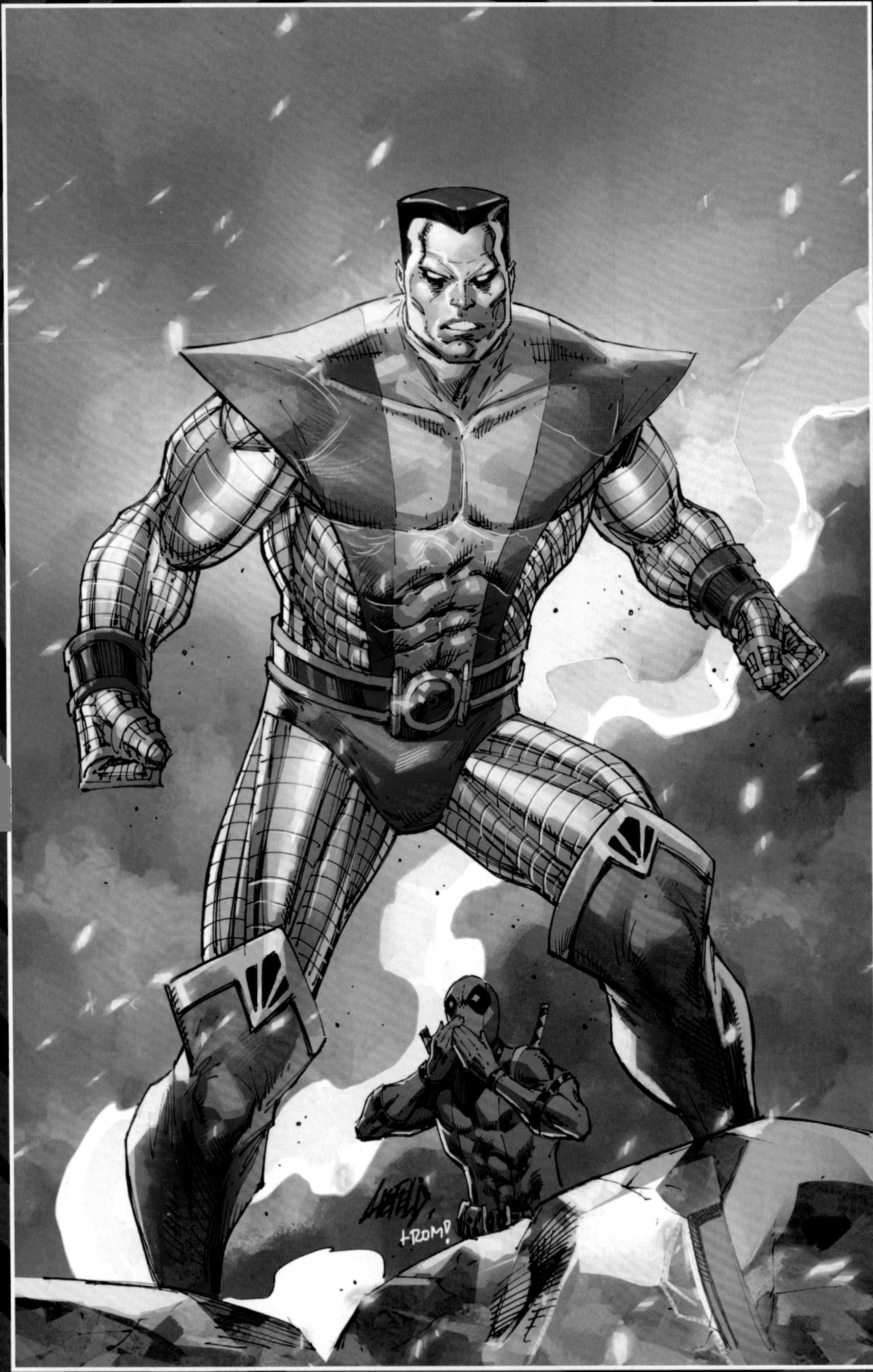

#13 VARIANT BY **ROB LIEFELD** & **ROMULO FAJARDO JR.**

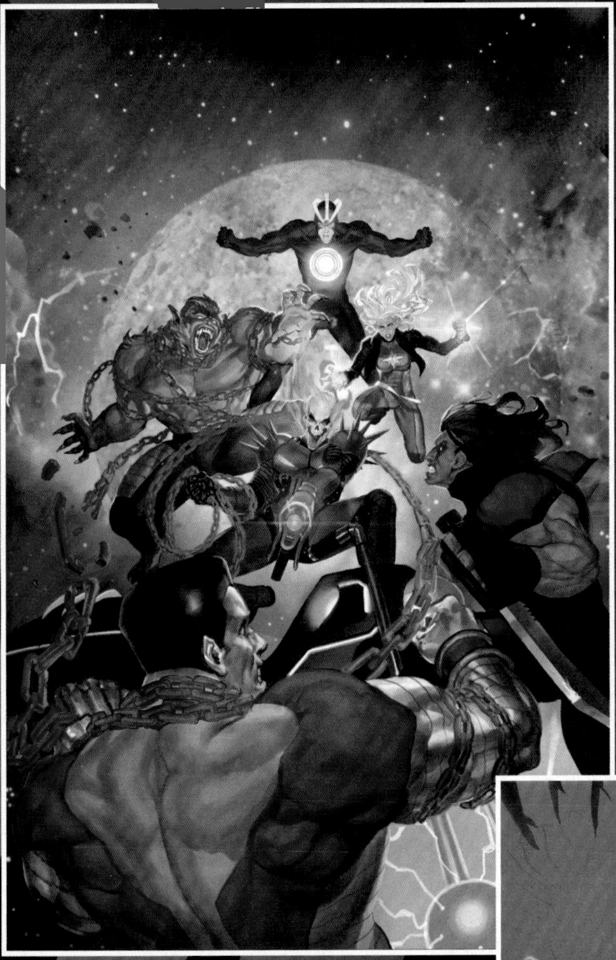

#15 COSMIC GHOST RIDER VS. VARIANT BY **AKCHO**

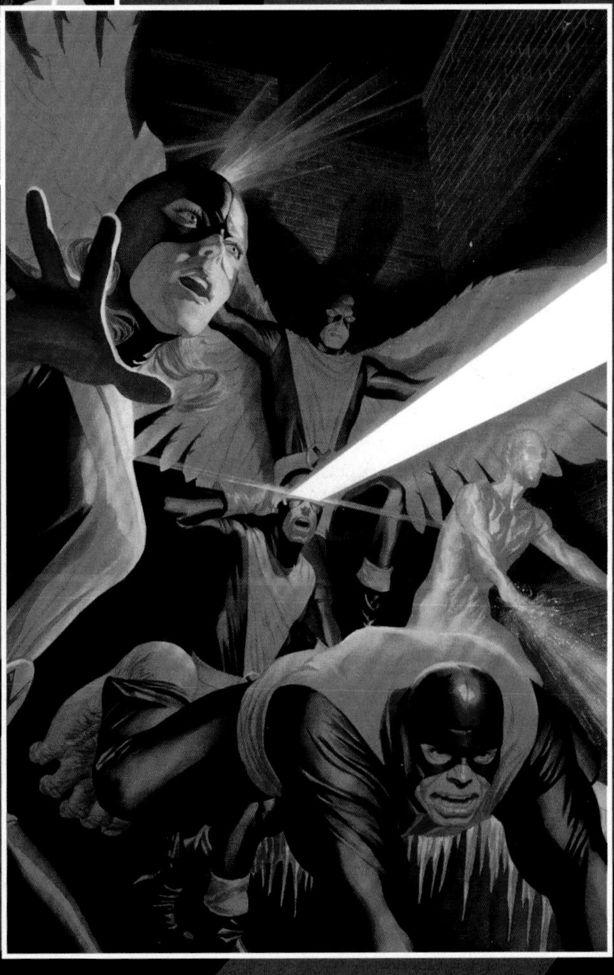

#17 UNCANNY X-MEN VARIANT BY **ALEX ROSS**

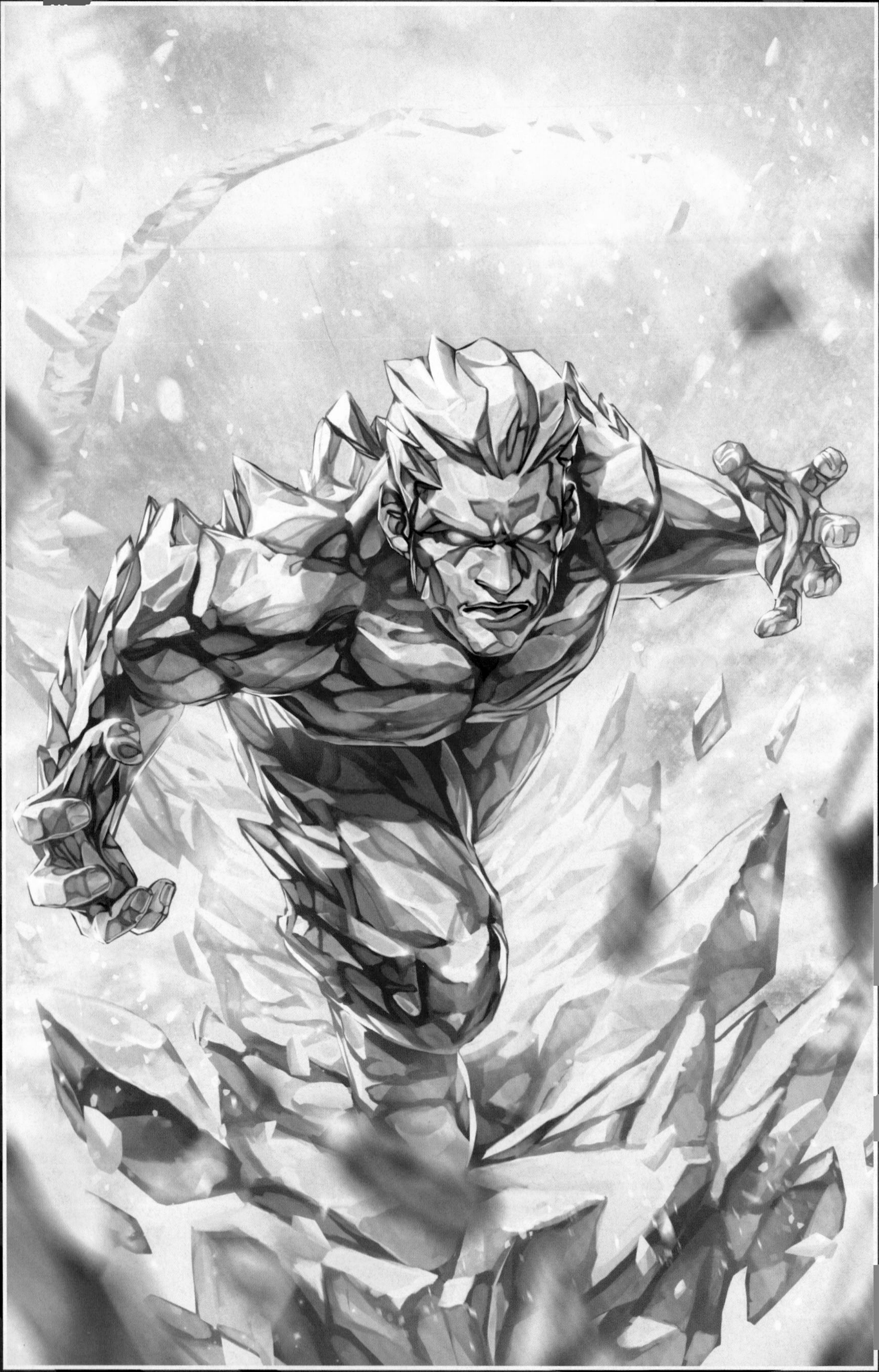

ANNUAL #1 VARIANT BY **JEE-HYUNG LEE**